A Short History of French Literature

From the Origins to the Present Day

BY

L. E. KASTNER

AND

HENRY GIBSON ATKINS

KENNIKAT PRESS
Port Washington, N. Y./London

840.9
K19s

71-5997

A SHORT HISTORY OF FRENCH LITERATURE

First published in 1925
Reissued in 1970 by Kennikat Press
Library of Congress Catalog Card No: 70-103229
SBN 8046-0866-0

Manufactured by Taylor Publishing Company   Dallas, Texas

PREFACE

In writing this book, a good many years ago now, it was the authors' aim to fill the gap which, by many teachers and students, is felt to exist between the numerous primers of French literature intended for British readers and such larger and more comprehensive works as those of Saintsbury, Dowden, Wright, and others. Their purpose remains the same to-day. No attempt has been made to give the impression of what would be an illusory completeness by the mere enumeration of writers of inferior rank. On the other hand, those of the first rank are dealt with at considerable length, while such writers of lesser importance as the authors have for various reasons felt bound to include are treated in smaller type—which serves the double purpose of indicating their relative position and of economizing considerable space. Biographies of the principal writers and brief summaries of the more significant works are likewise printed in the smaller type.

Instead of closing the survey, as do certain manuals, with the decline of Romanticism, or as others, with the waning of Naturalism, the history of French literature has been traced down to the present day. It may be objected that contemporary writers are too near to us to allow of an impartial and definitive judgment—which time alone will render possible. This truism, however, does not seem to preclude the desirability of bringing to the notice of British readers those living French writers whose names are not unlikely to survive, and to give in outline an account of the French literature of to-day such as may at least help to indicate its general tendencies.

In its present form the *Short History* represents a revision, within certain limits, of the whole text, to which considerable additions have been made in the last three chapters, so as to bring the sketch up to date.

The authors trust that the book in this new edition may meet with the same favour as in the past.

L. E. K.
H. G. A.

December, 1925.

CONTENTS

INTRODUCTORY

Origin of the French Language—The *Langue d'Oc*—The *Langue d'Oïl* and its Dialects—Prevalence of the Dialect of the Ile-de-France - - - - - - - - - - 1–5

BOOK I
Middle Ages

GENERAL VIEW

Characteristics of French Medieval Literature: Uniformity and Lack of Individuality—Distrust of Nature—Almost Total Absence of Sense of Art and Form—General Survey of French Medieval Literature - - - - - - 6–7

CHAPTER I—EPIC POETRY

Main Divisions: (1) The French or National Epic: First Period—Second Period—Third Period—Fourth Period—Division into Cycles—Smaller Cycles and later *Chansons de Geste*—Their Metrical Form—Their Scheme of Matter—Volume and Age of the *Chansons*—*Chansons de Roland*—Analysis. (2) The Epic of Antiquity: Benoît de Sainte-More—His Works—Lesser Authors. (3) The Breton Epic: Geoffrey of Monmouth—Divisions—Keltic Spirit of First Group—Marie de France — Béroul — Thomas — Second Group—Chrétien de Troie—Change of Spirit—His Works—Their Character—Third Group—The Holy Graal—Robert de Boron—Later Developments - - - - - 8–19

CONTENTS

CHAPTER II—LYRICAL POETRY

First Period: *Chansons d'Histoire* and *Chansons de Toile*—Second Period: Provençal Influence—Chief Representatives—Third Period: Its Characteristics—Guillaume de Machaut—Jean de Froissart—Eustache Deschamps—Christine de Pisan—Alain Chartier—His Prose - Pages 19–22

CHAPTER III—DRAMA

(1) Tragic Drama. The Liturgical Drama—The *Jeu d'Adam*—The *Jeu de Saint-Nicolas*—Miracles—The *Miracle de Théophile* — Mysteries — Divisions — Arnoul Greban — Performance of Mysteries—Theatrical Companies—*Confrérie de la Passion*. (2) Comedy in the Middle Ages: The *Jeu de la Feuillée*—The *Jeu de Robin et de Marion*—Clercs de la Basoche — Enfants sans Souci — The Farce — *Patelin* — Analysis—The Morality—The *Sottie*—Gringoire - 23–28

CHAPTER IV—SATIRICAL AND ALLEGORICAL POETRY

(1) Satirical Literature: Fables—The *Isopet* of Marie de France—The *Roman de Renard*—Its Branches—Characters and Characteristics—The *Fableaux*—Their Bulk, Age, and Origin—Authors of *Fableaux*—Rutebeuf—His Works—Later Developments of *Fableaux*—Other Kinds of Satirical Poetry— *États du Monde* — *Évangiles* — *Bibles* — *Débats* — *Disputes* — *Batailles* — *Congés* — *Chastiements*, &c. (2) Allegorical Literature: *Bestiaires*—*Lapidaires*—*Volucraires*—Philippe de Thaon—Richard de Fournival—The *Roman de la Rose*—Two Distinct Parts—Guillaume de Lorris and Jean de Meung—The First Part—Analysis—The Second Part as compared with the First—Importance of Jean de Meung—Rise of Allegory - - - - - 29–35

CHAPTER V—HISTORY AND MISCELLANEOUS PROSE

(1) History: Rhymed Chronicles—Gaimar—Wace—Benoît de Sainte-More—Garnier de Pont Sainte-Maxence—*Histoire de Guillaume le Maréchal*—The Great Prose Chroniclers—Geoffroy de Villehardouin—Jean de Joinville—Jean de Froissart: His Life—His *Chroniques*—Philippe de Commines: His Life—His *Mémoires*. (2) Miscellaneous Prose:

CONTENTS ix

Aucassin et Nicolette—Antoine de la Salle—Sermons—Brunetto Latini - - - - - - - - - 35–39

CHAPTER VI—LATER MEDIEVAL POETS

Charles d'Orléans: His Life—His Work and its Characteristics—François Villon: His Life—The *Grand Testament*—His Shorter Poems—His Position and Importance—The *Grands Rhétoriqueurs*—Jean Molinet—Jean Meschinot—Guillaume Crétin - - - - - - - - - - 39–42

BOOK II
Sixteenth Century

GENERAL VIEW

Renaissance and Reformation—First Period: Development of Individuality—Clément Marot—François Rabelais—Goodness and Divinity of Nature—Second Period: The Sentiment of Art—The *Pléiade* and Ronsard—The Reformation—The Latinization of Culture—Third Period: The Foundation of Literature on Psychological and Moral Observation—Amyot and Montaigne—The Philosophy of Reason—The Subordination of Literature to Social Life - - 43–47

FIRST PERIOD (1500–1549)

CHAPTER I—POETRY

Jean le Maire de Belges: His Works—Clément Marot: His Life—His Works—Connection with the Middle Ages—His Position—His Epigrams—In how far he is Typical of the Renaissance—Marguerite de Navarre—Her Poetic Works—Melin de Saint-Gelais: Character of his Verse—The School of Lyons: Maurice Scève—Louise Labé - 47–52

CHAPTER II—DRAMA

Nicole de la Chesnaye—Jean de Pourtalis - - - - 53

CHAPTER III—PROSE

François Rabelais: His Life—His Works—Short Analysis of *Gargantua* and *Pantagruel* — The Meaning of Rabelais'

CONTENTS

Buffoon Epic—His Philosophy of Life—His Style—Marguerite de Navarre: The *Heptaméron des Nouvelles*—Its Riskiness—Bonaventure des Periers: The *Nouvelles Récréations et Joyeux Devis*—Their Spirit—The *Cymbalum Mundi*—Jean Calvin: His Life—The *Institution de la Religion Chrétienne*—Calvin's Doctrine—Herberay des Essarts: The *Amadis des Gaules* - - - - - - 53–61

SECOND PERIOD (1549–1605)

CHAPTER I—POETRY

The *Pléiade*: Its Members—Their Ambition—The *Défense et Illustration de la Langue Française* — Other Theoretical Works—Three Principal Points in the Literary Reform of the *Pléiade*—The Formation of a Poetic Diction Distinct from that of Prose—The Substitution of the Older Forms of French Poetry by Classical Forms—A Reform of Versification—Pierre de Ronsard: His Life—His Works—Divisions and Characteristics—Ronsard's Genius—Joachim du Bellay: His Life—His Works—Their Originality—Lesser Members of the *Pléiade*—Baïf—*Vers Mesurés*—Belleau—Importance of the Reform of the *Pléiade*—The Protestant Poets—Guillaume du Bartas: The *Première* and *Seconde Semaine*—Du Bartas a Caricature of Ronsard—Théodore Agrippa d'Aubigné: The *Tragiques*—The *Aventures du Baron de Fœneste*—Degenerate Disciples of Ronsard—Philippe Desportes—Jean Bertaut—Vauquelin de la Fresnaye—Jean Passerat - - - - - - 62–72

CHAPTER II—DRAMA

The Programme of the *Pléiade*—Inauguration of Classical Drama—Medieval Drama dies hard. (1) Tragedy: Jodelle—Chantelouve—De Bèze—Louis Desmasures—The *Cléôpatre* of Jodelle—Characteristics of the Classical Drama of the Sixteenth Century—Scaliger—Grévin—Jean de la Taille—Garnier: The *Juives* and *Bradamente*—Montchrétien: The *Écossaise*. (2) Comedy: Jodelle's *Eugène*—Grévin—Jean de la Taille—Odet de Turnèbe—Larivey: Great Progress on his Predecessors—General Character of Sixteenth-century Comedy - - - - - - 73–78

CHAPTER III—PROSE

Prose-translators—Jacques Amyot: His Translations of Plutarch—Their Twofold Importance—Memoirs—Blaise de Monluc:

CONTENTS

Pages

The *Commentaires*—Brantôme: His Works—Their Literary Value—François de la Noue: *Discours Politiques et Militaires*—De Thou: *Historia mei Temporis*—Political Writers—Jean Bodin: The *République*—His Ideas—Étienne de la Boétie: The *Contr'un*—François Hotman: The *Franco-Gallia*—His Theories—Michel de l'Hôpital—The *Satire Ménippée*: Political Situation in France—Its Scheme and Authors—Treatises on Grammar and Language—Louis Meigret—Ramus—Henri Étienne: War against Italian Influence—Italian Elements—*Traité de la Conformité du François avec le Grec*—The *Précellence de la Langue Françoise*—The *Nouveaux Dialogues du Langage François Italianisé*—Claude Fauchet: The *Antiquitez Gauloises et Françoises*—*Recueil de l'Origine de la Langue et Poésie Françoise*—Étienne Pasquier: *Recherches*—Short Analysis—Michel de Montaigne: His Life—The *Essays*—Their Composition—The *Apologie de Raymond Sebond*—The Essence of Montaigne's Thought—Scepticism with regard to Metaphysical and Scientific Knowledge — Limitations of Montaigne's Scepticism—The Art of Life—His Theories on Education—His Style and Language—Summary—Pierre Charron: The *Traité des Trois Vérités*—The *Traité de la Sagesse*—Its Meaning—Guillaume Du Vair: Orator and Moralist -   78-95

BOOK III

Seventeenth Century

GENERAL VIEW

Classical Period Proper—Division into Periods—First Period: Struggle between Two Ideals—Malherbe—The *Précieuses*—The Academy—Vaugelas—Balzac—Second Period: Pascal—The Classical Ideal—*L'École du Naturel*—Third Period: Decline—New Ideals—Bayle—Fontenelle—Perrault—The Quarrel of the Ancients and Moderns—Language   -   96-101

FIRST PERIOD (1605-1659)

CHAPTER I—POETRY

Malherbe: The Reform Exemplified in his Work rather than carried out by him—Affects chiefly Versification—His Poetry—List of his Works—Mathurin Régnier: A Belated

Pages

Representative of the Sixteenth Century—His Satires—His Warfare with Malherbe—Another Opponent of Malherbe—Théophile de Viau—The *Hôtel de Rambouillet*—Catherine de Vivonne—Her Ambition—History of her *Salon*—Divisions—First Period—Second Period—Voiture: His Poems and Letters—Third Period—Other *Salons*—Later *Précieuses*—Good and Bad Sides of Preciosity—Pseudo-epics — Georges de Scudéry — Chapelain — Desmarets de Saint-Sorlin—Parodies—Paul Scarron - 101-109

CHAPTER II—DRAMA

Popular Drama—Alexandre Hardy: His Tragedies—His Tragicomedies—His Pastorals—Jean de Schélandre: *Tyr et Sidon*—Importance of its Preface—Théophile de Viau—Racan—Characteristics of the Popular Drama—Jean de Mairet: *Sylvanire*—Rules of the Three Unities Formulated—*Sophonisbe*—Inauguration of the Classical Tragedy on the Popular Stage—Its Main Characteristics—Rules of the Three Unities—Data—Partisans—Opponents—Triumph—Pierre Corneille: His Life—His Plays—Threefold Division—The *Cid*—Analysis—The Cabal against the *Cid*—*Horace*—*Cinna*—Analysis—*Pompée*—*Polyeucte*—Analysis—Corneille's Psychology—His Dramatic System—His Genius—His Verse—Rotrou: His Chief Plays—His Originality 110-123

CHAPTER III—PROSE

François de Sales: His Method—Honoré d'Urfé: The *Astrée*—Short Analysis—The Heroic-gallant Novel—De Gomberville—De la Calprenède—Madeleine de Scudéry: Her Originality—Reaction—Charles Sorel—The French Academy—Its History—Vaugelas: The *Remarques sur la Langue Française*—Balzac: His Rôle—René Descartes: His Life—List of Chief Works—The *Discours de la Méthode*—His Philosophical Method—The Influence of his Ideas—Blaise Pascal: Port-Royal — Arnauld (Antoine) — Jansenism—Life of Pascal—The *Provinciales*—The *Pensées*—Main Outline—Pascal the Creator of French Classical Prose - - - - - - - - - 123-133

SECOND PERIOD (1659-1689)

CHAPTER I—POETRY

Nicolas Boileau: His Life—*Satires*—*Art Poétique*—Short Analysis—Boileau's Literary Doctrine—His Influence—

CONTENTS

Jean de la Fontaine: His Life—List of Works—The *Fables*—Difficulty of Defining La Fontaine's Literary Position—Difference and Similarity with his Contemporaries - 133–138

CHAPTER II—DRAMA

Philippe Quinault—Molière: His Life—Classified List of Plays—The *Précieuses Ridicules*—*Tartuffe*—Opposition of the Religious Party—Reasons—Analysis—The *Misanthrope*—The *Avare*—Short Analysis—Aim of the Play—The *Bourgeois Gentilhomme*—*Georges Dandin*—The *Femmes Savantes*—The *École des Femmes*—Molière's Genius—His Position in the World's Literature—His Style—Jean Racine: His Life—List of Plays—*Andromaque*—Advent of a New Tragic Ideal—The *Plaideurs*—*Britannicus*—*Bérénice*—*Bajazet*—*Mithridate*—*Iphigénie*—*Phèdre*—Short Analysis—The Cabal against *Phèdre*—*Athalie*—Analysis—Racine's Dramatic Genius—Comparison with Corneille—Local Colour—Racine no *Précieux*—His Style - 139–152

CHAPTER III—PROSE

Cardinal de Retz: His *Mémoires* — La Rochefoucauld: His Maxims—Central Idea—His Style—Madame de Sévigné: Her Letters—The Comtesse de la Fayette: The *Princesse de Clèves*—Starting-point of the Modern Psychological Novel—The Realistic Novel—Antoine Furetière—Pulpit Oratory—Bossuet: His Life—Classified List of Works—Obituaries—The *Discours*—The *Politique tirée de l'Écriture Sainte*—*Histoire des Variations*—The *Maximes sur la Comédie*—Bossuet's Style—Louis de Bourdaloue: Causes of his Success—Fléchier—Protestants—Saurin - 153–160

THIRD PERIOD (1689–1715)

CHAPTER I—POETRY

Absence of Real Poetry—Development of Literature in other Directions - 160

CHAPTER II—DRAMA

Antoine de la Fosse—Régnard: His Merits—His Style - 160–161

CHAPTER III—PROSE

Pages

Jean de la Bruyère: The *Caractères*—Their Value—Style—Pierre Bayle: a Precursor of the *Philosophes* of the Eighteenth Century—The *Dictionnaire Historique et Critique*—Bayle's Doctrine—The Quarrel of the Ancients and Moderns—Charles Perrault—Fontenelle—Boileau—Fénelon: His Life—Classified List of Works—The *Maximes des Saints*—Madame Guyon and the Quietists—Dispute with Bossuet—The *Traité de l'Éducation des Filles*—The *Aventures de Télémaque*—The *Plans de Gouvernement*—*Lettre à l'Académie*—Its Importance—Jean Massillon—The Duc de Saint-Simon: His *Mémoires*—His Style - - - 161–169

BOOK IV
Eighteenth Century

GENERAL VIEW

Literature Changes its Ground—Two Great Names—Voltaire and Rousseau — Poetry: Voltaire — Lebrun — Delille — Tragedy: Voltaire — Comedy: Marivaux — Diderot — La Chaussée—Beaumarchais—The Novel: Le Sage—Prévost—Diderot—Rousseau—Bernardin de St. Pierre—Prose: The *Encyclopédie* - - - - - - - 170–175

CHAPTER I—POETRY

Jean Baptiste Rousseau: Hollow Rhetoric—Piron: His Epigrams—Voltaire: His Life—Character of his Verse—The *Henriade*—The *Pucelle*—Houdar de la Motte: Critic and Poet—Lebrun: His Excellence in the Epigram—Delille: Typical of his Time—Poetry by Recipe—Nicolas Gilbert—Parny—André Chénier: His Life—Greatest Poet of the Eighteenth Century—Classification of his Works—Poems of Classical Form—Didactic Fragments—Odes and *Iambes*—Language and Versification - - - - 175–183

CHAPTER II—DRAMA

Crébillon Père: His Chief Tragedies—His Dramatic System—Houdar de la Motte—Voltaire: Improvements and Innovations—Weak Psychology—Lack of Objectivity—Excel-

CONTENTS

lence of Workmanship—Chief Plays—Marivaux: Chief Plays—Poetic Fancy—Psychological Analysis—*Marivaudage*—Le Sage: *Crispin Rival de son Maître*—*Turcaret*—Destouches—Piron—Gresset—La Chaussée and the *Comédie Larmoyante*—Diderot and the *Drame*—Beaumarchais: His Life—The *Barbier de Séville*—The *Mariage de Figaro*—Development of the same Types in the *Barbier*—Political Significance - - - - - - - - 184–191

CHAPTER III—PROSE

Le Sage: The *Diable Boiteux* and *Gil Blas*—Marivaux: *Marianne*—L'Abbé Prévost: *Manon Lescaut*—His other Novels—Voltaire: His *Contes*—Diderot: The *Religieuse* and the *Neveu de Rameau*—J.-J. Rousseau—Bernardin de Saint-Pierre: His Life—His Twofold Importance—His Chief Works—*Paul et Virginie*—Unity of Prose outside Fiction—Fontenelle—A Herald of the *Encyclopédie*—His Life—The *Entretien sur la Pluralité des Mondes*—Its Importance—Montesquieu: His Life—The *Lettres Persanes*—The *Esprit des Lois*—Meaning of the Word *Loi*—Rough Summary—Appreciation of the Work—Voltaire as a Historian: The *Histoire de Charles XII*—The *Siècle de Louis XIV*—The *Essai sur les Mœurs*—Elimination of Providence—Progress of Reason—Voltaire's Philosophical Writings Proper—His Central Idea—His *Correspondance*—Summing up—Vauvenargues—The *Encyclopédie*—Its Scheme—Its Watchword—Diderot: His Life—His Philosophic Writings—His *Salons*—His Literary Importance—D'Alembert—Condillac—Helvétius—D'Holbach—Grimm—Turgot—Condorcet—Jean-Jacques Rousseau: His Life—List of his Works—His Leading Idea—Unity of his Work—The *Discours sur l'Origine et les Fondements de l'Inégalité parmi les Hommes*—The *Émile*—Analysis—*Julie ou La Nouvelle Héloïse*—Awakening of Sentimentality—The *Contrat Social*—The *Confessions*—Minor Works—His Great Influence on Literature—Buffon: His Life—The *Histoire Naturelle*—*Salons*—Mme du Deffand—Mme Geoffrin—Mlle de Lespinasse—Political Orators—Mirabeau—Robespierre, &c. - 191–225

BOOK V
The Transition (1789-1820)

GENERAL VIEW

Two Great Names—Mme de Staël and Chateaubriand—Mme de Staël's Importance—Her Definition of Romanticism—Chateaubriand's Work a Complement of hers—He realizes her Theories - - - - - - - 226–227

CHAPTER I—POETRY

Béranger: His Chief *Chansons*—His Ideas—His Qualities as a Popular Poet - - - - - - - 228–229

CHAPTER II—DRAMA

Delavigne: His Poetry—His Plays—Appreciation - - 229–230

CHAPTER III—PROSE

Madame de Staël: Her Life—List of Principal Works—The *Littérature*—*Delphine* and *Corinne*—*De l'Allemagne*—The *Considérations sur la Révolution*—Her Influence—Chateaubriand: His Life—List of his Chief Works—The *Essai sur les Révolutions* — *Atala* — The *Génie du Christianisme* — *René*—The *Natchez*—The *Martyrs*—The *Itinéraire*—The *Mémoires d'Outre-Tombe*—His Literary Rôle—Appreciation of his Genius—Joubert—Joseph de Maistre: Works—Ultramontanism—De Bonald—Benjamin Constant—Xavier de Maistre — Courier: Life — Writings — The Pamphleteer — Lamennais: Life—Works—Different Phases in his Development - - - - - - - - - 230–244

BOOK VI
Nineteenth Century

GENERAL VIEW

Division into Periods—First Period: Romanticism—Definition of Romanticism—Victor Hugo's Manifesto—Its Scope and Effects—Beginnings—Achievements—The Second Period:

CONTENTS

Realism and Naturalism—Definition—The *Parnassiens*—The Novel—Third Period: Difficulty of determining its exact Nature—Poetry—The *Décadents* and *Symbolistes*—The Novel—Foreign Influences—The Drama - - 245–253

FIRST PERIOD (1820–1850)

CHAPTER I—POETRY

Lamartine: His Life—Principal Works—The *Méditations*—Romantic Lyricism founded—No Progress in Later Work — *Nouvelles Méditations* — *Harmonies* — *Jocelyn* — *Chute d'un Ange*—Prose Works—Alfred de Vigny: Chief Works —*Poèmes Antiques et Modernes*— The *Destinées* — Prose Works—*Chatterton* and *Cinq-Mars*—De Vigny's Philosophy —Victor Hugo: Life — Classification of his Works — The *Odes et Ballades* — The *Orientales* — Other Lyrical Collections—The *Châtiments*—The *Contemplations*—The *Légende des Siècles*—Later Verse—Dramas—*Cromwell*—Its Preface —Victor Hugo's Dramatic System—Exemplified in all subsequent Plays—Analysis of *Hernani* and of *Ruy Blas* —The *Burgraves*—Prose Writings—*Notre-Dame de Paris* —Lesser Fiction—*Les Misérables*—Analysis—Other Novels —Victor Hugo's Genius—De Musset: Life—List of Chief Works—The *Contes d'Espagne et d'Italie*—The *Spectacle dans un Fauteuil*—The Four *Nuits*—The *Confessions*—His Comedies—His Lyric Genius—His Style—Gautier: Classified List of Chief Works—Cult of Form and Colour—Art for Art's Sake—The *Émaux et Camées*—His Prose Works—Minor Romantic Poets—Mme Desbordes-Valmore—Brizeux —Barbier—Moreau - - - - - - 253–271

CHAPTER II—DRAMA

Victor Hugo already Discussed—Dumas Père: His Life—Principal Plays—Appreciation as a Dramatist—Scribe: Chief Plays—No Dramatist—Great Skill in Scenic Art—Ponsard: The *École du Bon Sens*—Passes over to Romanticism—Value of his Plays - - - - - 271–274

CHAPTER III—PROSE

Victor Hugo already Considered—Historical Romances—Dumas Père: His Chief Novels and their Value—Main Divisions of Romantic Fiction—George Sand: Her Life—Classified List of Works—Novels of the First, Second, Third, and Fourth

Periods—Combination of Idealism and Realism—Early Realists—Stendhal: Founder of the Psychological Novel—Mérimée: Chief Works—Starts as a Romanticist—Goes over to Realism in his *Nouvelles*—His Position—His Remarkable Objectivity—Honoré de Balzac: Founder of Realism—His Life—The *Comédie Humaine*—Classified List of the Chief Novels—His Creative Genius—His System and Method—Phantasms of Romance—Lesser Novelists and Writers of Short Stories—Nodier—Eugène Sue—Souvestre—Karr—Murger—History—Thierry: Works—Appreciation—Guizot: His Life—His Chief Works—Leading Ideas and Method—Thiers: Realism in History—Mignet: The *Histoire de la Révolution Française*—Michelet: His Life—List of Works—The *Hoistire de France*—The *Histoire de la Révolution*—Evocation of the Past—De Tocqueville—Literary Criticism—Sainte-Beuve: Classified List of his Works—Importance of his Poetry—His System of Literary Criticism—Villemain: Historical Criticism—Quinet—The Philosophers—Victor Cousin—Pulpit Oratory—Lacordaire   274-290

SECOND PERIOD (1850-1925)

CHAPTER I—POETRY

The *Parnassiens*—De Banville: Classified List of his Works—Art for the sake of Artificiality—Excessive Cult of Poetic Form, and especially of Rhyme—Baudelaire: Decadence and *Satanisme*—The *Fleurs du Mal*—Leconte de Lisle: List of Works—Leader of the *Parnassiens*—Flawless Plasticity—Objectivity—Philosophy—Sully Prudhomme: His Poems—Begins with a Delicate Analysis of the Inner Life—Passes over to Philosophic Themes—Eugène Manuel: Popular Themes and Poetry of the Lower Classes—His Works—Coppée: His Works Classified—Continues Manuel—De Heredia: A Disciple of Leconte de Lisle—Colour—Originality in the Sonnet—*Décadents* and *Symbolistes*—Verlaine: His Works—His Innovations in French Lyrical Poetry—Importance of his *Art Poétique*—Appreciation of his Poetry—Mallarmé: Theorist of Symbolism—His Definition of Symbolism—Appreciation of his Poetry—De Régnier—*Vers Libre*—Gustave Kahn—De Régnier's Verse—Different Aspects—His Fiction—Jean Moréas: His Evolution—Verhaeren: His Earlier Work—His two Trilogies—His Plays—His Genius — Minor Symbolists: Vielé-Griffin — Samain—Outside Symbolism: Lahor—Rollinat—Jean Richepin—

CONTENTS

Symbolism a Spent Force—Present Day Poets: Paul Valéry—Francis Jammes—Louis Mercier—Paul Claudel—Péguy—Fernand Gregh—The Group of the *Humanistes*—The Neo-Classicists—Jean Marc Bernard—Charles Guérin—The *Unanimistes*: Jules Romains—Charles Vildrac—The *Fantaisistes*: Tristan Derème—The Independents: Paul Fort—The Poetesses: La Comtesse Mathieu de Noailles—Gérard d'Houville—Mme Delarue-Mardrus - - 290–307

CHAPTER II—DRAMA

Comédie de Mœurs—Dumas Fils: Chief Plays—Problem Plays—Skill as a Playwright—Brilliant Dialogue—Augier: His Chief Plays—His Solid Good Sense—Moral Scope of his Plays—Labiche—Sardou: His Plays Classified—His Mastery in Stagecraft—Appreciation of his Plays—Pailleron: The *Monde où l'on s'ennuie*—Jules Lemaître's Plays—The Problem Play: De Curel—Brieux—Naturalism: Becque—Hervieu—The *Théâtre Libre*—Its Influence—Henry Bataille—Bernstein—The Romantic Drama in Verse Revived: Rostand—His Earlier Plays—His *Cyrano* Defined—Earlier Romantic Drama in Verse: De Bornier—Coppée—Jean Richepin—Symbolism on the Stage: Maeterlinck—His Other Plays—His Prose Essays—The Dramatic Art of the Twentieth Century: Donnay—Lavedan—Octave Mirbeau—Emile Fabre—De Porto-Riche—Capus—Robert de Flers and Armand de Caillavet—Pierre Wolf—Romain Coolus—Georges Courteline - - - - - 307–316

CHAPTER III—PROSE

Flaubert: the Initiator of Naturalism—His Chief Novels—*Madame Bovary*—*Salammbô*—Partly a Romanticist—Objectivity—The Brothers De Goncourt: List of their Works—Their Preference of the Odd to the Typical—*Germinie Lacerteux* and its Dangerous Principle—Their Impressionist Style—Zola: Leader of the Naturalistic School in Fiction—His Novels Classified—His Method—His Merits and Demerits—Alphonse Daudet: His Novels Classified—In how far a Naturalist—Character and Originality of his Fiction—Maupassant: List of his Principal Works—The Short Story—His Manner and Style—Huysmans: Different Aspects of his Work—Villiers de l'Isle Adam: His Characteristics—Fiction outside Naturalism: Octave Feuillet—About—Cherbuliez—Erckmann and Chatrian—Pierre Loti: His Fiction Classified—Its Main

CONTENTS

Characteristics—Loti as a Word-painter—Anatole France: His Chief Novels Examined and Discussed—His Style—Maurice Barrès: Account of his Principal Works—The Metaphysician and Man of Action—The Nationalist—His Importance—Paul Bourget: The Psychological Novel—His Works Classified—His Characteristics—Fromentin—His *Dominique*—Lesser Writers of Fiction: Ferdinand Fabre: Regionalism—Theuriet—Pouvillon—Léon Cladel—Rod—The Brothers Margueritte—Hervieu—Marcel Prévost—Estaunié—Maindron—Paul Adam—The Novelists of the Twentieth Century: Henri Bazin—Henry Bordeaux—Claude Farrère—André Gide—Charles Louis Philippe—Marcel Proust—Romain Rolland—J. H. Rosny—War Novels: Georges Duhamel—Roland Dorgelès—Henri Barbusse—Renan: His Life—Principal Works—His Significance—Literary Criticism—Taine: His Chief Works—His System Explained and Criticized—Brunetière: His Theory of Evolution—Chief Works—Jules Lemaître: His Subjective Method—Anatole France as a Literary Critic: Also Subjective—Paul Bourget: Psychological Criticism—Émile Faguet—Gustave Lanson: Literary History—History: Fustel de Coulanges—His Method Defined by himself—His Importance—Ernest Lavisse - - - - - 316–339

INDEX - - - - - - - - - 341–345

SHORT HISTORY OF FRENCH LITERATURE

INTRODUCTORY

Origin of the French Language.—French, like Italian, Spanish, Portuguese, Provençal, Roumanian, and Rheto-Romance, is derived by a long succession of transformations from popular Latin, which was spoken over all the provinces or colonies of the *Imperium Romanum* or *Romania*.

This popular Latin speech was introduced into France, or Gaul as it was then called, by the soldiers of Julius Cæsar, who finally reduced the country in 51 B.C. In his train followed merchants and colonists, and an occupation began which lasted for four and a half centuries.

Already in the seventh century popular Latin or Romance had assumed distinct peculiarities, according to the countries in which it was spoken. As spoken in Gaul it is known by the name of Gallo-Roman or Gallo-Romance, not to be confounded with Low Latin, which is not a spoken but a written language.

By Low Latin is meant literary Latin as written by the uneducated, who made mistakes analogous to those of the modern schoolboy. All the scholars of the Middle Ages wrote in this dog Latin, which only disappeared in the sixteenth century, thanks to the great Humanists, who resuscitated the language of the great Roman classic writers.

INTRODUCTORY

The first thing Gallo-Romance did was to oust Keltic, the language of the Gauls, the original inhabitants. This transformation was effected all the more rapidly as the Gauls had never formed a nation or homogeneous whole capable of offering systematic resistance to the invaders. Moreover, they were intelligent enough and sufficiently civilized to recognize the moral and intellectual superiority of Rome and to profit by it. Their native idiom vanished as if by magic, leaving only very slight traces, more particularly as regards pronunciation.[1]

This state of things was disturbed by the Germanic invasions in the fifth century, by which date Keltic had absolutely vanished, while Greek, which the Romans had found established at Marseille, whither it had been brought by Phocean colonists, only survived till the first century of our era.

These Germanic invaders consisted of the West Goths in Aquitaine, the Burgundians in Burgundy, the Salian Franks in the north-east, and the Austrasian Franks in the east. In the same way and for the same reasons as the Kelts had abandoned their language in favour of Latin, so did these Germanic tribes in turn abandon theirs in favour of Gallo-Romance. The same fate befell the Normans under Rollo, who followed four centuries later (912) and settled along the Lower Seine. Yet the Germanic element[2] in the French language is not inconsiderable. It has been computed that about nine hundred words penetrated into Gallo-Romance, though a goodly number were lost in the passage to modern French.

[1] Excluding a goodly number of place-names, and some words of later (Breton) introduction, the following are among the commonest words of Gallic origin, most of them having already been adopted by Latin: *alouette, arpent, bec, bouleau, claie, lieue, marne, saie, truand, vassal*, &c.

[2] Apart from names of places and persons, and the other German words introduced in the sixteenth century (chiefly at the time of the Thirty Years' War), and gradually ever since, the Germanic element in the French language can be classed as follows:
   (a) Two adverbs (*trop* and *guère*).
   (b) Terms of war (*adouber, blesser, épier, éperon, épieu, fourreau*, the word *guerre* itself, *gonfanon, guetter, haubert, heaume*, &c.).
   (c) Terms pertaining to jurisdiction and administration (*alleu, ban, échanson, fief, gage, garantir, maréchal, saisir, sénéchal*, &c.).
   (d) Miscellaneous (*blanc, bleu, frais, gris, honte, loge, orgueil, renard, riche*, &c.).

INTRODUCTORY

On the other hand, Gallo-Romance lost ground in Armorica (the present Brittany), where certain Keltic tribes, driven from Britain by the Saxons, settled in the fifth century and reintroduced a Keltic dialect, which survives to-day.

The same thing happened in the sixth century, when the Vascons coming from Spain reinstated their language, Iberian (now called Basque), on the territory which they still in part occupy.

On Gallo-Romance soil originally one common language was spoken, which in course of time, and according to place, split up into an infinite variety of local speeches, from south to north and from east to west.

Certain more or less distinct peculiarities enable us to divide these different dialects into two main groups:

The **Langue d'oc** in the south,
The **Langue d'oïl** in the north,

both so called according to the custom existing in the Middle Ages of designating a language according to the word it employed to express affirmation.

A line drawn from the mouth of the Charente to the Alps, and passing through Limoges, Clermont-Ferrand, and Grenoble, forms, roughly speaking, the boundary-line between the two groups.

(1) **The Dialects of the Langue d'Oc** have now sunk to the rank of patois, i.e. of spoken dialects as distinguished from written dialects. This was not the case in the early Middle Ages, when the *langue d'oc* was not only the rival but the superior in many respects of the *langue d'oïl*.

The literature of the *langue d'oc*, or Provençal as it is now called from one of its chief dialects, already existed in the eleventh century, but its golden age is the twelfth century, the period of the famous lyric poets, the *troubadours*,[1] whose fame spread far beyond the limits of their native land, exercising great influence on the poetry of the north of France,

---

[1] Derived from the verb *trobare* = to find, to invent. In the *langue d'oïl* the word became *trouvère*, which is a nominative form (*tropator*).

and on that of Italy and Germany. This brilliant southern literature disappeared, yielding before that of the *langue d'oïl*, in the middle of the thirteenth century, as a result mainly of the crusade against the Albigeois or heretics of the south. In modern times a literary renaissance has been attempted; poets of rare talent, such as Jasmin (1798–1864), Roumanille (1818–1891), Aubanel (1829–1886), and above all, Mistral (1830–1914), have written remarkable poems in their native idiom, without, however, really succeeding in raising Provençal to the level of a literary language.

(2) **The Dialects of the Langue d'Oïl.**—Before the end of the seventh century general linguistic differences appeared in the north, sufficient to cause the language of that region to be regarded as a new language. In 659, Saint Mummolin was appointed in succession to Saint Éloi, bishop of Noyon, because he spoke not only German, but also Romance.[1] Other testimonies exist to the same effect in the eighth and ninth centuries, and about the middle of the ninth century we have a striking example of this Romance of the north in the famous *Serments de Strasbourg* (14th Feb., 842), which have been preserved by Nithard in his Latin history. In this important document the *langue d'oïl*, though still wavering on the border-line between Latin and French, appears fixed in its general traits. The oldest texts in the *langue d'oïl*, apart from the *Oaths*, are of the same century: the *Sequence de Sainte Eulalie*, in twenty-five lines, and a fragment of a homily on Jonas partly in Latin; in the tenth century we have a poem of greater length, *La Vie de St. Léger*, considerably altered by a southern transcriber; in the eleventh century the *Vie de St. Alexis*; later, the *Pèlerinage de Charlemagne*, and the *Chanson de Roland*, the first great literary work in French. From the twelfth century texts abound.

This old French literature was not peculiar to any particular province. Each dialect had its own literature, which

---

[2] *Quia prævalebat non tantum in teutonica, sed etiam in romana lingua* (*Acta Sanctorum Belgii Selecta*, iv, 403).

INTRODUCTORY

remained independent, or nearly so, till the fourteenth century. The chief dialects of the *langue d'oïl* are:

Francian or **French** proper, in the province of the Ile-de-France;

Burgundian, Franc-Comtois, Lorrainian, and **Champenois,** in the east;

Picard and **Walloon** in the north-east;

Norman in the north-west;

Poitevin, Angevin, Saintongeais, in the west;

And, out of France, **Anglo-Norman,** or Norman as it developed in England after its introduction by William the Conqueror and his followers.

But already in the twelfth century, the dialect of the Ile-de-France began to prevail as the standard literary language. This was not due to its superiority, but to the political predominance of that province, and to the extension of the influence of Paris, its capital. This progress continued in the thirteenth, and may be said to have been complete at the beginning of the fifteenth century, when the other dialects only remained as spoken languages, and even then only among the lower classes.

To sum up, modern French may be called a development of the Romance dialect of the Ile-de-France, which itself is a continuation and gradual transformation, under certain climatic and racial influences, of the popular Latin introduced into that part of Gaul during the four and a half centuries of the Roman occupation.

BOOK I
MIDDLE AGES

GENERAL VIEW

The three main characteristics of medieval literature are:

Its uniformity and lack of individuality. Speaking generally, nearly all the *Chansons de geste*, *Fableaux*, &c., might have been the work of the same author, so great is their similarity. Commines in prose and Villon in poetry are exceptions, no doubt, but they come quite at the end of our period, and instead of summarizing the peculiarities of medieval literature, they may be said to herald those of the Renaissance. Neither should it be forgotten that Villon left no disciples, and that those who did were his successors, the *grands rhétoriqueurs*, Molinet, Meschinot, and Crétin.

Its distrust of nature, the outcome of the teaching of primitive Christianity. In this respect Jean de Meung is an exception.

The almost total absence of any sense of art and form, and its replacement by set phrases and recurring formulas.

Although the literature of the Middle Ages already in the eleventh century produces works of real merit, and among the number the famous epic of Roland, its golden age is the twelfth century, the century of epic poetry. In the *Chansons de geste* proper, those of the National Epic, the warlike and feudal ideal is expressed; in the Breton Epic, the Epic of

GENERAL VIEW

Antiquity, and likewise in lyric poetry, arose new chivalric ideals, the new *courtoisie* and homage to women. The drama leaves the church, and prose makes its first appearance in sermons and translations.

In the thirteenth century literary activity hardly diminishes, but different tendencies set in. The epic vein is exhausted, and the *Chansons de geste* are in full decadence. Against the high ideal of chivalry and its overstrained sentiment the positive intellect and mocking temper of the people reacts. The *esprit gaulois* [1] has its revenge; a satirical and didactic literature arises in the *Fableaux*, the *Romance of Reynard the Fox*, and the second part of the *Romance of the Rose*. The prevailing taste is for moral allegory. The drama is still feeling its way, and prose asserts itself in the works of two great chroniclers, Villehardouin and Joinville.

The fourteenth century is an arid waste. The social and intellectual edifice of the Middle Ages slowly falls to ruins; writers only repeat those who have preceded them, and replace imagination by ingenuities and technical juggleries. The theatre is not yet definitely constituted, and in prose one great name only is found, that of Froissart, the famous chronicler.

In the fifteenth century, in spite of a vigorous effort in dramatic literature (mysteries, moralities, farces, and *sotties*), and the names of two great writers like Villon and Commines in verse and prose, the decadence that had manifested itself in the previous century continues in other branches. The minds of men were ripe to accept the new influences of the Renaissance.

[1] To give a definition of what is meant by *esprit gaulois*, in a concise form, is an impossibility. In its most general aspect it may be described as a revolt against and a parody of authority and respectability, a wish to shock *Mrs. Grundy*, which too often results in coarseness and even obscenity.

CHAPTER I

EPIC POETRY

Epic poetry in French literature is generally divided into three large groups:[1]

> The French or National Epic;
> The Epic of Antiquity;
> The Breton Epic or Épopée Courtoise.

The poems of the French Epic are known as *Chansons de geste*,[2] or songs of the deeds and achievements (*gesta*) of some heroic person; those of the Epic of Antiquity and of the Breton Epic as *Romans d'aventure*. In a few of the poems of the third group Breton and Byzantine sources are mixed, while in others the bases are events of the time, or national history and legend.

By far the most important is the French Epic, which was the first to develop. The two others are later and artificial.

The French or National Epic.—Though challenged in recent years, the theory that the French Epic is of Germanic origin still holds the field, at all events as regards the oldest songs. From the earliest times, so runs the theory, it had been the custom of the Germans to sing their heroes' deeds in lyrico-epic recitals. After their invasion of Gaul in the fifth century and their conversion to Christianity, they were rapidly assimilated by the Gallo-Romans whom they had conquered; but the Germanic blood, acting like a leaven, as it were, on the new amalgamated race, called forth similar lyrico-epic songs in the Gallo-Roman tongue from the fifth to the tenth century. To quote a famous philologist: " The French heroic epic is the product of the fusion of the

---

[1] This division dates back to the thirteenth century:
> *Ne sont que trois matières à nul home antandant*
> *De France et de Bretagne et de Rome la grant.*
> —Jean Bodel. *Chanson des Saisnes.*

[2] Later *geste* also meant *cycle.*

Germanic spirit, in a Romance form, with the new Christian civilization of France."

Of this, **The First Epic Period,** not a single monument has come down to us, but the Latin chronicles of the time are full of epic legends referring to the deeds of the Merovingians. All the events of which the French Epic has preserved the memory fall within this, the only period of spontaneous epic production.

We must not suppose, however, that the poems which arose in the space intervening between the fifth and tenth centuries were like the *Chansons de geste* such as we now know them. They were historical ballads or *cantilènes*, songs which were contemporary, or nearly so, with the events which they recalled and celebrated. They were essentially lyric-epic productions. Gradually as the events receded the lyrical element yielded to the epic, and the *Chansons de geste* were developed from these songs. We may regard the ninth century as the period of the transformation of the *cantilènes* into the *Chansons de geste*.

The Second Period of the French Epic reaches from 1050–1120. The three oldest epic poems which have come down to us—the *Chansons de Roland, Le Pèlerinage de Charlemagne,* and *Le Roi Louis* [1]—belong to this period. They are not original, but manipulations of old themes sung in the first period. The *Chanson de Roland* which we possess is certainly not the one which Taillefer the minstrel sang at Hastings; yet the original epic matter in these poems is on the whole free from heterogeneous and extraneous elements. They were couched in writing at a time when the original epic spirit could still be felt, though its creative power was dead. It is for that very reason that they are the finest *chansons* of the French Epic.

From the earliest times the epic matter tended to centralize about one person, Charlemagne, the champion of Christianity and chivalry against the hated Saracen. At the same time

[1] Known also as *Gormont et Isembart*.

local heroes were not neglected, as we see from the poems on Girard, Raoul, and Guillaume.

In the poems of **The Third Period** (1100–1180) additions and inventions are freely made to meet the requirements of the audience. Originally, and up to the end of the eleventh century, these epic songs were sung by the minstrel or *jongleur* as the warriors marched to battle, but in the twelfth century they became a mere pastime for the lords at meals and festivals. The *trouvère* or poet, who originally was sometimes a warrior, gradually tends to become a man of letters. He rarely sings his own compositions, but sells them to the *jongleur*. For the profession to be a lucrative one both for poet and minstrel they must please the audience, and the original epic matter being exhausted, novel themes must be found; fancy and invention, encouraged by the Epic of Antiquity and the Breton Epic, obliterate more and more the popular element.

During **The Fourth Period** (1150–1360) these tendencies were aggravated. It was the cyclical period proper; all the heroes, and consequently all the preceding *chansons* were arbitrarily connected by genealogical links on the assumption that we are more likely to be interested in a person related to others whom we already know. As early as the thirteenth century the greater part of the *Chansons de geste* had by this process been grouped into three principal cycles:[1]

The **Geste du Roi**, dealing with the Carolingian triad Pépin, Charles, and Louis, also called *Geste de Charlemagne*, after the central figure.

The **Geste de Garin de Monglane**, known also as the *Geste de Guillaume*, the subject of which is the defence of the south of France against the Infidels.

[1] Compare the following lines from *Girard de Vienne*, a *chanson* dating from 1210-1220:

> N'ot (eut) que trois gestes en France la garnie:
> Dou roi de France est la plus seignorie;
> Et l'autre après, bien est droit que vous die.
> Est de Doon à la barbe florie . . .
> La tierce geste . . .
> Fust de Garin de Montglane au vis (visage) **fier**.

The *Geste de Doon de Mayence*, on the feudal wars. A certain number of poems, however, resisted the attraction of the great cycles. Such is *Raoul de Cambrai*, based on historical events and representing the wars of the feudal barons among themselves; but the most important of this kind are the five songs which describe the struggle between the houses of Metz and of Bordeaux, forming a small cycle known as the *Cycle de Lorraine*.

The first crusade likewise called forth additional poems, forming the *Cycle des Croisades*, the last to develop. They are rather historical than epic.

Excepting the *Combat des Trente* (1351) and the *Chronique de Du Guesclin* (1384), barren attempts to revive the epopee at the time of the wars against England, and one or two others, no more *Chansons de geste* were composed after the fourth period, and soon after, those that existed were no longer sung. They were still copied into verse up till the end of the fifteenth century, but already before the middle of that century scribes began to turn into prose those that still offered some interest.

In the earlier *Chansons de geste* the decasyllabic verse is used, generally with the cæsura after the fourth syllable. The poems are divided into sections or *laisses* of varying length, the lines of each *laisse* being united by a single assonance or vowel-rhyme. Towards the end of the twelfth century assonance was abandoned in favour of full rhyme, and the decasyllabic line replaced by the Alexandrine or line of twelve syllables. In some *chansons* the two are mixed.

A marked peculiarity of many of these epic songs is the repetition of the same idea or incident under a different form in consecutive *laisses* of different assonances.

The *Chansons de geste* were sung to a very simple melody by the *jongleurs*, and accompanied by the *vielle*, a kind of violin.

The character of the earliest and purest of them, founded on a historical basis, is warlike and religious; gradually history is exaggerated, and a passion for the marvellous and fabulous invades everything. Love and gallantry, absent at first, gain ground apace under the influence of the Breton Epic. The style is occasionally grand in its simplicity, but more often monotonous, while the study of character is rude and elementary, and feeling for nature is conspicuous by its absence.

Leaving out of consideration the later refashionings both in prose and verse of the fourteenth and fifteenth centuries, it has been calculated that over a hundred *Chansons de geste* have come down to us. The three oldest have already been mentioned. These were followed in the twelfth century by about forty-five others, of which the best are perhaps: *Aliscans, Amis et Amiles, Le Charroi de Nîmes, Le Covenant Vivien, Garin le Loherain,* the oldest form of *Huon de Bordeaux,* and *Raoul de Cambrai.* By far the larger number of the rest are not later than the thirteenth century. They include: *Aimeri de Narbonne, Berte au Grand Pied* in its present French form, *Doon de Mayence, Garin de Monglane,* and *Les Enfances* (early exploits) *Ogier*.

The *Chanson de Roland,* as giving the best idea of the French epic in its unadulterated form, deserves special mention.

In the form in which we possess it—not the original one, as we have already noticed—the *Chanson de Roland* was composed during the first quarter of the twelfth century (between 1120 and 1125). As in the case of the bulk of these epic poems, its authorship is unknown. Some have wished to argue from the last line which concludes, or rather supplements, the Oxford text:

Ci falt la geste que Turoldus declinet,

that this Turoldus or Turold was the author; but as the meaning of the word *declinet* is doubtful, and as we cannot tell with any degree of certainty whether he was the poet, transcriber, or *jongleur*, this conclusion is unwarranted.

The *Chanson de Roland* consists of 4002 assonanced decasyllabic lines, divided into 291 *laisses* of an average length of 15 lines. It is founded on a historical event recorded by Eginhart in his *Libri Historiarium IV*, the surprise and defeat of Charlemagne's rear-guard returning from Spain, by the Basques in the valley of Roncevaux (15 Aug., 778). He tells that among those who fell was Hrodland (Roland), Count of the march of Brittany. In time the singers substituted the Saracens, the traditional foe, for the Basques, and from a simple historical event evolved the whole epic poem, of which we append a short analysis.

> Charlemagne, after seven years spent in Spain, has conquered the whole peninsula with the exception of Saragossa, which is still held by the Saracen chief Marsile, who sends word to Charlemagne that he is willing to submit and receive baptism. The Emperor accepts his offer, and resolves to send an ambassador to Marsile. Roland, the Emperor's nephew, proposes Ganelon, his father-in-law. Ganelon, thinking that Roland is plotting his death, swears to take vengeance. He arrives at Saragossa, and informs Marsile that the French will soon start on their homeward journey, and that Roland will be in command of the rear-guard. Marsile draws up his plans accordingly, and the traitor takes leave of him. The retreat of the Franks begins, and suddenly when the rear-guard has reached the pass of Roncevaux it is attacked by innumerable hosts of Saracens. Oliver, Roland's friend, beseeches him to sound his horn in order to recall the Emperor, who has already reached Gascony, but Roland refuses. The Franks, although greatly outnumbered, offer an heroic resistance, and after accomplishing prodigies of valour, all perish, save a small band of sixty warriors, who make a last stand round Roland, who at last decides to blow his horn (his *olifant*). Charlemagne hears the trumpet-blast and returns, but too late. The last of the Franks, Oliver and Archbishop Turpin, fall in their turn, but the Saracens, informed of the emperor's approach, take to flight. Roland remains alone, unwounded but dying, exhausted by the strife and his superhuman efforts in blowing his horn. The Emperor, who arrives in hot haste, bewails the fallen warriors and takes vengeance on Marsile; after which he returns to his capital, Aix, and brings the news to Aude, Roland's betrothed, who falls down dead on hearing the terrible tidings. The traitor Ganelon is tried, convicted, and quartered.

Taken as a whole, the *Chanson de Roland* is superior to any of the other *chansons*, though separate passages of great beauty occur in several of the earlier ones. Such scenes as Oliver's advice to Roland to blow his wonderful *olifant*, and the latter's proud refusal; Archbishop Turpin's address to the Frankish warriors before the fray, or the description of Roland's last moments, are worthy to take rank with the finest passages in the *Iliad*.

The Epic of Antiquity.—In the twelfth century the clerks thought they would rival the National Epic by adapting to the tastes of the public the strange and wonderful stories which they encountered in their Latin readings. To them the works of the Greco-Roman decadence were naturally more congenial than those of the classical period, as affording more suitable materials. They first hit upon the fabulous history of Alexander the Great, as contained in Julius Valerius, the Latin abbreviator of a Greek novel. The earliest of these romances of antiquity is the fragment of a poem on Alexander by one Albéric de Briançon. This fragment, which was composed quite at the beginning of the twelfth century, together with Valerius' version, gave rise in the second half of the twelfth century to the *Roman d'Alexandre*, due to three authors, Alexandre de Bernai, Lambert le Tort, and Pierre of St. Cloud, written in verses of twelve syllables, since called *Alexandrine*, although they had already been used in the *Pèlerinage de Charlemagne à Jérusalem*, a *Chanson de geste* of the end of the eleventh century. In these poems Alexander personifies the ideal knight of the time, and his largess, for which he became the model, is especially exalted, and in order to make the narrative more attractive, monstrous wild beasts, mermaids, amazons, rain of fire, and magic fountains are introduced with a liberal hand.

All the other productions of the Epic of Antiquity, with one exception, were written in the octosyllabic line. Of these the *Roman de Troie* (1165 *c.*), dedicated to Aliénor of Anquitaine, and comprising no less than 30,000 lines, is the work of **Benoît** de Sainte-More, the best poet in this group. His source is not the *Iliad*, but translations of two lost Greek novels; several episodes are invented, of which the most notable is that of Troilus and Briseida, which, after passing through Latin and Italian, gave rise to Shakespeare's play of *Troilus and Cressida*.

The *Roman d'Énéas*[1] (1160 c.), a kind of courtly and chivalric travesty of the *Æneid*, is by an unknown author, as is also the *Roman de Thèbes* (1160 c.), based on a glossed text of Statius, to which considerable additions were made.

Benoît, by his conventional and metaphysical conception of love, may be called the forerunner of the poets of the Breton Epic, whose casuistic love code was also considerably furthered by several renderings of Ovid's *Ars Amoris*.

Much in the same spirit as those already mentioned is the *Roman de Jules César* (in Alexandrine verse) by Jacot de Forest, copied from the prose *César* (1240 c.) of Jean de Tuin, who himself had drawn almost exclusively on Lucan's *Pharsalia*.

The Breton Epic.—The Breton Epic is the product of the contact of French society with the Kelts. This contact took place mainly in England at the time of the Norman Conquest, and to a lesser degree between Normans and Bretons on the continent of France, by means of Keltic harpers, who wandered about England and France singing their *lais* or songs on Keltic traditions, the historical basis of which rests on the wars against the Saxons (fifth and sixth centuries), but which had absorbed anterior mythological elements. The popularity of these *lais* was greatly increased by **Geoffrey of Monmouth's** *Historia Regum Britanniae* (1136 c.), which purported to be a history of the Britons, but which in reality is a compound of Nennius,[2] Keltic popular tales, and his own imagination. Geoffrey's book acted as a stimulant; at the

---

[1] Through the medium of Heinrich von Veldeke's translation the *Roman d'Énéas* introduced *courtoisie* into German literature.

[2] Towards the end of the tenth century an anonymous writer, who became known later under the name of Nennius, wrote a short *History of the Britons*, in which Arthur is mentioned for the first time.

same time it is wrong to regard it as the source of the Breton Epic, although it may have been used to some extent by later writers in the " matter of Britain ".

The Anglo-Norman and French poets, prompt at seeing which way the wind blew, and always on the alert for new material, lost no time in competing with the Keltic bards. Some wrote *lais*, others extended or amalgamated them into longer poems, while yet others mixed in them traditions and inventions the origin of which was not Keltic at all.

The huge mass of the Breton Epic falls naturally into three large divisions, each of quite a different nature:

The first division includes the **Lais** and the poems referring to **Tristan;**

The second those that deal with **Arthur and the Knights of the Round Table;**

The third, of later date, comprises the poems on the **Holy Graal,** and its mystic band of guardians and *questers.*

The spirit of the poems of **Group I** is essentially Keltic: adventures, exploits, chivalry, tourneys, and religion find little place in them; they are mainly stories of tender or deep passion, enshrouded in a veil of mystic melancholy.

Most of the *lais* we possess are due to a poetess, **Marie,**[1] of French birth, who lived at the court of Henry II of England. She translated, or adapted from Keltic or Anglo-Saxon, a dozen or more of these short stories in verse, of which the best are *Lanval*, a knight beloved of a fairy who in the end leads him away with her; *Eliduc*, the twofold love of a knight and the resignation of his lawful wife; *Bisclavret*, the story of a werwolf, and *Chevrefeuille*, an episode in the story of Tristan and Isolt.

The story of Tristan is closely connected with lost *lais* of mythological origin quite foreign to the Arthurian cycle with which it was afterwards connected. The scattered traditions relating to the adventures of Tristan were united into a single poem in England by **Béroul** (†1150 *c.*), whose work has only

---

[1] Known as Marie *de France.*

come down to us as a fragment. About 1170 **Thomas**, another Anglo-Norman poet, also composed a poem on Tristan, which we likewise only possess in fragmentary form.

In the poems of **Group II** the Keltic spirit is entirely absent. This change is manifest in the works of **Chrétien de Troie**, the most famous of the poets who have treated the *matière de Bretagne*. A new ideal of chivalry had sprung up among the feudal aristocracy. Chrétien determined to follow the fashion, and in this he was aided by his lucid positivism, which is the very opposite of the mystical melancholy Keltic mind, and also by his position as poet of the court of Champagne, whose countess Marie, and her mother Aliénor of Aquitaine, had introduced into the north of France the refined manners of the south and the love-poetry of the troubadours, which at the time were looked upon as the ideal of chivalry.

Chrétien's poems, which all belong to the Breton Epic, include his lost *Tristan*, composed about 1160; followed by *Erec*, then by *Cligès*; a few years later (1170 c.) by *Lancelot* and by *Ivain* or *Le Chevalier au Lion*, and lastly (1175 c.) by *Perceval*, or *Le Conte du Graal*, which he left unfinished.

Adventures, tourneys, marvellous exploits, which are merely ornaments in the *lais* or the poems on Tristan when they do occur, tend to become an end in themselves. Arthur has nothing in common with the mysterious Keltic chief whom the fairies have carried off to the Isle of Avallon, but becomes the embodiment of what a perfect knight should be; a brilliant king whose court is the centre of ideal politeness, gracious manners, sumptuous festivals, and refined love — not the passion of the poems on Tristan or even of the *lais* of Marie de France, but the metaphysical *courtoisie* of the southern troubadours.

Form is Chrétien's chief merit, and his poetry offers the best example of twelfth-century French.

Group III.—The ideal of a worldly and too facile life,

as represented in the romances of the court-poet of Champagne, seems to have shocked a few serious and austere Christian minds. In these Keltic traditions themselves they found a means of protesting against the frivolity of the *Romans de la Table Ronde.*

Chrétien, in his fragment of *Perceval*, makes mention of a certain dish or *graal*. With his continuators this *graal* became the vessel in which Joseph of Arimathea gathered the Lord's blood, and towards the beginning of the thirteenth century a poet of Franche-Comté, **Robert de Boron,** tried to connect the history of this holy *graal* with the Breton Epic, in a trilogy of poems: *Joseph d'Arimathie, Merlin* (which introduced the famous enchanter into the cycle), and *Perceval,* lost, but early turned into prose.

In Boron's productions the religious side of the Holy Graal episode is developed and love plays no part.

Still more austere and rigidly ascetic is a *Quête du Saint Graal,* composed in the thirteenth century; Galahad, a figure of immaculate perfection, replaces Perceval, and woman is cursed and shunned as the embodiment of sin.

But these romances of the Graal were too much in contradiction with the tastes and aspirations of feudal aristocracy to represent anything but the pangs of a few tormented minds. For the lords and ladies of the thirteenth and fourteenth centuries the ideal knight was Ivain or Lancelot, and not Perceval or Galahad.

The poems of the Breton Epic are written in the octosyllabic line with full rhyme, and, unlike the *Chansons de geste,* were meant to be read and not sung.

Gradually from the beginning of the thirteenth century the prose romances seem to have superseded the poetical and helped to spread the fame of the Breton Epic, which in the Middle Ages was immense, as the numerous Italian, German, English, Spanish, and Portuguese translations, continuations, and imitations testify.

Returning to France from Spain in the sixteenth century

EPIC POETRY

in the guise of the *Amadis des Gaules*, they became the main source of inspiration for the chivalric and pastoral novels of the seventeenth century.

CHAPTER II

LYRICAL POETRY

First Period.—There is little doubt that lyrical poetry of a popular kind existed in the north of France already in the tenth century. It consisted of dance-songs, of which only a few refrains, incorporated in songs of a later epoch, have been preserved. These popular dance-songs were called *Chansons d'histoire* on account of their semi-narrative character, or *Chansons de toile*, no doubt because they were sung by women when weaving. They are written in verses of ten or eight syllables with assonance, and consist of four or five strophes with a refrain. The characters are limited to two or three, the dramatic and epic element predominating. None of these poems occurs later than the close of the twelfth century.

Second Period.—About 1170, Provençal influence came and interrupted this current of popular and spontaneous poetry. Communication between the north and the south had already taken place in the Holy Land at the time of the Crusades, but the direct medium was Aliénor of Aquitaine, and her daughter Marie who had married the Count of Champagne. Her court, together with Paris the capital, became the centre of courtly poetry, which was in full vogue during the last years of the eleventh and the beginning of the twelfth century. The earliest singers were persons of noble rank and birth, but gradually poetry was abandoned by the nobility, and fell into the hands of the *bourgeoisie*.

The lyric poetry of the troubadours of the south was moral, satirical, and political, although its main theme was love. That of their northern imitators is almost exclusively amorous.

It is essentially a poetry of the intellect and of the imagination, embodying the ideal of the brilliant society of the south which had been imported into the north. In this society great importance was attached to certain rules of social etiquette which were designated by the name of *courtoisie*, and in which an elaborate code of love represented that passion as ennobling, and woman as the object most worthy of worship.

The spontaneous cry of passion is rarely heard in these songs, which reflect the thoughts of the poet about love and not his own personal feelings. Their real merit lies in their grace, elegance, and prettiness, as well as in their artistic qualities.

They are generally made up of five, six, or seven strophes, invariably divided into three parts ($2 + 2 + 1$; $2 + 2 + 2$; $2 + 2 + 3$), with varying and complicated rhyme schemes. In most cases the poet was also a musician and composed his own melody; the form of each strophe was invented anew for each song, and was considered the property of the inventor; he was not supposed to repeat it himself, and no other poet could use this *son* (melody) without acknowledgment, unless it was for polemical purposes.

Different names were applied to these songs according to their form and nature (*pastourelle*, *estampie*, *tençon*, *jeu parti*, &c.).

Chrétien de Troie, who introduced *courtoisie* into the Breton Epic, was one of the first to write songs in the manner of the troubadours, but the chief representatives of this artificial lyric in the *langue d'oïl* are: **Conon** or **Quesne de Béthune** († 1219), who sang at the court of Marie; **Gace Brulé**, a knight of Champagne; **Gui**, the governor of the castle of Coucy († 1203), and **Thibaut de Champagne**, king of Navarre († 1253), the best and most original of them all.

In the hands of the commoners who practised the art, particularly in the *puys*,[1] or poetical competitions of the north

---

[1] The word *puys* means properly *peak*, *height*. Thus was called the platform on which the judges sat, and from which the competing poets recited their verses.

of France, the courtly lyric became more personal and satirical. Of these the most famous are **Adam de la Halle, Jean Bodel,** and **Baude Fastoul,** all three belonging to Arras.

The Third Period of French lyric poetry in the Middle Ages begins with the fourteenth century.

During this period varieties of lyric poetry having a more or less fixed form were developed, reduced to rule, and almost exclusively used. The *ballade* especially, the *rondeau*, the *virelai*, and the *chant royal* were the established forms.

The initiator of this new school was one Guillaume de Machaut, and his principal followers were Eustache Deschamps, Froissart the famous chronicler, Christine de Pisan, and Alain Chartier. Their poetry was a continuation of the artificial lyric of the south, in which art and grace were replaced by pedantic subtlety and scholastic dialectics. As they had little to say they determined to replace poetic inspiration by elaborating the technique of verse. A poet was truly great if he could write poetry with *annexed*[1] rhymes, still greater if he could rise to the *equivocal and retrograde*[2] rhyme or other such juggleries, although occasionally Machaut's followers essay to make passing events the subject of poetry, and in this way give us some idea of the men and manners of their age.

Their style was as complicated as their technique, and allegory, which had become almost obligatory since the Romance of the Rose, holds sway. Hence such strange titles as *L'Horloge Amoureuse*, *Traité de l'Épinette Amoureuse*, *L'Arbre des Batailles*, &c.

Guillaume de Machaut (1305 *c.*–1377) wrote no less than 80,000 verses. Occasionally in an odd *ballade* or *rondeau* the form is good, but in the whole of his production it can safely be said that there is not a line of real poetry.

Jean de Froissart (1337 *c.*–1404 *c.*) is the author of about

---

[1] A rhyme was known as *annexed* when the last syllable of one verse becomes the first of the verse following.
[2] A *rime équivoque et rétrograde* was one in which the last syllable of one verse becomes the first *word* of the verse following.

25,000 lines of lyric and didactic poetry very little superior to that of his master.

Eustache Deschamps (1340 c.–1406 c.) is a pupil of Machaut in form, but not in spirit. He it was especially who tried to find subjects for poetry in the events of his life and times, his best-known poem being the *ballade* on Du Guesclin:

Estoc d'honneur et arbre de vaillance.

Deschamps' works are very voluminous, and comprise no less than 1450 *ballades*, *rondeaux*, and other light pieces, besides a long satirical poem on women called *Le Miroir de Mariage* in 13,000 lines, and an *Art de Dictier et de Faire Ballades et Chants Royaux* (1392)—the earliest poetics in French.

Deschamps was a grumbler and a pessimist, but he had a real love for his country and for the poor.

Christine de Pisan (1363–1431) was of Italian parentage and birth, but came to France when quite a child. Left a widow at an early age, she was obliged to turn to literature to keep herself and her children. Her best verse productions are in the forms established by Machaut and his school, but often pedantic and marred by hurried composition,

Alain Chartier (1392 c.–1430 c.) was considered in his day as the greatest writer of the time. As a poet he is prosaic in the extreme. As a prose writer, though he did not often succeed in freeing himself from allegory and abstraction, he deserves to be remembered for his patriotism, and for his harmonious eloquence, acquired by a diligent study of the ancients, especially Seneca. A few pages in Alain Chartier are the best prose before the sixteenth century. They will be found in the *Quadriloque Invectif* (1422), in which France beseeches the representatives of the Three Estates to have pity on her wretched state.

CHAPTER III

DRAMA

(1) **Tragic Drama.**—The tragic drama of the Middle Ages is a continuation and expansion of the liturgical drama, which itself had developed from the church service, to which interpolations were gradually added for the greater edification of the faithful. Christmas and Easter especially were the seasons when these representations were given. The language was at first exclusively Latin and in prose, gradually verse was introduced, and French used side by side with Latin. The earliest play in which the vernacular (of Poitou) competes with Latin is *Sponsus* (1150 *c.*), a paraphrase of the parable of the Foolish Virgins. Finally, French ousted Latin, and as the audience and actors became more numerous the play passed from the church into the public street or square. The actors, who at first were priests supported by laymen, became later almost exclusively laymen.

Secular drama played outside the church by lay actors is fully established in the twelfth century. The oldest play of this kind in French (but with interspersed liturgical sentences in Latin) is the *Jeu d'Adam*, written in England by an unknown author in the twelfth century. The verse is octosyllabic, and the play is made up of three juxtaposed parts: the fall of Adam and Eve, the death of Abel, and a procession of Messianic prophets who announce the coming of the Redeemer. The style is simple but vigorous, and the coaxing of Eve by the devil shows considerable psychological insight.

Of the thirteenth century only two religious plays remain. The first, the *Jeu de S. Nicolas*, was composed by **Jean Bodel** of Arras, and played there, no doubt by a *puy* on the occasion of that saint's day. It consists of a mixture of tragic and comic scenes—a handful of Christians in combat against the Saracens, and tavern scenes teeming with life and realism.

The second is a so-called **miracle** play, or the recital of some miraculous event attributed to the Virgin or the Saints. It was written by the *trouvère* **Rutebeuf,** and styled *Miracle de Théophile:* an ambitious priest who sells his soul to the devil, but is saved in the end by the intervention of the Virgin Mary.

Of the fourteenth century forty-three *Miracles de Notre Dame* have been preserved. They formed the repertoire of some literary guild. Their literary value is not great, and they are only interesting for their strange blending of mysticism and realism. The authors of these Miracles drew on very varied sources: the apocryphal gospels, legends of saints, *chansons de geste,* and romances.

One of these, *L'Histoire de Griselidis,* a dramatized *fableau,* is entirely profane, and much more like a *morality* than a miracle.

In the fifteenth century a new kind of religious play appears, the **mystery,**[1] a distant offspring of the liturgical drama, which marks the culminating point of the medieval drama. A mystery can be defined as the exposition in dialogue of an historical event drawn from the Scriptures or the lives of the Saints. They were object-lessons intended to teach the masses the essential truths of religion.

According to subject, they can be divided into three large cycles:

The Cycle of the Old Testament;
The Cycle of the New Testament;
The Cycle of the Saints.

The first group is a kind of biblical encyclopedia, which, under the name of *Mystère du Vieux Testament,* includes a fusion of mysteries originally distinct. In the Cycle of the New Testament the most famous production is the *Passion* of **Arnoul Greban,** written about 1450, and embracing the

---

[1] The word *mystère,* in this sense, is derived from the Latin *ministerium,* and has no connection with the Greek word *mystery.* Originally the term *mystère* was applied to *tableaux vivants.* It was first applied to dramatic performances in the royal privilege which conferred upon the association known as the *Confrérie de la Passion* the right of performing sacred plays (1402).

entire earthly life of our Lord in 34,000 lines, which required 150 performers and four days for the delivery. But Greban, in alliance with his brother Simon this time, went one better, and composed the *Actes des Apôtres*, comprising 61,908 verses, and for which 498 actors were requisitioned. It was played with great success at Bourges in 1536, the performance extending over forty days.

Two mysteries, the subjects of which are taken from profane history, form an exception: the *Siège d'Orléans* and the *Destruction de Troie*, the last of which was probably never played.

In the Middle Ages the performance of a mystery set a whole city in motion. The costs were defrayed by the clergy, the town, or sometimes by a guild. The actors, who were amateurs, were recruited from all classes of society—advocates, priests, artisans, burgesses, &c.—by means of the *cry* or proclamation, which announced the enterprise, and invited volunteers to offer their services. On the day preceding the first day of performance the personages in their different costumes paraded the streets (*la montre*). We have already mentioned the large number of actors and the extraordinary length of time that some of these plays required. In them time and place were treated with the utmost freedom. The vast stage represented simultaneously all the localities in which the action was supposed to take place—paradise, Nazareth, Jerusalem, the sea, hell, as the case might be—and none of the actors quitted the stage. Nothing that could appeal to the eyes or senses was neglected; devils shot in and out of trap-doors, manikins were burnt or wracked, flames darted from the jaws of a dragon figuring the mouth of hell, while, when the case required it, an infernal din was kept up by the " master of the secrets " and his myrmidons in the invisible depths below the stage.

The oldest theatrical company giving regular performances was the celebrated *Confrérie de la Passion*, composed of burgesses and artisans, which already existed in 1398. In 1402 it received state recognition and the sole right to play sacred plays in Paris. This guild first gave its performances in the large hall of the Hospital of the Trinity, but in 1539 it migrated to the Hôtel de Flandres, and thence to the Hôtel de Bourgogne. On the model of this association similar ones were formed in the provinces.

The repertoire of the *Confrérie de la Passion* was at first composed exclusively of mysteries, but farces were ultimately introduced, and the Christian drama stifled under the growing abundance of popular and burlesque scenes, which had been added partly because the solemnity of the matter demanded relief, but still more because the actors found it pleased the audience better. The Parliament of Paris took fright; the Protestants were scandalized, as were also the lovers of classical art. In consequence that assembly decreed on the 17th of November, 1548, that the *Confrérie de la Passion* should be forbidden in future to play sacred dramas, though they were allowed to perform mysteries on profane subjects. About 1588 the *confrères* ceased to play, and yielded their hall to other actors; the opposition to classical tragedy became weaker and weaker, and at the end of the century the medieval tragic drama was as good as dead.

(2) **Comedy in the Middle Ages.** — The origins of French comedy are uncertain. The two oldest comedies, *Le Jeu de la Feuillée* (1260 *c.*) and *Le Jeu de Robin et de Marion* (1283 *c.*), have nothing in common with later productions, a fact which has led some authorities to suppose that they are the remnants of an early comic drama the history of which has remained unknown to us. Both these plays were written by **Adam de la Halle** of Arras.

The *Jeu de la Feuillée*, so called because it was played under a bower, probably by some *puy*, is a kind of review of the year in 1096 verses. Adam himself, his father and his wife appear, while his neighbours, friends, and enemies are also presented to us in a series of pictures, in which obscene realism and graceful fancy alternate.

The *Jeu de Robin et de Marion* is a kind of comic opera, a *pastourelle* in dialogue. The shepherdess Marion sings of her love for Robin while watching over her sheep; a knight appears and tries to win her love; she escapes from him, rejoins her companions, and after a series of rural diversions all join hands and execute a dance.

Of comedy in the fourteenth century only two dialogued pieces by Eustache Deschamps occur, which were not intended for the stage.

It was at this period that two societies were organized which were destined to play much the same part with regard to comedy as the *Confrérie de la Passion* did in the serious drama. These were the *Clercs de la Basoche* or *Clercs du Parlement*, and *Les Enfants sans Souci*. The *Basoche* had formed a corporation since 1303, but it was not till the beginning of the fifteenth century that they obtained the right to play farces and moralities.

About the same time some young men of the upper classes, who styled themselves *Les Enfants sans Souci*, likewise obtained the privilege to perform farces, and other pieces which received the name of *sotties*. Thus during the fifteenth century farces, moralities, and sotties, were the kinds cultivated.

The **farce,** of which we have one solitary specimen belonging to the thirteenth century, was a play the sole object of which was to amuse. It has a great deal of analogy with the *fableau*; in fact farces were often only *fableaux* in action. About 150 have come down to us. The best are *Le Cuvier*, a satire against women; *Le Franc Archer de Bagnolet*, a hit at boastful swashbucklers; and above all, *L'Avocat Patelin*, composed about 1470, by an unknown author:

> Patelin is a poor briefless barrister; his wife pesters him for some cloth to make a gown; he promises to gratify her wish, and wends his steps to the draper's. After having coaxed and beguiled him to let him have some cloth, he sets off, promising to pay the draper when the latter calls. The draper turns up duly and finds Patelin in bed with a raging fever, raving in every dialect. He must be mistaken; such a man could not have been lately in his shop and

bought some cloth. He goes away, convinced that he has been dreaming or been deceived by the devil. In the meantime the draper has dismissed his shepherd, Thibaut Aignelet, because he stole his wool and ate his sheep. The shepherd asks Patelin to defend him before the court; the latter, agrees; tells his client to affect idiocy, and to reply to all questions with "bée". The stratagem succeeds, and Thibaut gets off scot-free. Patelin asks for his fee, but can obtain no other answer but "bée", thus falling into his own trap.

The **moralité**, as its title implies, was meant to inculcate certain moral truths. Their character is very varied—mostly comic, sometimes quite serious, but always didactic; and the personages are generally allegorical figures, such as *Bien Avisé*, *Raison*, *Malechance*, *Oysance*, &c.

The **sottie** is much like the farce, except that its satire is more aggressive. It was used with a direct political purpose by Louis XII:

> *Le roy Loys douziesme desiroit*
> *Qu'on les jouast à Paris, et disoit*
> *Que par tels jeux il sçavoit maintes faultes*
> *Qu'on lui celoit par surprinses trop caultes* (cunning).

Thus **Pierre Gringoire**, a member of the *Enfants sans Souci*, in his *Sottie du Prince des Sots* (1512) backs up the king in his quarrel against Pope Julius II, who appears accompanied by *Simonie* and *Hypocrisie*, and introduces himself with the words:

> *Je ne me puis de mal faire abstenir,*
> *Ma promesse ne vueil* (veux) *entretenir;*
> *Ainsi qu'un Grec suis menteur détestable,*
> *Comme la mer inconstant, variable.*

The comic drama of the Middle Ages did not disappear entirely on the advent of the Renaissance; it had created a tradition which was continued in the sixteenth century and which is still felt in modern comedy.

CHAPTER IV

SATIRICAL AND ALLEGORICAL POETRY

(1) **Satirical Literature.** — Various renderings of the Æsopic fables were made from the twelfth century onwards, by way of the Latin fables of Phædrus and Avianus, with additions of Eastern origin. The most interesting of these is the *Isopet* (a generic name in the Middle Ages for any collection of fables whether Æsopic or not) of **Marie de France** (about 1180), the author of the more famous *lais*. These fables, mingling with the animal stories which had existed in popular tradition from the earliest times, may have helped to call forth the world-renowned **Roman de Renard,** one of the capital works of the Middle Ages, the different *branches* of which, taking them all together, cannot fall much short of one hundred thousand lines.

These branches are: the *Pèlerinage de Renard* and the *Jugement de Renard*, which both belong to the end of the twelfth century, and of which the authors are not known; *le Couronnement de Renard*, written soon after 1250, and *Renard le Nouvel*, the work of a poet of Lille, Jacquemart Gelée, nearly half a century later; *Renard le Contrefait*, composed at Troyes before 1328.

In the Animal Epopee the principal characters, characters which have become individualized, are: Reynard the Fox—whose name became so famous that it was applied to the whole class, and turned out the older word *goupil*—He it is who is the chief actor, while around him are grouped *Isengrin* the wolf, *Noble* the lion, and their wives; *Bruin* the bear, *Bruyant* the bull, *Brichemer* the stag, *Tibert* the cat, *Couard* the hare, *Chanteclair* the cock, *Pinte* the hen, and many others. The primitive form of the *Roman de Renard*, in which these scattered animal-stories were first grouped round one central hero, and which belongs to the early part of the twelfth century, is lost, but it can in part be reconstructed from the

Latin *Isengrinus* (1150 c.), and from the German *Reinhart Fuchs*, a rendering from the French by an Alsatian, Heinrich von Glichezâre (1180 c.).

In the primitive form and the earliest branches of the Romance of Reynard, wonderful skill is exhibited in keeping the characters mere beasts, while assigning to them human arts. The spirit is one of frank gaiety, untroubled by any didactic or satirical intention. Not so in the later branches. When it was perceived how easily the doings of the fox and his companions lent themselves to social and political satire, the beasts were more and more transformed into men; the whole became a huge and often dull *bourgeois* parody of the church and nobility, in which rascality and trickery (*renardie*) triumph over force. Things are still worse in *Renard le Contrefait*, which closes the series. It is nothing more than a kind of encyclopedia woven into the story, which itself has received distinct additions. Far inferior in execution to the other branches, it owed its prodigious success to allegory, at a time when allegory had invaded the whole of literature.

The same *bourgeois* spirit is apparent in the **fableaux** (the form *fabliau* belongs to the Picard dialect), short tales in verse—almost invariably octosyllabic couplets—dealing, for the most part from the comic point of view, with incidents of ordinary life. About 150 of these *fableaux* have come down to us. Their average length is from 200–300 lines. The period of their greatest popularity extends from the close of the twelfth to the beginning of the thirteenth century, though they appear as early as 1159 and as late as 1340.

It may be that a few of these stories have come down to us from the East, albeit the great majority of them only call for an inventive effort that does not exceed the capacity of the most ordinary experience. Their chief aim is to amuse. Too often, however, amusement is sought in ribaldry and obscenity. Many are satirical, but in this connection it should be noticed that the authors carefully avoid attacking powerful personages, and confine their attention to the peasant, the village priest, and, above all, to woman in general.

The *fableaux* are mostly by anonymous writers. Of the authors whose names are recorded the best known are: **Huon le Roi,** who wrote one of the most charming and least offensive of these tales, the *Vair Palefroi*; **Courtebarbe,** the author of *Les Trois Aveugles de Compiègne*; **Jean Bodel,** whose best are *Brunain* and *Gombert et les deux Clercs*; **Gautier le Long,** who composed the *Valet qui d'Aise à Malaise se met* (by marriage), and *La Veuve*; also **Bernier,** to whom we owe *La Housse Partie*, and **Rutebeuf,** the greatest poet not only of the thirteenth century, but of the whole of French literature prior to Villon.

His best work are the satires against the religious orders, the mendicant friars, and indeed against all clerics, students alone excepted; but, besides *fableaux*, and the *Miracle de Théophile* which is noticed under dramatic literature, he wrote the *Mariage Rutebeuf* on his own unhappy conjugal relations; the *Dit des Ribauds de Grève*; the *Dit de l'Herberie*, an amusing parody of a quack; and numerous religious pieces. Little is known of Rutebeuf, except that he lived a Bohemian life at Paris, in constant distress and misery, the result of lavish habits, a passion for gambling, and an unhappy marriage. His poems, judging by the allusions which they contain, must have been written between 1255 and 1280. They are in the dialect of the Ile-de-France. His most striking qualities are force, spirit, and colour, and some of his best productions reveal a touching personal note that reminds one of Villon, although, unlike Villon, he is almost entirely lacking in pathos.

Consequent on considerable changes both in society and literature, the *fableau* disappeared as a branch of literature in the second half of the fourteenth century. In the fifteenth it is represented by the prose *conte* and by the farce. The *conte* in verse belongs to a much later period.

Other species of satirical poetry are the so-called *états du monde*, in which universal satire is expressed. The oldest and most interesting of these is the *Livre des Manières*, by **Étienne de Fougères** († 1178). Here likewise may be classed the *Bible*[1] of **Guiot de Provins** and that of **Hugues de Berzé**, satirizing the whole of contemporary society.

Other poems mocked at certain classes of society only, clerks, peasants, usurers, and more especially woman. Of the last kind the wittiest is the *Évangile des Femmes*, recast and interpolated several times from the beginning of the twelfth century onwards. It is divided into quatrains of twelve syllables, in the last line of which the praise accorded in the first three lines is sarcastically upset.

Political satire, too, was full of life in the Middle Ages; at the beginning of the thirteenth century **André de Coutances** composed the biting *Roman des Français*. Neither were our neighbours across the Channel less sparing of satire in *La Paix aux Anglais* (1264), in *La Charte aux Anglais*, or in *Le Dit de la Rebellion d'Angleterre*, at the beginning of the fourteenth century.

Papal and royal vices were also attacked.

Half-way between satirical and allegorical poetry may be placed certain other pieces intended mainly to amuse. Such are the *dits*, short poems on events of daily life, usually; the *débats*, *disputes*, and *batailles*, generally between two allegorical personages; the *congés*, the *testaments*, the *fatrasies* or nonsense verse, and the *chastiements*, counsels on education and conduct, in which the didactic element has a large share.

(2) **Allegorical Literature.**—The earliest is found in the so-called **bestiaires**, treatises on natural history, in which descriptions of symbolic animals, full of fanciful science and fabulous traditions, serve as a basis for moralizing and religious instruction. When precious stones or birds served as a pretext to inculcate the lesson they were called *lapidaires* or *volucraires*. These fairy tales of science were borrowed

---

[1] Called *bibles*, not because they had anything in common with the Bible, but to indicate that they contained the truth, and the truth only.

from Latin versions, which themselves were derived from Greek and Eastern sources. The earliest versified *bestiaire* is that of **Philippe de Thaon** (before 1135), dedicated to Queen Aélis of Louvain. In its symbolic zoology the lion and the pelican are the emblems of Christ, the unicorn is God, the crocodile is the devil, and so on. Philippe is also remembered as the author of the *Comput*, a popular astronomy in verse, containing a calendar for the use of priests. In the thirteenth century **Richard de Fournival** († 1260), in his *Bestiaire d'Amour*, made use of these animal-stories for the interpretation of human love.

No doubt the rise of allegory was in part furthered by such productions, although it would appear to have spread in the main from sermons and theological treatises, in which the Seven Deadly Sins and other abstractions were treated as entities.

The representative poem of allegorical literature, and moreover the most remarkable literary achievement of the Middle Ages, is the **Roman de la Rose.**

The Romance of the Rose is not a homogeneous whole. It consists of two distinct parts, written at different periods by two different poets, the one representing the aristocratic ideal and the other the democratic spirit of the *fableaux* and of the *Roman de Renard*. The first part, of 4669 octosyllabic lines, was written in the first quarter of the thirteenth century by **Guillaume de Lorris,** an inhabitant of the little town situated between Orleans and Montargis; the second part, of 18,148 octosyllabic lines, was composed some forty years later (about 1278) by **Jean de Meung**.

Guillaume's poem is a scholarly allegorical code of courtly love, inspired by Ovid and Chrétien de Troyes. He tells us as much in the opening lines:

> *Ce est li rommanz de la rose*
> *Ou l'art d'amorz est tote enclose.*

The Rose is the emblem of the beloved lady. To pluck the

rose in the garden of Delight is to win the maiden, but to achieve this end is no easy matter:

> Wandering one May morning by the river banks, the dreamer —for all the incidents are placed in the setting of a dream—finds himself outside the walls of the domain of the god of Love; on the walls are painted figures of Hatred, Envy, Sadness, Old Age, Poverty, and other evil powers. Introduced by *Dame Oiseuse* (Idleness), he is attacked by Cupid, who, taking him at vantage, empties his quiver on him; he yields himself a prisoner, and learns Cupid's commandments on the evils and gains of love. Led by *Bel Accueil*, the lover approaches the Rose, but he is driven back by her guardians, Shame, Fear, *Danger* (Resistance, Refusal), *Malebouche* (Slander), and Jealousy, the last of which shuts up *Bel Accueil*, his friend, in a tower. The poem ends with a lament of the lover.

Such in brief is the outline of Guillaume's share of the Romance of the Rose. When Jean de Meung took up the parable in his continuation, he maintained, indeed, the essential thread of the allegory, and finally made the lover cull the rose, but the story in his hands becomes a mere pretext for satirical digressions, affording large scope for his vast erudition: dissertations on pauperism, property, government, the Church, justice, instinct, the nature of evil, the origin of society, witchcraft, marriage, woman in general, and a thousand other topics. His share of the work is a vast satirical encyclopedia, which supplements the pictures of medieval life offered by the later branches of the *Roman de Renard*.

Jean de Meung was the first popularizer of rationalism, of Nature as the guide of life: the true predecessor of Voltaire and more especially of Rabelais. The very contrast between the two parts of the Romance of the Rose contributed not a little to its enormous success, which spread far beyond France. In the following century it was severely censured, chiefly on account of its violent attacks against women, by Gerson and Christine de Pisan, but despite that, continued in favour right into the sixteenth century, thanks to Clément Marot's edition.

The *Roman de la Rose* did more than any other single poem

to assure the final victory of allegory, which for a period of two hundred years pervaded the whole field of literature.

CHAPTER V

HISTORY AND MISCELLANEOUS PROSE

History at first was written in Latin by clerks and monks; for the lay public the *Chansons de geste* and narrative poems took the place of history.

The first of these rhymed chronicles is due to **Geffrei Gaimar,** whose *Histoire des Anglais*, in octosyllabic verse, was written between 1147 and 1151.

Soon after **Wace,** born in Jersey about 1100, and later Canon of Bayeux, composed his two large historical poems, the *Roman de Brut* (1155), in 16,000 lines, and the *Roman de Rou* of the same length. The first is a compilation of Keltic traditions, drawn mostly from Geoffrey of Monmouth, in which Brut or Brutus, the grandson of Æneas, is represented as the ancestor of the Britons; the second sketches the history of the Dukes of Normandy from Rou or Rollo to Henry the First (912-1106).

Before Wace could finish his history he was replaced by the more fashionable **Benoît de Sainte-More,** to whom we owe the *Chronique des Ducs de Normandie*.

To the twelfth century also belongs the poem on *Saint Thomas le Martyr* by **Garnier de Pont Sainte-Maxence,** notable for the fine scene in which the murder of Becket is described.

Still more remarkable is the historically very important *Histoire de Guillaume le Maréchal*, Earl of Pembroke, of 20,000 lines or so, by an anonymous writer.

When it was found that verse was not conducive to accuracy in history, the rhymed chronicles were replaced by prose narratives. At the beginning of the thirteenth century a French nobleman, who had taken part in the fourth crusade, instead of entrusting the recital of his exploits to some clerk, took it into his head to give an account of them himself in French prose. His name was **Geoffroy de Villehardouin.** He was born in Champagne about 1160, and died in 1212 on his fief at Messinopolis in Thrace. There it was that he composed during the last years of his life the *Chronique de la Conquête de Constantinople* (1207 *c.*), the first great prose chronicle, than which no other single work gives a better idea of chivalry and feudalism.

Jean de Joinville (1224–1317), the next of the great chroniclers, wrote at the beginning of the fourteenth century, but his work, both in style and spirit, belongs to the same century as that of Villehardouin.

He was past eighty when Jeanne of Navarre, wife of Philippe le Bel, invited him to write the "*saintes paroles et les bons faits*" of Saint Louis, whose devoted companion he had been during his six years' crusade (1248–1254). His book, the *Vie de Saint Louis*, was completed in 1305 only, and as the Queen had died in the meantime, it was dedicated to her son, afterwards Louis X.

Joinville is interesting chiefly on account of his keen observation and the colour of his style.

Prose takes complete possession of the historical field with **Jean Froissart,** the last of the chroniclers proper.

> **Jean Froissart** was born at Valenciennes in 1338. Of his early years we possess no reliable information. The following are the chief facts of his later life: in 1361 he journeyed to England, receiving a gracious welcome from his countrywoman, Queen Philippa of Hainault, wife of Edward III, who appointed him Clerk of her Chamber. From 1364 to 1368 he travelled widely, visiting Scotland, Aquitaine, and Italy where he met Chaucer and Petrarch. At the death of his benefactress he returned home; became curate of Lestines, and later canon of Chimai (1385). As his canonry did not make residence obligatory, and as he was in want of materials for his Chronicle, he set out once more on his travels, returning to England for a three months' stay in 1395. That same year he came back to France, and seems to have died soon after 1404.

The *Chroniques* of Froissart include the period 1326-1390, and deal mainly with the affairs of France, England, and Scotland, although they likewise supply information in regard to Germany, Italy, Spain, and even occasionally touch on Hungary and the Balkan peninsula. Froissart's information, gathered during his wanderings in many lands, is often untrustworthy or partial. His merit lies in the vivid picturesqueness of his descriptions and in his brilliant, sympathetic picture of chivalry.

Next in order comes **Philippe de Commines,** who forms a link between the fifteenth and the sixteenth centuries.

Philippe de Commines was born at the castle of Commines, near Courtrai, about 1445. In 1464 he entered the service of the court of Burgundy, but in 1472 he passed over to the cause of Louis XI, becoming one of his most trusted advisers. On the King's death he incurred the displeasure of his successor, Charles VIII, and for eight months he was imprisoned in an iron cage; but in 1491 he was restored to a measure of favour; he accompanied Charles to Italy, and there met the famous Machiavelli. He held places and pensions under Louis XII, and died in 1511.

His *Mémoires* (1488-1495), which were not published till 1523, are the earliest French example of history as distinguished from the chronicle. For the knight-errantry of Froissart he substitutes a diplomatic shrewdness and a wide curiosity, applied not only to individuals but also to nations; he abandons brilliant descriptions for psychological observation and searchings after the causes of events. In his politics he is aristocratic and monarchical, but not despotic; his ideal government is constitutional and parliamentary; his ideal king one who knows how to listen to advice, and who leaves the decision of peace or war to the nation. Hence his admiration for England: " *De toutes les seigneuries du monde dont j'ai connaissance où la chose publique est mieux traitée, où règne moins de violence sur le peuple, où il n'y a nul édifice abattu ni démoli par la guerre, c'est l'Angleterre.*"

Commines, together with Villon in poetry, is the first of modern writers. Froissart and his predecessors ignore the mass of humanity; not so Commines, whose sympathy for the humble and the oppressed is quite a modern trait, as is also his thirst for knowledge and his undogmatic religion.

Miscellaneous Prose.—Among the miscellaneous prose writings of the Middle Ages, the exquisite *chantefable* of *Aucassin and Nicolette*, mainly in prose, but partly in assonanced *laisses* of seven-syllable verse, deserves more than passing notice. It was written about 1150 in the Picard dialect by an anonymous author. It is the story of the love of Count Garin of Beaucaire for the beautiful Saracen maiden Nicolette.

By far the best prose writer of the later Middle Ages is **Antoine de la Salle** (1386-1461 *c.*), who composed *Le Petit Jean de Saintré* (1456), the first, in point of time, of the long series of realistic novels in French literature, but who is not the author, as is frequently asserted, of either the anonymous *Quinze Joies de Mariage*, that pearl of medieval misogynic literature, or of *Les Cent Nouvelles Nouvelles*, a collection of obscene tales, suggested by Boccaccio's *Decameron*.

> Of written sermons the first occur in the twelfth century. Of these the best are those of **Maurice de Sully,** Archbishop of Paris, which do not offer sufficient literary merit to account for the extraordinary popularity which they enjoyed at the time.
>
> In the succeeding period the palm must be awarded to **Gerson** (1363-1429), who has already been noticed as a bitter enemy of the Romance of the Rose, although he himself experienced its influence.
>
> In the fifteenth century the two preachers, **Olivier Maillart** (†1502) and **Michel Menot** († 1518), courted favour by descending to the language of the populace. Their style is vivid, but often coarse.

Noteworthy also among the miscellaneous prose writings is the *Trésor* (1265 *c.*), by Dante's master, **Brunetto Latini,** chiefly on account of the author's remarkable testimony to the supremacy of the French language in his time: " *Et se* (si) *aucuns demandoit por quoi cist livres est escriz en romans selonc le langage des François, puisque nous somes Ytaliens, je diroie que* *ce est por deus raisons: l'une, car nous somes en France, et l'autre por ce que la parleüre est plus delitable et plus commune à toutes gens."*

CHAPTER VI

LATER MEDIEVAL POETS

With the fifteenth century the literature of the Middle Ages closes. Without being an epoch favourable to poetry or to literature in general, it is not the same dreary waste as the fourteenth century. It was in the fifteenth century that the medieval drama produced its masterpiece, the famous farce of *Patelin*, that Commines wrote his *Mémoires*, and that two genuine poets appeared, Villon, a man of the people, and **Charles d'Orléans**, the last representative of the graces and refinements of chivalric society.

Charles, duc d'Orléans (1391-1465), was the son of an Italian mother, Valentine of Milan, and of Louis of Valois, who was murdered by John the Fearless. In alliance with the infamous Bernard d'Armagnac, he did his best to avenge his father. He commanded at Azincourt (1415), and was taken prisoner and carried to England, where he spent twenty-five years in captivity, hunting, hawking, and composing light verse. At the age of forty-nine he returned to France, and passed his last years (1440-1465) in Epicurean ease at his little court of Blois, where he had gathered around him a small circle of poets.

His work consists of 102 *ballades*, 400 *rondels*, and 131 *chansons*. He was in no way an innovator in poetry; he made use of old forms, and, like his predecessors, he remained faithful to Dame Allegory, although he transformed the old material by an exquisite sense of art. His range is small, and his ideas lack depth, but the music and grace of his light verse, especially of his *rondels*, has rarely been surpassed. His favourite subjects are the changing seasons, the songs of the birds, lovers' fancies, and counsels against melancholy and care; **or,** in his later years at Blois, when the springtide of love was past for him, the deceiving arts of the fair and the folly of those who place their trust in them.

His style is clearness itself, and he is almost as easy to read as a modern poet.

A poet of infinitely greater genius was **François Villon**.

> **Villon.**—François de Montcorbier, or Des Loges, for his patronymic is not known for certain, was born at Paris, in 1431. He owes the name of Villon to an ecclesiast Guillaume de Villon, who took an interest in him and sent him to the University of Paris, where he took his M.A. degree. Till 1455 Villon had steered a straight course, but having killed his adversary in a duel he was compelled to flee from justice. Receiving letters of pardon six months afterwards, he returned to the capital. It was on the occasion of his first departure that he composed the *Petit Testament*, a collection of mock bequests to various friends and enemies with autobiographical details and allusions. The consequences of his first crime no doubt threw Villon into bad company. Resourceless and ostracized he joined a band of thieves, and was condemned to be hanged for a burglary committed by his gang; but the capital punishment was commuted to banishment. His chief work, the *Grand Testament*, an amplification of the smaller one, alludes directly to these events in the two famous *ballades*, *Des Pendus* and *De l'Appel*.
>
> We next come across Villon in 1461 at Meung-sur-Loire, in the cell of the local prison, where he had been confined by the Bishop of Orleans. Louis XI, passing through Meung after his recent consecration, to celebrate the event set all the prisoners at liberty, and among them our poet.
>
> From that moment we lose all trace of the reckless vagabond. He was dead when the *Grand Testament* appeared in 1489.

Villon's fame as a poet rests on the *Grand Testament*, which was completed in 1461. He conceived the idea of it during his incarceration at Meung, and finished it soon after his liberation. It consists of 178 stanzas each containing eight octosyllabic lines, in which about a score of minor pieces, chiefly *ballades* and *rondeaux*, some written previously, are inserted. The poet on the point of leaving this life casts a sorrowful glance over the past, confesses and laments the errors of his wild youth, and asks forgiveness of God. He thanks his friends and protectors, curses his enemies, and bequeaths to each fanciful legacies, as in the *Petit Testament*. The chief attractions of Villon, however, are not the satirical portions of his jesting bequests, but rather those short poems interspersed in the body of the work, such as the famous *Ballade des Dames du Temps jadis* with its still more famous refrain "*mais où sont les neiges d'antan?*" (but where are last year's snows?), in which the poet rises to the conception of the universal and all-levelling law of death. Almost as familiar is the epitaph in form of a *ballade* which Villon wrote on himself and his companions when expecting to swing with them: *La Ballade des Pendus*. In this song of death, in which there is an antinomy of grim humour and of simple but infinite pathos, the skeletons of Villon and of his fellows are supposed to address the passer-by who contemplates them, dangling on the gibbet of Montfaucon.

Most touching, too, is he in the expression of repentance for his lawless and debauched life. A proof that this repentance was sincere is afforded by the *Ballade que Villon feit à la Requeste de sa Mère*. Neither was he lacking in patriotic fervour and in ingenuous faith.

But his merit as a poet is not only intrinsic. He is a past-master in the technique of verse, handling with extraordinary skill the most artificial forms of poetry, such as the *rondeau* and the *ballade*. In fact, he has never been equalled in the latter.

Villon represents popular tradition. In contrast with the aristocratic Charles d'Orléans, he is exclusively a representative of the *esprit gaulois*, the father of that *élite* of essentially French minds to which belong Marot, Rabelais, Régnier, La Fontaine, Molière, and Voltaire. But more than that, he is the first modern French poet—modern in his abandonment of the traditional machinery of allegory and abstraction; in the complexity of his feelings, passing from mirth to despair, from beauty to horror—modern in that his poetry reflects his own personality.

Villon is the first great French poet, yet he cannot be classed among the greatest, his range being too narrow and limited.

After the death of Charles d'Orléans and of Villon the poetry of Machaut and his companions blossomed forth anew under the name of *rhetoric*. The most typical of the *grands rhétoriqueurs* are **Jean Molinet** († 1507), **Jean Meschinot** († 1509), and **Guillaume Crétin** († 1525), parodied by Rabelais under the name of Raminagrobis.

In fantastic, puerile, and inane metrical tricks they even went one better than their predecessors. The following lines from Crétin's works will give an idea of what they could do:

> *Pour vivre en paix et concorde, qu'on corde*
> *Guerre, et le chant qu'accord d'elle cordelle;*
> *Qui pour chanter à sa corde s'accorde,*
> *Mal prend son chant; amour telle est mortelle.*
> *Guerre a toujours, Dieu scait quelle sequelle;*
> *Livres en sont de plainctz et crys escripts;*
> *De guerre sourt beaucoup plus pleurs que ris.*

The fame of the *grands rhétoriqueurs* was as great in their day as it is now incomprehensible, and lasted till well into the sixteenth century. Even a true poet like Clément Marot was unable to free himself entirely from the shackles of these *facteurs* in poetry, as they most appropriately styled themselves.

BOOK II
SIXTEENTH CENTURY

GENERAL VIEW

Two leading influences dominate the literature of the sixteenth century—that of the **Renaissance** and that of the **Reformation**. The Renaissance strove to revive Antiquity in its ideas and in its art; the Reformation to return to a more primitive and purer form of Christianity.

In order to facilitate the study of the main influences that characterize the development of French literature during the sixteenth century, it is advantageous to make two main divisions. A third, extending from about 1585 to the first years of the seventeenth century, is a period of transition betokening new ideals.

First Period (1515-1549).—The signal for the Renaissance came from Italy and was given by the Humanists, who lent fresh life to the forgotten sense of Antiquity. The Middle Ages had not ignored the Latin classics, and had even translated and imitated them, but only as a means of arriving at a better understanding of Christianity and of improving moral life. The chief innovation effected by the Humanists of the sixteenth century sprang from their desire to study and understand Antiquity " for its own sake ", and by so doing, to transform the very basis of education and intellectual culture. Moreover, though the men of the Middle Ages were fairly well acquainted with Latin literature, they were almost wholly ignorant of Greek, which was looked upon as the language of the chief heresies. The Humanists were the first to give Greek an equal place with Latin. Other causes which led to the Renaissance were the consequences of the Italian wars of Charles VIII, Louis XII, and Francis I. Contact with Italy acted as a kind of revelation upon the Frenchmen of those days. To this must be added the peculiar charm of the Italian climate and manners. The Italy of the Renaissance, invaded, devastated and trampled under foot by these men of the North, bewitched its rough conquerors, as Greece of yore had captivated the Romans. They conceived the idea of a new life, freer, more ornate, more *human* in a word, than the one they had been leading for so long. The whole of Europe became Italianized, almost unawares, and in less than fifty years the remnants of medieval tradition had disappeared. No doubt many of the tendencies peculiar to the Renaissance already existed out of Italy, but it was the Italian genius which gave the decisive impulse.

The primary characteristic of the new spirit is **the development of individuality,** than which we can imagine nothing more directly opposed to the Middle Ages. It is for that reason that **Villon** and **Commines** may be considered the first modern writers. They are already *somebody*. With **Clément Marot** this trait becomes more accentuated; his poems are filled with himself and himself alone.

From this free exercise and development of the faculties another idea springs, which can be called the leading idea of the Renaissance, and of which **François Rabelais** is justly looked upon as the living incarnation—**the idea of the goodness or divinity of nature,** the contradiction and negation of what the Schoolmen and the theologians had taught for more than a thousand years. Rabelais was the first, with the exception of Jean de Meung in the thirteenth century, among French writers, to teach that the great foes of man were custom, rule, authority and restraint; that by every means in his power it is man's duty to attack and destroy these enemies; and finally, that the perfection of education is the liberation of the instincts.

Second Period (1549–1585 *c.*). — While Rabelais was publicly and openly setting forth the religion of Nature, another sentiment which he lacked was springing up and developing among a few of his contemporaries—**the sense of art,** in which the Middle Ages were so grievously deficient, and which is also largely characteristic of the Renaissance. Having rediscovered Nature and freed the individual, the Renaissance felt that the development of neither could be left absolutely to chance, and strove to make imitation of nature and individual development dependent on the realization of beauty. The poets of the **Pléiade,** and especially **Ronsard** their leader, were the first to perceive the full force of this new sentiment, and to reveal it to their contemporaries. They aimed at producing "works of art", and their ambition accounts for and explains their subsidiary efforts—their scorn for old literary forms, their imitation of classical rhythmical combinations, and their application of pagan mythology to French poetry. What they tried to wrest from Antiquity was not its philosophy, but only its art. Thus they were the first to point out the importance in literature of form and style, which are among the essential factors of French Classicism.

When men found out that a glorification of nature could lead to a justification of immorality, and that they were paying too dearly for the benefits of the Renaissance, the **Reformation** broke out. Nothing could be more erroneous than to represent the Reformation as analogous in its principles to the Renaissance. It is precisely the contrary. The only point they have in common is that, for a short time, they fought for the emancipation of the individual, and consequently stood face to face with the same enemies—the Schoolmen and the theologians. In preaching the Reformation Luther and Calvin not only attacked the Papacy and Catholicism; their object was to destroy the Renaissance, which was a new birth of pagan Antiquity, whereas the Reformation represented a return to primitive Christianity, as we have already said. This explains the opposition which the Reformation encountered at first in France. The country had not emancipated itself from the bonds of scholasticism and asceticism immediately to relapse into the tyranny of Protestant Puritanism. France, after having tasted the sweets of art and of independence, refused so early to be weaned, or to take up again one of the Germanic elements which it had cast aside as being too " Gothic ". The race asserted itself and went its own way.

The first effect of this transformation was what has been happily called the **Latinization of Culture.** Towards 1560, or thereabouts, in spite of the efforts of a few enthusiasts like **Henri Étienne,** the language of Homer more and more takes refuge in the seclusion of the colleges, and becomes once again the object of the attention of none but scholars and erudites. The dramatists of the sixteenth century no longer go to Sophocles or to Aristophanes for lessons in their art, but rather to Seneca or Plautus, and French writers in general, finding that Latin had qualities more in keeping with the genius of their race, returned to Latin tradition after the short poetic intoxication evoked by Greece.

Third Period (1580–1605). — During this period the remaining traits of the classical period begin to appear in outline. Firstly, **the foundation of literature on psychological and moral observation** announced by **Amyot's** translation of Plutarch, and carried out in the *Essays* of **Michel de Montaigne.** Nature, while remaining our guide, must be submitted to rule and discipline. Although the French people refused to accept the sombre and despairing morality of Calvin, they saw the necessity of reacting against the growing licentiousness of morals, and gradually **the philosophy of Reason** took the place of that of Nature. Finally, **the subordination of literature to social life,** which was to prevail in French literature for a period of nearly two hundred years, appears clearly in the works of the last writers of the century, who felt that the development of self might lead to the ultimate destruction of society. This is the central idea of French Classicism, and to see it fully at work we shall have to wait till the seventeenth century.

FIRST PERIOD (1500–1549)

CHAPTER I

POETRY

Among the immediate predecessors of Clément Marot one alone, **Jean le Maire de Belges,** born about 1473 at Bavay (Latinized into Belges), in Hainault, deserves more than passing mention, chiefly on account of the real influence which he exercised in his time, and also because of his prose work, *Les Illustrations des Gaules et Singularitez de Troie*. Both Marot and the school of Ronsard proclaimed him a master. Du Bellay, in the literary manifesto of the *Pléiade*, declares that he was the first to illustrate France and the French language: "*Luy donnant beaucoup de motz et de manières de parler poétiques, qui ont bien servi mesmes aux plus excellens de nostre tens*", while the English grammarian Palsgrave adduces his authority in his *Esclaircissement de la Langue Françoyse*.

Although Jean le Maire's work may be said in some points to foreshadow the Renaissance, he nevertheless belongs essentially to the school of the *grands rhétoriqueurs*, of whom he was by far the greatest.

Of his verse, the best examples are the two *Epîtres de l'Amant Vert à Madame Marguerite* (1505). The "green lover" is Queen Margaret's green parrot, who dies of grief at her departure, and from the nether regions writes to his beloved mistress an account of his journey.

In the *Illustrations des Gaules et Singularitez de Troie* Le Maire attempts to prove the Trojan origin of the French people, a favourite theme in the Middle Ages and sixteenth century. It is a medley of crude erudition, in which turgidity and bombast alternate with graceful fancy.

By far the greatest among the poets of the first half of the sixteenth century is **Clément Marot**.

> **Clément Marot** was born at Cahors about 1496. He was the son of Jean des Mares, surnamed Marot, one of the later *rhétoriqueurs*. About 1518 Clément entered the service of Princess Margaret, afterwards Queen of Navarre. In 1525 he followed the King, Francis I, to Italy, and is said to have been wounded and taken prisoner at the battle of Pavia. Soon afterwards he was imprisoned on a charge of heresy, in spite of his protestations:
>
> > *point ne suis luthériste*
> > *Ni zwinglien et moins anabaptiste;*
> > *Je suis de Dieu par son fils Jésus-Christ* (1525).
>
> He was liberated in the following spring, thanks to the intervention of Margaret, his patroness; but having made many enemies by his witty satires, aimed especially at the Sorbonne, and strongly suspected of leaning towards Protestantism, he first fled to the court of the Queen of Navarre (1534), whose sympathies were on the side of the Reformers, and later to that of the Duchess of Ferrara. He returned to France in 1536, but only on condition of a formal abjuration. The great success of Marot's translation of the Psalms awakened the suspicions of the Sorbonne; they complained to the King, and Marot thought it best once more to leave France. He made his way to Geneva, but his morals lacked the austerity required of a follower of Calvin, and he went on to Turin, where he died in 1544.

The works of Marot are composed: of translations and allegories, such as the translation of the first two books of the *Metamorphoses*, and his *Temple de Cupido*, or again his *Enfer*; of *chants royaux*, *ballades*, and *rondeaux*; of occasional pieces: *étrennes*, *blasons*, *complaintes*, &c.; of his translation of fifty of the Psalms.

Both by poetic inspiration and education Marot is closely connected with the preceding century. His learning is that of the Middle Ages:

> *J'ai lu des saints la légende dorée,*
> *J'ai lu Alain, le très noble orateur*
> *Et Lancelot, le très plaisant menteur.*
> *J'ai lu aussi le Roman de la Rose,*
> *Maistre en amours, et Vatere et Orose*
> *Contant les faits des antiques Romains.*

As a proof of his interest in earlier literature can be quoted his edition of the *Roman de la Rose*, and of Villon's works—" our Ennius ", as he calls him. He changed very little in the traditional medieval verse-forms and rhythmical combinations, and Boileau exaggerates when he says of him in the *Art Poétique*: " *Et montra pour rimer des chemins tout nouveaux* ". His immediate masters were the *grands rhétoriqueurs*, from whose puerilities he could never completely free himself,[1] and although he had dipped into Virgil, Ovid, and Catullus, he is essentially a national and popular poet. His temperament had much in common with that of Villon, whom he surpassed in clearness, grave and sly humour, though he could never attain to the simple pathos of the earlier poet. Charming a poet as Marot is, he cannot be ranked among the greatest; he was too much lacking in intensity of feeling, picturesqueness of vision, and vividness of style. Except in the translation of the Psalms, where the subject lent him some dignity, his work is in the main pretty rather than beautiful, light rather than strong, graceful rather than grand. He never could rise to higher flights. This must be borne in mind in order properly to understand the reform attempted by Ronsard and his associates in the second half of the century. Marot's great service to French poetry is that he restored naturalness and simplicity, and substituted native grace and delicacy for the artificial excess of ornament and allegory of the *grands rhétoriqueurs*. He is one of the most famous representatives of the *esprit gaulois*; he looks back to Villon and forward to La Fontaine.

---

[1] Cp. the *equivocal* rhymes (*mortel être* : *tel être; sous France* : *souffrance; argentier* : *large et entier*, &c.) which occur in his works, or the famous *ballade* of thirty-nine lines with rhymes in *ac*, *ec*, *ic*, *oc*, and *uc*.

Of his verse the most characteristic examples are the epistles and epigrams. Among them the best are the fable of the Lion and the Rat; the two famous epistles to the King, one *Pour avoir été dérobé*, and the other *Du Temps de son Exil à Ferrare*; the epigrams on Semblançay, or the one to the Queen of Navarre. Some of his *ballades*, too, are delightful, and everyone has read the famous rondeau, *Au Bon Vieux Temps un Train d'Amour regnoit.*

In the epigram Marot has never been surpassed; indeed his language is so closely connected with this form that all French writers since have used the "Marotic style" when writing this kind of verse.

In point of style and language he was a purist, as is proved by the fact that he is almost as easy to read as a modern writer.[1] It is probably for that reason he has at all times been a favourite with his countrymen.

We have seen that in more than one respect Marot continues the Middle Ages, but in two points he is a real child of the Renaissance, namely, in his belief in the goodness of Nature, and in the personal note which pervades his whole work.

Among Marot's disciples the most notable is **Margaret of Navarre** (1492–1549), sister of Francis I, his patroness. Her poetry presents a strange mixture of gallantry and mysticism. In the *Chansons spirituelles*, which betray the spirit of the Reformation, she exhibits genuine feeling; the verses written during her brother's illness, praying for his recovery, being especially touching:—

> *Oh, qu'il sera le bien venu*
> *Celui qui, frappant à ma porte,*
> *Dira; Le roi est revenu*
> *En sa santé très bonne et forte!*
> *Alors sa sœur, plus mal que morte,*
> *Courra baiser le messager*
> *Qui telles nouvelles apporte*
> *Que son frère est hors de danger.*

[1] Already in the seventeenth century La Bruyère had noticed this peculiarity: "*Marot par son tour et par son style semble avoir écrit depuis Ronsard: il n'y a guère entre Marot et nous que la différence de quelques mots.*"

She also composed humorous epistles like those of Marot, and *dizains* on the model of Petrarch, but in her later years her verse is almost exclusively religious: " *Elle aimait fort composer des chansons spirituelles,*" says Brantôme, " *car elle avait le cœur fort adonné à Dieu* ". The greater part of her works were collected by a publisher of Lyons in 1547, under the title of *Marguerites de la Marguerite des Princesses*.[1] This collection includes, besides poems, four mysteries and two farces, thus showing how varied was the talent of this most gifted woman, who so admirably represents the genius of her time. She is also the author of a series of prose tales, which will be noticed elsewhere.

The man who passed as the greatest poet after Marot's death was **Melin de Saint-Gelais** (1481–1558), to whom, along with Marot, is due the introduction of the Italian sonnet, so much favoured in the second half of the century. His fame was short-lived, and was eclipsed by the appearance of the *Pléiade*.

Saint-Gelais, who was a servile imitator of the Italians, sought for elegance, but fell into mannered prettiness and mawkishness; Melin *tout de miel* being a frequent pun among his contemporaries. He was the literary purveyor of court amusements in his *rondeaux*, *quatrains*, and poetical *mascarades*. Like Marot and most of his followers, he affected much the *blason*, which celebrates an eyebrow, a lip, a jewel, a flower, or a precious stone.

The transition from Marot to Ronsard is to be traced chiefly through the so-called **School of Lyons,** at the head of which stands Maurice Scève, and which includes also Louise Labé, *la belle cordière*, as she was called, besides several other women poets, and Antoine Heroët (1492–1568).

The works of **Maurice Scève** († 1564) consist of *Délie, Objet de plus Haute Vertu* (1544), a collection of 449 *dizains* in honour of his lady-love, which offer a strange combination

---

[1] Other poems of hers, of which the most striking is the Dantesque *Les Prisons*, have been recently discovered and published.

of mysticism and intentional obscurity, though certain passages are marked by great intensity of feeling. Less significant is *Le Microcosme* (1562), a descriptive poem in Alexandrine verse, of three cantos each of a thousand verses, in which the history of man on earth is set forth.

Maurice Scève was the first poet in the sixteenth century to have a real feeling for art, the first to seek inspiration in higher themes and break with court and occasional poetry.

It is for that reason that the *Pléiade* saw in him a kindred spirit. In one of his sonnets Du Bellay celebrates him as—

> *Gentil esprit, ornement de la France,*
> *Qui d'Apollon saintement inspiré,*
> *T'es le premier du peuple retiré,*
> *Loin du chemin tracé par l'ignorance.*

Étienne Pasquier gave proof of a correct appreciation of Scève's position when he wrote in his *Recherches* (1560): "*Le premier qui franchit le pas fut Maurice Scève, Lyonnais*", but he was also right when he added that *Délie* was written "*avec un sens si ténébreux et obscur que, le lisant, je disois estre très-content de l'entendre, puisqu'il ne vouloit estre entendu*". It was Marot's gracefulness and Scève's higher aspirations that Ronsard and his school tried to combine.

Louise Labé (1526–1566) wrote (*a*) a dialogue in prose, *Le Débat de Folie et de l'Amour*, an allegory after the old school; (*b*) twenty-four sonnets, of which one is in Italian; and (*c*) three elegies.

Her romantic personality, and the fact that she was idolized by so many contemporary poets, has led to an over-estimation of her poetic worth; yet her sonnets and elegies, though often incorrect and stiff, are songs of a true passion felt, as she declares, "*en ses os, en son sang, en son âme*". Amid much antithesis and metaphor, one often meets lines of genuine inspiration:

> *D'un tel vouloir le serf point ne désire*
> *La liberté, ou son port le navire,*
> *Comme j'attends, hélas, de jour en jour,*
> *De toi, ami, le gracieux retour.*

CHAPTER II

DRAMA

The history of the Medieval Drama has been discussed in a preceding chapter. We noticed there that up to the end of the first half of the sixteenth century it held undisputed sway, that in 1548 the Parliament of Paris had to forbid the *Confrérie de la Passion* to continue to represent sacred subjects, and that this date marks the official end of the old drama.

Of those who wrote medieval plays in this period (1515–1549), besides Gringoire, **Nicole de la Chesnaye** and **Jean de Pourtalis** deserve to be noticed. The first wrote the allegorical *Condamnation du Banquet*, and the latter is the supposed author of the *Contredits de Songe-Creux* (1531), a satirical review of society, in prose and verse.

CHAPTER III

PROSE

Among the prose writers of the first half of the sixteenth century the greatest name is that of **François Rabelais,** whose real figure has been obscured by popular tradition, which fashioned a new Rabelais after the model of his book. Rabelais was not a buffoon or a drunkard, but one of the most learned men that ever lived, who in his moments of leisure and for his own amusement, composed one of the greatest books in the world's literature.

> **François Rabelais** was born about 1494 at Chinon in Touraine, and received his first schooling at the Abbey of Seuilly, near his birthplace. He became a novice of the Franciscan order, and entered the monastery of Fontenoy le Comte, where he had access to a large library; acquired Greek, Hebrew, and Arabic, and studied all the Latin and Old French authors within his reach, as well as medicine, astronomy, botany, and mathematics. But the Francis-

cans, growing jealous of his wide learning, took away his books, and Rabelais left the monastery. In 1524 he was allowed to pass over to the Benedictine order. In 1530 he entered the University of Montpellier, but soon left for Lyons to get his first book, parts of Hippocrates and Galen, published. He remained there as physician to the hospital. In 1532 and the following year he was engaged on literary work. In 1534 he accompanied Bishop Du Bellay to Rome, and again in 1536. From 1537 (when he took his doctorate) to 1539 he taught at Montpellier. He then went back to Lyons, returned to Paris in 1540, and once more made things right with the Church, obtaining permission to enter the collegiate chapter of St. Maur des Fossés instead of a monastery. Francis I, who was well-disposed towards Rabelais, died in 1547; the authorities attacked Rabelais for impiety, and he was obliged to escape to Metz and thence again to Rome, in the company of Cardinal Du Bellay, who himself was suspected of liberal tendencies. Through the protection of his friends he was enabled to return in 1549, and obtained the living of Meudon, near Paris, which he gave up in 1553. On the appearance of the fourth book of his great work a new storm broke out; both Catholics and Protestants demanded that it should be suppressed and the author burnt, but the influence of his patrons prevailed once more. Rabelais probably died the next year (1553) at Paris.

Apart from his medical books, the fragment of an almanac, and his satirical prophecy for the year 1533, the *Pantagruéline Prognostication*, Rabelais' work consists of a long buffoon epic on a fabulous dynasty of giants, Grandgousier, Gargantua his son, and Pantagruel, son of Gargantua. This epic is made up of five Books, the first devoted to Gargantua and his parents, and the last four to Pantagruel.

The date of the composition of the several Books is as follows: Pantagruel, First Book, 1533; Gargantua, 1535, which is the refashioning of a Chap Book published by Rabelais in 1532 under the title of *Chronique Gargantuine*; Pantagruel, Second Book, 1546; Pantagruel, Third Book, 1552.

Finally, a fourth book on Pantagruel, the Fifth Book of the whole work, appeared in 1564. This Fifth Book is certainly not entirely by Rabelais, but it is impossible to distinguish what is not his own. Its satire is much too bitter and bold to be entirely the work of one of the shrewdest and most prudent of men, who was prepared to maintain his opinions "*jusques au feu, exclusive*". It sounds more like a Huguenot pamphlet. A short analysis of the five Books follows:

First Book. *Gargantua.*—Relates the birth, childhood, and education of Gargantua; his arrival in Paris on his big mare, and his successful war against King Picrochole. At the end of the war Gargantua constructs the famous Abbey of Thelema to reward the zeal and gallantry of the monk, brother Jean des Entamures. In the earlier part of the book the most interesting pages are those where Rabelais contrasts the medieval education, the one which Gargantua received at first, which consists mainly in drinking, eating, sleeping, and learning by heart, with the more modern, which he afterwards receives from his new tutor Ponocrates, and which embraces a union of bodily and mental exercise, hitherto kept apart, strict observation of the laws of hygiene, daily practice in all kinds of athletics, outdoor lessons in astronomy, and instruction derived from amusement itself.

Second Book, *Pantagruel.*—The plan of this book is almost identical with that of the first, though more fanciful and less didactic. It relates the birth, education, and wars of Pantagruel. But the main point of difference is that we are for the first time introduced to the incomparable Panurge, the fellow of Shakespeare's Falstaff in his lack of morals and inexhaustible wit, who becomes the devoted and inseparable companion of Pantagruel.

Third Book.—This book, save for one short episode, is entirely occupied with the adventures and exploits of Panurge, who for his services in the late war is appointed Lord of Salmigondin, " an estate producing a revenue of 6,789,106,789 royals certain, besides a varying income arising from periwinkles and locusts, which might amount to 2,435,768 or 2,435,769 gold *moutons* ". After leading a dissipated life for some time, Panurge is suddenly alarmed at the idea of being without anyone to look after him in case of illness. He consults his master as to whether it would not be wiser for him to marry, a question which, from now till the end of the fifth book, determines the course of the story. Panurge consults in turn the *sortes Virgilianæ*, the sibyl of Panzoust, the old poet Raminagrobis, Herr Trippa, the greatest professor of astronomy, geomancy, chiromancy, and other sciences. None of these giving a satisfactory answer, he turns from the wisdom of the ancients to that of the moderns: the theologian Hippothadeus, the physician Rondibilis, the judge Bridoye, who gives his decisions by a throw of the dice, are approached for advice, but none can give a decisive reply. In despair Panurge and his friends go to the fool Triboulet, who recommends them to try the oracle of the Divine Bottle, *la Dive Bouteille*, which can only be reached by a long and perilous journey in unknown seas, and among islands little visited.

Fourth Book.—They embark at St. Malo. The ships are laden with every kind of provisions, and they start on their distant expedition, which is described in detail in the last two books. The quest is long and perilous; in each island at which the party touch some social or ecclesiastical abuse is held up to ridicule: the Island of Procuration, the land of litigation and chicane, where the Pettifoggers and Catchpoles live—by being beaten; the Island of Tapinois (Sly-Land), where reigns Prince Quarême-Prenant, the personification of Lent, "the standard-bearer of the ichthyophagists, the father and foster-father of physicians"; the Ile Farouche, inhabited by the fanatical Protestants; the blessed Island of Papimanie, where the fanatical Papists dwell, &c.

Fifth Book.—On the fourth day the pilot sights the Ile Sonnante, or Isle of Ringing, another satire on the Catholic Church, and this time a bitter and angry one. Next the lawyers and judges are again and more severely handled under the name of Chats Fourrés (Furred Cats), at whose head stands Grippeminaud. Shortly after the travellers arrive at the port of Matæotechny (Vain Art), in the kingdom of Queen Quintessence, whose officers "cut fire into streaks with a knife", or "try to catch the wind with nets". Finally they reach their journey's end, and consult the oracle, whose reply is the word "*Trincq*"—drink, that is of the pure water and wisdom of knowledge. Such a question as that of Panurge is not worthy to attract the attention of a sage.

The exuberant mirth and rich epic life of Rabelais' story no doubt contains a deeper meaning than appears on the surface. The writer himself in the preface declares that the reader must " break the bone in order to suck the marrow ", if he wishes to get at the hidden truth. In the same passage, however, he speaks of the " *doctrine absconce* " and the " *mystères horrifiques* " which his story contains. These bombastic expressions show plainly that Rabelais is jesting, jesting at the mania of the Middle Ages of wishing to interpret all things allegorically. They are obviously a warning not to give way to a systematic allegorical explanation of the whole. Rabelais relates much purely out of love for his subject, especially the coarse jests and obscenities with which the work abounds, and those who seek a deeper meaning here resemble the officers of Queen Quintessence, who try to catch the wind with their nets. The opinion that Rabelais' book is a complicated puzzle cannot too much be guarded against; the satire of Scholasticism, of lawyers, of the mad adventures of chivalry, of monks, and of the Romish court, when it occurs, is obvious enough, and not very revolutionary either, if we except the Fifth Fook, which is certainly interpolated. Rabelais' main object was to amuse, occasionally to instruct and moralize, but without feint or disguise.

What is still plainer is Rabelais' philosophy of life, his militant faith in Nature and instinct, the source of the eighteenth-century ethics and of modern French Realism, to which he has given concrete form in the famous Abbey of Thelema, an abbey whose rule has but one single clause: " Do what thou wilt, because men who are free, well born, well educated, and conversant with honourable company, have naturally an instinct which prompts them to virtuous actions and withdraws them from vice. This is called honour...."[1]

Since Nature is good, and we hold our faculties from her, let us develop them to the utmost extent, unhampered by ascetic restraint or by other artificial trammels in ethics or philosophy; let man be as *complete* a man as it lies in his power to be. Such is Rabelais' ideal, as it was to be that of Goethe more than two hundred and fifty years after.

Rabelais' style is racy and picturesque, full of the most original and attractive imagery; but too often his power of verbal invention gets the better of him, and then his language becomes a verbal orgy — metaphors, synonyms, proverbs, Latinisms, neologisms, and endless enumerations being jumbled together in the utmost confusion. He was a very great writer, but totally devoid of any feeling for beauty.

[1] Cp. also the allegory of Physics and Antiphysics (*Pantagruel*, iii, 32).

The influence of Rabelais is seen in the numerous story-writers of the time. Not to mention several authors, who directly imitated or parodied Pantagruel, the two most famous names are those of **Bonaventure Des Periers,** and the poetess **Margaret of Navarre** (1492-1549), whose collection of tales appeared in 1558 under the title of *Heptaméron des Nouvelles*. The series, which was designed to equal in number that of Boccaccio's *Decameron*, is incomplete. A company of ladies and gentlemen detained by floods on their return from the Pyrenean baths, beguile the time by telling these tales. Margaret was directly inspired by Boccaccio, save that her stories are all real; " *une chose différente de Boccace, c'est de n'éscrire nouvelle qui ne fût véritable histoire* ", as she informs us in the preface. Most of them are borrowed from court life. The hero of No. 25 is Margaret's own brother, King Francis I; and No. 10 is the story of the authoress's own life. Only about half a dozen farcical stories occur, the greater number being love stories nearly as free as those of the *Decameron*. The riskiness of the *Heptaméron* is a little surprising, in one who was known to her contemporaries as a good and pious lady; but then we must not forget that they are only shocking according to the proprieties of our time, and that Margaret wrote in the sixteenth century, at a time when it was thought quite legitimate to laugh at the immoralities of monks and priests. In short, the grossness of some of the stories merely exemplifies the grossness of the language and manners of the times. The *Heptaméron*, as is proved by the *Dialogues*, which separate the *days*, was written for the purpose of moral edification, strange as that may seem to us.

Bonaventure Des Periers (1510 *c.*-1544 *c.*) is the author of the posthumous *Nouvelles Récréations et Joyeux Devis* (1558), in which Rabelais' influence is evident, although Des Periers is more temperate, and does not lapse into the exaggerations of Rabelais' wit and the exuberances of his style. He is more in the spirit of the old French farces and *fableaux*. The *Joyeux Devis* are almost solely a collection of anecdotes, in which love stories give way to farces. The majority of the tales have their scene in France: "*Je ne suis point allé chercher mes contes à Constantinople, à Florence ni à Venise*", says the author in the delightful introduction, where he adds with more subdued Pantagruelism, "*Je vous donne de quoi vous réjouir, qui est la meilleure chose que puisse faire l'homme*". Most of them, too, are taken from hearsay or from the author's own experience. The tone is occasionally free, but more often quite harmless.

Des Periers also wrote the *Cymbalum Mundi* (1537), a violent attack against the Gospels, and the theologians, both Catholic and Protestant. As a poet he belonged to the school of Marot. He likewise attempted *vers mesurés*, or quantitative verse, and translated Horace into *vers blancs*, or unrhymed verse.

While Rabelais was exuberantly proclaiming his doctrine of the goodness of Nature, a stern and sombre counter-cry came from **Jean Calvin**, the leader of the Reformation in France, the representative of the new spirit of intransigent reform, and attempted restoration of primitive Christianity.

> **Jean Calvin** was born in 1509, at Noyon in Picardy, where his father was *procureur-fiscal*, and secretary of the diocese. He studied theology, and then law at Orleans. From Orleans he went to Bourges, where he learned Greek, and began to preach the reformed doctrines. He made his literary *début* with a Latin commentary on Seneca's *De Clementia*. After the famous discourse of Nicolas Cop, rector of the Sorbonne, which had been inspired by Calvin, the latter was obliged to quit Paris and take refuge at Angoulême. As persecution was raging hotly against the *heretics*, Calvin no longer felt safe in France, and proceeded to Bâle. In 1536 he issued his famous work the *Christianæ Religionis Institutio*. The same year he went to Ferrara in Italy, revisited his native town, sold his paternal estate, and set out for Strasbourg by way of Geneva, where the reformer Farel persuaded him to remain and assist in his work. But the party of the *libertins*, or free-thinkers, gaining the upper hand, Calvin and Farel were expelled from the town (1538). The same year he settled in Strasbourg, where he married. In 1541 the Genevans, wearying of libertine licence, invited Calvin to return, and after some hesitation he accepted the invitation. During fourteen years he carried

on a struggle against the *libertins*, overcame all opposition, and finally set up an autocratic theocracy in Geneva, which became the religious centre of the French Reformation. He died in 1564.

Calvin was a young man of twenty-seven, living obscurely in Bâle, when the imprisonment and burning of the Reformers by Francis I, rousing him to indignation, called forth his famous letter to Francis (1535). Silence, he said, would have been treason. In this letter, which the year after was prefixed to his great theological work the *Christianæ Religionis Institutio*, he protests against the accusations of those who had wished to persuade the King that the followers of the Reformation were nothing but rebellious and seditious subjects. In 1541 Calvin translated the *Institutio* into French. The *Institution de la Religion Chrétienne* is the first theological treatise written in the French language, and by opening up a wide field of thought to those ignorant of Latin, is epoch making.

It is composed of four Books: of God; of Jesus as Mediator; of the Effects of His Mediation; of the Exterior Forms of the Church. Like Luther, Calvin founded his doctrine exclusively on the Word of God as contained in the Bible. But while Luther accepted everything from the Catholic Church which did not directly contradict the Bible, Calvin rejected everything that could not be expressly referred to God's Law.

Calvin's central idea is the doctrine of predestination, as contained in the Epistle to the Romans, ix, 10–23: Man is a fallen being; his will and his righteousness are both powerless to obtain salvation; God, of his mere good pleasure, predestines some men to eternal life without any regard to their goodness or virtue, and condemns others to eternal death " in order through their damnation to glorify His majesty "; the Son of God came to earth to redeem the elect only. At the same time, and in the midst of this grim theology, Calvin finds room to deliver attacks against the sacraments of the Church, the celibacy of priests, the authority of the Holy See, &c.

In the case of Calvin the style is indeed the man—stern, imperious, lofty, and gloomy.

The *Institution* is the first great prose work of the sixteenth century.

In contrast also to the positive spirit of Rabelais and his followers stands the famous *Amadis des Gaules* (1540–1548), translated from the Spanish of Montalvo and his successors by **Herberay des Essarts** († 1550 *c.*). It is a continuation, as it were, of the Romances of the Round Table and its chivalric ideals, which, coming back to France from Spain, were fashioned by the author to suit the tastes of his contemporaries. The characteristics of the *Amadis* are knightly adventures, courtly gallantry, daring deeds of arms, and a love of the supernatural. The leading personages, besides Amadis, the son of King Perion of Wales and of an Armorican princess, are Galaor his brother, Oriane his future wife, and their son Esplandion. Des Essarts only translated the first eight books, but he had imitators and continuators. In the same way as Montalvo's four books had multiplied to twelve, so did the eight of Des Essarts extend to twenty-four (1550–1613), but it was the first eight books which became especially popular, being translated into English, German, and Dutch. " *On y pouvait cueillir toutes les belles fleurs de notre langue* ", says Pasquier.

The extraordinary vogue of the *Amadis des Gaules* lasted till the advent of the seventeenth-century pastoral and chivalric romances, which it had called into existence.

SECOND PERIOD (1549-1605)

CHAPTER I

POETRY

The second half of the century marks the advent of a new poetic school, whose ideal finds expression in a group of writers who styled themselves the **Pléiade**, and at whose head stands **Pierre de Ronsard**.

After deafness, consequent on a serious illness, had closed for him the avenue to public life, Ronsard resolved to seek fame in another path, and to throw himself ardently into the study of Antiquity. With that end in view he shut himself up in the Collège Coqueret. There he met a number of students animated with the same desire, and who also shared the lessons of the principal, Jean Daurat, the famous Hellenist. Around Ronsard gathered the " Brigade ", composed of **Baïf, Joachim Du Bellay, Remi Belleau,** and Ronsard himself, which, by and by, with the addition of **Pontus de Thyard, Jodelle,** and their common master, **Daurat,** was to become the *Pléiade*, in allusion to the seven stars of the Pleiads, and also to their Greek prototypes of the court of the Ptolemies.

Dissatisfied, after a careful study of Greek and Latin models, with the state of the French language and literature, they conceived for that language an ideal of literary beauty which should rival that of Antiquity.

In the first place, it was necessary to clear the ground, and thus a great part of their doctrine is purely negative, and in direct opposition to their predecessors, Clément Marot and his school. In the second place, they asserted in face of the pedantry of the Humanists, the "*latiniseurs*" and "*grécaniseurs*", that the native tongue was capable of such rivalry, and proposed to show by what means it could be made to attain this end.

At length, in 1549, they flung out their manifesto, the most important study in literary criticism of the century. The treatise was by Du Bellay, but breathed the spirit of Ronsard. It was styled *Défense et Illustration de la Langue Française*. During the same year and the next Ronsard and Du Bellay published poetical works illustrating the theories of the seven associates. The excitement in the camp of Marot and his followers was great, but in spite of a counter-manifesto, the struggle did not last long, and already in 1550 Ronsard was fully established and looked upon as the Prince of Poets.

To obtain a just insight into the theories of the *Pléiade* it is necessary to take into consideration, besides Du Bellay's manifesto, the *Art Poétique* (1565), and the two prefaces of the *Franciade* (1572–1573 or 4), both due to Ronsard, which form a complement, and generally a confirmation of the *Défense et Illustration*. The literary reform of Ronsard and his school bears on three principal points:

The creation of a poetic diction distinct from that of prose. Struck by the fact that the poetic language of the Greeks has a vocabulary, forms, and turns of its own, the *Pléiade* tried to create a language peculiar to poetry—richer, more expressive, and more sustained than prose. To this end they did not borrow, wholesale, words from Greek or Latin, as has sometimes been supposed.

The well-known lines [1] of Boileau on Ronsard have no foundation in fact. The *Pléiade* sought to innovate with discretion, and, apart from the Greek and Latin words which were already current in the sixteenth century, they only borrowed mythological adjectives and classical proper names. Far from encouraging poets to talk a kind of Latinized French, Ronsard especially recommends them to write " in French ", and warns them against the pedantry of those *écoliers limousins*

---

[1] *Ronsard qui le* (Marot) *suivit par une autre méthode,
Réglant tout, brouilla tout, fit un art à sa mode,
Et toutefois longtemps eut un heureux destin.
Mais sa muse, en français parlant grec et latin,
Vit dans l'âge suivant, par un retour grotesque,
Tomber de ses grands mots le faste pédantesque.
Ce poëte orgueilleux, trébuché de si haut,
Rendit plus retenus Desportes et Bertaut.—Art Poétique,* l.

who prefer *collauder* and *contemner* to *louer* and *mépriser*.¹ What does occasionally impart to the poetry of the *Pléiade* a foreign look is the excessive use of mythological adjectives and classical proper names. Compare, for example, the following lines from Ronsard's *Odes*:

> *Mais tout soudain, d'un haut style plus rare,*
> *Je veux sonner le sang Hectoréan,*
> *Changeant le son du Dircéan Pindare*
> *Au plus haut bruit du chantre Smyrnéan;*

and also certain turns and constructions inspired by the study of the poetry of the ancients, to which they had recourse for the attainment of their proposed select and aristocratic idiom for verse. They recommend the use of adjectives for nouns or adverbs (" *le frais des eaux* ", " *il vole léger* "); of paraphrases like " *le Père foudroyant* ", instead of Jupiter, and "*la Vierge chasseresse*", instead of Diana, &c. The other innovations which they introduced were eminently French, and consist of no more than 200 new words, borrowed, according to their doctrine, from old French (*greigneur, souloir, déduit, guerdon, los*, &c.); from the dialects (*harsoir = hier soir, besson = jumeau, bers = berceau*, &c.); from the technical vocabulary (*creuset, brisées, erre, havet, maillet*, &c.), or composed either by *provignement* or derivation (*enrocher, engemmer, blondoyer, vanoyer, sourcer, doucelet, seulet*, &c.), or by juxtaposition (*chevre-pied, fier-humble, donne-vin*). The first manner of juxtaposing words is alone blameworthy; the two others are in the spirit of the language (cp. *aigre-doux* and *portefeuille* in modern French); but the later followers of the *Pléiade*, and especially Du Bartas, brought them into discredit by using them too freely and injudiciously.

The substitution of classical forms for the older forms of French poetry. On this point the *Défense et Illustration* is very explicit; *rondeaux, ballades, virelais, chants-*

---

¹ Compare also Ronsard's words in the second preface to the *Franciade*: " *C'est un crime de leze-majesté d'abandonner le langage de son pays, vivant et fleurissant pour vouloir deterrer je ne sçay quelle cendre des anciens* ".

royaux, chansons, are to be cast aside, and replaced by odes like those of Horace or of Pindar, by the elegy, epigram, or sonnets in the manner of Petrarch. *Fatrasies*, too, and *Coq-à-l'âne* must give way to regular satire, and moralities and farces yield to tragedy and comedy modelled on Seneca and Plautus.

A reform of versification. On matters of versification the *Défense* says very little. Du Bellay is content to recommend the cultivation of rich but not over-curious rhymes. As if conscious of the gap, Ronsard gives fuller information. In fact, the innovations in rhyme and rhythm are the personal work primarily of Ronsard. More liberal than Du Bellay, he permits *enjambement*, or the carrying over of a clause begun in one line into the next without any break. He also allows hiatus on the ground of classical example; but, more important, to Ronsard is due the reintroduction of the Alexandrine, especially in lyrical poetry, and the honour of having imposed it on later writers as the French verse *par excellence*, and also of having created almost all the rhythms used after him, and even some which have not been utilized since.

In conclusion, we cannot do better than quote the following lines from Ronsard, which so eloquently sum up the aspirations of the *Pléiade*, and the reforms attempted and carried out by them and their leader:

> *Je vy que des François le langage trop bas*
> *A terre se trainoit sans ordre ny compas:*
> *Adonques pour hausser ma langue maternelle,*
> *Indonté du labeur, je travaillay pour elle,*
> *Je fis des mots nouveaux, je r'appelay les vieux,*
> *Si bien que son renom je poussay jusqu'aux Cieux.*
> *Je fys, d'autre façon que n'avoyent les antiques,*
> *Vocables composez et phrases poëtiques,*
> *Et mis la Poësie en tel ordre qu'après*
> *Le François fut égal aux Romains et aux Grecs.*

By far the most important members of the *Pléiade* are **Pierre de Ronsard** and **Joachim Du Bellay**.

Ronsard was born in 1524 near Vendôme, of an old family, perhaps of Hungarian origin. At an early age he entered the service of the son of Francis I, and afterwards that of James V of Scotland. After his return to France he was sent on various diplomatic missions. These and the fatigues of court life undermined his health, and he was struck with deafness, and, as we have seen, resolved to devote his life to the study of Antiquity and art. Already, a year after the publication of the *Pléiade's* manifesto, Ronsard was recognized as the greatest living poet, and during a period of forty years was destined to occupy this lofty position. Never was man placed so high by the universal admiration of his contemporaries; his works were imitated in nearly all European literatures; Tasso sought his advice; the Italians placed him above Petrarch; Mary Stuart and Queen Elizabeth vied with each other in sending him gifts, and his deafness made men compare him to Homer. His death, at the close of 1585, was felt as a national calamity, and princely honours were paid to his tomb.

Ronsard's poetic work can be divided into four periods.

From 1550 to 1554, fresh from the teachings of Daurat, he is an exaggerated and indiscreet Humanist—the devoted follower of Pindar and Petrarch. The first three books of the *Odes* are an attempt at a resuscitation of the former, and though Ronsard could not rise to the height of his original, yet the study of Pindar trained him in the handling of sustained periods of verse, and interested him in complex lyrical combinations. Then followed the *Amours de Cassandre*, closely modelled on Petrarch, and partaking rather of the artificial character of old French " *courtois* " poetry than of the passionate character of modern lyricism.

From 1554 to 1560 he abandons Pindar, and imitates the poets of the Alexandrine school, a collection of whose works had just been published by Henri Étienne, under the impression that they were those of Anacreon. In 1555–6 he composed *Les Amours de Marie*, a blending of voluptuous ardour and melancholy; the fourth and fifth book of the *Odes*, Gallic in tone and spirit, and recalling the *chansons* of Marot; and some *Hymnes* after the pattern of Callimachus, in which description and rhetoric prevail.

From 1560 to 1574 Ronsard was in part a court poet. In this period he also wrote the *Discours sur les Misères de ce Temps*, aimed at the Huguenots, and which may be said to have endowed French literature with the Satire, and began his epic poem *La Franciade*, fortunately left unfinished. In this poem Ronsard discourses on the travels of a fabulous son of Hector, Francus, who, after the fall of Troy, pursued by fate, finally lands in Gaul and conquers that country.

From 1574 to 1584 his work, though less in bulk, is more mature and original. This is the period of his admirable *Sonnets à Hélène*, in which the poet is really himself.

Ronsard's genius is mainly elegiac and lyrical. He is exquisite whenever by chance his intentions as a scholar tally with his temperament, or whenever the poet gets the better of the Humanist. He is unsurpassed in the so-called secondary kinds of poetry, but in higher themes inspiration too often fails him. Before all else he is a master of his instrument—the creator of endless rhythms and verse-combinations unknown to his predecessors.

After Ronsard, the brightest light in the poetical constellation is undoubtedly **Joachim Du Bellay.**

> **Joachim Du Bellay** was born in 1522 at Lyré, near Angers, of an illustrious family. After an unhappy youth, which left indelible traces of melancholy on his character, he proceeded to Poitiers to study law. Soon after he became acquainted with Ronsard and joined Daurat's band. The same year as the *Défense et Illustration de la Langue Française* (1549) he published a collection of sonnets probably in honour of Mlle de Viole, under the anagram "Olive". In 1553 he accompanied, as *Intendant* his cousin Cardinal Du Bellay to Rome, but a diplomatic career proved uncongenial to him. Abandoned by the cardinal and his friends, his health grew rapidly worse, and he died in 1560.

Du Bellay's *Sonnets à Olive*, written in the style of Petrarch, are, with a few exceptions, strained and affected, falling far short of their model. Later, Du Bellay recanted, and went so far as to write a satire against the Petrarchists. At Rome for the first time the poet found his true self: he is no longer a pure imitator, but translates into verse his most intimate feelings. In the *Antiquités de Rome* [1] he expresses the sentiment of ruins for the first time in French literature. Du Bellay had started for Rome full of enthusiastic hopes, which his first impressions did not belie. He was soon undeceived: the cynical intrigues of the Pontifical court, the corruption of Roman society, indifferent health, the torments of an unhappy love, and a longing for his " sweet " province of Anjou—all this tended to embitter his natural melancholy and to depress his spirits. A reflection of this mood is found in the sonnets of his *Regrets*, partly satirical, which appeared in 1559, and are indisputably his best work. About the same time Du Bellay, by the publication of the *Jeux Rustiques*, charming rural songs, of which the best are the well-known *Vanneur de Blé* [2] and *Vénus*, showed that his poetic genius was not one-sided. These were followed by *Le Poëte Courtisan*, a biting satire against court poetasters.

Du Bellay is the most original and modern of the poets of the *Pléiade*. Though he was the enthusiastic spokesman of the new School, his lyrical inspiration often triumphed over the somewhat narrowing spirit of his associates. This struggle between originality and theory explains a certain number of contradictions in his poetical productions, as well as in the *Défense*.

The other members of the *Pléiade* are of comparatively little importance, with the exception of Jodelle (*vide* Drama). They offer nothing which cannot be found in Ronsard and Du Bellay, and much which is only a caricature of their genius.

Thus **Antoine de Baïf** (1532–1589) strove to revive the quantitative metrical system of classical verse. He wrote several volumes of *vers mesurés*, as they were then called. Most of the poets of the sixteenth century tried their hand at such verse, but soon abandoned the attempt as contrary to

---

[1] Translated by Spenser under the title of the *Ruins of Rome*.
[2] Translated by Andrew Lang in *Ballads and Lyrics of Old France*.

the genius of the language. Baïf has been blamed for having forged comparatives and superlatives after the Latin pattern: *doctior, doctisme*, &c. This he did, but only jestingly.

Remi Belleau's (1528–1577) poetry is purely of the descriptive kind, but occasionally redeemed by a delicate feeling for nature. His most interesting production is the *Pierres Précieuses*, an adaptation of the medieval *lapidary* to the taste of the Renaissance.

Ronsard and the *Pléiade* inaugurated the French classical school. Their work was continued by Malherbe, and brought to perfection later by Boileau. They maintained that the true poet could not do without study and art; that nature unassisted does not produce masterpieces, and that the ancients alone must be our guides. What they often failed to perceive was the link which unites Antiquity and truth, imitation and originality; the masterpieces of Greece and Rome are admirable not because they belong to Antiquity, but because they are founded on imitation of nature, and on reason. The second great fault of the school, due to its intellectual and limited outlook, is that they dried up for two centuries the spring of popular and spontaneous poetry. Yet they did not suppose, like some of the writers of the seventeenth century, that the total play of emotion must be rationalized by the understanding; occasionally a poem is the outcome of personal and sincere feeling.

The Reformation, too, had its poets: Guillaume Salluste, Seigneur du Bartas, a contemporary of Ronsard, and Théodore Agrippa d'Aubigné whose capital work only appeared in the seventeenth century, but who in spirit is wholly of the sixteenth century.

Guillaume Salluste du Bartas (1544–1590) began by the publication of *Judith* (1573), an epic poem, in which the Catholics saw an apology for regicide. This was followed up by his chief work, *La Première Semaine* (1578), and its continuation, *La Seconde Semaine* (1584). The first *Semaine* is a long epic poem on the creation of the world, an adoration of the Almighty in the marvels of nature, while the second *Semaine* is a kind of universal history. The popularity of this epic was immense, and in a few years it had passed through thirty editions. Although its conception is not without grandeur, and a few passages of real beauty are to be found in the midst of much laboured and rhetorical description, it is difficult for us now to account for this contemporary enthusiasm, confined, as it may largely have been, to the followers of the Reformation who wished to oppose Du Bartas to Ronsard. The style and language of Du Bartas are absolutely devoid of art—rough and barbaric. His rhymes, too, are often provincial. He is a kind of caricature of Ronsard, and, together with Baïf, is responsible for the discredit into which the chief of the *Pléiade* subsequently fell. He makes an especial abuse of the Homeric compounds introduced by the *Pléiade* (" *Le feu donne-clarté, porte-chaud, jette-flamme* ", " *Mercure eschelle-ciel, invente-art, aime-lyre* ", &c.). A list of more than three hundred such compounds has been compiled from his works. To gain effect he also affects the repetition, in nursery wise, of the first syllable of a word (" *les flo-flottantes et bou-bour-donnantes ondes* "). Although admired by Milton, Byron, and Goethe, Du Bartas is but a very mediocre poet, always copious, rarely majestic, and nearly always turgid. His works as a whole are unreadable now, in spite of a few fine passages scattered over the body of the *Semaines*.

Théodore Agrippa d'Aubigné (1552–1630) was a greater poet. In his early verse, *Le Printemps*, *Hécatombe à Diane*, &c., he is nothing but a belated Ronsardist, lacking in taste, while in *La Création*, closely modelled on Du Bartas, he is even more flat and frigid than his master. But these were only initiatory efforts. The passions of the Reformation period awoke him to his true poetic vocation, and from a poet of the court and of love, transformed D'Aubigné into an angry satirist. The *Tragiques* is the first notable work in French after the manner of Juvenal. It was begun in 1577, after the battle of Castel-Jaloux, and continued on different occasions till 1594, but did not appear as a whole till 1616. It presents a picture of the ills which afflicted France during the religious struggles. In the first three cantos, entitled *Misères, Princes, La Chambre Dorée*, D'Aubigné describes the civil wars, the corruption of the court, and the infamy of the tribunals, ready to sell Justice to the highest bidder. The last four cantos, *Feux, Fers, Vengeance, Jugement*, show the martyrs of the new faith dying at the stake and in the dungeon, or butchered on St. Bartholomew's Eve; and in spite of these persecutions the steady growth of the Reformed Church, the executioners struck by divine vengeance on this earth or condemned to eternal torture by the tribunal of God.

The *Tragiques* as a whole is wearisome reading. Force, imagination, abundance of images, a few fine lines,[1] occur side by side with obscurity of diction, superfluity of detail, repetition, and painful effort.

Victor Hugo was well acquainted with the *Tragiques*, and many a passage in his *Châtiments* shows the influence of D'Aubigné.

Other works of D'Aubigné are *Sa Vie à ses enfants*, which covers the period between 1557 and 1618; *L'Histoire universelle*, a vindication of militant Calvinism (1553–1601); a religious pamphlet called *La Confession de Sancy*, which has been called, and not without justice, the first of the *Provinciales*, and in which D'Aubigné represents a worthy Huguenot nobleman, who has become converted to the Catholic faith, and confesses his past errors. It is a model of ironical satire. After the *Tragiques*, D'Aubigné's best-known production is the satirical tale *Les Aventures du Baron de Fœneste*. De Fœneste (derived from φαίνεσθαι) relates in half-Gascon French, and in boastful and partly ironical language, his experiences during his travels, on the field and chiefly at court, to the Huguenot M. D'Enay (from εἶναι). D'Aubigné contrasts the man who *appears*—the sponging and penniless

---

[1] Cp. *Les corbeaux noircissant les pavillons du Louvre; Ils sont vêtus de blanc et lavés de pardon; L'air n'est plus que rayons, tant il est semé d'anges; A l'heure que le ciel fume de sang et d'âmes.*

courtly Panurge, whose whole life is founded on show, and who with his last penny purchases a tooth-pick, instead of bread, to show that he has dined copiously—with the man that *is*, the man who lives on his estate, among his rustic neighbours, tilling his fields and serving his people and his native land.

Ronsard's influence lasted till the end of the sixteenth century; but the poets of that period, instead of imitating the classics and attempting higher themes, preferred the antitheses and hyperboles of the lighter and softer Italian lyrics. They are absolutely devoid of originality and creative power; often the prettiest passages in their poetry are only plagiarisms from beyond the Alps. Form is their chief merit.

> These remarks apply especially to **Philippe Desportes** (1546–1606), the typical court poet. He composed sonnets, odes, elegies, and mascarades, and translated parts of Ariosto's *Orlando Furioso*, and also the Psalms. His verse is elegant and graceful, but not infrequently marred by conceits and affectation.
>
> **Jean Bertaut** (1552–1611) wrote amatory and religious lyrics in imitation of Desportes. He is less artificial, but still more affected than his master.
>
> **Jean Vauquelin de la Fresnaye** (1536–1602) deserves notice as the author of the first collection of regular satires, which, however, were largely borrowed from the Italians Sansovino and Ariosto. To him we also owe an *Art Poétique* (1575), in which the tenets of the *Pléiade* are formulated.
>
> More interesting than these is **Jean Passerat** (1534–1602), a poet of the Gallic tendency of Villon and Marot. His *Œuvres* (1606), consisting of sonnets, elegies, epigrams, eclogues and light verse, are witty and in good taste. The eclogue *Catin*, and the *vilanelle*, *J'ai perdu ma tourterelle*, will always appeal to the reader of French literature.

CHAPTER II

DRAMA

The blow dealt to the medieval drama by the decree of the Parliament of Paris (1548) was followed up the year after by an appeal in Du Bellay's *Défense et Illustration*, inviting future playwrights to turn to Antiquity for their models, and to replace the medieval plays (miracles, mysteries, moralities, farces, and *sotties*) by regular comedy and tragedy based on classical models: " *Quant aux comedies et tragedies, si les roys et les républiques les voulaient restituer en leur ancienne dignité qu'ont usurpée les farces et moralitez, je seroys bien d'opinion que tu t'y employasses.*"

Jodelle responded to this invitation, and three years after the *Défense* he inaugurated the modern drama with the tragedy of *Cléopâtre* and the comedy of *Eugène*, which were both performed on the same day by Jodelle himself and some of his friends in the Collège de Boncourt, in presence of the Court. As Ronsard says, Jodelle

> . . . *le premier d'une plainte hardie*
> *Françoisement sonna la grecque tragédie,*
> *Puys, en changeant de ton, chanta devant nos rois*
> *La jeune comédie en langage françois.*

Nevertheless, the new drama won its way but gradually. Profane mysteries perpetuated the traditions of the Middle Ages; the exclusive privilege which the *Confrérie de la Passion* enjoyed prevented the training of actors capable of interpreting the new art, and the school of Jodelle was reduced to having its plays performed by students or the nobility in colleges or at Court. It was purely academic and learned, whereas the popular drama of the Middle Ages held the stage, and could alone be used as a vehicle for satire or polemic. Moreover, as the decree of 1548 applied to Paris only, plays of a sacred character (mysteries) continued to be written and acted in the provinces, together with the older repertoire, or were dubbed by the name of tragedy and tragi-comedy, probably with the idea of balking the authorities. Such plays are *Les Enfants dans la Fournaise* (1561), *Le Triomphe de Jésus Christ* (1562), *L'Holopherne* (1580), *Le Caïn* (1580), and *La Macchabée* (1596), which are nothing but mysteries; while *Philanire* (1560), *L'Amour d'un Serviteur* (1571), *Lucille* (1576), and *Akoubar* (1586) bear close relationship to the morality.

Thus, while the old medieval repertoire continued to be served up anew on the popular stage, fresh plays on the same lines, though in gradually decreasing numbers, were added to it till quite the end of the century.

Finally, the force of circumstances induced the *Confrérie de la Passion* to make a compromise with the new school, and towards 1588 they hired out their privilege and their hall (Hôtel de Bourgogne) to a troop of comedians who, thanks to the goodwill of Henry IV and the return of peace (1593), were able to play classical tragedy and comedy. The medieval drama took refuge in the provinces, and languished till it was finally eclipsed by the splendours of the drama of the seventeenth century.

Tragedy.—The way for a reform in dramatic poetry, comedy as well as tragedy, had been to some extent prepared by plays written in Latin, the work of Buchanan, Muret, and others, and also by translations from Sophocles and Euripides.

The first tragedy in French representing the new school was, as we have seen, Jodelle's *Cléopâtre* (1553). His example was soon followed by a number of other poets, whose tragedies can be grouped according to subject into classical or religious plays; while a third group, which can be called political, owes its birth to the desire of the Protestants and their adversaries to use the stage for polemical purposes. Such are, e.g., *La Guisade* (1589), *Le Guysien* (1592), and **Chantelouve's** *Coligny* (1575), in which the theme is the murder of the illustrious admiral.

Lastly, the Protestant reformer **De Bèze**, in *Le Sacrifice* *d'Abraham*, and **Louis Desmasures**, in three tragedies on the life of David, attempted a kind of compromise between the medieval mystery and classical tragedy.

The chief representatives of French tragedy, based on classical models, in the sixteenth century are: Étienne Jodelle, Jacques Grévin, Jean de la Taille, Robert Garnier, and Antoine de Montchrétien.

The *Cléopâtre* of Étienne Jodelle (1532–1573) was the first French " regular " tragedy. The plot was borrowed from Plutarch. The play is divided into five acts with choruses. In acts ii, iii, and v the decasyllabic line is used, but the Alexandrine appears in acts i and iv. There is hardly any dramatic action, and the play is scarcely more than a succession of declamations. These faults, though in a lesser degree, are shared by all Jodelle's successors in the sixteenth century. They are due to the influence of Seneca, whose works were copied in preference to those of the great tragedians of Greece, firstly, because the scholars of the time had a better knowledge of Latin than of Greek, and secondly, because the perfection and admirable simplicity of Greek models were much more difficult to imitate than Seneca's declamatory style —it was easier to versify awe-inspiring catastrophes than to depict real characters and passions. Seneca's influence was also reinforced by **Scaliger's** Latin commentary on Aristotle's *Poetics* (1561), wholly founded on the tragedies of the Roman poet.

Lack of action in *Cléopâtre* is not atoned for by the style, which is loose, turgid, and pompous. It is the first French play in which Unity of Time appears. Like its successors, it is oratorical and lyrical, but not dramatic. The date of Jodelle's second tragedy, *Didon se sacrifiant*, is uncertain. It is still more devoid of action than *Cléopâtre*, albeit superior in point of style. The Alexandrine measure is used throughout, and since then it has ranked as the standard verse of tragedy. Whatever the merit of Jodelle's two plays may be, they are important historically: the choice of subjects, the small number of characters, the simplicity of action, the tendency to observe the Unities, mere narrative in lieu of dramatic action, and a sustained effort to attain *le style noble*, all suggest classical tragedy.

Le Mort de César (1560) of **Jacques Grévin** (1538-1570) shows some improvement on his predecessor, especially as regards the style, which is less obscure and ponderous.

Jean de la Taille (1540-1611) was the first to treat Biblical subjects in accordance with the precepts of the new school. He chose King Saul as the hero of a tragedy, "*faite selon l'art et à la mode des vieux auteurs tragiques*": *Saül Furieux* (before 1562). In 1573 he composed *Les Gabéonites*, a continuation of *Saül*. Both these plays, in the midst of much that is purely oratorical and declamatory, offer certain scenes that are not without dramatic life.

Garnier and Montchrétien represent the height of French tragedy in the sixteenth century.

Robert Garnier (1544-1590 c.) wrote eight plays, of which the first six (*Porcie, Cornélie, Marc Antoine, Hippolyte, La Troade,* and *Antigone*), closely modelled on Seneca, show little improvement on those of his predecessors. After his Latin or Greek tragedies he issued a sacred tragedy, *Sédecie* or *Les Juives* (1583), his masterpiece. The play, which takes its name from the choruses, composed of Jewish maidens, exhibits the revolt of the Jewish king and his punishment by Nebuchadnezzar. We notice in it a marked improvement in action; and a genuine feeling for the spirit of the Bible has enabled the poet to trace real characters in the persons of Nebuchadnezzar and Amital. His heroic and majestic style, which in places recalls Corneille, was much admired by his contemporaries; in one of his sonnets Ronsard exclaims:

> *Quel son masle et hardy! quelle bouche héroïque*
> *Et quel superbe vers entens-je icy sonner!*

while the lyrical utterances in the plaintive songs of the chorus prove that Garnier was assuredly a poet if not a dramatist. Unity of time is observed in Garnier's plays, but unity of place is neglected.

The year before *Les Juives* he wrote *Bradamente*, an example of the new form of tragi-comedy, or tragedy with a happy ending. The subject is romantic, and borrowed from cantos 44-46 of Ariosto's *Orlando Furioso*. Rüdiger, after surmounting endless dangers, wins his Love, Bradamente, sister of the four sons of Hemon. Both place and time are freely treated. The dialogue is free from sententious maxims; comic and tragic scenes are interwoven, and no choruses appear.

Of the six tragedies left by **Montchrétien** (1575 c.-1621), by far the best is *L'Écossaise ou Le Désastre*, in which he depicts the sad fate of Mary Queen of Scots. As far as dramatic action is concerned, *L'Écossaise* is a retrograde step on Garnier. The first two acts are filled with sententious political tirades, in which Elizabeth and her councillors debate as to whether Mary shall die or not; in acts iii and iv the prayers and lamentations of the unhappy Queen leave room for nothing else, while the last act is devoted to a minute account of her execution. The two rivals do not even meet. The charm of the play lies in the beautiful lyrical passages, superior even to those in Garnier, the elegiac softness of which has won for Montchrétien the name of "the Racine of the sixteenth century". His tragedies connect the sixteenth century with the classical school of the seventeenth century.

Comedy in the sixteenth century, if we omit translations and imitations from Aristophanes, Plautus, and Terence, is neither Greek nor Latin. It is derived mainly from the medieval farce and from Italian comedy.

As in tragedy, **Jodelle** was the first to show the way, his *Eugène* appearing in 1552. In spite of the fact that it is called a comedy, and of its polemical prologue, it is little more than an old farce decked out in more regular and rhetorical language.

Two years after, **Grévin** wrote *La Maubertine* (the woman from the Place Maubert) and *La Trésorière*, in which Jodelle's influence is obvious; this was followed by *Les Esbahis*, freely modelled on a translation from the Italian of Ch. Étienne. In each of these three plays the octosyllabic line is used, as in the medieval farce.

In imitation of his Italian models **Jean de la Taille** employs prose for the first time in the *Corrivaux* (1573). **Odet de Turnèbe** (1553–1581) also used prose in *Les Contents* (1584).

The most remarkable name in the history of sixteenth-century comedy is that of **Larivey** (1540–1611). He was of Italian origin, but Gallicized his name (*il Giunto = l'arrivé*). He adapted from the works of contemporary Italian dramatists with great tact and discretion. To suit the requirements of French readers he changed the locality of the scenes, the names of the characters, suppressed or added passages and parts with so much judgment that his adaptations are nearly always superior to the originals. But his chief title to fame consists in his style, teeming with popular and proverbial expressions, which did so much to advance the art of dialogue. Of the dozen plays due to the pen of Larivey nine have come down to us, of which the best by far is *Les Esprits* (the Ghosts), imitated from the *Aridosio* of Lorenzino de' Medici.

In general the comedy of the sixteenth century in its intrigue bears a close similarity to the imbroglio of Italian comedy; its types of character are purely conventional (merchants, panders, ruffians, bullies, parasites, and bourgeois), and in general the language is even more grossly indecent than that of medieval farce.

CHAPTER III

PROSE

Among prose-translators we find such well-known names as Ronsard, Du Bellay, Belleau, Baïf, Du Vair, &c., but none of these can compare with **Jacques Amyot**, of Melun (1513–

1593), professor of Greek and Latin at the University of Bourges, and afterwards tutor to the sons of Henry II, and finally Bishop of Auxerre. His first translation, *Théagène et Chariclée*, appeared in 1547, and was destined to have great influence on the development of the French novel. In 1559 followed *Les Amours Pastorales de Daphnis et Chloé*, from Longus; and the same year he completed for his princely pupils the translation of Plutarch, which he had previously begun at the request of Francis I. To Henry II he dedicated the translation of the *Vies des Hommes Illustres de Plutarque*, and to Charles IX the *Œuvres Morales* (1572).

Amyot's translations from Plutarch had an enormous success, opening up a source of moral and historical culture for which his fellow-countrymen had long thirsted: " Plutarch," says Montaigne, " is my favourite book since it has become French ", and he always quotes according to Amyot's version. In another passage of his *Essays* (ii, 4) he adds: " *Nous autres ignorants (du Grec) estions perdus, si ce livre ne nous eust relevé du bourbier: sa mercy* (thanks to it), *nous osons à cett' heure et parler et escrire; les dames en regentent* (teach) *les maistres d'eschole; c'est notre bréviaire.*" Montaigne's words show the importance of the Plutarch translations in helping to spread the knowledge of Antiquity, and as a book for ladies. From the time of Amyot's translation Plutarch is known in French literature as *Amyot*. But such success was impossible without excellence in execution; Amyot gives the sum of Plutarch's ideas, and penetrated so deeply into the Greek author's thought that he may be said to have made it his own; in fact he not infrequently surpasses the original in clearness and precision. There may be mistranslations in his version, but he is no philologist; his main object was to place the ideas and life of the ancient world at the disposal of French readers, and to enrich the literature of his country,

afin que sans danger,
Le Français fût vainqueur du savoir étranger,

as Ronsard says. Amyot went out to conquer fresh fields, but *conquistadores* are apt to be violent, and he did not scruple to Gallicize the antique conditions of life to suit his public, translating vestal maidens by "*religieuses*", and providing Alexander the Great with "*huissiers à verge*" and "*gentils-hommes de la chambre*". Local colour, however, is after all only a poetic ornament, and this slight blemish is amply atoned for by the fact that Amyot, anticipating Montaigne, helped to found French literature on a moral and psychological basis.

Beginning with the reign of Henry II (1548) Memoirs and Biographies abound. We shall proceed to discuss the most important.

For fifty-five years **Blaise de Monluc** (1502–1577) held a command in the army of the king—of this his scars remind him, which cover his whole body with the exception of his right arm. Finally a gun-shot tore away half his face, and compelled him to wear a mask. Retiring from the Service in 1574 as Marshal of France, he decided " *d'employer le temps qui me reste à descrire les combatz auxquels je me suis trouvé pendant cinquante et deux ans que j'ai commandé, m'asseurant que les capitaines qui liront ma vie, y verront des choses desquelles ils se pourront aider, se trouvans en semblables occasions, et desquelles ils pourront aussi faire profit et acquérir honneur et réputation*". The outcome of this resolve was the *Commentaires* (printed in 1592), which Henry IV is said to have called the " soldier's Bible ".

Monluc was a faithful and brave servant of his master, his watchword being to gain honour in the service of the King. He laments the victims of war, and is conscious that their curses are weighing down upon him—but the King commanded. He could unfortunately, he says, enforce obedience by means of cannon only. He would have done still more harm to the Huguenots if it lay in his power, for they are the King's enemies; yet he is no fanatical Catholic, and would have no objection to becoming a Huguenot " if the King first of all changed his faith "—his religion, too, is " *au service du roi* ".

Monluc's directness of speech, and the rough soldierly humour of the narrative, enlivens the *Commentaires* with what has been described as " the poetry of war ".

The " *révérend père en Dieu* ", as **Brantôme** (1540–1614), the secular possessor of ecclesiastical benefices, styled himself, was also a soldier like Monluc, but more of a courtier. He was as fickle and unsteady as Monluc was true and staunch; he was, he tells us himself, " *du naturel des tabourineurs* (drum-players), *qui aiment mieux la maison d'autrui que la leur* ", a *condottiere*, who roamed all over the East, and crossed over to Scotland on the same ship as Mary Queen of Scots when she left France for the last time. In 1583 a fall from a horse maimed him for life, and, confining him to his estates, prompted him to write his experiences—feats of war, love stories, scandals, duels, &c.

Brantôme's works, which did not appear till 1665–1666, include: *Vies des Hommes Illustres et des Grands Capitaines Étrangers*; *Vies des Hommes Illustres et des Grands Capitaines Français*; *Vies des Dames Illustres, des Dames Gallantes*; and *Anecdotes touchant les Duels*.

His style is pleasant and chatty, but his vision is neither wide nor profound; he feels interest only for what clatters, glitters, or amuses, and shows a disconcerting incapacity to distinguish between vice and virtue: in his eyes the court of Charles IX " *est une école de toute honnêteté* "! The fact that the whole of sixteenth-century society parades before us in his works gives them a historical importance far in excess of their mediocre literary value, which is only occasionally redeemed by a fine portrait like that of Mary Queen of Scots, of De l'Hôpital, or of Marguerite de Valois.

Here, as in other branches of literature, the Protestants did not lag behind. The chief literary contributions of the Huguenot leader **François de la Noue** (1531–1591) are the *Discours Politiques et Militaires* (1587), written during his captivity in the castle of Limburg. These twenty-five discourses treat in almost equal proportion of political, moral, and military matters. The military discourses describe the wars of the years 1562–1570, those of Condé and Coligny, which the author relates with the greatest modesty and impartiality.

La Noue's *Discours* were one of the sources used by **De Thou** (1553–1615) in the great *Historia mei Temporis*, an important work written in Latin. La Noue was a man of fervent belief, but tolerant, a true and good man. The opponents whom he combated with sword or pen, the wild Monluc and the Humanist Montaigne, are unanimous in their praise of his character and conduct.

He was also a moralist, and wrote a *Discours contre les Amadis*, a protest against the excessive vogue of these romances, and also against the imitation of Spanish manners.

Among the political writers of the sixteenth century, the greatest and most impartial is **Jean Bodin** (1530–1596), the author of the *République*. It is a book of political philosophy, a subject whose "holy mysteries" have been profaned by writers like Machiavelli and other "*courtiers des tyrans*". Bodin chose his title obviously in direct opposition to that of Machiavelli's *Prince*. The work, written in a clear and concise style, sets up the conditions of a form of government equally distant from the two poles of anarchy and tyranny. Bodin comes to the conclusion that "*une monarchie royale et légitime*", in which he sees a picture of the Family, can alone fulfil these conditions. He had in his mind the material and moral welfare of the people; was no advocate of tyranny, condemned slavery, and held that religious persecution can only lead to a weakening in religious belief. Like Montesquieu in the eighteenth century, he devotes attention to the adaptation of government to the varied conditions of race and climate.

Étienne de la Boétie (1530–1563), the friend of Montaigne, under the influence of the current of revolutionary ideas which developed during the first part of the century, composed the *Discours de la Servitude Volontaire*, or the *Contr'un*, a youthful and ardent attack on tyrants. After La Boétie's death, Montaigne attempted to protect the memory of his friend, in a well-known passage of the *Essays*, as a good and peace-loving citizen, although he could not help confessing that La Boétie " *eust mieux aymé estre nay à Venise qu'à Sarlat* ", thereby implying that he was a republican at heart.

François Hotman (1524-1590), the eminent Protestant jurist, is famous for his Latin political treatise, the *Franco-Gallia* (1573, translated 1574), in which he represents the institutions that the Huguenot party demanded as being those which for a long time governed France, and which alone can help to retrieve her prosperity. According to Hotman, these ideal institutions can be found in the history of Gaul and of the early Frankish monarchy: in Cæsar's time the peoples of Gaul formed a federation of free states, at the head of which was a General Assembly of deputies elected by the whole of the country. After the Roman conquest and the conquest of Gaul by the Franks, this federation was replaced by an elective monarchy, beginning with Childéric, in which the King could be deposed by the States-General composed of the nobles, the magistrates, the merchants, and artisans. The clergy formed no order and exercised no power. The sensation caused by the *Franco-Gallia* has been compared to that produced by the *Contrat Social* in the eighteenth century.

> Other political writers are **Michel de l'Hôpital** (1504-1573), the advocate of tolerance, in the *But de la Guerre et de la Paix*, addressed to Charles IX.
>
> Also **Henri Étienne** and **D'Aubigné**, both noticed elsewhere.

Here belongs likewise the famous pamphlet, **La Satire Ménippée** (published in 1594), so called after the *Satira Menippea* of the Roman satiric poet Varro, who in his turn had taken as his model the Greek Menippus, the pupil of Diogenes. The *Satire Ménippée* is a striking answer to the intrigues of the fanatical League against Henry IV of Navarre, the lawful heir to the throne of France, and at the same time a literary annihilation of all hostile pamphleteers. The authors of the *Ménippée*, of whom there were half a dozen, were not Huguenots, but peace-loving Catholics, who feared that in the end civil war would ruin France and deliver her up to Spain; but as the partisans of the League opposed Henry IV chiefly because he belonged then to the Reformed Church, they were compelled to turn their shafts against the Pope and his adherents. The political situation in France just before the birth of this famous satiric pamphlet was as follows: Henry III had been murdered by the fanatical monk Clément; Henry of Navarre (Henry IV) and the Duc de Guise were competitors for the succession, which had been refused to Henry IV as professing the Protestant faith. Philip II of Spain was also scheming to buy the French crown for his daughter, the Infanta of Spain, and was backed up by the Pope. A convocation of the *États Généraux* remained without any result. It is the proceedings of this assembly that the authors of the *Ménippée* took as the object of their lampoon.

The first part consists of a prologue by **Jean Leroy,** canon of Rouen, introducing two quacks, one of Spain, the other of Lorraine (the Guises were of Lorraine), who vaunt the virtues of the *Catholicon* of Spain, a divine electuary to which anything is possible. The following lines will give an idea of the miracles which it can at need accomplish. There are a score such miracles. We quote numbers three and sixteen, as being brief.

III. " *Qu'un Roy casannier* (Philip II) *s'amuse à affiner* (refine) *ceste drogue en son Escurial, qu'il escrive un mot en Flandres au pere Ignace, cacheté de Catholicon, il luy trouvera homme, lequel* (*salva conscientia*) *assassinera son ennemy* (Prince of Orange), *qu'il n'avoit peu* (pu) *vaincre par armes en vingt ans.*"

XVI. " *Voulez-vous bientost estre Cardinal? Frottez une des cornes de vostre bonnet de Higuiero* (= fig tree, another expression for Catholicon); *il diviendra rouge, et serez fait Cardinal, fussiez-vous le plus incestueux et ambitieux Primat du monde.*"

Then follows the opening of the States-General and the

speeches begin, speeches in which each of the speakers of the League, the Lieutenant, the Legate, Cardinal de Pelvé, Monsieur de Lyon, the Rector Roze, and others, betray their ambition, greed, egoism, and hypocrisy. Finally, Monsieur d'Aubray, the representative of the bourgeois class, closes the sitting with a long harangue in which he demands order, toleration, the lawful king, and at the same time unmasks the dark schemes of the nobility and their foreign allies.

Although the civil war was not quelled till 1598, what the *Ménippée* demands was already an accomplished fact when that pamphlet appeared in 1594, but at the same time it did a great deal to strengthen Henry IV's newly-acquired position and authority.

The authors, apart from Leroy, were **Nicolas Rapin,** a French and Latin poet, who contributed to the speeches and epigrams interspersed in the body of the work; **Jean Passerat,** who wrote part of the French and Latin epigrams; **Florent Chrétien,** a speech in macaronic Latin; **Pierre Pithou,** the author of the Harangue de M. d'Aubray, and **Gilles Durant,** of certain verses.

During this period a great number of treatises on language and grammar appeared, either proposing reforms, combating foreign influence, or setting forth new ideas.

The disorder reigning in the French language at this period, and more especially in spelling, which by false etymology was made to resemble Latin more closely by the introduction of superfluous letters,[1] prompted **Louis Meigret** of Lyons to publish a *Tretté de la Grammere fransoęse* (1550), in which he advocates phonetic spelling, regardless of supposed etymological derivation, that "*grande superstition*", as he calls it. Although Meigret found a few ardent supporters, such as **Ramus,** Baïf was the only one of the important writers of the sixteenth century to follow his recommendations. Ronsard and Du Bellay sympathized, but preferred to follow tradition,

[1] Instead of *écrire, sais, fait, recevoir*, &c., they wrote *escribre, sçais, faict, recepvoir* &c.

while Pasquier, Montaigne, and others, could see no good in such an innovation. This lack of unanimity, and also the opposition of publishers, made success impossible.

Among philologists three names deserve special mention: H. Étienne, Pasquier, and Fauchet. Resistance to the Italianizing of the language called forth the linguistic works of **Henri Étienne** (1531–1598).

Italian elements had been introduced wholesale during the first half of the sixteenth century. The French expeditions to Italy (1483–1547); the immigration of Italian architects, actors, painters, &c., and the influence of Catherine of Medici, the wife of Henry II, were all responsible for this foreign mania, so much affected by the Court. The innovations were chiefly terms referring to court life (*altesse, grandesse, disgrâce, carrosse, carnaval, courtisan, escorte*, &c.); terms of art and amusements (*baldaquin, fresque, feston, concert, sonnet*, &c.); and of war (*soldat, cavalerie, fantassin, escadron*, &c.). The courtiers did not stop there, and, to be in fashion, made it a point to introduce in their conversation as many Italian words as possible.

Henri Étienne determined to check this abuse. In 1565 he published the *Traité de la Conformité du François avec le Grec*, which, while admitting in the main that French is derived from Latin, strives to show that it stands in close spiritual relationship to Greek, and is thus deserving of equal consideration, and from that very fact superior to other modern languages, especially Italian, that being the point that he really wants to bring home. Étienne's ideas in this respect are identical with those of the *Pléiade*.

In the *Précellence de la Langue Françoise* (1579) he affirms the inferiority of Italian once more, and in the *Nouveaux Dialogues du Langage François Italianisé* (published anonymously at Geneva in 1578) he derides the "*gâte-français*" in the person of Philausone, "*gentilhomme Courtisanopolitois*", who in the preface addresses his readers in the following terms:—

"*Messieurs, il n'y a pas longtemps qu'ayant quelque martel en tête (ce qui m'advient souvent pendant que je fais ma stanse en la cour) et à cause de ce étant sorti après le past pour aller un peu spaceger, je trouvai par la strade un mien ami, nominé Celtophile.*"

A long dialogue of over six hundred pages takes place between Philausone and his opponent Celtophile, in which Italian imitation, not only in language but in manners, is severely criticized.

Étienne, as a Protestant, also hates the Italians, and thinks that the only neologisms which Italy can furnish are the names of things which France did not know till she came into contact with her, such as *poltronnerie, charlatan, intriguant*, &c. Party feeling comes out strongly in his *Apologie pour Hérodote* (1566), which, under pretext of establishing the veracity of the Greek historian by comparing his tales with the events of the civil war, is really a covert attack on the Catholics.

Claude Fauchet (1530–1601) is the creator of Political History and of the History of Literature. The *Antiquitez Gauloises et Françoises* (1579–1599) is remarkable for great erudition and for its originality. It consists of two books, of which the first is devoted to the history of the Gauls and to that of the Franks down to 751, and the second to the history of Pépin and his successors from 751 to 840. The *Recueil de l'Origine de la Langue et Poésie Françoise*, by the same author, establishes for the first time the Latin origin of French: "*La longue seigneurie que les Romains eurent en ce païs, y planta leur langue.*" Fauchet is wrong, however, in assuming that French is the outcome of a mixture of Gallic and Latin, but he should not be measured according to present-day standards; by the mere fact of proclaiming that French had nothing in common with Greek he was far in advance of his contemporaries. The second part of the *Recueil* is taken up with critical notices of one hundred and twenty-seven Old French poets and quotations from their works.

Unfortunately the learned and original researches of Claude Fauchet passed almost unnoticed, a fate which also befell the works of Étienne Pasquier (1526–1615), the author of the

Recherches de la France (begun in 1560), dealing in ten volumes with the political, literary, and administrative history of the country.

> In **Book I** Pasquier gives a picture of the Gauls and Franks, whose supposed Trojan origin he rejects, as had done Fauchet.
> In **Book II** he studies the social organization of the early Gauls.
> In **Book III** he discourses on the relations of the court of Rome with the State.
> In **Book IV** he examines questions referring to ancient legislation.
> **Books V** and **VI** sets forth certain events in French history: the trial of Jeanne d'Arc, the revolt of the Connétable de Bourbon, &c.
> **Books VII** and **VIII** contain studies on the origin of the language, the literary history of the sixteenth century, and versification.
> **Book IX** treats of French Universities, especially of that of Paris.
> **Book X** describes the rivalry between Frédégonde and Brunehaut.

Books VII and VIII are by far the most important from a modern point of view, and still indispensable to the student of sixteenth-century literature. Pasquier's productions are almost equal to those of Fauchet scientifically, and far superior from a literary point of view.

Among the moralists of the sixteenth century none is so celebrated as **Michel de Montaigne,** the author of the *Essays*, than which few books have exercised a greater and more lasting influence on the literature and thought of the world. Montaigne was a favourite with Bacon, and especially with Shakespeare, who made numerous borrowings from the *Essays*.

> **Michel Eyquem, Seigneur de Montaigne,** was born in 1533 at the Château de Montaigne, in Périgord. His grandfather was a merchant of Bordeaux. His father, after serving in the army for some time, became mayor of Bordeaux. Montaigne himself tells us much of his youth and the original ideas of his father on education: how he had him put out to nurse in one of the villages on his estate, roused him from sleep to the sound of music, and made him learn Latin exclusively till the age of six. Montaigne's mother was Antoinette de Loupes (Lopez), of a Jewish family which had

emigrated from Spain. From six to fourteen (1539-1546), young Montaigne was a pupil of the College de Guyenne, the best school in France, the Head of which was the famous scholar, André de Govea. Montaigne tells us that his masters there were Buchanan and Muret, who wrote Latin plays for the scholars, and how he took part in them. Neither does he hide the fact that he was careless, lazy, and read, on the whole, merely as his fancy dictated.

From 1546-1554 his course is doubtful, but he probably studied law at Bordeaux or Toulouse. At the age of twenty-one he became a member of the *Cour des Aides* at Périgueux, and three years later he was appointed Councillor of Parliament at Bordeaux. There Étienne de la Boétie was his fellow-member, and a close friendship sprang up between them, which lasted till La Boétie's early death in 1563.

At thirty-three Montaigne married Françoise de la Chassaigne, the daughter of a Councillor of the Parliament of Bordeaux, and in 1568, on the death of his father, he became the head of the family. The year after he translated the *Theologia Naturalis* of the Spaniard, Raymond de Sebond, and in 1570 he resigned his post and retired to his Château de Montaigne. In 1572 he commenced to write essays, and published two books in 1580. From June to November of that year we find him travelling in Switzerland, South Germany, Tyrol, and Italy. While near Lucca he was elected mayor of Bordeaux, and though he at first refused the dignity, he gave way on receiving a letter from Henry III commanding him to accept. On the whole, he seems to have filled the duties of the post with great tact, in spite of a somewhat hurried departure just at the time when the plague broke out with renewed vigour. In 1588 Montaigne went to Paris to arrange for the publication of the *Essays,* and soon after made the acquaintance of Mlle de Gournay, his adopted daughter. He died in 1592, leaving to his wife and Mlle de Gournay the task of issuing a definitive edition of his Essays, which appeared in 1595.

Montaigne's *Essays* consist of three Books, on the most varied subjects, whose titles frequently afford no clue whatsoever to their contents, and are only mere pegs to hang ideas upon;[1] he chatters on in a disconnected way on a thousand topics, and often completely loses sight of his original theme,

[1] We quote a few at haphazard: *A Trick of certain Ambassadors, Of Cannibals, Of Smells and Odours, Of Books, Of Thumbs, A Custom of the Isle of Cea, How a Man should not Pretend to be Sick,* &c.

yet he does so with an object in view; he avoids all systematic exposition for fear of appearing pedantic.

The *Essays* are the effort of a man to make the knowledge of himself the basis of a knowledge of the human race, and to deduce a rule of conduct from this knowledge. If we bear this in mind we shall not blame Montaigne for continually talking about himself. He takes himself as a representative of " *la moyenne humanité* ", and by exposing himself to view he exposes all of us, because a single person can, as it were, sum up the species, and, according to Montaigne, " *porter la forme entière de l'humaine condition* ". This he did generally at first, but in time he got over any timidity he may have felt of continually speaking of himself: " *J'ose non seulement parler de moi, mais parler seulement de moi.*"

In other words, Montaigne is the first French writer who made moral and psychological observation the true basis of literature.

The foundation and essence of Montaigne's ideas are contained in the ironical *Apologie de Raymond Sebond*, a fifteenth-century professor of Toulouse, whose *Theologia Naturalis* Montaigne had translated in 1569. In this famous essay, the twelfth chapter of the second Book, he wrote an eloquent tirade against the value of human understanding and reason, in so far as metaphysical and scientific knowledge is concerned.

It cannot be denied that our natural reason gives us a kind of animal knowledge (" *brute connaissance* ") of the existence of God (Deism), but no more.

Of scientific knowledge, of the " *âneries de l'humaine sapience* ", he speaks with sovereign disdain. Lately, he says, Copernicus has proved that the earth moves, although we had been taught for thousands of years that it is the sun that does so—" who knows if in another thousand years a third doctrine will not be established, and overthrow the two others? What else shall we have to learn by that fact except that it is indifferent to us who is right?" Montaigne even deprecates the value of scientific endeavour and research, and denies that knowledge increases either our happiness or usefulness in this life. We do not know that the two most learned men of antiquity, Aristotle and Varro, had "*aucune particulière excellence en leur vie*". The sum of this excellence is not to be found among the learned, but among the ignorant and lowly ("*ignorance abécédaire*"), or among those men who are really wise, who after long striving see that they know nothing and cannot know anything ("*l'ignorance qui se sait, qui se juge*"). These two classes, in their modesty, are good citizens and good Christians, but the men of the third class, the so-called cultured men, are the bastards ("*métis*") of society, dangerous and discontented disturbers of the peace, who pretend they know everything, and want to improve on all things: "*Esprits surveillants et pédagogues des causes divines et humaines*". The desire to know everything is the ruin of mankind: "*Du cuider naît tout péché*". Thus "*il nous faut abêtir pour nous assagir*", famous words which will be taken up later by Pascal.

The human mind is a "dangerous vagabond", in whose footsteps misfortune is bound to follow if it is not held in check and prevented from forming personal opinions dangerous to tradition ("*opinions communes*"). This is the doctrine of a peace-loving man scared by the excesses of the civil and religious wars. How far removed from the spirit of the Renaissance! With Montaigne begins the reaction of the seventeenth century, in which free inquiry is replaced by the *opinions générales*—by authority.

For the same reason, because he had been so brought up and because he was an enemy of all innovations which only engender unrest, Montaigne lived and died a Catholic, and condemned the Reformation as a presumptuous revolution. But Montaigne's scepticism is not universal. If he denies the possibility of attaining certainty in metaphysical and scientific matters, no man was ever more convinced of the worth of life on this earth, of the art of "enjoying his being loyally", which he held to be the " fundamental and most illustrious of our occupations ". This task is difficult indeed, for nothing is constant here below (" *le monde n'est qu'une branloire perpétuelle* "); the safest and most pleasant plan is to follow Nature, in whose goodness and excellence Montaigne, like Rabelais, was an ardent believer. Virtue consists in a life true to nature and is thus " *une qualité plaisante et gaie* ".

Notwithstanding, Montaigne admires those who, like Socrates, find strength enough in their natural reason to check the passions by means of the will. The discipline of our natural impulses, but not the violent asceticism of the Middle Ages, which he hates, is his ideal, although he owns that he did not come up to it himself: " *Je n'ai pas corrigé par la force de la raison mes complexions* (disposition) *naturelles.*"

Whosoever, like Montaigne, considers practical morals as the sole object worthy of occupying us, must necessarily feel particularly interested in the great problem of education, and to it he has devoted a large amount of space in the *Essays*. To us, especially as compared with Rabelais, his views on education are perhaps the most attractive part of his book.

In matters of education (see i, 23, 24, and 25, and ii, 17), Montaigne is too much prepossessed in favour of that facile and smiling virtue to which " *des routes ombrageuses, gazonnées et doux-fleurantes* " lead, but we can only approve when he has a hit at those " ushers who pillage science in books and lodge it at the tip of their lips only to disgorge it and scatter it to the winds ", or " who fill the memory of their pupils, but leave their understanding and conscience void and empty ".

The pupil should be taught to do " *ce qu'il doit faire estant homme* "; his faculties, reason, and judgment must first be developed; in a word, we must *educate* and not merely *instruct*. If the pupil's judgment is not sane, and if he does not make knowledge really his own, let him rather play tennis, says Montaigne; his body at all events will be the better for it.

As for the method to be pursued, the master should not confine himself to books; every place and occasion should be utilized. Montaigne also recommends the learning of modern foreign languages, and protests against the great amount of time wasted on Latin and Greek. Travelling and intercourse with others are not forgotten, while corporal punishment and the brutality of schoolmasters are mercilessly attacked.

The chief faults of Montaigne's system are that individual effort plays so small a part, and that athletic training is too much neglected. In practice his theories lead to the method of the Jesuits, the developing of social and worldly qualities: virtually the *honnête homme* or gentleman of the seventeenth century.

Montaigne's style is original and all his own: concise and crisp, with sharp and sudden sallies, full of vivid imagery, unexpected turns and word-combinations, very different from the solid and monotonous style then in vogue. His is the style of merry and animated conversation: " *Le parler que j'aime, c'est un parler simple et naïf, tel sur le papier qu'à la bouche* ".

His language is not so original; he invented little in vocabulary and syntax, and he uses Latinisms freely like most of his contemporaries. He reintroduced old words, and used Gascon words if they suited his purpose better than French words, but in this respect he only practised what the *Pléiade* had recommended, and what Ronsard actually did. He did not pretend to invent, and considered the French language quite rich enough if properly handled.

To sum up, it can be said of Montaigne that in scientific and metaphysical affairs he demands absolute submission under the tutelage of ecclesiastic guidance—a doctrine of servitude. All his curiosity and attention were bestowed upon questions of practical morals, in the indefatigable discussion of which he placed himself under the guidance of Antiquity as opposed to Medievalism—a doctrine of freedom.

During the last years of his life Montaigne enjoyed the friendship of a disciple who was already famous for his eloquence as a preacher. This man was **Pierre Charron** (1541–1603), the author of two noted contributions to the literature of the latter years of the century. In 1593 he published *Les trois Vérités contre les Athées, Idolâtres, Juifs, Hérétiques et Schismatiques*. The "three truths" that Charron tried to prove are—that there is a God; that He is known to the Christians only; and thirdly, that He is worshipped as he should be by the Roman Catholics only. This was followed in 1601 by the *Traité de la Sagesse*, in which most critics have only seen a systematic exposition of Montaigne's scepticism, but which is really an attempt to establish the authority of religion on a rational basis, and the scepticism of which is explained by the fact that Charron wished to show that the most reasonable thing for man to do is to despair of ever being able to attain to Truth through Reason.

Very few of the ideas contained in the *Sagesse* belong to Charron. Three contemporaries, Bodin especially, Montaigne and Du Vair, are unscrupulously copied. The book is "*quêté par ci par là*", as the author tells us, and intentionally so, for his object was to give a synthesis of the ideas of his time and not to write an original work. This is proved by the attention Charron pays to arrangement, a preoccupation which constitutes the chief originality of the book.

The *Traité de la Sagesse* met with great success. The Sorbonne condemned it, and Charron began to smooth down the passages that had been censured, "*pour fermer la bouche aux malicieux et contenter les simples*", but died in 1603, while still engaged on the task.

Much was learnt from Charron by one of the best prose writers of the sixteenth century, **Guillaume Du Vair** (1556–1621), orator and moralist, who for some unexplained reason has fallen into unmerited oblivion. No man before him did so much to further French eloquence, partly by the publication of his works on that subject (*Actions et Traités Oratoires* and *De l'Éloquence Française*), and partly by his translations of Æschines, Demosthenes, and Cicero. His works bearing on philosophy are the *Philosophie des Stoïques*, and the *Traité de la Sainte Philosophie*, in which he gives up as hopeless the idea of secularizing moral philosophy, and, seeing no way of remedying corruption but by a return to Christian morality, proclaims its necessity, thereby anticipating Pascal.

BOOK III
SEVENTEENTH CENTURY

GENERAL VIEW

The seventeenth century is the Classical[1] period proper of French literature. At no time, except perhaps during the middle portion of the nineteenth century, has such a galaxy of talent appeared, and certainly none at any time has so admirably represented what are the leading characteristics of French genius. As the result of causes which will be discussed in their place, the seventeenth century may be said to be almost devoid of poetry, if by that we understand imagination, sensibility, and individuality; but in compensation it has produced the three greatest French dramatists that have ever lived—**Corneille, Molière,** and **Racine,** the second of whom is generally looked upon as unsurpassed in comic art; the father of modern philosophy—**Descartes**; the greatest fabulist and the greatest pulpit-orator in the world's literature in **La Fontaine** and **Bossuet,** not to mention a host of other names of the highest rank, such as Pascal, Boileau, La Rochefoucauld, La Bruyère, Fénelon, St. Simon, &c.

The literature of the seventeenth century falls naturally into three periods:

1605 to 1659, a period of preparation and of struggle between old traditions and new ideals.

[1] The wider acceptation of the term includes the eighteenth as well as the seventeenth century.

1659 to 1689, the golden age of French Classicism, in which these ideals were embodied in a series of great masterpieces.

1689 to 1715, a period of transition, during which the classical ideal gradually wanes, and is replaced by the appearance of new ideas heralding the critical and scientific spirit of the eighteenth century.

The literature of the sixteenth century had been revolutionary and individualistic. That of the seventeenth is social, and its characteristics can be deduced from its identification with the social ideal.

During the first period public opinion completed the subjugation of the spirit of individuality, lack of discipline, and licence, which had already begun under the reign of Henry IV. This result, however, was not reached without a hard struggle; writers like **Régnier,** De Viau, and other belated representatives of a past age, fought stoutly against the new spirit and in favour of the prerogatives of the *esprit gaulois*, and we know that they had no inconsiderable following. The honour of having turned the tide in favour of the new ideal is generally attributed to **François Malherbe.** This opinion is no doubt due to the hackneyed lines in Boileau's *Art Poétique*:

> *Enfin Malherbe vint, et, le premier en France,* &c.;

but we think it more reasonable to ascribe the transformation which took place between the years 1610 and 1630 to the influence of the *salons*, or social and literary gatherings of certain society ladies known afterwards as *Précieuses*. Though the *Précieuses* were responsible for certain faults, which will be noticed in due course, yet from the very fact of their being no longer a negligible quantity in literature, they made ample amends. They delivered literature from pedantry, they polished language and manners, and moreover assured the victory of the social ideal, which made it obligatory for writers to give expression to *common* or general ideas rather than to particular opinions. In this way they set up the vogue for those branches of literature known as *universal*, the essential characteristic of which is that their very life depends upon the existence of a public to encourage them.

In 1635 the **Academy** was founded, and although it took the direction of the language out of the hands of the *Précieuses*, it had little effect upon their social influence, and acted in the same direction, as did also the works of **Vaugelas** and of **Balzac**. In time, however, the influence for good of the *Précieuses* was more than counterbalanced by their affectation, reinforced by Italian *concetti*, and later by Spanish pomposity. A masterpiece became necessary to bring back literature to the right path. In 1656 **Pascal's** *Lettres Provinciales* appeared, and not only was the language *fixed*, to use Voltaire's term, but also the characteristics of French classical literature and of the classical ideal, as illustrated by the masterpieces of Molière, La Fontaine, and Racine, the representatives of the golden age of French literature, for whom Nature became the model, the aim and end of art.

Here it is necessary to examine the restrictions to which this rule of rules was subjected, and we shall see that the literature of the *École du Naturel* was a faithful imitation of Nature, but only of a part and not the whole. Nature is the model, but the fidelity of the artistic imitation can only be discerned by good sense and reason. Thus it was not the study of Nature in all her forms and aspects that they strove to imitate, but only *la nature raisonnante*, that is to say, the essential and the general, and from this it follows that the lower attributes, the accidental, the ephemeral, and the local, must be eliminated as not conforming to the general scheme of nature. And, in order to make sure that their imitation was faithful, and that they might not fail to distinguish the constant from the variable and the essential from the accessory, all the writers of this age turned to the great poets of Antiquity for their models, not because they had any pedantic preference for them as ancients, but because the fact of their work having stood the test of time for so long, in spite of wars, revolutions, and the changes of modern civilization, proved conclusively that it must be founded on truth to the constant and universal in human nature.[1]

Another characteristic of the literature of this period is that, in its aims, and generally in regard to its modes of expression, it is moral, but only in so far as morality is indispensable to the existence of society.

Lastly, as the poet was solely concerned with general ideas, he could only excel in the manner in which he expressed them, and this naturally led to the perfection of form in poetry; while, on the other hand, the strict domination of reason was accompanied by many disadvantages, such as the elimination of dumb nature[2], of individuality, and even of imagination and sensibility, which are usually considered the prerogatives of poetry.

To us who are accustomed to a more complex conception of nature, and who consider that the height of genius is the combination of the typical and the individual, it may seem at first sight that the great writers of this period have represented psychological abstractions rather than real living characters. As a rule this charge is not applicable to the greatest among them, and though their conception of art and truth may differ from ours it is identical with that of the ancients, and if we admire Sophocles we ought not to grudge our praise to Racine. One cause of our comparative lack of appreciation is that they failed in local colour, though at bottom an artist can only successfully represent what he sees; but perhaps the main reason is that we miss in them that wonderful admixture of poetry and reality which makes the greatness of Shakespeare and his compeers.

---

[1] This point is brought out clearly in several passages of Boileau's *Réflexions Critiques sur Longin:* " *Il n'y a en effet que l'approbation de la postérité qui puisse établir le vrai mérite des ouvrages;*" or again: " *L'antiquité d'un écrivain n'est pas un titre certain de son mérite, mais l'antique et constante admiration qu'on a toujours eue pour ses ouvrages est une preuve sûre et infaillible qu'on les doit admirer.*"

[2] No doubt the domination of reason was furthered by Descartes' philosophy, although we do not think that his mechanical view of nature can be made wholly accountable for the absence of external nature in seventeenth-century literature, seeing that it is already absent in the literature of the Middle Ages and of the sixteenth century, and only appeared for the first time in the eighteenth century.

Hardly had the literature of the seventeenth century reached its height when it began to decline. France lost her political predominance, manners grew coarser, cliques reappeared, and the atheists or *libertins* of the early years of the century could no longer be kept down even by the eloquent diatribes of Bossuet. The ideas of Descartes, too, were distorted and used as a weapon against religious belief, while **Bayle** in his first work, *Les Pensées sur la Comète* (1682), by opposing the "*evidences of reason*" to the truths of religion, drove the attack home, and dealt a fatal blow to tradition and authority, on which literature had hitherto rested. A few years later **Fontenelle**, the bulk of whose work belongs to the eighteenth century, by the publication of the *Entretiens sur la Pluralité des Mondes* (1686), acting as an intermediary between science and the world of fashion, suggested that science is the best way to truth. Finally, **Charles Perrault**, by championing the Moderns in the famous *Quarrel of the Ancients and Moderns*, upheld the idea of human progress, and instead of depicting man in general, as found in the ancient classics, writers now strove to depict the manners and ideas of their own time.

Language.—Modern French proper dates from the seventeenth century. Henceforth the French language may be considered as fixed in its main outlines, although such a term is of course only relatively correct. The individualistic and independent spirit of the sixteenth century had rendered a standard language impossible; each writer followed his own fancy: "*le langage escouloit toujours des mains*", as Montaigne tells us. Here as elsewhere the seventeenth century replaced anarchy and disorder by regularity and uniformity. The language spoken by the better part of the Court and authors was adopted as the model; a kind of aristocracy in words was established, a large number being excluded as lacking in elegance or nobility, and the creation of new words was strictly prohibited. In this way the language lost in force and picturesqueness, but gained in clearness and precision: "*La phrase,*" says a famous scholar, "*a une noblesse d'allures,* *une majesté toute naturelle; une tendance générale des esprits à l'analyse psychologique, un goût prononcé pour les abstractions, rendent cette langue capable d'exprimer nettement et fortement les idées générales les plus abstraites et les nuances les plus fines de l'analyse, et de soutenir sans effort le poids des conceptions les plus profondes. La pensée la plus puissante ou la plus subtile trouve en elle un instrument d'expression d'une délicatesse sans égale. Elle est devenue le vêtement le plus souple qui puisse dessiner les formes de l'idée sans la voiler."*

FIRST PERIOD (1605-1659)

CHAPTER I

POETRY

The literary reform which took place at the beginning of the seventeenth century is generally put down to the credit of **François de Malherbe (1555-1628)**. This is incorrect in the main. All he did was to apply to poetry, better than anyone before him, a new literary ideal in conformity with the desire for peace, order, and discipline, which was then making itself felt throughout France, as opposed to the individualistic tendencies of the sixteenth century. The change, as we shall see, was the work not of a single man, but of the *salons* or literary and social gatherings of the time. Moreover, we know that Malherbe's finest poems, which during his lifetime were scattered through, and to some extent lost in the anthologies of the day, did not appear in collected form till 1630, two years after his death, and that he did not leave any disciples, rightly so called. Thus we are led to the conclusion that Malherbe experienced the consequences of the transformation far more than he brought it about or even conceived it. As exemplified in his works it bears on two points—language and versification.

In language he "selected" from the vocabulary of the *Pléiade*; he rejected all base, dialect, technical, and archaic words, all Latinisms and compounds, and urged that writers should employ the standard[1] French only, as accepted by the people of Paris. At the same time, and in spite of the disdain he affected for his predecessors, he did not break with them so much as some have pretended. His general conception of poetry is that of Ronsard; like him he indulged in *concetti*, and drew, too, largely on mythology, and his sentiments are also purely pagan. In matters of versification he was more drastic: he insisted on rich and exact rhyme; he rejected rhyme between a simple word and its compound (*jour* : *séjour*; *mettre* : *permettre*, &c.); between words too easy to couple, such as *montagne* and *campagne*, and between short and long syllables. Other precepts on this score are to be found in a copy of Desportes' poems, to which Malherbe added marginal critical notes. There he forbids *enjambement* or overflow, inversion, hiatus, cacophony, and absence of cæsura.

Of verse-combinations he only accepted a few of those bequeathed by Ronsard; but all he wrote, he wrote with the greatest care, and never allowed his muse to infringe the "rules of duty"; he polished and repolished his verses till every trace of dissonance had disappeared. Two or three stanzas would often cost him reams of paper, and his friend Racan, in the *Vie de Malherbe*, tells us that he used to say that "*après avoir fait un poème de cent vers ou un discours de trois feuilles, il fallait se reposer dix ans tout entiers*".

Malherbe's merit and his originality lie in his excellence as an artisan in versification. He was the first to add to the classical doctrine of Ronsard that polish, harmony, and correctness which are among the leading characteristics of the literature of the seventeenth century, and without which no

---

[1] It is in this sense that we are to understand Racan's famous words in his life of Malherbe: "*Quand on lui demandoit son avis de quelque mot françois, il renvoyoit ordinairement aux crocheteurs du port au Foin et disoit que c'estoient ses maistres pour le langage.*" By that Malherbe did not mean to enjoin that authors should write like market-porters, but that they should use no word or turn that would be unintelligible to such people.

masterpiece is possible. On the other hand, Malherbe lacks the essentials which make the poet. It would be almost impossible to be more deficient than he is in enthusiasm, imagination, sensibility, and naturalness. His ideal, as was the case with Ronsard as he grew older, tended towards the entire elimination of the personal element from poetry, and its transformation into rhetoric. This change responded exactly to the taste of the time, and proved salutary in some branches of literature, but was naturally the death-knell of lyric poetry proper, which did not reappear till the beginning of the nineteenth century with the Romantic Movement.

As can be easily imagined, Malherbe's methods did not lead to great and rapid production. His works consist of his *Poems*, in all 125 pieces, the first of which, *Les Larmes de Saint Pierre*, appeared in 1587, and the last, *Les Vers Funèbres sur la Mort d'Henri le Grand*, not until the edition of 1630; his *Commentaire sur Desportes*; a few translations from the Latin, and his *Correspondance*.

Just as a new ideal was about to rise on the ruins of the old, the latter suddenly threw out an unexpected and brilliant light. In 1608 a collection of nineteen satires appeared, which placed **Mathurin Régnier** (1573–1613), their author, in the first rank of French poets.

When Régnier began to write he was only a belated disciple of the sixteenth century, who strove to retain the licence of the manners of a past age. This is why Boileau, while granting that no poet before Molière was so well acquainted with the ways and characters of men, blames Régnier for his *rimes cyniques* (ribald rhymes), although a satirist cannot always be expected to avoid calling a spade a spade. In his *Satires*, imitated or remodelled from Horace, Pliny, Juvenal, and the Italians Berni and Aretino, he attacks courtiers, parasites, hypocrites and braggarts. The two best are *Macette*, the portrait of a pious hypocrite, no unworthy ancestor of the family of Tartuffe, and the one (Satire IX) directed against the overweening criticism of Malherbe, in defence of the *Pléiade*, which had been attacked by Malherbe, in the person of the poet Desportes, Régnier's uncle.

If Régnier stood up for Ronsard and Desportes, it was more out of opposition to Malherbe than because he himself followed the precepts of the *Pléiade* or of its later followers. In fact, Ronsard's literary ideal was more like that of Malherbe than that of Régnier; the *Pléiade* fought for art and form like Malherbe, though less consciously, while Régnier, continuing the Gallic tradition of Villon and Marot, discarded the artificial and aristocratic idiom of the *Pléiade* for a more popular, coloured, and picturesque style.

The real antagonism between Malherbe and Régnier is to be sought in the fundamental conception they each formed of poetry. The former was guided solely by reason and discipline; the latter by native genius and imagination, as is sufficiently attested by the following lines of Régnier's ninth satire, *La Défense des Anciens Poètes*:

> *Cependant leur savoir ne s'étend seulement*
> *Qu'à regratter un mot douteux au jugement,*
> *Prendre garde qu'un " qui " ne heurte une diphtongue,*
> *Épier si des vers la rime est brève ou longue;*
> *Ou bien si la voyelle à l'autre s'unissant*
> *Ne rend point à l'oreille un vers trop languissant;*
> *Et laissent sur le vert* (abandon) *le noble de l'ouvrage.*

Or by another passage in the same piece, where Malherbe's weak point is severely censured:

> *Nul aiguillon divin n'élève leur courage;*
> *Ils rampent bassement, faibles d'inventions,*
> *Et n'osent, peu hardis, tenter les fictions,*
> *Froids à l'imaginer; car s'ils font quelque chose*
> *C'est proser de la rime et rimer de la prose,*
> *Que l'art lime et relime, et polit de façon*
> *Qu'elle rende à l'oreille un agréable son.*

Yet to some extent Régnier rendered the same service to French poetry as Malherbe; like him he turned away from the languid elegance and mawkishness of the degenerate disciples of Ronsard to the observation of life. For that reason the later classical school felt that they could not reject entirely the work of him who is the first great French satirist before Boileau.

Another opponent of Malberbe was **Théophile de Viau** (1590–1626), like Régnier, a *libertin* [1] or upholder of the literary and philosophic ideas of the century of Montaigne. As a poet his contemporaries esteemed him too highly, but on the other hand, Malherbe, and afterwards Boileau, unjustly depreciated him. Some of his pieces, such as *La Solitude*, show considerable lyric gifts, and charm the ear by their free and musical movement, while others, although often marred by the most offensive vulgarity, evince a keen feeling for nature (cp. *Lettre à son Frère*, in verse).

His judgments in literary matters were sound and original, and in his fragmentary *Histoire Comique* he appears as an early partisan of the Moderns against the Classicists:

" *Ces larcins qu'on appelle ' imitation des auteurs anciens ', se devraient dire: des ornements qui ne sont point à notre mode. Il faut écrire à la moderne: Démosthène et Virgile n'ont point écrit en notre temps et nous ne saurions écrire en leur siècle; leurs livres quand ils les firent étaient nouveaux, et nous en faisons tous les jours de vieux. L'invocation des Muses à l'exemple de ces païens est profane pour nous et ridicule.*"

One of Théophile's (for thus was he called by his contemporaries) most beautiful pieces is the *Élégie* [2] *à une Dame*, in which, siding with Régnier against Malherbe, he vindicates the rights of free poetic inspiration:

> *Mon âme imaginant n'a point la patience*
> *De bien polir les vers, et ranger la science;*
> *La règle me déplaît; j'écris confusément;*
> *Jamais un bon esprit ne fait rien qu'aisément,* &c.

The Hôtel de Rambouillet and the Précieuses.—Peace and social order had returned to France with the Monarchy,

---

[1] In the seventeenth century the term *libertin* applied as much, if not more, to freedom of thought as to licence in morals.
[2] Would now be called an " epistle ".

but the individualistic, unruly, and licentious spirit of a former age had not been entirely subdued, and still left traces on the court of Henry the Fourth, which to many still appeared very much lacking in polish. In 1608 a distinguished lady, **Catherine de Vivonne**, Marquise de Rambouillet, the daughter of a great Roman lady, whose father had been French ambassador at Rome, decided to retire from the unmannerly court of Henry, and to throw open her mansion for literary and social gatherings, where lords and ladies, on a footing of temporary equality with men of letters, might exchange ideas on literature, refinement, and good taste. Such is the origin of the *Hôtel de Rambouillet*, the first of those literary and social *salons*, as they were called, which were destined to have so great an influence on French literature, and which lasted, with ups and downs, till the outbreak of the French Revolution.

Although gatherings seem to have taken place as early as 1613, the real importance of the *Hôtel de Rambouillet*, and its famous *chambre bleue*, where the Marchioness used to receive her friends, dates from 1618. The aim of the Marquise and her circle was to carry out the ideal of refined and polite society which D'Urfé had depicted in his romance of *Astrée*. No one could have been better fitted for this task than Catherine de Vivonne, in praise of whose accomplishments, beauty, and nobility of character all contemporaries are unanimous.

The history of the *Hôtel de Rambouillet* falls into three periods. From 1620 *c.*–1630 the circle takes in recruits and prospers. The guests include Richelieu, the sprightly Mlle Paulet, who dances, sings, and plays the lute to admiration— for such worldly diversions were not debarred; and among authors, Malherbe, Racan his friend, Chapelain, Vaugelas and Balzac. The second and most brilliant period extends from 1630 to the death of Voiture in 1648. Only a few gaps had taken place among the lords and ladies of the *salon*, and these were quickly filled up and fresh adherents added—La Rochefoucauld, the Duke de Montausier, the Marquise de

Sablé, the future Duchesse de Longueville; and among literary lights, Corneille, Ménage the grammarian, but above all the plebeian **Vincent Voiture** (1598–1648), the soul of the assembly, who held his place on the tacit understanding that he should always be witty. Voiture may be looked upon as the incarnation of the aspirations of the famous *Hôtel*. He wrote verse, most of which is insipid, but he is better known for his letters, addressed to the Marchioness and the lords and ladies of her entourage, which, though occasionally far-fetched and over-ingenious, are always vivacious and witty. Thanks to the personal influence of the Marchioness herself, who seems to have been a person of good sense, till about 1640 the talk of her *salon* remained free from exaggerated affectation. Balzac writes in 1638: "*On n'y parle point savamment, mais on y parle raisonnablement, et il n'y a lieu au monde où il y ait plus de bon sens et moins de pédanterie.*" Soon after, however, the epidemic broke out; some voted for the conjunction *car*, and others against; heated discussions took place which should be the approved spelling, *muscardin* or *muscadin*, *sarge* or *serge*, and words which appeared insufficiently "noble" were ruthlessly rejected. When Julie and Angélique became of age to share their mother's authority in the *salon*, these faults were aggravated—Corneille's *Polyeucte* was censured, and after a reading of Chapelain's inane epic on the Maid of Orleans, the Duchess of Longueville could not help remarking that it was "perfectly beautiful, but extremely tiresome". Then it was that Montausier, who had sighed twelve long years for Julie's hand, offered her the famous *Guirlande de Julie*, in which every flower represented in a drawing had its appropriate poem, and all conspired to the praise of Julie. Things became still worse in the third period (1648 to 1665, in the latter of which years the Marquise de Rambouillet died), though a few more additions were made, and Mme de Sévigné, Mme de la Fayette, and Fléchier joined the fashionable assembly. The quarrel of the *Uranistes* and *Jobelins* (1649) split the society into two factions

—some for Voiture's sonnet on Urania, and others for Benserade's on Job—and introduced a spirit of coterie and rivalry. It was then that the terms *précieux* and *précieuse* were first applied to the frequenters of the *Hôtel*, and similar literary sets formed on its model. Of these the most famous is that of Mlle de Scudéry (*les samedis*), the originality of which consisted in having adapted preciosity to the requirements of the middle classes, and that of Mlle de Sablé, where maxims especially were the fashion.

In time the *salons* of Paris were copied and their faults exaggerated by provincial coteries. Chapelle, writing from Montpellier in 1656, says: "*A leurs petites mignardises, à leur parler gras et leurs discours extraordinaires, nous vîmes bientôt que c'était une assemblée de précieuses.*" It was these later imitations that chiefly contributed to render preciosity ridiculous. In 1659 Molière dealt the *précieuses*, or rather their degenerate followers, a severe blow in his satiric comedy of the *Précieuses Ridicules*, but it was not a death-blow, for he felt obliged to deliver a second thirteen years later in the *Femmes Savantes* (1672); in fact, the spirit of preciosity did not die out, and the tradition continued with interruptions during the whole of the seventeenth century. The cabal against Racine's *Phèdre* was, as it were, a revenge for the *Précieuses Ridicules*; yet, with the advent of the classical ideal, preciosity was confined more and more to mere cliques. All that is remembered usually of the *précieuses* is the characteristics by which they lent themselves to ridicule, and it must be owned that they had many such. They strove by introduction of *pointes*, conceits, and forced metaphors to express all they said in a language comprehensible to the initiated alone, and unintelligible to the people. It is interesting to read in this connection the two comedies of Molière, or the *Grand Dictionnaire des Précieuses* of Somaize (1661), that clumsy advocate of their cause. There we learn that "*la belle mouvante*" is the hand; that by "*les commodités de la conversation*" is meant an arm-chair; that "*le supplément du soleil* " stands for the moon; and " *se délabyrinther les cheveux* " for to comb one's hair. Nevertheless, all their metaphors have not disappeared, and a few picturesque and graceful ones have withstood the test of time. Such are: *travestir sa pensée, avoir l'abord peu avenant, des cheveux d'un blond hardi*, &c.

But these faults were more than outweighed by the real services which preciosity rendered to French literature during the first three decades of the century. It refined the language by clearing it of a certain pedantic overgrowth, and of a coarseness that disgraced it; it enriched it by determining the exact meaning of words, by adopting, inventing, or creating new modes of expression, and above all by teaching the force a word acquires when put in its right place; lastly, it gave it polish, although it is quite true that in so doing it drew too sharp a dividing line between the speech of the people and that of polite society.

Noticeable about this time is a sudden, and, in quantity at any rate, considerable outburst of epic verse. Greece had had its Homer, Italy its Virgil, and its Tasso, whose *Jerusalem Delivered* had but lately achieved European fame, and men began to ask why France should not also have her great epic poet. The outcome was six huge epics in the space of fifteen years, which only deserve mention from the fact that they passed for some time as masterpieces, and a few years later afforded excellent material for Boileau's satiric bent.

The chief are the *Alaric* (1651) of **Georges de Scudéry;** *La Pucelle* (1656) by **Chapelain;** and *Clovis* (1657) by **Jean Desmarets de Saint-Sorlin,** which indirectly gave rise to the famous *Quarrel of the Ancients and Moderns* at the end of the century.

The vogue of these pseudo-epics called forth parodies, of which the most famous are *Le Typhon, ou La Gigantomachie* (1644), by **Paul Scarron** (1610–1660), and the *Virgile Travesti* (1648–1652), by the same author, which was considered a model of its kind.

CHAPTER II

DRAMA

The academic, classical, and Italian drama of the sixteenth century, from Jodelle to Montchrétien, was purely literary, rhetorical, and lyrical. It appealed only to a small chosen class of learned readers, and was never produced on the public stage.

From 1600 to 1630 **Alexandre Hardy** (1570–1631), the chief playwright and provider of the *Hôtel de Bourgogne*, and a few followers, established a new dramatic art, in which their one and only guide was the requirements of a popular audience. Of the 600–700 plays which this French Lope de Vega is said to have composed, he published only 40, namely, 11 tragedies, 24 tragi-comedies, and 5 pastorals.

The tragedies (*Marianne, Dido, La Mort d'Alexandre*, &c.) Hardy shaped according to the necessities of the stage. The choruses which he had at first introduced were afterwards dropped as injurious to dramatic action. For him the taste of the public was decisive. In the same way as he curtailed the lyric element of tragedy, so did he curtail eloquence and rhetoric in favour of action. His characters, too, are more numerous. His heroes meet and die on the stage, and he seldom makes use of messengers. Tragic action with Hardy can last for days and even months, and several places are often represented concurrently on the stage, as in the old mysteries. He inclines more and more to tragi-comedy, which, together with the pastoral, crowded out regular comedy during the first thirty years of the century.

Hardy's tragi-comedies proper are a regular medley of tragedy and comedy, in which the action lasts for years. In eight of them Heliodorus' novel of *Theagenes and Clariclea* is dramatized, and in five others we have adaptations of Spanish novels by Cervantes, Montemayor, and Agreda.

The pastoral plays are mostly love stories, the heroes of

which are burgesses and peasants dressed in shepherd's garb.
The scene is transferred to Arcadia, and in the plot miracles
and witchcraft find a place. Doubtless Hardy was influenced,
as he tells us, by Tasso's *Aminta* and Guarini's *Pastor Fido*,
as well as by Montemayor's *Diana* and D'Urfé's *Astrée*. In
the Pastoral he uses the decasyllabic line.

Hardy is probably the worst writer who ever composed a
play, but he was the first to make a true appeal to the people,
and by showing a genuine appreciation of theatrical effects he
transformed an academic pastime into a public performance.

Another representative of this popular and irregular drama
is **Jean de Schélandre** (1585-1635), whose real name was
Daniel d'Anchères. His play of *Tyr et Sidon*, a vast drama
in two parts, which shows all the freedom of the mysteries
in varying locality and mingling heroic matter and buffoonery,
is chiefly known for its preface by the famous scholar and
ecclesiast, François Ogier. This curious example of literary
criticism is a furious onslaught upon the "Three Rules",
which critics were then striving to impose upon the drama,
and which prevailed so tyrannically a few years later. Ogier
congratulates De Schélandre on having refused to accept
such trammels; protests vigorously against a servile imitation
of Antiquity, and urges poets to look in new paths for new
beauties, more in conformity with the genius of the time and
of the race. But Ogier's preface passed unnoticed, and was
forgotten to such an extent that the same ideas appeared
entirely new and audacious when they made their second
appearance, exactly two hundred years later, in Victor Hugo's
preface to *Cromwell* and in the other manifestoes of the
Romantic School. Nobody in 1827 suspected that Ogier had
already loudly proclaimed that dramatic truth consists in a
blending of heroism and buffoonery, of tragedy and comedy.

The following are Ogier's exact words: "*Dire qu'il est
malséant de faire paraître en une même pièce les mêmes personnes
traitant tantôt d'affaires sérieuses, importantes et tragiques, et
incontinent* (immediately) *après de choses communes, vaines et*

comiques, c'est ignorer la condition de la vie des hommes, de qui les jours et les heures sont bien souvent entrecoupés de ris et de larmes, de contentement et d'affliction selon qu'ils sont agités de la bonne ou de la mauvaise fortune."

Jean de Schélandre was not a great enough poet to make the Shakespearian drama triumph in France, in spite of one or two beautiful speeches in the tragic part of the play, such as that of Abdolomin, King of Sidon, bending under the double burden of long years and a heavy crown.

Théophile de Viau, the lyric poet, is the author of the tragedy of *Pyrame et Thisbé* (1617 c.), which appeared with great success, and which Boileau has pilloried by his ridicule of two very absurd lines in it:

> *Ah! voici le poignard qui du sang de son maître*
> *S'est souillé lâchement! Il en rougit, le traître!*

" *Toutes les glaces du Nord ensemble* ", says Boileau, " *ne sont pas à mon sens plus froides que cette pensée* "—and he was right; yet *Pyrame et Thisbé* contains many lines of striking lyric beauty, and the dialogue in parts recalls the great name of Corneille.

Lastly, *Les Bergeries* of **Racan** (1589-1670) deserves notice as perhaps the best pastoral play in French literature.

The chief characteristics of the popular drama of the early part of the seventeenth century are: contempt of rule and regularity, neglect of reason and truth, free play of fancy and imagination, increased mixture of tragedy and comedy, no regard for propriety of speech and action, and mingling of all styles.

The spirit of licence and abnormality displayed by Hardy and his school could not but displease a public whose ideal now lay in order and regularity.

In the preface to *Sylvanire* (1629), a tragi-comedy, **Jean Mairet** (1604-1686), at first an adherent of Hardy, formulated the doctrine of the " Three Unities ". In 1634, two years before Corneille's *Cid*, the first tragic masterpiece

DRAMA

in French literature, Mairet applied the rules in his tragedy of *Sophonisbe*, which inaugurated the classical tragedy of France on the popular stage, and marks the beginning of a new era in French dramatic literature. A noted French theatrical critic has said of the play: " *La tragédie de Mairet est loin d'être un chef-d'œuvre; mais elle a mérité d'être regardée toujours comme notre plus ancienne tragédie classique. Avec cette pièce était fondé ce genre dramatique destiné à une carrière illustre, quoique courte. Les traits essentiels du genre étaient trouvés; la noblesse du style, l'exclusion absolue du comique, le raffinement dans l'analyse et l'expression des sentiments; la tendance oratoire dans le langage, la simplification et l'arrangement logique de l'intrigue; la conception abstraite et puissante des caractères. Les règles étaient observées, un peu moins rigoureuses, mais telles au fond que Chapelain allait les imposer bientôt à Corneille.*"

The Rules of the Three Unities.—Before passing on, it is necessary to discuss fully these three famous Rules which, from Mairet's day up to the beginning of the present century, came to be regarded in France as the laws of a literary species. The so-called three Rules of Unity are those of Action, Time, and Place.

Briefly stated, these rules enjoined that there should be only one action or plot in a play, that the action should take place entirely within the space of twenty-four hours, and that the scene of the action should be the same throughout the play.[1] According to the critics of the sixteenth and of the seventeenth century, these rules found their justification in the *Poetics* of Aristotle, a claim which is without foundation. The Unity of Action, without which it would be impossible to write a good play, is the only one of the three which is formulated in the *Poetics*. Of the Unity of Time all Aristotle says is, when comparing Epic poetry with Tragedy, that the latter " endeavours as far as possible to confine itself to a

---
[1] Cp. Boileau, *Art Poétique* (iii, 45 and 46):
*Qu'en un lieu, qu'en un jour, un seul fait accompli,
Tienne jusqu'à la fin le théâtre rempli.*

single revolution of the sun, or but slightly to exceed this limit; whereas the epic action has no limits of time ". Thus Aristotle, far from laying down a hard-and-fast rule, only gives a piece of information; and in addition to this, it should not be forgotten that the action in Greek plays was naturally much simpler, and that the Greeks themselves often did not observe the twenty-four hours limit. As for the Unity of Place, it is a pure invention, about which we find not a word either in Horace or Aristotle, and which only took equal importance with the other two at a much later date, and seems at first to have been disregarded.

A considerable controversy arose during the sixteenth and at the beginning of the seventeenth century over these rules, the Classicists upholding and their adversaries opposing them. Finally the Classicists triumphed, owing largely to the influence of Richelieu, and Chapelain, his right-hand man in literary matters.

The most important *data* to be observed in the history of the struggle are the following:

1549.—The **Pléiade** adopted the precepts of Aristotle. These precepts replaced the previous theories of Fabri's *Rhétorique* (1544), and of Sibilet's *Art Poétique* (1548) which give little more than the rules of old French poetry (*ballades, rondeaux, virelais*, &c.).

1561.—**Scaliger** in his Latin *Poetice* supplied a full commentary on Aristotle's *Poetics*, and in consequence all sixteenth-century writers knew Aristotle largely.

Scaliger says that music is not essential, but he is inconsistent, for he does not recommend the dropping of the choruses. He declares further that the style must be sublime, that tragedy must represent the higher ranks of life, and have incidents more important than those of comedy; that the action must be completed in six or eight hours, and that a play must be divided into five acts. He gives no definite rule about the Unity of Place, although he does not find it reasonable that a person should be made to go from Thebes to Athens in a few minutes. Like all the partisans of the Unities, he treated them as a question of verisimilitude.

1562.—**Grévin,** in the preface to the *Mort de César*, recommends that music should be banished, and that Æschylus, Euripides, and Sophocles should be taken as models.

1572.—Jean de la Taille, in the preface to *Saül*, was the first rigorously to formulate the three Rules of the Unities: "*Il faut toujours représenter l'histoire ou le jeu en un même temps, et un même lieu*".

1573.—Ronsard, in the preface to the *Franciade*, recommends that the action of a tragedy or comedy should take place within the space of twenty-four hours.

Among those who wrote against or did not observe the Rules are:—

1582.—Jean de Beaubreuil, who in the preface to *Régulus* objects to the Unity of Time.

1598.—Pierre de Laudun Daigaliers, in his *Art Poétique Français*, rejects the Unity of Time on the ground that if it is observed we only get incredible actions and no better tragedies.

1628.—François Ogier, in the preface to Jean de Schélandre's *Tyr et Sidon*, where he defends his friend for having rejected the Rules, and blended together tragedy and comedy.

Every nation, says Ogier, has its own particular taste, and it is the duty of poets to adapt themselves to it; the French are impatient, desire novelty and variety, and are wearied by long reports of messengers and long tirades. The Greeks had special reasons for keeping their style, the chief being that it formed part of their religion, although it cannot be denied that they crowded into one day more than is reasonable. Therefore the modern dramatist should give up the Unities, replace reports by action, and mix tragedy and comedy, since real life is made up of laughter and tears.

We have already noticed that none of the authors of the popular drama, which flourished during the first thirty years of the seventeenth century, observed the Rules. To their excessive irregularity was due the victory of the Rules, Racan, for example, giving actions which last for years.

After 1625 the Rules were followed by some dramatists; in 1629 they were formulated by **Mairet** in the preface to *Sylvanire*, and applied five years after by the same poet in the tragedy of *Sophonisbe* (1634). In 1635 Richelieu was converted. Thanks to his influence and the advocacy of **Chapelain**, the Rules finally prevailed, and afterwards came to be looked upon as essential in every tragedy or comedy worthy of the name.

Pierre Corneille is the father of French classical tragedy as it occupied the stage for two centuries. If not the greatest, he is the first in time of the galaxy that makes the literary glory of the age of Louis XIV, though his best work was done before that monarch's accession to the throne.

Pierre Corneille was born in 1606 at Rouen. The history of his life, if one separates it from the history of his plays, is of little importance. He was the eldest son of Pierre Corneille, *Maître des eaux et forêts* at Rouen. From 1615 he frequented the Jesuit college of his native town, where he distinguished himself by skill in Latin verse composition. After leaving the college he studied law, and was admitted to the bar in 1624, though it is doubtful whether he ever pleaded, and accident co-operated with genius to turn him to dramatic work. His first play was the comedy of *Mélite*, acted at Paris in 1629, which proved a great success. For a time Corneille belonged to the band of poets (*La Société des Cinq Auteurs*) employed by Cardinal Richelieu to work out his dramatic plans but not possessing the "*esprit de suite*" which the Cardinal required of his poets he soon withdrew from his service, and with only one long interruption devoted the whole of his life to dramatic art.

After the failure of his last play, *Suréna* (1674), he retired from the stage for good, and died at Paris in 1684, a poor man, "*saoul de gloire et affamé d'argent*", as he one day said to Boileau. A dramatist, however prolific, could not live in those days on the proceeds of his plays; patrons, too, were stingy, and the grants allowed him by Louis XIV were small and spasmodic. He might have added to his income, as all his brother-playwrights did, by writing flattering dedications and nicely turned occasional verse, but he was not gifted in that direction, and his upright character spurned such means.

The plays of Corneille fall naturally into three periods. During the first (1629-1636) he wrote almost nothing but comedies. Apart from *Mélite* (1629), he composed *Clitandre* (1632), *La Veuve* (1633), *La Galerie du Palais* (1633), *La Suivante* (1634), *La Place Royale* (1635), and *L'Illusion Comique* (1636). All these early comedies owe nothing to foreign writers; they consist of incidents taken from everyday life and but slightly "romanced", written in a language which is a perfect imitation of that of the *précieuses*. To this period belongs also

Médée (1635), taken from Seneca and Euripides, the best tragedy up to that time.

The second period (1636-1651), consisting mainly of tragedies, opens with *Le Cid* (1636), which placed Corneille at once above all his predecessors and contemporaries. This was followed by four tragedies of great beauty: *Horace* (1640), *Cinna* (1640), *Polyeucte* (1643), and *Pompée* (1643), which along with the *Cid* may be accounted Corneille's masterpieces. Then came *Le Menteur* (1643), the best comedy previous to Molière, the first French comedy of character, and the first French comedy written in polite language, without low wit or indecency. The next year (1644) appeared *La Suite du Menteur*, the same high standard hardly being maintained. Then Corneille's productions become weaker. In 1645 *Rodogune* was issued, and, although it was preferred by the author himself to any of his plays, much of the pleasure we experience in reading it is spoiled by the highly improbable, at times almost ridiculous, situations it contains. Yet it deserves special mention on account of the fifth scene, one of the finest in French drama. *Rodogune* was followed by *Théodore* (1645), a story of Christian martyrdom much inferior to *Polyeucte*; *Héraclius* (1647), containing much fine poetry, but marred by a still greater complication of plot than in *Rodogune*, and by the blustering part of Pulchérie; the operatic play *Andromède* (1650), based on Ovid; and the two tragi-comedies, *Don Sanche* (1650) and *Nicomède* (1651), the two last superior pieces of the dramatist.

The third period (1652-1674) comprises the plays of his old age and decadence. The first is *Pertharite* (1652), the failure of which caused Corneille to abandon dramatic poetry for six years, and devote himself to a translation into French verse of the *Imitatio Christi*. In 1659 Fouquet, the Mæcenas of the time, persuaded him to reconsider his decision, and *Œdipe*, a play which became a great favourite with Louis XIV, was the result. Then came in rapid succession *La Toison d'Or* (1660), *Sertorius* (1662), *Sophonisbe* (1663), and *Othon* (1664), plays of little merit; *Agésilas* (1666) and *Attila* (1667), killed and buried by Boileau's cruel epigram:

> *Après Agésilas,*
> *Hélas!*
> *Mais après l'Attila*
> *Holà!*

Tite et Bérénice (1670), written in competition with Racine's *Bérénice*, although unknowingly; *Pulchérie* (1672) and *Suréna* (1674), two signal failures.

We will now pass on to consider Corneille's masterpieces at greater length.

The first great play of Corneille, and indeed of the whole theatre of France, is *Le Cid* (1636), a skilful adaptation of a play by the Spanish poet Guillén de Castro.

> The plot is briefly as follows:—Don Roderigo (surnamed the "Cid" or "Lord" by the Moors he has conquered) is in love with Chimène, the daughter of Don Gomez, Count de Gormas, and has been accepted as her suitor. The aged Don Diego, Roderigo's father, who has just been appointed governor to the King's son, asks Don Gomez to give his daughter's hand to his son. Don Gomez, jealous of the honour won by Don Diego, refuses his consent and openly insults the old man. Roderigo's father, in his powerlessness, appeals to his son for revenge: "*Venge-moi,*" he cries, "*venge mon honneur et le tien, va provoquer le père de Chimène.*"
> Roderigo obeys his aged father's bidding, defies Don Gomez and kills him. Thereupon Chimène, in spite of her love for Roderigo, appeals to the King to avenge her father's death. In the meantime Roderigo has saved Sevilla, threatened by the Moors, and the King can no longer punish the hero who has rendered him such signal service. Then Chimène appeals to the King's courtiers, and promises her hand to the knight who will bring back to her Roderigo's head. Don Sancho, Roderigo's rival, accepts the offer, but is vanquished and spared by his generous foe. Presently Don Sancho appears and lays his sword at the feet of Chimène, who, believing that he has conquered, curses him and openly declares her love for Roderigo. Finally she learns the truth, but is still doubtful whether she ought to accept the hand of a man who has so lately killed her father. After some debating the King advises her to take a year to consider the matter, and as she makes no

objection to this proposal, we may take it for granted that in the end the two lovers are united.

The success of *Le Cid* was so great that all dramatic authors, save the worthy Rotrou, rose against Corneille. The obscure Claveret accused him of plagiarism, and Scudéry launched his *Observations sur le Cid*, in which he tried to demonstrate that the play was worthless. No principle, no doctrine of art, was at stake. It was purely a case of jealousy, and among the jealous was Cardinal Richelieu, who posed as an author. He was also angry with Corneille for having introduced duelling into the play at a time when he was striving hard to repress it, and for glorifying Spain at an inopportune moment. He consequently determined to put an end to the quarrel concerning the *Cid*, by pressing the Academy to draw up its *Sentiments sur la Tragi-Comédie du Cid*. Chapelain was approved as a fit person to do so. The Academy found fault with the violation of dramatic proprieties, but could not deny Corneille's genius, while public opinion was too strong for the Cardinal and his friends, and maintained its original verdict. To quote the hackneyed lines of Boileau:

> *En vain contre le Cid un ministre se ligue;*
> *Tout Paris pour Chimène a les yeux de Rodrigue.*

Nevertheless Corneille, who had shown a tendency towards a freer dramatic system and a return to Spain, seems to have been very much impressed by the *Sentiments de l'Académie*, and after a retirement of several years, we see him reverting to regular tragedy and antique subjects. In *Horace* (1640), based on Livy's account of the combat between the Horatii and Curiatii, Corneille's main object was to depict the sublimity of Roman patriotism, and its triumph over the passion of love, which the poet henceforth will always sacrifice to honour or to duty. In *Le Cid*, Chimène had finally pardoned, after a struggle, and love had gained the upper hand. In *Horace* Camille, the betrothed of Curiatius, curses her brother

Horace, the conqueror of her lover; she is stabbed to death by Horace, and Horace is absolved.

In *Cinna* (1640), Corneille dramatized the conspiracy against the Emperor Augustus, as related by Seneca.

> Cinna, grandson of Pompey, is enamoured of Émilie, but she will only consent to marry him if he takes revenge on Augustus, her father's murderer. Cinna agrees, and forms a plot to kill the Emperor and restore the Republic. Presently Maxime, who also loves Émilie, reveals the conspiracy through motives of jealousy. Cinna, summoned before the Emperor, seeing all is lost, prepares to meet his doom, but finally the Emperor, after an inward struggle, resolves to extend his pardon to all the conspirators. Cinna and Émilie, touched by so much magnanimity, melt into tears and swear eternal friendship to the Emperor.

The subject of *Pompée* (1643) is taken from the *Pharsalia* of Lucan. Despite several impressive scenes, such as the one where Cornelia, Pompey's widow, reveals to Cæsar, her enemy, the plot hatched against him, the play is not free from the excessive declamation and bombast of Corneille's model. But of all Corneille's plays the one in which he followed most closely the classical dramatic system is *Polyeucte*, performed at the end of 1642 or early in 1643. A story of Christian martyrdom was a bold venture, and when the play was read at the *Hôtel de Rambouillet*, "the Christianity was found extremely displeasing" to people who thought heathenism good enough for literature, a view which, as we shall see, was also shared by Boileau.

> The scene of *Polyeucte* is laid in Melitene, the capital of Armenia, in the palace of Felix, the Roman governor. The events are supposed to take place in the year A.D. 250. Christianity has penetrated into the Roman empire, but is still persecuted. Felix has given his daughter Paulina in marriage to a rich nobleman of the name of Polyeuctes, after having refused her hand to Severus, a man of small fortune and of no position. In the meantime Polyeuctes has become a convert to the Christian faith, and in the midst of a solemn sacrifice in the temple, along with his friend Nearchus, pulls down the altars of the false gods. Nearchus is condemned to death, and meets his fate without a murmur.

Polyeuctes is thrown into chains, and all means are used to make him repent his rash deed; but the prayers of Felix and the supplications of Paulina are all in vain. Paulina, who loves Severus at the bottom of her heart, is none the less devoted to her husband; she urges Severus, who has meanwhile risen to high honours, to intercede in favour of Polyeuctes, telling him that were she to become a widow, she will never consent to become his wife. Severus does as he is bid, but all his efforts prove useless. Polyeuctus by order of Felix is led out to meet his doom, and by his glorious end wins Paulina for God:

> *Mon époux en mourant m'a laissé ses lumières,*
> *Son sang dont tes bourreaux viennent de me couvrir*
> *M'a dessillé les yeux, et me les vient d'ouvrir.*
> *Je vois, je sais, je crois, je suis désabusée,*
> *Je suis chrétienne enfin . . .*

Corneille's imagination was distinguished by a leaning towards the extraordinary which was natural to him, and at the same time encouraged by the agitated period in which he lived. His characters are not ordinary men and women, but heroes and heroines, who, sacrificing their natural impulses, find the expression of their heroism in the triumph of the will over all obstacles that interfere with its development:

> *Je suis maître de moi comme de l'univers.*
> *Je le suis, je veux l'être.* (Auguste in *Cinna*.)
>
> *Qu'importe de mon cœur, si je sais mon devoir.*
> (Aristie in *Sertorius*.)
>
> *. . . Je suis fort peu de chose,*
> *Mais enfin de mon cœur moi-même je dispose.*
> (Dircé in *Œdipe*.)

Or the characteristic lines in *Agésilas*:

> *Un roi né pour l'éclat des grandes actions*
> *Dompte jusqu'à ses passions,*
> *Et ne se croit point roi, s'il ne fait sur lui-même*
> *Le plus illustre essai de son pouvoir suprême.*

Hence Corneille's fondness for improbable and complicated situations, on the ground that the greater the difficulties to surmount, the more heroic the character will be; hence the comparative absence of psychology, due to the fact that he often invented or adapted a situation and afterwards created his characters to fit it, instead of leaving them to develop naturally; and hence also his contempt for the passion of love, which he regarded as unworthy of occupying the first place in tragedy: "*J'ai cru jusqu'ici*", Corneille writes to his friend St. Evremond, "*que l'amour était une passion trop chargée de faiblesse pour être la dominante dans une pièce tragique.*"

In his old age these peculiarities became more marked, and to such an extent as to become serious defects. His heroes' will is glorified for its own sake; formerly they had triumphed over their passions after a struggle, now they cannot fail or falter. Love after having been banished from his tragedies is reintroduced in the guise of the most frigid gallantry; his nobility and elevation degenerate into affectation and bombast, and the bent of his imagination takes the altered shape of a mania for unreasoned inventions, innovations, and complications.

In his best tragedies, Corneille's characters have the simplicity and grandeur of magnificent statues, but also something of their immobility. From their very conception they arouse admiration rather than pity or fear; but, although the inflexible self-reliance with which they meet their doom is at times apt to pall, yet all praise is due to the author for having laid before humanity so sublime and noble an ideal.

When at his best, nobody, perhaps, has ever written in verse better than Corneille; the virile eloquence of his lines is unsurpassed, as are his swift replies line by line, but he was not always inspired, and Molière was right when he said: " My friend Corneille has a familiar spirit, who inspires him with the finest verse in the world; but sometimes the spirit deserts him, and then it fares ill with him."

Second only to Corneille as a playwright stands **Jean Rotrou** (1610–1650), his friend and one of the " five authors " employed by Richelieu. In his youth, impatient of restraint and unwilling to submit to the rules of classical tragedy, he squandered his talent in comedies and extravagant tragi-comedies, but with years he learnt much from his great contemporary, and before his death he had written four pieces, two of which, *Saint Genest* (1645) and *Venceslas* (1647), are at least equal to Corneille's tragedies of the second class. *Saint Genest*, imitated, but in no servile manner, from the Spaniard Lope de Vega, is one of the most striking plays of the seventeenth century. It is the story of an actor who, playing the part of a Christian martyr before the Emperor Diocletian, is suddenly struck by divine grace, proclaims himself a Christian, and suffers martyrdom. Interwoven with the story is some amusing by-play depicting contemporary theatrical life. *Venceslas*, his masterpiece, represents in true Corneillian style the inward struggle of a king constrained to choose between duty and parental affection.

Other plays of Rotrou that will repay the reader are: *Laure Persécutée* (1638); *Don Bernard de Cabrère* (1647), his best tragi-comedy; and *Cosroès* (1649).

Rotrou is an unequal and careless writer, but when in his happiest mood, he has a lyric note, absent in all the dramatists of the seventeenth century, which recalls our Elizabethans.

CHAPTER III

PROSE

Might not spiritual truth be made more attractive to mundane society if presented in its most gracious and pleasing aspect? Such was the question that **François de Sales** (1567–1622), Bishop of Geneva, proposed to answer in the affirmative, when, at the King's request, he published a collection of spiritual letters addressed to a relative, under the title of *L'Introduction à la Vie Dévote* (1609). De Sales saw that it would be futile to require from people " *qui vivent parmi le monde et les cours* " the sum of Christian renunciation and self-denial; imperfection is man's lot, " *et nous ne pouvons aller sans* *toucher terre* "; yet, though he may have strewn the path to heaven with roses, under the angelic bishop's docility and sweetness there lay strength. " *Suaviter in modo, fortiter in re* " might have been his motto. Never was style more in keeping with the man—flowery and mystical, yet insinuating.

The long reign of the *précieuses* had been prepared, as we have noticed, by a novel which for a long time enjoyed a success as marvellous as almost any in literary history. This famous book was the pastoral romance of *Astrée*, by **Honoré d'Urfé** (1568-1625), composed of five volumes, published at different times from 1610 to 1619, and comprising over five thousand pages. Even at a time when the *Astrée* had lost its popularity Mme de Sévigné did not hesitate to acknowledge her weakness for it, and the great La Fontaine could write:

> *Étant petit garçon je lisais son roman,*
> *Et je le lis encore ayant la barbe grise.*

D'Urfé's immediate model was the *Diana* (1560) of the Spaniard Montemayor, who himself had imitated largely the Italians Sannazaro (*Arcadia*), Tasso (*Aminta*), and Guarini (*Pastor Fido*).

> The scene of the *Astrée* is laid in the fields of D'Urfé's native Forez on the banks of the Lignon, in Merovingian antiquity. The shepherd Céladon, banished by his beloved Astrée on suspicion of faithlessness, in his despair throws himself into the waters of the Lignon; saved by the nymphs he resists the love of the princess Galatea, but does not dare to appear before Astrée as long as she has not revoked her order of banishment, which she finally consents to do, but only at the end of the fifth volume. The two lovers are united in marriage, and the banks of the Lignon become a scene of universal joy.

But the main plot is often only an excuse for numerous historical episodes, contemporary allusions, and gallant conversations, in which the different varieties of love are depicted and discussed after the manner of the amorous casuistry of the fashionable ladies of the time.

PROSE 125

The influence of preciosity, combined with that of Spain and of the political events of the time, gave rise to the heroic-gallant novel, the tradition of D'Urfé's *Astrée* combining with that of the older *Amadis*. The shepherds and shepherdesses were replaced by heroes and heroines, clad in antique garb; romantic episodes and high deeds were blended with dissertations and polite conversations reflecting the social ideal.

> **Marin le Roy de Gomberville** (1599–1674), in *Polexandre* (1629–1637), unites the kind of motive found in the *Amadis* with geographical interest. The hero wanders over the whole world in pursuit of those who dare to sigh for the love of the fair Alcidiane, and also to discover the mysterious island on which the princess dwells. In this way we are taken to Morocco, the Canary Islands, the West Indies, &c.
>
> **Gautier de Costes de la Calprenède** (1609–1663), in *Cassandre* (1642), *Cléopâtre* (1647), and *Faramond* (1661), exhibits a kind of universal history: the dissolution of the Macedonian empire, the decline of Rome's power, and the foundation of the French monarchy; but this is only the background, his heroes and heroines being mere idealizations of the lords and ladies he had met in the *salons* of Paris. Like all these prolix romances those of De la Calprenède are unreadable now, although his reputation was not so ephemeral as that of his contemporaries, and lasted till the eighteenth century.

Madeleine de Scudéry's (1607–1701) two chief novels are *Artamène ou Le Grand Cyrus* (1649–1653), and *Clélie* (1654–1660). Her originality consists in having done openly and knowingly what her predecessors had done unconsciously. To the adventures in *Polexandre* and to the historical details in *Cléopâtre* she added allusions to and portraits of the men and women of the *précieux* society of the day. Cyrus is none other than Condé; Lydiane is Françoise d'Aubigné, the future Mme de Maintenon; Mandane is the Duchess of Longueville; and so forth. By attempting to study the curiosities and shades of the passion of love Mlle de Scudéry occasionally succeeds in analysis of character; in fact her novels, especially *Clélie*, may be said to foreshadow the psychological novel in French literature.

The insipid gallantry and the high-pitched emotions of courtly shepherdesses and pastoral cavaliers produced a natural reaction. In 1622 **Charles Sorel** (1599–1674) published the *Histoire Comique de Francion*, and five years later the *Berger Extravagant*, the Don Quixote of France, which recounts the pastoral follies of a young Parisian bourgeois, whose head has been turned by the fashionable novels of the day. Another burlesque of the heroic novel is the *Roman Comique* (1651) of **Paul Scarron**, the master of the school of realism in the seventeenth century.

The greatest of the literary societies of France, the **French Academy**, sprang from a private society of men of letters in Paris, which about the year 1629 used to meet at the house of one Conrart, a wit and scholar of the time, for the discussion of literary questions. At first they were but nine, but fresh members were added by degrees, among others the poet Boisrobert, a favourite of Richelieu, who was kept informed by him of these gatherings. The Cardinal, pleased with the account of the society, offered his protection and official recognition. After some hesitation they accepted, and under the title of *Académie Française* they held their first sitting on 13th March, 1634; but the Parliament of Paris only registered the letters patent in July, 1637, and that only on an express order of the King, and on the condition that the Academy should meddle with nothing but the embellishment and improvement of the French language. From the outset the number of members was raised to the Forty at which it has ever since remained, and each week one of the members was appointed to read a paper. Their chief occupation, however, was the compilation of a dictionary, which has become famous under the name of *Dictionnaire de l'Académie*, and of which the first edition appeared in 1694.

The Academy by undertaking its dictionary, and projecting a grammar, took away from polite society the direction of the language, although its object was the same as that of the *précieuses* and their followers. The efforts of both tended to make the language gain in dignity and precision, but impoverished it by the elimination of its picturesque and forceful elements.

That the Academy has not always been impartial in the election of its members will be evident when it is remembered that Descartes, Pascal, Molière, J.-J. Rousseau, Beaumarchais, H. de Balzac, Michelet, and Béranger never belonged to it.

It received much help from **Vaugelas** (1585–1650), one of its early members, who had the reputation at the time of knowing his own language better than any man, and whose decisions were looked upon as laws: " *Si félicité n'est pas français,*" wrote Chapelain, " *il le sera l'année prochaine. M. Vaugelas m'a promis de ne pas lui être contraire, quand nous solliciterons pour lui.*"

In 1647 he published his *Remarques sur la Langue Française*, which served as a guide to his fellow-members in their literary labours. He proposed first of all to make the French language " *vraiment maîtresse chez elle, et de la nettoyer des ordures qu'elle avait contractées* "; secondly, he asserted that the test of correct language is the manner of speaking of the best part of the Court. But although he established the sovereignty of court usage he never dreamt of shutting the door upon all change; he knew and declared that this was impossible. His object was to regulate the language, to give it stability as far as essentials only are concerned: " *Je pose des principes, qui n'auront pas moins de durée que notre langue et notre empire.*"

One of the most active of the Academicians was **Jean Louis Guez de Balzac** (1597–1654), who was the first to apply to prose the principles which had guided Malherbe in verse. That the latter was a poet alone explains the fact that his reputation survived that of Balzac.

Balzac's letters and political treatises were admired for the pureness of their eloquence and the harmonious cadence of their periods. He foreshadowed to a great extent the limpid, if somewhat colourless prose of the Classicists, and also taught his countrymen the art of being eloquent without having anything to say.

If Balzac was devoid of ideas no man ever had more than his great contemporary and friend **René Descartes,** the founder of modern philosophy, as opposed to scholastic disputes and subtleties, from whom all systematic thinking is professedly derived.

> **Descartes** was born at La Haye, near Tours, on the 31st March, 1596, of a family of noble rank. When eight years of age he was sent to the Jesuit college at La Flèche, where he remained for eight years. Dissatisfied with scholasticism, and eager to learn from life and the close observation of men what he had been unable to find in books, he determined at the age of twenty-one to enlist as a volunteer. The outbreak of the Thirty Years' War soon gave him plenty of employment. First he served for two years in Holland, then he passed into the Catholic army of the Duke of Bavaria. On the approach of winter the army was obliged to take winter quarters at Neuburg on the Danube. It was there that he conceived for the first time the principles of a new philosophical method: "*N'ayant par bonheur aucuns soins ni passions qui me troublassent, je demeurais tout le jour enfermé seul dans un poêle* (room heated by a stove) *où j'avais tout loisir de m'entretenir de mes pensées.*" In consequence he left the army in 1621, travelling, with occasional sojourns in Paris, till 1629, when he returned to Holland, where for twenty years he meditated and wrote, often shifting his residence, but little disturbed save by the controversies of philosophy and the orthodox zeal of Dutch theologians. An invitation from the Queen of Sweden, who desired to learn his philosophy from his own lips, was accepted in 1649. The rigours of a northern temperature, combined with change of habits, proved fatal to his health, and he died at Stockholm of inflammation of the lungs, in 1650.

His chief works consist of the *Discours de la Méthode* (1637), the first philosophic treatise of importance written in the French language; the posthumous *Traité des Passions* (1650), also in the vernacular; the *Meditationes* (1641) and *Principia* (1644), written in Latin.

The key to Descartes' philosophic method is contained in the famous *Discours de la Méthode*, which must have been elaborated between the dates 1619 (Neuburg) and 1637 (publication). His philosophy has its starting-point in universal doubt. Everything being abandoned, is there any possibility of finding any new and clear foundation from which to build up our knowledge? Evidently in the fact of doubt alone. What is doubt? Doubt is an act of thinking. Thinking is inconceivable without a person to think. Thus, doubt implies the mental existence of a doubter, and the famous Cartesian proposition—*Cogito, ergo sum*, " I think, therefore I exist ", naturally follows. But how and why have we attained this certainty? Simply because we perceive it so clearly and distinctly that its denial is impossible. Hence follows the first and fundamental rule of Descartes' philosophy—to accept as true what we perceive clearly and distinctly, and nothing beyond. One of these clear and distinct perceptions is the idea of God as the absolutely Perfect Being. God the Perfect Being cannot deceive, and therefore whatever our consciousness clearly testifies may be implicitly believed. Mind or spirit is pure consciousness, and matter is mere extension; these attributes are mutually exclusive, and can be united (as in man) only through the intervention of God. Animals in which the rational soul is absent are mere automata.

The influence of Descartes' ideas, which were in harmony with those of his time, reacted upon the literature of the whole of the seventeenth century, although their full force was not felt till about thirty years after the publication of the *Discours de la Méthode*. The orators and poets of the second half of the century show little taste for the picturesque in nature, and devote themselves wholly to the study of man. This is partly attributable to the strictly mechanical view of nature taught by Descartes. Like him, too, the writers of this period sought for general truths, and subordinated imagination to reason. In point of style Descartes, unlike his contemporaries, is heedless of form. He has made little progress on the writers of the beginning of the century, yet he possesses great qualities —vigorous precision, clearness, and certain flights of imagination, which produce all the more effect amid the solid mass of abstract reasoning.

By far the greatest writer of this period was **Blaise Pascal**. A consideration of his works is inseparable from the history of Port-Royal and of Jansenism.

Port-Royal was a convent of Cistercian nuns, about eight miles from Versailles. It was founded in the thirteenth century for nuns only, but soon after its establishment obtained from the Pope the privilege of receiving such members of the laity as should desire to live in religious retirement without being compelled to take monastic vows. The community was removed to Paris in 1626; and from this time the old establishment of Port-Royal des Champs, as the convent near Versailles was called, was exclusively devoted to the use of a lay community. This community soon numbered among its permanent inmates some of the most distinguished scholars of the age, **Antoine Arnauld** (1612–1694), Le Maistre, Nicole, Lancelot, and others. Their life was divided between study, instruction, and manual labour. One of their greatest public services was the foundation of a famous school, for which they prepared well-known educational books.

Port-Royal, however, is best known for its adhesion to the **Jansenist Movement**. In 1640 appeared the *Augustinus* by **Cornelius Jansen**, Bishop of Ypres, in which, summarizing the doctrines of St. Augustine against the Pelagians and Semi-Pelagians, he repudiated the ordinary Catholic dogma of the freedom of the will, and affirmed that man was predestined either to eternal life or everlasting damnation, and that he could only be saved if possessed of divine grace. This austere doctrine, which is practically identical with that of Calvin, and directly opposed to the more worldly and accommodating system of the Jesuits, was introduced into Port-Royal by the Abbé de St. Cyran, a friend of Jansen. From that time the abbey of Port-Royal became the fortress of Jansenism in France, and in the great controversy which soon afterwards broke out, the doctrines of the great Dutch theologian found their staunchest adherents and supporters in Antoine Arnauld and Pascal.

Blaise Pascal was born at Clermont-Ferrand in 1623. His precociousness was extraordinary; at the age of sixteen he had written a Treatise on Conic Sections, which excited the admiration of Descartes. But the intensity of study, preying upon a nervous constitution, consumed his health and strength; at an early age he suffered from temporary paralysis. When about twenty-three he fell under the religious influence of St. Cyran, read eagerly in the writings of Jansen, and resolved to live for God alone. But to restore his health he was urged to seek recreation, and by degrees the interests and pleasures of the world took hold on him; from 1649-1653 he lived not only in the world, but in a style beyond his means. However, the religious spirit was still alive in his heart, and needed only to be reawakened. The reawakening came in 1654 through his sister Jacqueline, who had abandoned the world two years previously and entered the community of Port-Royal. From this time Pascal subjected himself to the most rigid mortification, self-denial, and absolute obedience to his spiritual director. He joined Port-Royal, and henceforth, till his death in 1662, he threw himself with passionate devotion into its cause.

Apart from Pascal's achievements as a mathematician and physicist, his two great works are the *Lettres Provinciales* (1656-1657), and the posthumous *Pensées*.

Although the *Augustinus* had not been avowedly written as a work of controversy, but simply to set forth the doctrine of St. Augustine, the Jesuits had long marked Jansen and St. Cyran as theological foes, opposed to their doctrines. As soon as Jansen's book appeared it was received with loud clamour, and prohibited by a decree of the Inquisition in 1641; in the following year it was condemned in general terms by Urban VIII in the bull *In Eminenti*. On the other side, Arnauld, the leading theologian of the Port-Royalists, wrote an apology for Jansen (1644), and a second apology appeared from his pen the following year. The Jesuits determined that they would not be beaten. In 1653 five propositions, professedly extracted from Jansen's *Augustinus*, were condemned by a papal bull.

A great blow had been struck, and the insulting triumph of the Jesuits knew no bounds. They refused absolution to the Duc de Liancourt, for no other reason but that he was on friendly terms with Port-Royal, and had refused to withdraw, at their demand, his granddaughter from its protection. Indignant at such an outrage, Arnauld rushed anew into the controversy; and on a question concerning divine grace he was condemned in 1656 by the Sorbonne. "You who are young, clever, and inquiring," said Arnauld to Pascal, "you ought to do something." The words were not lost, and the next day Pascal produced "A Letter written to a Provincial by one of his Friends ". A second was issued a few days later. These flew from hand to hand, and the fury of the Jesuits was boundless. Never before had been seen such delicate and yet scathing irony, such incisive argument, wedded to such perfect felicity of phrase and rare distinction of style.

Of the eighteen letters which make up the *Provinciales*, the first three and the last three, which deal with the affairs of Arnauld and the Sorbonne, are of little importance as compared to the twelve intervening letters, in which Pascal by a change of tactics set up the real and fundamental question: the question which of the two parties, Jesuits or Jansenists, would in the future direct public opinion, and more generally, which of the two moral ideals, the worldly or the intransigent, would triumph. These letters discuss at length the whole subject of the moral theology of the Jesuits, with all its subtle equivocations and casuistries invented for the extenuation of sin. They constitute the most powerful blow ever directed against their order, and one from which it has never fully recovered.

The *Provinciales* occupied Pascal till the spring of 1657, and during the following year he began to busy himself with a scheme of a great Apology of the Christian Religion. Of this projected apology Pascal left fragments only, known as the *Pensées*. A garbled edition appeared in 1670, but it was not till 1844 that an authentic text was issued. Several attempts to reconstruct the plan of Pascal's apology have been made in vain, but the main outlines of his thought can be clearly discerned: Man is so constituted that he can never be satisfied until he rests in knowledge of the truth. But man is a complicated being, an incomprehensible phenomenon made up of good and evil. How then is this duality in human nature to be solved so that man may find happiness? It cannot be settled by the two great opposing systems of philosophy at all times—the rational, dogmatic, and stoical on the one hand, and the sceptical and epicurean on the other. The riddle of human nature, according to Pascal, can only be solved in one way—by a recognition of the truth taught by religion, that human nature is fallen from its true estate, that man is a dethroned king; and this dissonance in man's nature can only be overcome in one way—through union with God made man—with Jesus Christ, the centre in which alone we find our weakness and the divine strength. In Him all contradictions are reconciled.

Pascal is the creator of French classical prose, just as Corneille is of French classical verse. With the *Provinciales* a standard was set up which has in all essentials remained unchanged ever since.

SECOND PERIOD (1659-1689)

CHAPTER I

POETRY

The recognized critic of the classical school, the "Legislator of the French Parnassus", is **Nicolas Boileau**, surnamed Despréaux.

Boileau was born in Paris of an old stock of lawyers on the 1st of Nov., 1636. He received his early education at the Collège d'Harcourt, and later at that of Beauvais. At first he studied law and theology, but, inheriting a competence, devoted himself to literature. His first publications were *Satires* (1660-1665), in which he waged successful war against all that seemed to him false and despicable in art. He became the champion of a new school, the friend and upholder of the great writers of the age of Louis XIV, of La Fontaine, Molière, and Racine especially. The *Satires* were followed by the first *Épîtres*, by the *Art Poétique* (1674), by the first cantos of the clever serio-comic poem *Le Lutrin*. In 1677 Boileau was appointed, together with Racine, to write the history of the King, and renounced for the time the profession of poetry. The last period of his life, down to his death in 1711, was taken up with polemics with the Moderns. To this period belong the *Réflexions Critiques sur Longin* (1694), the *Ode sur la Prise de Namur* (1693), the three last *Épîtres* (1695), and the three last *Satires* (1694, 1698, 1705).

All Boileau's most important contributions to literature, both in verse and prose, fall under the head of literary criticism. His work in that direction was at first purely militant and destructive. In the *Satires* he delivered relentless attacks on the dangerous tendencies that were at work in French literature—the conceits of the *précieuses*, the insipid jargon of the heroic-gallant novel, and the mawkishness of dramatists such as Quinault. Once this task was accomplished, Boileau felt bound to replace the negative criticism of the *Satires* by formal precepts on literature. This he did in the *Art Poétique* (1674), his capital work, though he was too much of a satirist at heart to forgo the opportunity of once again attacking the worthless poets in whose faults he found justification for his new rules. Thus the criticism of the *Art Poétique* falls into two distinct categories—the statement of his poetic doctrine, and the estimate of the poetry of his time, which is practically the same as in the *Satires*. Boileau's *Art Poétique*, which owes much of its doctrine and many of its details to Horace, and in a lesser degree to Aristotle, consists of four cantos.

Canto I contains general precepts on the art of poetry, with a short digression on the history of French versification, conspicuous for the ignorance Boileau displays of earlier French poetry.

Canto II defines the special laws of the shorter poems—the

Idyll, the Elegy, the Ode, the Sonnet, the Epigram, the Ballade, &c.

Canto III is entirely devoted to the history and laws of tragedy, epic poetry, and comedy.

Canto IV, like the first, contains general precepts, and ends with the praises of Louis XIV.

The *Art Poétique* is essentially dogmatic. In order properly to understand Boileau's literary doctrine it is necessary to consult the *Épîtres* and the *Réflexions sur Longin*, in which his theories are explained at length.

What, then, are the leading principles of this doctrine?

Its starting-point is the imitation of nature:

Jamais de la nature il ne faut s'écarter (iii, 414).

Fidelity to nature is the real test for all poetry. But this rule of rules calls for restrictions. The poet must not imitate all that is to be found in nature, but only what conforms to the strict rule of reason and good sense:

Tout doit tendre au bon sens (i, 45).

A consequence of this was that the lower attributes of human nature were refused poetic treatment, for what we have in common with all animals is just the opposite of reason. In the same way the accidental, the ephemeral, and local must be eliminated, as only falsifying the true nature they disguise, and the author must avoid anything that is of a particularly personal character, and deal only with those ideas and sentiments which he has in common with everyone.

Finally, Boileau's third tenet recommends the imitation of the ancients, not because they are the ancients, but because no one since has imitated nature with the same fidelity as they did. They will serve as a touchstone.[1]

By referring art to reason and truth Boileau was an emancipator; but the strict domination of reason in his doctrine led

---

[1] Cp. Pope in a passage on Virgil in his *Essay on Criticism*, directly inspired by Boileau:
Learn hence for ancient rules a just esteem;
To copy Nature is to copy them.

to the exclusion of "exterior" nature (plants, the stars, the sky, the elements, &c.), and to the belief that the only study for man was man. It also tended to proscribe imagination and sensibility, although it is too often overlooked that in the very first lines of the *Art Poétique* Boileau lays stress on genius as the one essential without which all is in vain. Lastly, it led to the perfection of form in poetry, for as the poet was concerned only with general ideas, he could excel only by the manner in which he expressed them.

Boileau's influence as a critic was immense, and lasted till the rise of the Romantic School at the beginning of the nineteenth century. The study of foreign literatures, of archæology, and of the Middle Ages was necessary to complete his doctrine, and show its one-sidedness. It was in the hands of the writers of the eighteenth century, who interpreted it to their own tastes, that it became deadening and sterilizing. In this way Boileau was made to answer for the faults of degenerate disciples whom he would have been the first to repudiate.

Modern critics may differ in their judgment of Boileau, but none have ever disputed the genius of **Jean de la Fontaine,** the greatest fabulist in the literature of the world.

La Fontaine was born on the 7th of July, 1621, at Château-Thierry, where his father was *maître des eaux et forêts*. He does not seem to have exerted himself overmuch at school. At nineteen he entered the Oratory, thinking that he had a vocation for the Church. But he soon gave up this idea and married a pretty girl of fifteen, Marie Héricart, of whom he soon got tired. In 1659 he agreed to a division of property and left his wife. He came to Paris, where, under the protection of different patrons belonging to the nobility (The Duchesse de Bouillon, the Prince de Condé, Mme de la Fayette, and Mme de la Sablière), and following his natural bent, he drifted into that careless and easy-going existence which lasted till his conversion, just before his death in 1695.

Besides his *Fables*, of which we shall speak last of all, La Fontaine is the author of five books of *Contes*, whose *gau-*

loiserie or riskiness connects him with the tradition of the *fableaux*; five larger poems of mediocre value, of which the best are *Adonis* (1658) and *Philémon et Baucis* (1685); various shorter pieces, including six " elegies ", nine " odes ", thirteen " ballades ", and twenty-five " epistles "; a tedious paraphrase of *Psyché*; and twelve plays which prove that La Fontaine was destitute of dramatic talent.

The *Fables*, which consist of twelve Books, were published and written at different times—the early ones in 1668, and the last Book not till 1694.

To assign his correct position to La Fontaine in the literature of his epoch is no easy task. His ideal of life, his Epicurean morals, connect him with the libertine group of the beginning of the century, and with the older irreverent and Gallic writers, such as Rabelais and Des Périers. His language, too, and his verse are hampered by none of the conventionalities of the time. The speech of the " *honnêtes gens* " suffices not to render the manifold echoes of his universal sympathy. His is an original, forceful, and picturesque language; he introduces old words if they suit his purpose better (*cuider, engeigner, déduit, liesse, chevance,* &c.), or popular phrases (*tirant sur le grison, il avait du comptant, tout cousu d'or*), nor does he draw the line at words of any class (*bique, goujat, hère, racaille, ripaille,* &c.). In versification his measures and rhythm vary according to the sentiment expressed, and he does not shrink from employing *enjambement* or overflow, if the effect is heightened thereby.

What distinguishes him above all things from most of his illustrious contemporaries is the fact that he is a poet, in the sense that we can always recognize the unobtrusive but perpetual intervention of his own personality in his work.

While these qualities make of him a man unique of his kind in the age in which he lived, it does not sever all connection between him and contemporary literature. His artistic ideal is in close conformity with that of Boileau, Molière, and

Racine. Speaking of Molière's *Fâcheux*, La Fontaine says:

> *Nous avons changé de méthode,*
> *Jodelet n'est plus à la mode,*
> *Et maintenant il ne faut pas*
> *Quitter la nature d'un pas.*

But instead of depicting man only he made animals his special study, and, what is more, he is the only writer of his century who introduced "exterior" nature into his works. In his *Fables* La Fontaine invented nothing. He took his subjects on all sides, from the ancients (Æsop, Phædrus, Babrius, &c.), or from sixteenth-century writers (Marot, Des Périers, Rabelais, &c.):

> *J'en lis qui sont du Nord et qui sont du Midi,*

transforming his models by his wonderful gifts as a poet and a psychologist:

> *Mon imitation n'est point un esclavage;*
> *Je ne prends que l'idée et les tours et les lois*
> *Que nos maîtres suivaient eux-mêmes autrefois.*

And this is why he has so much enlarged and extended this branch of literature, some of his *Fables* being *contes* or *fableaux* (*Le Curé et le Mort*, *La Laitière et le Pot au Lait*, *La Jeune Veuve*, &c.), others idylls (*Tucis et Amarante*), others elegies or epistles. Each of them is a little drama in itself, and together they form, as he has himself said,

> *Une ample comédie à cent actes divers*
> *Et dont la scène est l'univers.*

On this scene, under the disguise of animals, the foibles of his contemporaries and of humanity at large are exposed with a quiet and unobtrusive moral:

> *En ces sortes de feinte il faut instruire et plaire,*
> *Et conter pour conter me semble peu d'affaire.*

CHAPTER II

DRAMA

The two greatest names in the whole of French dramatic art fall within this period—Molière in comedy, and Racine in tragedy.

During the interval between Corneille and those two great writers, the most popular playwright was **Philippe Quinault** (1635-1688), the author of seventeen plays, both tragedies and comedies, in which he followed the taste set by the novels of La Calprenède and Mlle de Scudéry.

The affected and insipid gallantry [1] of Quinault's plays is unbearable now, but he is still remembered for the graceful and harmonious verse of the librettos (1671-1686) written for Lulli's operas.

It is quite refreshing to turn from the languid graces of Quinault to the robust good sense of **Molière,** the greatest name in the whole of French literature.

Jean-Baptiste Poquelin, known by his stage name of **Molière,** was born at Paris in January, 1622. He was the son of a wealthy upholsterer, who held the office of *tapissier valet de chambre* to the King. From 1636 to 1641 he was a pupil of the Collège de Clermont (now *Louis le Grand*). Before leaving school he had inherited his father's charge, but his bent did not lie that way. In 1643 he gave up his post, and in spite of his father's opposition he organized a theatrical company with the help of the Béjarts. They called it *L'Illustre Théâtre,* but in spite of its pompous title its success was not great, and Molière was imprisoned for debt. Soon after he and his companions determined to try their fortune in the provinces. They departed at the end of 1646 or the beginning of 1647, and stayed away from Paris for eleven years. At Lyons, Molière published, in 1655, *L'Étourdi,* his first regular five-act comedy. Success began to smile, and he resolved to return to the capital; on the 24th of October of the year 1658 he played for the first time in the presence of the King, the pieces represented being Corneille's *Nicomède* and the *Docteur Amoureux,* one of Molière's lost

---

[1] Cp. Boileau's famous lines:
> Les héros chez Quinault parlent tout autrement,
> Et jusqu'à " je vous hais " tout se dit tendrement.

farces. Louis XIV was so much pleased that he gave Molière permission to set up in Paris as the *Troupe de Monsieur*, and to play alternately with the Italian actors in the Petit Bourbon theatre. In 1659 he staged *Les Précieuses Ridicules*, which inaugurates the series of those famous plays which Molière was to produce with little interruption for fourteen years. In 1662 he married Armande Béjart. His last play was the *Malade Imaginaire* (1673), during the representation of which he was seized with a violent fit of coughing, which burst one of the vessels of his lungs. There was just time to take him home, where he died one hour after the accident.

The most important plays of Molière can be classed as follows:—

Character comedy: *Tartuffe* (1664), *Don Juan* (1665), *Le Misanthrope* (1666), *L'Avare* (1668).

Comedy of manners: *Les Précieuses Ridicules* (1659). *L'École des Maris* (1661), *L'École des Femmes* (1662), *Georges Dandin* (1668), *Le Bourgeois Gentilhomme* (1670), *Les Femmes Savantes* (1672).

Heroic comedy: *Dom Garcie de Navarre* (1661).

Pastoral comedy: *Mélicerte* (1666).

Farces: *Sganarelle* (1660), *Le Médecin malgré lui* (1666), *Les Fourberies de Scapin* (1671), *Le Malade Imaginaire* (1673).

Comédie-ballet: *La Princesse d'Élide* (1664), *L'Amour Médecin* (1665), *Le Sicilien* (1667), *Psyché* (1671), with the assistance of Pierre Corneille, Quinault, and the composer Lulli.

Critical comedies: *La Critique de l'École des Femmes* (1663), *L'Impromptu de Versailles* (1663).

Of his plays, of which about one half are in prose and the other half in verse, the best are *Tartuffe*, *Le Misanthrope*, *L'Avare*, *Les Femmes Savantes*, *Le Bourgeois Gentilhomme*, *Georges Dandin*, and *L'École des Femmes*, while the first three will generally be esteemed his masterpieces.

Along with these, the *Précieuses Ridicules* (1659) deserves more than passing attention, as being his first really great play, and the first dramatic satire on cultured society in

France. The shaft was aimed at the ridiculous only among the *précieuses*, the imitators of the *Hôtel de Rambouillet*, who abounded in Paris, but more especially in the provinces; at least so said Molière in his preface, and the *précieuses* evidently took him at his word, for we know that the Marquise and her set were present at the first performance. Whatever may have been Molière's intentions, it dealt the class as a whole a severe blow.

The play ends with the confusion and exposure of the two *précieuses*, Cathos and Madelon, and a healthy moral on the part of Gorgibus, their father and uncle. Its success was immediate and universal, and even to-day it has lost little of its comic force.

Molière was above all a believer in the goodness of Nature. All those he attacks in his works are such as disfigure or tamper with it. Of these not the least dangerous is the religious hypocrite, the *Tartuffe* of his next play, of which the first three acts appeared in 1664, and were acted before the court at Versailles. Immediately the devout protested indignantly, and the King yielded by prohibiting the play, but Molière finished his work, and read or performed it at the houses of several of the great noblemen of the time. In 1667, on the authority of a verbal promise from the King, and having softened down a few of the bolder passages, Molière performed the piece under the title of *L'Imposteur*. After the first representation, M. de Lamoignon, President of the Parliament of Paris, ordered the theatre to be closed. Molière, however, was not to be beaten; he sent a second *placet* to the King, who was then besieging Lille. The King was well-disposed, but the Archbishop of Paris threatened with excommunication anyone who should even read the play. It was not till 1669, when circumstances were more favourable, that Louis XIV granted the desired permission.

The reason for the storm of indignation roused by the play on its first appearance was the opinion held by his accusers that Molière had attacked religion itself. They were not altogether wrong, in so far as religion is conceived as a restraining force. Molière belonged to the sixteenth century in these matters. Like Rabelais and Montaigne, he thought that Nature and good sense were sufficient as guides of conduct —just the opposite of the original form of Christian morality, which is resistance to Nature. This explains the indignation of the high ecclesiastics of the time, and the naïve fright of the Jansenist Baillet, who, in his *Jugements des Savants*, begins his article on Molière with the following words: " *M. de Molière est un des plus dangereux ennemis que le siècle ou le monde ait suscités à l'Église de Jésus-Christ.*"

The following is the main outline of the story of *Tartuffe*:

> Under the cloak of sham devoutness the hypocrite Tartuffe has managed to introduce himself into the house of Orgon, a wealthy Parisian bourgeois, who in his blindness welcomes him as a pattern of virtue, and in spite of the warnings of Cléante, his brother-in-law, goes so far as to entrust him with the management of his household, and entreats his wife and family to conform and submit cheerfully to all his orders; not only making over his fortune to him, but even offering him his daughter's hand in marriage. In vain does Cléante attempt once more to expose the mean impostor's hidden baseness and wickedness. Encouraged by his patron's protection, Tartuffe next begins to make love to Orgon's wife; on being informed of this, Orgon declares that he will only believe what he sees with his own eyes. Hiding one day under the table, Orgon sees for himself Tartuffe's perfidy and wickedness; and when he wishes to turn Tartuffe out of the house, the latter declares that it is he who is the master, and that it is for Orgon to quit. Suddenly an officer puts in an appearance, bearing a sealed letter from the King; but, to every one's surprise, the letter is a warrant for the apprehension of Tartuffe (instead of Orgon), whose arrest was hourly expected, owing to an incriminating report.

The great manner of Molière was continued in the *Misanthrope* (1666): Alceste is a cynic, but honourable, and with a real disdain for vice in his misanthropy. Rousseau on this account, and others after him, have treated the play as a vindication of insincerity against truth, and as making virtue itself ridiculous on the stage. This charge, however, seems uncandid; neither the rudeness of Alceste nor the misanthropy from which it springs are to be called virtues. Alceste is not ridiculous because he censures vice, but because he is a maniac.

The next play, *L'Avare* (1668), is Molière's best piece in prose. Here he borrowed from *Les Esprits* of Larivey, the *Belle Plaideuse* of Boisrobert, and especially from Plautus' *Aulularia*, carrying out his saying, "*Je prends mon bien où je le trouve*"—if indeed the words are authentic— and surpassing them all in his wonderful psychic picture of the Miser in whom avarice destroys all family bonds.

A short analysis of the play follows:

> Élise, the daughter of the miser Harpagon, is in love with Valère, who one day saved her life, and has introduced himself into the house in the guise of a steward, while Cléante, her brother, is enamoured of Marianne, a charming young neighbour. But Harpagon is thinking of marrying Marianne himself, and decides that Cléante shall marry "a certain widow", and his daughter M. Anselme, an old gentleman, who is ready to take her without a dowry. Cléante, who is refused by his father the supplies of money necessary for his maintenance, is obliged to borrow at an exorbitant interest from a usurer, who turns out to be his father. Lively scenes ensue now between father and son about the projected marriage, the miser finally turning his son out of doors. In the meantime La Flèche, Cléante's servant, has stolen a casket full of gold which the miser had hidden in his garden, and will only restore it on certain conditions. Craving to get back his money, Harpagon is obliged to forgo his own marriage, and to consent to the union of Marianne with Cléante, and of Élise with Valère. M. Anselme, who proves to be the father of Valère and Marianne, promises to give the couples a large dowry, and to pay all expenses; while the old miser expresses perfect satisfaction with the arrangement, on condition that he is not asked to disburse a penny, and that he will be presented with a new coat for the wedding day.

As the aim of this play has sometimes been misunderstood, it is interesting to note what was the opinion expressed by Goethe, in his *Conversations with Eckermann*: " Molière is so great that one is astonished anew every time one reads him.

He is a man by himself—his pieces border on tragedy . . . no man has the courage to imitate him. His *Miser*, where vice destroys all the natural piety between father and son, is especially great, and in a high sense tragic."

The *Bourgeois Gentilhomme* (1670) and *Georges Dandin* (1668) have the same object of moral satire; on the one hand, a vainglorious bourgeois eager to ape the aristocracy, on the other, the pride and meanness of the nobility itself. In the *Femmes Savantes* (1672) Molière returned to the subject of the *Précieuses Ridicules*, but with maturer powers and greater art. It was the same folly which he attacked under a different form; science was the fashion, and the pedantic ladies of the time were patronesses of physics, astronomy, and anatomy.

Following up the lesson of *L'École des Maris* (1661) in *L'École des Femmes* (1662), Molière shows that woman ought to be withdrawn from the inferior intellectual and moral condition in which she is kept by the tyrannical egotism of man.

Molière is a purely French and Gallic genius. His ancestors are not the ancients, as in the case of Corneille and Racine, but the old authors of *fableaux* and farces, as well as the sixteenth-century writers, Rabelais and Régnier. All his comedies, from the early farces to the *Misanthrope*, represent different stages of the same spirit of independence, characteristic of the literature of the sixteenth century. This explains why he cared so little about the famous Rules of Unity: " *Je voudrais bien savoir* ", he says in *Le Fâcheux*, " *si la grande règle de toutes les règles n'est pas de plaire.*" His belief in the goodness of Nature, and his persistent refusal to comply with any restraint or discipline, are also typical of the *esprit gaulois*.

By his indifference to conventional processes, by his continuous and indefatigable production in spite of all obstacles, by the plentitude of his art, unhampered by any of the slow and studied methods of a Boileau or a Pope, he deserves to

DRAMA

take rank among such world geniuses as Homer, Plautus, Shakespeare, and Rabelais.

The French have claimed for him a superiority over all earlier and later writers of comedy. On the whole, there is no reason to gainsay the universal verdict of the nation. Shakespeare was a greater genius because he excelled in tragedy as well as comedy, and also because, apart from being a great dramatist, he is one of the greatest poets of the world, while Molière was hardly a poet at all. The influence of Molière in comedy has been immense, greater by far than that of any other writer cultivating this particular branch. All succeeding French writers of comedy derive directly from him. Neither was his influence less in England (cp. Fielding and Sheridan)—in fact, one might almost say that for two hundred years Molière's comedy has determined the form of European comedy.

Molière has at all times been taken to task for his style; but it is too often forgotten that his verse as well as his prose are meant to be spoken on the stage, and not to be read. Thus it is not fair to judge his comedies as books; a great many of the so-called faults of his style are due to the fact that such and such a phrase or expression is meant for the ear and not for the eye.

The typical representative of the literary ideal of the *grand siècle*, or rather of its golden age, is **Jean Racine**.

> **Racine** was born on 22nd December, 1639, at La Ferté Milon. After he had passed through the town school of Beauvais, he was sent to that of *Port-Royal*. Here he studied hard, especially Greek, which he knew better than any of his fellow-writers. At nineteen he came to Paris to complete his studies, and an ode in honour of the King's marriage, *La Nymphe de la Seine*, made his name widely known. In 1661 he went to Uzès in Languedoc, hoping in vain to obtain a benefice from his uncle, the vicar-general of the diocese. He returned to Paris early in 1663, and soon after composed a second ode, which brought him a gratification of 800 livres. In the meantime he had made the acquaintance of Boileau, Molière, and La Fontaine. His principal efforts were now directed to the stage. Assisted by Molière, he gained

some recognition for his first tragedy, *La Thébaïde ou Les Frères Ennemis* (1663). This was followed by *Alexandre* (1666), which after the sixth performance was withdrawn from Molière's theatre and entrusted to the rival actors at the *Hôtel de Bourgogne*. This incident, added to the fact that Racine persuaded Mlle du Parc, Molière's best actress, to leave him, led to an estrangement between the two great poets. In 1666 appeared Nicole's *Visionnaires*, condemning the dramatist as an "*empoisonneur public*", and Racine, believing that he had been personally aimed at, issued a reply in which he mercilessly ridiculed the men who had been his teachers at *Port-Royal*. During the next ten years Racine produced his dramatic masterpieces. Moved by religious scruples, and mortified at the continual cabals formed against his plays, he turned from dramatic work (1677), made his peace with *Port-Royal*, and married in June of the same year. It was in 1689 only, at the request of Mme de Maintenon, that he wrote *Esther*, his first Biblical play, which was followed in 1691 by *Athalie*, also a scriptural drama. In his later years he lost the King's favour, chiefly on account of his Jansenist tendencies, and died in 1699.

Apart from his two initiatory efforts, *La Thébaïde* (1663), a poor imitation of Corneille's manner, and *Alexandre* (1666), in which he closely followed Quinault, Racine's plays consist of *Andromaque* (1667), *Les Plaideurs* (1688), his only comedy, *Britannicus* (1669), *Bérénice* (1670), *Bajazet* (1672), *Mithridate* (1673), *Iphigénie* (1674), *Phèdre* (1677), and the two Biblical plays, *Esther* (1689) and *Athalie* (1691).

The series of Racine's masterpieces was opened by *Andromaque* (1667), which had as great a success as Corneille's *Cid* thirty years previously. The plot of *Andromaque* was taken partly from Book II of the *Æneid* and partly from the *Andromache* of Euripides, though some points of importance, mainly with regard to the character of the heroine, have been essentially altered. It marked the advent of a new tragic ideal, the very opposite of that of Corneille, the substitution of human passion, and especially love, for the heroic crises of the will, and for that reason it was but coldly received by the partisans of the older dramatist who found the hero Pyrrhus "too violent". Racine retorted in the preface that "*tous les héros ne sont pas faits pour être des Céladons* ";[1] while Subligny, an obscure author of the time, took advantage of the occasion to write a parody, *La Folle Querelle*, which he took to Molière, who did not refuse it. Since the " plot " of *Alexandre* Molière thought he had a right to reprisals.

Racine's next play, *Les Plaideurs* (1688), gave a new proof of his brilliant talent for satire, which he had already displayed in his letters against the Port-Royalists. It is a caricature of lawyers written by Racine to avenge himself for the loss of a law-suit concerning the priory of Épinay. In the preface Racine tells us that he received some help from " his friends ". These friends were the little group who were in the habit of meeting at the inn of the *Mouton Blanc*, namely Boileau, La Fontaine, Furetière, and a few others. The matter of the *Plaideurs* may be due to several hands, but the form obviously belongs to Racine alone. The play was coolly received. People insisted, says the author, on examining " *mon amusement comme on aurait fait une tragédie* ", but the play being performed at court a month later, the King laughed loudly and the courtiers followed suit.

Till now the enemies of Racine had maintained that he could depict the passion of love only. To prove the contrary he borrowed from Tacitus the subject of his next play, *Britannicus*[2] (1669), a masterly exposition of Nero's adolescence in crime and of his struggle against his ambitious mother Agrippina. The first preface to *Britannicus*, together with that to *Bérénice* (1670), Racine's next tragedy, is especially important as containing the declaration of his dramatic system.

The subject of *Bérénice*, Titus sacrificing his love for the Jewish queen to political considerations, had been proposed at the same time to Racine and Corneille by Louis the Fourteenth's sister-in-law, the sprightly Henrietta of England. *Bérénice* is not one of Racine's best plays, but, needless to say,

[1] It will be remembered that Céladon is the sentimental hero of D'Urfé's *Astrée*.
[2] Cp. Boileau's allusion in the *Epître* vii:
    Et peut-être ta plume aux censeurs de Pyrrhus
    Doit les plus nobles traits dont tu peignis Burrhus.

far superior to that of Corneille, whose powers were now fast waning.

In his next play, *Bajazet* (1672), Racine brought on the stage an almost contemporary event of Turkish history, related to him by Count de Cézy, French ambassador at the Porte.

His enemies had this time to lower their flag; yet Mme de Sévigné could not grant that Racine had equalled her darling Corneille, and put down most of the success of *Bajazet* to the marvellous acting of Mlle Champmeslé, a famous actress of the day: " *Bajazet est au-dessous (d'Andromaque) . . . Racine fait des comédies* (plays) *pour la Champmeslé; ce n'est pas pour les siècles à venir. Si jamais il n'est plus jeune, et qu'il cesse d'être amoureux, ce ne sera plus la même chose. Vive donc notre vieil ami Corneille! Pardonnons-lui de méchants vers en faveur des divines et sublimes beautés qui nous transportent.*"

The year after (1673) *Mithridate* appeared. In this play Racine freely availed himself of the historical traditions contained in Appian, Plutarch, Florus, and Don Cassius.

It could not be said that he had equalled Corneille on his own ground in *Britannicus*, but in *Mithridate*, together with the figure of Monimia, that emblem of feminine grace and delicacy, he exhibits a picture of large political interests in a manner hardly surpassed by his rival. Racine shows his hero Mithridate unhappy in love and in policy, his son Xiphares being his rival in the former and his other son Pharnace in the latter. When Mithridate sees himself betrayed by Pharnace, who has joined the Romans, his mortal enemies, he kills himself, but dies reconciled with Xiphares and Monimia, the princess they both loved.

This play, which is said to have been the favourite tragedy of Louis XIV and Charles XII of Sweden, was followed by *Iphigénie en Aulide*, first performed at Versailles before the Court (August, 1674), and half a year later at Paris. Racine for the most part imitated the *Iphigenia* of Euripides; but instead of adopting the *dénoûment* of the Attic tragedian, he followed another ancient tradition. In his version Eriphile, jealous of Iphigenia, who gains the love of Achilles, denounces her rival to the Greeks in order to see her sacrificed, and kills herself when it appears that she is herself the victim demanded by the gods.

It was not till January, 1677, that Racine produced his next tragedy, *Phèdre*, which he preferred to all his other plays: "*Je suis pour* Phèdre *et M. le prince de Condé est pour* Athalie", he replied to Boileau, who asked him which of his own tragedies he liked best. The plot was again borrowed from one of Euripides' plays, *Hippolytus*, although with important changes in the action and characters, partly suggested by the *Phædra* of Seneca:

> Phedra, the wife of King Theseus, is in love with her step-son Hippolytus. In her despair she resolves to die, but learning that her husband has expired, she declares her love to Hippolytus, who repels her advances. Suddenly the report spreads that Theseus is safe and on his way home. Phedra to exonerate herself allows her nurse Œnone to persuade the King, who has now arrived, that Hippolytus has wished to obtrude his love upon her. Theseus in his wrath banishes his son, and calls upon Neptune to punish him. The suicide of Œnone, whom Phedra has cursed in her remorse for her criminal suggestion, opens the King's eyes, but too late. Hippolytus has been dragged to death by his runaway steeds. Phedra takes poison, and as she expires confesses the crime of which Œnone was the instigator.

If not the most perfect of Racine's masterpieces, *Phèdre* is generally acknowledge to be the most powerful. Never before had such a marvellous presentation of human agony been exhibited on the French stage; but tragic passion displayed in all its force and horror shocked the *précieux* followers of Quinault and of the heroic-gallant novel. The Duchess de Bouillon and her brother the Duc de Nevers made up their minds that the play of Racine should fail. They ordered a rival play on the same subject from Pradon, a feeble playwright of the time, and by engaging the front seats in the two theatres for six successive nights, and leaving them empty in the one where Racine's *Phèdre* was being performed, made it appear as if it was a failure. Immediately a violent literary quarrel broke out, and on both sides insulting sonnets were exchanged. The Duc de Nevers threatened to horsewhip Racine and Boileau who had sided with him, and would probably have carried out his threat had not the Prince de Condé intervened and put a stop to the dispute.

The cabal had been baffled, but Racine, who was in the highest degree sensitive, irritated by the endless intrigues of his adversaries, and troubled in his conscience by religious scruples, determined to quit the stage. The Jansenists were regaining their ascendancy over him, and already in the preface to *Phèdre* we notice that he is very eager " *de réconcilier la tragédie avec quantité de personnes célèbres par leur piété et par leur doctrine, qui l'ont condamnée dans ces derniers temps* ", a direct allusion to his old master's words that playwrights were " public poisoners ".

Racine did not return to dramatic work till twelve years after (1689), when he accepted an invitation from Mme de Maintenon to compose a Biblical drama for her pupils, the young ladies of the educational establishment of St. Cyr. The result was the play of *Esther* (1689). So great was the success that the same lady asked the poet for a second drama of a religious character, and he produced what is generally recognized as his most perfect play, *Athalie* (1691), a unique blending of grace and majesty.

He took the plot from 2 Chron., xxii and xxiii, and called the play *Athalie*, partly because Athaliah is the central figure, partly because her name appeared to him better known than that of Joas:

> Athaliah has caused her grandchildren to be murdered in order to reign in their stead, and introduce the cult of idols. One of these children, Joas, has escaped, and been brought up in the temple in the fear of God by the high-priest, Joad, and his wife, Josabet. Athaliah comes to the temple, followed by Mathan, who has renounced his true God to become a priest of Baal. She relates to Mathan and Abner, one of the officers of the King of Judah, a terrible dream, in which a child stabbed her to the heart. She

recognizes that child in the person of young Joas; orders him to be led into her presence, and requests that the boy shall be delivered up to her. Joad refuses, and Athaliah leaves the temple with threats. The high-priest sees that no time must be lost, and crowns Joas King. Presently Abner arrives with an order from Athaliah to Joad to yield up the child, and also a treasure concealed in the temple. He feigns to yield, and lures Athaliah into the temple, where she falls a victim to the Levites armed against her by the high-priest.

Racine is the creator of character-tragedy, of tragedy true to life, as opposed to the tragedy of Corneille, whose inventive powers were applied to the creating of situations to which he afterwards accommodated his characters. A consequence of this principle is that the exceptional, extraordinary, and " complex " action of Corneille's plays is replaced by " *une action simple, chargée de peu de matière* ", turning upon everyday experience. Compare, e.g. Corneille's Cinna, a conspirator when the curtain rises, and at the end of the play the minister of the prince he wished to murder, with Mithridate, a father the rival of his son; or Rodrigue, obliged by his honour to kill his mistress's father, and the same day betrothed to the daughter of his victim, with the subject of *Britannicus*, the struggle between a son and his ambitious mother. Another consequence of Racine's dramatic system was the unprecedented importance given in his tragedies to the passion of love, as being the most general of all, the most natural, and perhaps the most tragic, and finally as being the passion which, while it remains identical in its essence, best displays the diversity of human character. Here again Racine was doing the opposite of what Corneille recommended and actually did.

Racine has been blamed for having depicted under ancient names courtiers of the time of Louis XIV, but no drama can avoid reflecting contemporary manners, however careful the author may be of local colour — a consideration which, like historical accuracy, only concerned him in so far as it was needful with his courtly audience for verisimilitude. Local colour at best is only an outward ornament, and may help the writer to add poetry to truth; but the object of the drama is to depict human passions, and not to restore forgotten epochs of civilization by an effort of erudition. Racine's characters only belong to Antiquity by name; outwardly they are noblemen of the time when one man was the state, and intrinsically real and lasting types of humanity.

Although it cannot be denied that occasionally his heroes do talk the jargon of gallantry *à la Quinault*, it is wrong to make a *précieux* of Racine. His contemporaries on more than one occasion found that he invested his characters with too much inborn ferocity, and it was his abhorrence of his own fictions which was the inward cause of his conversion. If any fault can be found with his characters it is that they sometimes tend in their generality to become psychological abstractions rather than real living beings.

His style, except as regards the invariable elegance of its form, has been described as " bordering on prose ". This simplicity makes it an incomparable vehicle for psychological analysis:

> *J'aimais jusqu'à ces pleurs que je faisais couler* (Brit.).
> *Prends soin d'elle, ma haine a besoin de sa vie* (Baj.), &c.

This mode of writing is exactly the contrary of that of the *précieux*, who express very simple things in very complicated language.

> Of the contemporaries of Racine the only one who is not entirely forgotten is **Thomas Corneille** (1625-1709), a younger brother of the *grand* Corneille. He began by writing comedies mostly imitated from Spanish models, and in 1656 produced *Timocrate*, an insipid tragedy in the manner of Quinault, the greatest theatrical success of the century. Later he imitated Racine in *Ariane* (1672), and his brother in the *Comte d'Essex* (1678).

CHAPTER III

PROSE

In this period prose developed considerably in the direction of Memoirs. Of these the most remarkable are the *Mémoires* (1662-1679) of Paul de Gondi, **Cardinal de Retz** (1614-1679), in which he relates the events of the Fronde [1] and the part he played in it.

Too passionate to be impartial, his *Mémoires* nevertheless present a living picture of his time as a whole. They abound in portraits, which were then coming into fashion, and in political considerations.

The same period is also covered by the *Mémoires* of the Duc de la Rochefoucauld, the author of the more famous *Maximes*.

The life of **François de la Rochefoucauld,** Prince de Marsillac (1613-1680), falls naturally into two parts: one active and adventurous, when he threw himself ardently into the struggle of the Fronde; the other of bitter disillusion amid a chosen circle of devoted friends, of whom not the least important was Mme de Sablé, a later *précieuse*, at whose *salon* he was an assiduous visitor. It was there, with the help of the hostess and a few of her friends, that he elaborated those maxims which are the quintessence of preciosity. Their value must not be overrated, in spite of the wonderful conciseness and polish of their lapidary style. The central idea that runs through them all is, briefly, that every virtue is the product of vices, while these are resolvable into selfishness, " in which all virtues are lost like rivers in the sea ". A few quotations will bring this out more clearly:

> We all have strength enough to endure the misfortunes of others.

---

[1] Fronde is the name (taken from the sling used by the boys of Paris in their mimic fights) given to certain civil dissensions from 1648 to 1654. The Old Fronde was a protest of the people against increasing taxation and the usurpation of their parliamentary rights. The New Fronde, which developed from it, was a struggle between the discontented nobility and the prime minister, Mazarin, whom they wished to overthrow.

In the adversity of our friends we always find something which does not displease us.

People sometimes think that we hate flattery, but we hate only the way they flatter.

Our passions are the only orators that always convince.

Such are the moral comments on life of one who was unable to gaze on the world with an impartial mind. Although it is impossible to deny the partial truth of La Rochefoucauld's charges, we cannot admit that his maxims are universal; they are purely the reflection of his mood, after a bitter experience of life, or, at most, of the society with which he was conversant. On that account they were very popular with his contemporaries; Boileau, La Fontaine, and especially Mme de Sévigné, all admired them.

The character and influence of La Rochefoucauld's style have been happily characterized by Voltaire in the following passage: " *Un des ouvrages qui contribuèrent le plus à former le goût de la nation et à lui donner un esprit de justesse et de précision est le Livre des Maximes de François, Duc de La Rochefoucauld. On lut avec avidité ce petit recueil. Il accoutuma à penser et à renfermer des idées dans un tour vif, précis et délicat.*"

Epistolary art also finds many a notable representative in this age. It may be said to have reached perfection in the letters of **Mme de Sévigné** (1626–1696).

Left a widow at the age of twenty-five, she devoted herself entirely to the education of her two children, especially of her daughter; and when the latter, who had meanwhile married M. de Grignan, left her to follow her husband into Provence, of which he had been appointed governor, she began with her daughter that famous correspondence which continued till her death, and which has earned for her so high a place in the literature of her country. Her letters are not rhetorical studied exercises decked out for the public like those of Balzac, but a delightfully natural and graceful exchange of thought, in which she allows her imagination to run away with her pen, but is never false to her sound judgment and robust good sense. Mme de Sévigné's twenty-five years of letters to her daughter are also valuable as revealing in detail the Court and fashionable world in the reign of Louis XIV.

A letter-writer also, and a faithful friend of Mme de Sévigné, was Marie Madeleine, **Comtesse de la Fayette** (1634–1693), the founder of the modern novel. Her first work of fiction, *Zayde* (1670), already marks an advance on the longwinded and insipid productions of Mlle de Scudéry, while *La Princesse de Clèves* (1678), her masterpiece, represents real and natural sentiments in precise language. It is the starting-point of the modern psychological novel.

The realistic novel was continued by **Antoine Furetière** (1620–1685), also the compiler of a *Dictionnaire* (1690) of the French language, for which he was unjustly expelled from the Academy as a plagiarist. His *Roman Bourgeois* (1666) is a pessimistic and satirical narrative of middle-class life in Paris, with a second part directly aimed at Sorel, his forerunner in this branch of literature.

At no period of French literature has pulpit oratory been represented by a series of more famous names. The greatest pulpit orator of all times, and one of the greatest French prose writer of the seventeenth century, was **Jacques Bénigne Bossuet.**

> **Bossuet** was born at Dijon on the 27th of Sept., 1627. At an early age he was sent to the school of his native town; and when fifteen years of age he proceeded to Paris, where he finished his studies. He was ordained in 1652, and placed at the head of a mission sent to Lorraine to convert the Protestants of that province. Here it was that he composed his first polemical work against the Protestants. In 1659 he was summoned to Paris, where he preached for ten years with immense success. In 1669 he pronounced the funeral oration on Henrietta of France, being rewarded with the bishopric of Condom, and soon afterwards (1670) was appointed tutor to the Dauphin, the King's son. From that date he devoted himself entirely to the education of his royal pupil, and with that object wrote some of his most important works. The remaining portion of his life, save that he delivered a few funeral discourses between 1683 and 1687, was

wholly devoted to controversial works in defence of the Catholic faith. Despite this he did not neglect the duties of his diocese; "*faisant honte,*" says Saint-Simon, "*dans une vieillesse si avancée, à l'âge moyen et robuste des évêques et des docteurs les plus instruits et les plus laborieux*". He died on the 12th of April, 1704.

The chief works of Bossuet may be classed under the following headings:

Works of Edification and Piety, which include sermons, panegyrics, and funeral orations; the *Élévations sur les Mystères* and the *Méditations sur l'Évangile*. Of these only six of the funeral orations and one sermon appeared during his lifetime.

The works composed in connection with the education of the Dauphin, which are: the *Discours sur l'Histoire Universelle* (1681), the *Politique tirée des Propres Paroles de l'Écriture Sainte*, the *Traité de la Connaissance de Dieu et de soi-même*, the *Abrégé de l'Histoire de France*, which only appeared in 1747.

The controversial works, which comprise the works against the Protestants, the principal being *L'Exposition de la Doctrine de l'Église Catholique* (1671), and *L'Histoire des Variations des Églises Protestantes* (1688); the works relating to the "Quietists" or "new mystics", of which the most important is the *Relation du Quiétisme* (1698); the works written against Richard Simon, the first man to apply scientific learning to the explanation of the Scriptures. These include the *Défense de la Tradition et des Saints Pères*, which was published in 1753.

Miscellaneous writings, of which the principal is the *Maximes sur la Comédie* (1693).

We shall consider his most important works in the order named.

Bossuet pronounced several famous funeral orations, of which the best are those on Henrietta, Queen of England (1669); on her daughter Henrietta of England, Duchess of Orléans (1670); on Marie-Thérèse of Austria, Queen of France (1683); on

Anne de Gonzague de Clèves, Princesse Palatine, in which the *libertins* or freethinkers of the time are mercilessly attacked (1685); on Michel le Tellier, chancellor of France (1686), glorifying the revocation of the Edict of Nantes; and on Louis de Bourbon, Prince de Condé (1687).

Before Bossuet, the chief aim in the funeral discourse had been to please the audience much more than to instruct and edify. We know what ideas the preachers who preceded him had on that subject, from one of the most distinguished of them under Louis XIII, the eloquent François Ogier. Ogier acknowledges that obituary orations are merely meant for ostentation, diversion, and pomp; that since the pleasure is for the rich, " exquisite viands " are required. A funeral oration is like a tournament or a review, and the orator must display all his art and " all the flowers of his eloquence ". Such was the ideal before Bossuet. He changed it completely by applying to the funeral oration the same method as in his sermons and panegyrics; instead of considering life, he only considers death, which furnishes the lesson and acts as a foundation for it.

Bossuet has sometimes been accused of flattery and insincerity in his obituary orations. No doubt he respected all the conventionalities which the audience and the occasion imposed upon him, but at the same time he spoke or hinted at all the truth which he was capable of conceiving. His views on the revocation of the Edict of Nantes, and on the Revolution in England, were those of all his contemporaries in France. He said what he thought, and these events are judged in the same way in his other writings.

Of the works composed for the Dauphin the most significant is the *Discours sur l'Histoire Universelle* (1681), which is made up of three parts: *Les Époques, La Suite de la Religion*, and *Les Empires*. The first part is a rapid and masterly *résumé* of the world's history from the creation to the reign of Charlemagne. In the third part Bossuet follows the fate of the large empires of Antiquity, showing that human affairs in general depend on Providence, but at the same time attributing a large part in them to will and genius: "*A tout prendre, il en arrive à peu près comme dans le jeu, où le plus habile l'emporte à la longue*". In the second part we have a kind of apology of religion, or rather of the Catholic creed, the truth of which is proved, according to Bossuet, by the continuity of one and the same tradition. It contains the essence, as it were, of the great prelate's thought.

In the *Politique tirée de l'Écriture Sainte* he teaches that kings are absolute, but nevertheless bound to respect the rights and laws of the nation, and also that they are answerable to God for their actions. Lover of tradition as he was, he prefers a monarchy to any other form of government, yet he admits other forms, provided they are enduring and likely to afford protection to the subjects: "*Je respecte dans chaque peuple, le gouvernement que l'usage y a consacré et que l'expérience fait trouver le meilleur.*"

Bossuet's polemic against Protestantism is best represented by the *Histoire des Variations des Églises Protestantes* (1688), a complement of the second part of the *Discours* and of the *Exposition de la Foi Catholique* (1671). The title sufficiently indicates that the author's aim was to prove that the Protestant Church did not possess the obviousness, the infallibility, or the immutability of the Catholic Church, and that therefore it must be false. In order to drive home his argument he exhibits Luther, Zwingli, Calvin, Wicliffe, Huss, and their different doctrines in a series of striking pictures, couched in sober but vigorous language. The fifteenth and last Book terminates with a prayer that God may bring back these rebel sects to the flock of the faithful, although Bossuet is careful not to explain why they left it.

The *Maximes sur la Comédie* (1693) are the development of a letter that Bossuet had addressed to Father Caffaro, an ecclesiast who, in a dissertation prefixed to the comedies of Boursault, had declared that a good Christian could without any scruples visit the theatre. He refutes this view in this little masterpiece of serried argument and passionate eloquence, which will always be remembered for the cruel anathema on Molière: " *La posterité saura peut-être la fin de ce poète comédien, qui en jouant son* Malade Imaginaire *ou son* Médecin par Force, *reçut la dernière atteinte de la maladie dont il mourut peu d'heures après, et passa des plaisanteries du théâtre, parmi lesquelles il rendit presque le dernier soupir, au tribunal de Celui qui dit: ' Malheur à vous qui riez, car vous pleurerez '.*"

Bossuet's severity might lead us to believe that he inclined to Jansenism, but this was not the case, although he is equally distant from the casuists and Jesuits: " *Deux maladies dangereuses ont affligé de nos jours le corps de l'Église; il a pris a quelques docteurs une malheureuse et inhumaine complaisance, une pitié meurtrière, qui leur a fait porter des coussins sous les coudes des pécheurs.* . . . *Quelques autres, non moins extrêmes, ont tenu les consciences captives sous des rigueurs très injustes; il ne peuvent supporter aucune faiblesse; ils traînent toujours l'enfer après eux et ne fulminent que des anathèmes.*"

Pomposity has become the traditional term to apply to Bossuet's style, but as a matter of fact, with the exception of a few passages in the funeral orations, it is simple and lively, and always in perfect harmony with his thought.

The Jesuit **Louis de Bourdaloue** (1632–1704) was preferred in his time to Bossuet as a pulpit orator. The only event of importance in his career was a mission undertaken after the revocation of the Edict of Nantes, with the purpose of converting the Protestants of the south of France to the Catholic Church. His whole life was devoted to preaching, confessing, and consoling.

His prodigious success as a preacher has been attributed to the allusions his sermons may contain, but the primary cause of his popularity lay in the sustained clearness and simplicity of his style, which, while disclaiming all the artifices of rhetoric, occasionally borders on dryness. So severe and outspoken was the moral teaching of this Jesuit that he may well be called " the living refutation of the *Provinciales* ".

Besides his numerous sermons, he pronounced two funeral orations.

Around Bossuet and Bourdaloue a group of sacred orators gather, but all, with the exception of Fénelon, are inferior. Contemporary testimony speaks of the grace and seductive charm of Fénelon's homilies, which were improvised and never set down on paper.

> **Esprit Fléchier** (1632–1710), the fashionable bishop of Nîmes, and the haunter of *salons*, introduced the mannered prettiness of the *précieux* into his sermons and funeral orations, of which the best is that on the famous general Turenne.
>
> Among the Protestants, **Jacques Saurin** (1677–1730), who preached in England and Holland, took Bossuet as his model. His language is energetic, but often unpolished.

THIRD PERIOD (1689–1715)

CHAPTER I

POETRY

In this period of transition poetry practically ceases; versifiers are plentiful, but real poets are conspicuous by their absence. Literature develops in other directions, affording larger scope for that critical and scientific spirit which was to come to full bloom in the following century.

CHAPTER II

DRAMA

With the exception of Regnard, the same may be said of the drama.

One only of the tragic poets of this period deserves even a passing notice:

Antoine de la Fosse (1653–1708) composed one tolerable play, *Manlius* (1698), imitated from the *Venice Preserved* of the English dramatist Thomas Otway, who in turn had taken his plot from the *Conjuration des Espagnols contre Venise* (1674) of the abbé de St. Réal.

Molière certainly found more talented followers than Corneille or Racine. The most important of these is **François Regnard** (1655–1710), who, in his autobiographical romance *La Provençale*, describes the vicissitudes of his early adventurous life. There we read of his capture and sale as a slave by Algerian corsairs, his bondage in Constantinople, and his ransom. After wanderings which extended even to Lapland, he found his vocation in the success of *Le Divorce* at the *Théâtre Italien* in 1688. From 1696 to 1708 he continued to issue comedies, of which the best are: *Le Joueur* (1696), *Le Distrait* (1697), and *Le Légataire Universel* (1708).

Next to Molière, Regnard is the greatest comic writer of his age. He lacks the depth of characterization of his illustrious predecessor, but makes up largely for this by his inexhaustible wit and gaiety. A friend telling old Boileau one day that Regnard was mediocre, he answered: "*Il n'est pas médiocrement gai.*"

His style is the perfection of comic versification.

Florent Carton Dancourt (1661–1725) composed forty-seven comedies in prose, exhibiting the world of finance (*La Femme d'Intrigues*, 1692, and *Les Agioteurs*, 1710), or the world of shady morality (*Le Chevalier à la Mode*, 1687, and *Les Bourgeoises à la Mode*, 1692). His plays are merely topical, but witty, and valuable from a sociological point of view.

CHAPTER III

PROSE

The life of **Jean de la Bruyère**, born in Paris, 1645, was most uneventful. After having been chosen to aid Bossuet in educating the Dauphin, he became tutor to the Duc de Bourbon, grandson of the great Condé, and received a pension from the Condés until his death in 1696.

Apart from the unimportant *Dialogues sur le Quiétisme* (1699), his only work is *Les Caractères ou les Mœurs de ce Siècle* (1688), appended to a translation of the *Characters* of the Greek writer Theophrastus.

The book was revised and enlarged till it reached its definite form, which consists of sixteen chapters dealing with literature, personal merit, women, the heart, society and conversation, the gifts of fortune, the town, the Court, men in high stations, the King and commonwealth, man, judgments, fashion, customs, the pulpit, and in a closing chapter with the *esprits forts* or freethinkers of his time. The *Caractères* consists of maxims and portraits, the latter increasing rapidly as the editions were multiplied, in which the manners and certain individualized types of his time are depicted: " I give back to the public what it has lent me ", said La Bruyère. He was taken at his word, and forthwith the public appeared, key in hand. He protested, but it must be acknowledged that in the majority of cases the keys fitted; Cydias, the wit, is none other than Fontenelle, Émile masks his protector Condé, Mme de Montespan sat for Irène, and Théodecte is easily identified as Mme de Maintenon's brother.

La Bruyère's insight into character is shrewd rather than profound; he notes every outward betrayal or indication of the heart with infinite minuteness, but he rarely succeeds in divining its hidden mechanism. He was above all things a stylist, replacing the classical style by one crisp and concise, which at its best recalls Voltaire, to whose judgment nothing need be added: " *Un style rapide, concis, nerveux, des expressions pittoresques, un usage tout nouveau de la langue, mais qui n'en blesse point les règles.*"

A herald of the sceptical outlook and varied learning of the " philosophers " of the eighteenth century was the *Dictionnaire Historique et Critique* (1697) of **Pierre Bayle** (1647–

1706), professor of philosophy at Rotterdam, of whom Diderot could say: "*Nous avons eu des contemporains dès le règne de Louis XIV.*"

The Dictionary was originally intended to be one of pure erudition, having for its sole object to trace and rectify the errors in other dictionaries of the same class; but his searching study of systems of philosophy and of history had engendered in Bayle a sort of scepticism, and thus his work became the arsenal of rationalism.

It consists of articles on famous men representing mythology, ancient history and geography, the history of religions, philosophy, and European history and literature during the sixteenth and seventeenth centuries, with copious notes not infrequently taking up three-quarters of the page, and containing the most interesting and original matter. It should be noted that Bayle was completely ignorant of the sciences, and that they find no place in his book. In this point he differs essentially from his successors, who found in science a consolation for all they had helped to overthrow.

Bayle's doctrine aims at shaking the very foundation of religion by dint of confronting its teaching with that of reason, and by showing that morals can stand without its aid. However he did not attack his adversaries or put forth his ideas openly; his method is one of insinuation, practised generally by a system of references to other articles or notes which contain the absolute negation of the question he has just been discussing with apparent impartiality or left undecided.

The leading idea of the eighteenth century, the idea of human progress, first emerged in the famous **Quarrel of the Ancients and Moderns,** which had its origin in an academic disputation as to whether Christian heroism and Christian faith afforded more suitable material for a Christian poet than the history and fables of Antiquity. As early as 1657 the poet Desmarets de Saint-Sorlin had composed the epic of *Clovis*, in which none of the gods of classical mythology took any part, and all the supernatural work was accomplished by the Deity and the angels and devils of the Christian religion. Desmarets, conscious that he was going against all hitherto accepted canons, attempted to defend his rejection of the gods of mythology in a number of prefaces and treatises (1670-1674), in which he did not scruple to deal the ancients more than one blow. He thus tended to generalize the question, and by putting the whole of Antiquity on trial, he became the chief upholder of the Moderns in the early days of the famous quarrel. On the other side stood Boileau, who replied in the third canto of the *Art Poétique* (1674) that the mysteries of the Christian religion could not be decked out with the ornaments of poetry without loss to that simple faith and reverence with which they should be regarded.

Shortly before his death Desmarets, addressing the following lines to his friend **Charles Perrault** (1628-1703), bequeathed his cause to him:

> *Viens défendre Perrault, la France qui t'appelle,*
> *Viens combattre avec moi cette troupe rebelle,*
> *Ce ramas d'ennemis qui, faibles et mutins,*
> *Préfèrent à nos chants les ouvrages latins,* &c.

For some time slight skirmishes only took place. Finally, in 1687 the battle opened in earnest, and the quarrel assumed a new importance with Charles Perrault's poem on the *Siècle de Louis le Grand*, read before the Academy, and in which, partly to flatter the King, the modern French poets were placed above the ancients. After the affirmation of his thesis Perrault attempted to prove the truth of it in the famous *Parallèles des Anciens et des Modernes* (1688-1697), adducing six principal reasons for the superiority of the moderns: the fact that they came later, the greater exactness of their psychology, their more perfect method of reasoning, the art of printing, Christianity, and, finally, the protection of the King.

From the first Fontenelle had sided with Perrault, and backed him up with his *Digression sur les Anciens et Modernes* (1688).

The partisans of Antiquity protested, La Fontaine in the *Épître à Huet*, La Bruyère in the *Caractères*, and Boileau in the *Réflexions sur Longin* (1694), which, in the midst of much worthless matter, points out what is the real reason for the veneration in which the ancients are held: "*L'antiquité d'un écrivain n'est pas un titre certain de son mérite, mais l'antique et constante admiration qu'on a toujours eue pour ses ouvrages est une preuve sûre et infaillible qu'on les doit admirer.*" But at bottom Boileau was in a false position; he was a modern himself, and felt the impossibility of maintaining the inferiority of the moderns. He finally became reconciled with Perrault, and accepted his thesis, though in a modified form, in the famous letter of 1700. There Boileau grants that the century of Louis XIV, the *grand siècle*, is equal not to the whole of Antiquity, but to any single century of Antiquity.

The quarrel, which seemed appeased, broke out again at the beginning of the eighteenth century, between Houdar de la Motte, who had refashioned the *Iliad* to suit the taste of his times (1714), and the learned Mme Dacier, furious at this travestying of Homer.

Respect for religion and Antiquity connect the great divine **François de la Motte Fénelon** with the seventeenth century, but his political opinions, his intellectual curiosity, and the sensitiveness of his temperament betray the immediate precursor of the eighteenth century.

> **Fénelon** was born 6th August, 1651, at the castle of Fénelon, in Périgord. At twenty he entered the seminary of St. Sulpice in Paris, being admitted to holy orders in 1675. Three years later he was appointed director of an institution for women converts to the Catholic faith, and soon after placed at the head of a mission sent to preach among the Protestants of Poitou. In 1689 he was appointed tutor to the young Duke of Burgundy, grandson of Louis XIV, a position which he held for the next six years. Fénelon was a born teacher, who combined the manners of a *grand seigneur* with all the refinements of an accomplished churchman; gentle, but also hard and inflexible if the case required it. This subtlety and complexity of character explains the ascendancy he exercised over his royal pupil, and all those who came in contact with

him: "*Il fallait faire effort pour cesser de le regarder,*" says Saint-Simon. In 1695 the King, displeased with his views on religion and politics, presented him with the bishopric of Cambrai, more to get rid of him than to reward him. From 1695 to 1699 he was engaged with Bossuet, his former friend and patron, in the unhappy quarrel concerning the Quietists. After 1699 he lived almost exclusively for his flock; but in the revived Jansenist dispute he engaged earnestly on the side of orthodoxy. He died in 1715.

The varied character of Fénelon's works is a proof of the originality and flexibility of his intellect. They include:

Theological and controversial works, of which the chief are the *Traité de l'Existence de Dieu* (1712), and the *Maximes des Saints* (1697); educational and moral works: the *Traité de l'Éducation des Filles* (written 1681, published 1689), besides the *Fables*, the *Dialogue des Morts*, and the *Aventures de Télémaque* (1699), all composed for his pupil; political writings, of which the most notable are the *Plans de Gouvernement*, and the *Direction pour la Conscience d'un Roi* (1711); critical works: the *Dialogues sur l'Éloquence* (1718), and the *Lettre à l'Académie* (1716).

Of Fénelon's polemical works the most noteworthy are the *Maximes des Saints*, which led to his controversy with Bossuet.

In 1687 Fénelon had made the acquaintance of Madame Guyon, the celebrated Quietist mystic; and, convinced of the unfairness of the outcry which made her responsible for the grosser mysticism of other sects, he advised her to submit a work written by her to Bossuet. In the condemnation of Madame Guyon's book by Bossuet, Fénelon acquiesced; but when he received the manuscript of that prelate's *Instruction sur les États d'Oraison*, in which the points at issue were more fully set forth, he suddenly changed front and forestalled Bossuet by the publication of the *Maximes des Saints*, in which he upheld certain doctrines of the Quietists, a sect whose tenets inculcated complete abnegation of the will, and its replacement by absolute surrender to the Divine love.

Bossuet was not slow to perceive the dangerous tendencies

of a creed which in theology leads to indifference towards dogma by rendering the priest superfluous as an intermediary between God and man, and in morals abandons the mind and body to the instincts. Hence the fury and bitterness of his attack, for according to him the whole Church was at stake. He replied to Fénelon in his *Relation sur le Quiétisme* (1698), caused his book to be censured by the French bishops, and won the King over to his side. Finally the matter was referred to the Pope, who issued a brief in which twenty-three propositions chosen from the *Maximes des Saints* were condemned, and Fénelon submitted without demur.

The *Traité de l'Éducation des Filles* (1681), written for the daughters of the Duchess of Beauvillier, makes of Fénelon one of the founders of feminine education. It rests on two general principles: the *rôle* which woman will be called upon to play in the family and in the world, and on the development of natural gifts.

The leading idea of the *Dialogue des Morts* (1699) is that politics must be guided by moral principles.

The *Aventures de Télémaque* (1699) is a pedagogic romance, combining moral teaching with instruction in Greek mythology and antiquities. It narrates the wanderings of Telemachus in search of his father Ulysses, under the guardianship of Mentor. Fénelon's pupil, for whom it was written, is advised to avoid an excessive love of pleasure, war, and pomp—the very faults of the French monarchy at the end of Louis XIV's reign. The King perceived that the satire was meant for him, and hence his anger when *Télémaque* was published surreptitiously in 1699. The politics of *Télémaque* are more or less Utopian, and intended to be so. Fénelon's ideas, ideas which he thought attainable, are to be found in the *Plans de Gouvernement*—a limited monarchy in which the King can only demand of his subjects what is necessary for the good of the State, and in which authority would be shared with a powerful and Christian nobility mediating between the Crown and the people. Here, too, he was having a sly hit at Louis XIV, under whose reign the French monarchy had become despotic, whereas Fénelon's ideal form of government is aristocratic and parliamentarian.

The *Lettre à l'Académie* (1716) deserves special notice as being the most important critical work of the century, next to Boileau's *Art Poétique*.

Like Boileau, Fénelon is an admirer of the ancients, but instead of formulating rules he merely gives impressions, some of which are strikingly original. The French Academy, just as its great Dictionary was approaching completion, wondered what it could do next. Each of its forty members was consulted, and Fénelon gave his opinions in the *Lettre à l'Académie*, proposing a grammar, treatises on rhetoric, poetics, tragedy, comedy, and history, and at the same time imparting his views on language and literature. In the opening chapter he complains of the poverty of the language; speaks with admiration and regret of the coloured and suggestive language of the sixteenth century, and if it were possible would go back to the methods of the *Pléiade* for enriching it. He also condemns the use of rhyme. In tragedy he finds too much pomp, and a monotonous abuse of the passion of love; in comedy he attacks the moral teaching of Molière, but cannot help admiring his genius. In the ninth chapter, on history, he recommends the resuscitation of the past, the exposition of the life of peoples and of the progress of civilization. A last chapter is devoted to the Ancients and Moderns. Both sides appealed to Fénelon, but he was careful not to commit himself, although his works as a whole point clearly enough to his preference for the disciples of Antiquity.

The line of the great pulpit orators of the seventeenth century is closed by

Jean Baptiste Massillon (1663–1742), who, by ignoring dogma, ruined a branch of literature which depends upon it for its very existence. Massillon was a rhetorician and not an orator; an adept at suiting religion to an audience of fine ladies and gentlemen; facile and abundant, but lacking in force and fire. His works comprise over sixty sermons, ten panegyrics, and six funeral orations, including that on Louis XIV, notable for the noble simplicity of its opening words: "God alone is great, my brethren."

Louis de Rouvroy, **Duc de Saint-Simon,** was born at Versailles in 1675, and lived till 1755, albeit his work belongs both in spirit and subject to the seventeenth century.

The *Mémoires*, which cover the period from 1691 to 1723, rank him as the greatest memoir writer in a literature which has never been surpassed in that branch. They were probably begun in 1694, and reached their final form in 1740. On his death they were impounded by the Foreign Office, and although several garbled abstracts and extracts were in circulation during the eighteenth century, it was not till 1829 that the first authentic edition appeared. All his life Saint-Simon was a disappointed and dissatisfied man, an irreconcilable noble who dreamed of the time when the high nobility, and especially the peers (he was one himself), shared the power with the King. Hence his hatred for Louis XV and his Court, "*ce long règne de vile bourgeoisie*", hence his likes, and especially his dislikes, which make it impossible for him to be impartial. But if his prejudices blind his judgment, they render his power of vision all the keener, and no writer has ever surpassed him in making a vanished past live again.

His style, too, is equal to the intensity of his imagination; often confused and irregular, but always living and the exact reflection of his emotions.

BOOK IV
EIGHTEENTH CENTURY

GENERAL VIEW

The history of French literature in the eighteenth century is the history of the revolution which took place in social and political theories and ideas, and in general modes of thought, from the close of the reign of Louis XIV with the death of that monarch in 1715, to the outbreak of the great Revolution in 1789. Never was a period more important for the evolution and development of human thought, and never was a literature more closely bound up with the ideas of its own day and generation than that of France during the epoch under consideration. The literature of the whole century busied itself in fact with, comparatively speaking, little else than those great problems of human life which were stirring France to its depths, and which the Revolution was shortly to blazon forth to the whole civilized world. The great men of letters of the period were the teachers and preachers of their day. They did not, like those of other ages, concern themselves with questions of abstruse philosophy, nor with questions of æsthetics, nor with ideals of purely literary achievement. Their watchword was no cry of " art for art ". Living in a time of transition, when old ideals were being ruthlessly swept away, the only man who could get a general hearing was the one who had a new gospel to preach.

By far the greatest names are those of **Voltaire** and **Rousseau**; and if Voltaire is called the teacher of the age, Rousseau may well be called its preacher. As Voltaire was the schoolmaster of the eighteenth century, so Rousseau was its priest —the expounder of its esoteric mysteries. Thus, while Voltaire taught to all, and was the acknowledged sovereign, the followers of Rousseau were inspired by him with a greater enthusiasm and a deeper conviction.

Voltaire's influence was the wider, Rousseau's the more profound; and while Voltaire's name is written large on the whole century, it was Rousseau who was the direct forerunner of the Revolution, and whose writings contain in germ the doctrines of the men of '90.

The history of poetry pure and simple in the century is not a long one, and if little is to be recorded, still less can be said to attain the highest rank. That such would be the case is only to be expected from the general tendencies then at work, for the speculative and didactic spirit is directly opposed to the highest achievement in the field of pure poetry. Great verse-makers we should expect, and do actually find in numbers—one of them, indeed, among the greatest masters of this more mechanical art. The "poetry of reason" was the poetry that appealed to most, and La Motte in his declaration in its favour was supported by many of the greatest writers of the day, and among them **Montesquieu** and **Buffon**, who looked upon prose as the ideal vehicle of thought, and poetry as excellent only in so far as it shared its obviousness and directness. Prose, they argued, is best, because it says what is to be said in the briefest and clearest way; and rhyme and rhythm, and all figures of speech, are bad in so far as they tend to obscure and confuse. It must be admitted that these extremists were opposed in form by the majority of their contemporaries, who, however, while contesting their views, were closely allied to them in spirit, and though calling themselves poets and championing the cause of poetry, were completely unable to appreciate its inner meaning.

But in all those aspects of verse-writing for which the only requirements are great technical skill, wit, reason, and lucidity of thought and conception, many of these eighteenth-century poets excelled. They are hardly surpassed in the writing of epistles, satires, criticism, verse-pamphlets, and all the lighter occasional forms. In one characteristic branch, the epigram, they have perhaps never been equalled. But in the higher conception of poetry which lies above and beyond mere correctness of versification, and clearness, and even brilliance of wit, the epoch under review, with one notable exception at the very end, is entirely wanting. More and more as the century advanced imitation took the place of nature, the borrowing of ready-made metaphors that of direct inspiration, mere words and paraphrase that of imagination. And this is the explanation of the astonishing fact that the critics of the day thought they had at last found their greatest epic writer in Voltaire, their greatest lyric poet in **Lebrun,** and last and most wonderful of all, their greatest descriptive poet in that paraphrase personified, **Delille.**

The dramatic work of the century reached, on the whole, a far higher standard of merit than its poetry. The traditions of the brilliant seventeenth century were still living and powerful, and playwrights were stimulated both by the prestige and the material advantages to be won by success on the stage. Accordingly not only were the two old-established *genres* of tragedy and comedy still cultivated, but an entirely new type arose in the so-called *drame*.

Tragedy was a mere imitation of that of the preceding century, and rapidly tended to become stereotyped. The example of Racine and the theory of Boileau were enforced with relentless rigour, one man only, La Motte, making a bold and praiseworthy but unsuccessful attempt to break these convential shackles. Voltaire alone, in spite of unfavourable conditions, succeeded by his wonderful cleverness and marvellous technique in giving life to the dry bones, and in writing tragedies of real merit.

Of comedy much better things are to be said. Not only was the comedy of the last century continued, but two men have to be noticed, to each of whom is due a distinct and original development. **Marivaux** was responsible for a style which was called after him *marivaudage*, the main characteristics of which are that love is placed at the centre of interest; love casuistry, and a certain sentimental introspection taking to a great extent the place of external action. **Beaumarchais**, in works of supreme distinction, introduced upon the stage an original type of political and social satire. Lastly, there arose an entirely new kind of dramatic writing, called somewhat vaguely *drame*, and sometimes divided into the two classes of *tragédie bourgeoise* and *comédie larmoyante*, though this distinction was neither very clearly marked nor very rigorously observed. The main characteristic of this new *genre*, which was introduced by **La Chaussée**, was a mixture of tragic and comic elements, rendering possible a closer reproduction of the conditions of actual life than could be attained under the old division of all dramatic writing into pure tragedy and pure comedy. Thus very considerable activity prevailed in dramatic composition in the eighteenth century, and though tragedy had lost its vital force, and was in a state of decadence, comedy had not only enough vigour to proceed with energy along the old lines, but such vitality as to develop fresh and original phases, and even to give birth to a new kind of dramatic art.

The novel occupies a very important place in the literature of the century. Not only did the "Encyclopedists" make use of it as an instrument for the propagation of their views and outlook on life, but there were three writers who initiated new types of fiction. **Le Sage**, the immortal author of *Gil Blas*, was the creator of the *roman de mœurs*, the novel of manners and social conditions rather than of characters. Marivaux invented a peculiar type of love story, treating of the delicate traffic and casuistry of love in somewhat over-refined and elegant language; while the **Abbé Prévost,** famous as the author of *Manon Lescaut*, identified his name with pathetic and often dolefully sentimental stories of love and adventure.

But the really important novels of the period were didactic, the novels with a purpose. Each of the three most prominent writers of the age wrote such, and no literary form could have been better fitted for the end they had in view, or more successful in their hands. Voltaire in his many short prose *contes* expressed his views on all the subjects which were of deepest interest to himself and his contemporaries; **Diderot** in his novels, and especially in *Le Neveu de Rameau*, produced profound and searching criticisms on human nature and social life. Rousseau, most important of all the writers of fiction of the day, was not only the first to compose didactic novels of absolutely first-rate importance, but exercised the most far-reaching influence on the literature of France and of the whole of Europe by the introduction into literature of sentiment and descriptions of nature. His fervid passionate language was entirely new to his contemporaries, and had no small share in the wonderful success and ascendancy of his works. *La Nouvelle Héloïse* was the first novel which aimed at exercising direct influence on men's minds, and it was a sermon to which all listened, and which thousands obeyed. Lastly, **Bernardin de St. Pierre**, the disciple of Rousseau in the painting of nature, did for tropical and exotic scenery what Rousseau had done for the more familiar landscapes of the countryside. Thus in range, in quantity, and in excellence of individual work, the fiction of the period is of very great value and significance.

The prose writings other than fiction show the same trend noticed in all other branches, only that the purpose is here open and avowed, and not veiled by the exigencies of any form of art. Already with **Fontenelle** the doctrinal spirit begins to appear, and its characteristics become more and more accentuated with the growth of the numbers and power of the *philosophes*, to culminate eventually in the *Encyclopédie*.

As in the seventeenth century the great subject had been man and the study of the human heart, the great interest of the eighteenth century is society and its different conditions and variations. The seventeenth century had regarded literature as an art, the eighteenth regards it as an instrument for the propagation of its views and the furtherance of its aims. These aims comprised a twofold revolt—in political and social matters, a revolt against traditional and established authority, and in religious matters (here the influence of the English philosophers, known as the Deists, played a part), a revolt against orthodox religion and revelation. Last of all, in the *Encyclopédie* we see in a pronounced form most of the tendencies of the earlier part of the century; it is not only a storehouse of information on the learning and interests of its age, and a guide to the spirit by which that age was animated, but also a great monument in the history of human speculation, and one of the most striking phenomena in the whole history of letters.

The change which took place in the language from the seventeenth to the eighteenth century corresponds to that which is seen in literature. The long period of the seventeenth century is replaced by a short, rapid, broken phrase, more easy to handle and more suitable for the treatment of the manifold topics which engaged the attention of the great propagandists of the time.

CHAPTER I

POETRY

First in point of time of the poets of the century comes **Jean Baptiste Rousseau** (1671–1741), a man of little importance apart from his literary work. He was at one time a great friend of Voltaire, but they afterwards quarrelled, and Rousseau became the object of the bitter onslaughts of his former friend. Throughout the eighteenth century he had a very great reputation as a lyricist, and no man was more reprinted than he. Apart from his numerous *Odes*, which were mostly panegyrical and in the rhetorical style of his master Boileau, his work was a curious mixture of the sacred and the profane —paraphrases of the Psalms and cantatas in startling contrast to light epistles, and not uncommonly licentious epigrams. Rousseau was a disciple of the *Art Poétique*, and tried to make up by style for want of genuine feeling. He is always artificial and impersonal; his generalizations and abstractions are the very negation of the spirit of lyric poetry. Yet his verses are neat, sonorous, not without considerable technical skill, and this sufficed to give and assure him a great reputation in his day.

Alexis Piron (1689-1773), though he did not write much, must be mentioned here on account of his epigrams, which are among the most brilliant of that brilliant century. Many of them are directed against his fellow-authors. They are whimsical, full of charming fancy, droll and comical, little gems of language, as polished and sparkling as human speech can be.

In this as in all subsequent chapters of this book the name of **Voltaire** is written large.

François Arouet was born at Paris in 1694, the son of Maître Arouet, a rich notary. The name of **Voltaire** he did not take till 1718. He was educated by the Jesuits at the *Collège Louis le Grand*, where he made some influential friends, and on leaving school was early introduced to the society of wits and aristocratic freethinkers. Soon malicious and satirical verses began to circulate in his name, and one of these he had to thank for a residence of eleven months in the Bastille, in 1717. This steadied him, and turned his thoughts to more serious matters, and at the end of six years' hard work he had already won the reputation of being the greatest poet of France. In 1726 he was again thrown into the Bastille for having shown, in a quarrel with one of the great nobles, a manly independence not tolerated in those days in men of his class, but was allowed out at the end of a few days on condition of transferring his abode to England. There he spent the two years 1726-1728, enjoying the acquaintance of many of the greatest politicians and men of letters, and studying English literature, politics, and above all philosophy and science. These years were of very great importance for his character and development, and gave him the opportunity of becoming acquainted with English life and ways.

During the four years following his return he displayed wonderful literary activity, and work followed work.

In 1734 an order of arrest was issued against him on account of his *Lettres Philosophiques*, giving his impressions of England, and he fled from Paris, never permanently to settle there again. For the next ten years he lived at Cirey on the Swiss frontier with Madame du Châtelet. At the end of that time he once more returned to Paris, where he was loaded with honour upon honour, and made in turn Academician, Royal Historiographer, Gentleman of the Chamber, with other offices. However, after a while he quarrelled with Mme de Pompadour, and left the Court. In 1750 he went on the invitation of Frederic the Great to Berlin, where at first he was fêted like a king, and presented with a magnificent establishment. The glamour, however, soon wore off, Voltaire's sensitive vanity was wounded, and in 1753 he left Prussia in a way that contrasted painfully with his triumphal entry three years before. After some wanderings he settled in 1755 near Geneva in a house which he called *Les Délices*. Soon after he bought on the frontier, but in France, an estate at Ferney, and there passed the last twenty years of his life in peace, as the *grand seigneur* presiding over the affairs of his village, and as the sovereign of European letters receiving at his court pilgrims from far and wide, keeping up a correspondence with the learned and distinguished of all the civilized world, and the object of the sentimental idolatry of his own countrymen.

In 1778, at the age of eighty-four, he went on a visit to Paris, was received there with indescribable enthusiasm, idolized alike by high and low, and in the midst of this reign of triumph died after three months, his end being probably accelerated by the undue strain and excitement.

Voltaire is typical of the verse-makers of his century, and the fact that he was considered a great poet is a comment on the debased taste of his time. Of the highest poetry, that indefinable power of imaginative suggestion which lies outside mere correctness of form and brilliance of wit, he knew nothing. In all verse for which a light and pleasing fancy, a keen intellect, and reasonableness are sufficient, he was a master. He has never been surpassed, and rarely equalled, in the verse of gallantry, in the writing of epistles, and in all branches of what are known as *vers de société*. In all such forms his wonderful wit is apparent; he always finds the word that tells, the *mot propre*. His unfailing vivacity and naturalness, which make his prose so excellent, become virtues. Yet all these qualities fail to make a great poet, and when Voltaire attempts a serious work it seems as though his very clearness and limpidity of thought and his very mechanical perfection of form are against him. The subtle charm of poetry cannot live in the white light of this intellectual glare. Thus the *Henriade* (1723), his most ambitious poetic venture, in spite of the wonderful clearness of many of its incidents, is lacking in spontaneity, is too artificial, and is dreary in the extreme. It was a praiseworthy attempt on the part of Voltaire to give his country a great epic, and was hailed by his contemporaries as a complete success. It deals with the times of the three Henries, Henry III, Henry IV, and the Duke of Guise, and ends with the battle of Ivry in 1590.

It is a mere military narrative, amplified by various rhetorical devices, dreams, love stories, and though all the machinery of epic poetry is utilized, the epic spirit is absent. After a brief success, it has come to be esteemed at its true worth. His other epic attempt, the shameless burlesque, *La Pucelle* (1730), is less tiresome merely because the serious and pretentious attitude has not to be kept up, and Voltaire can give free play to his ever-ready wit. His miscellaneous verse-writings are too numerous to mention, and all, whether *contes*, epistles, satires, epigrams, or didactic poems, are marked throughout by the highest skill in the manipulation of verse and perfection in all the externals of poetry, together with the almost complete absence of the poetic spirit itself.

Houdar de La Motte (1672-1731) deserves to be mentioned in connection with his poetical criticism and theories, and his verse-translation or rather adaptation of Homer, in which he left out some half, and reduced the rest to a dead level of conventionality to meet the false and artificial taste of his day. In his *Réflexions sur la Critique*, an answer to the attacks on his Homer, he made some valuable and suggestive remarks on the dispute of the " Ancients and Moderns ", in which he was on the side of the latter. As a critic he exercised a considerable, and on the whole far from beneficial, influence on his age. He wrote, in addition, *Odes*, mostly on abstract and moral subjects, dull methodical discourses rather more in the nature of sermons than poems.

Écouchard Lebrun (1729–1807), absurdly called by his contemporaries " Lebrun Pindare ", wrote frigid and commonplace odes and lyrics in the manner of his day. In these forms he was not particularly different from numbers of others. In his epigrams, however, he represents the highest point to which the art was carried even in that age of brilliant epigrammatists. He frequently used the epigram as a vehicle of literary criticism. His best are wonderful in their inevitable felicity of expression, absolute perfection of form, and condensation of thought without obscurity.

The most famous exponent of the art of writing poems without poetry is **Jacques Delille** (1738–1813), who is almost unreadable now, but interesting as typifying a whole period. He was born in Auvergne, but went early to Paris, where he was educated at the Collège de Lisieux. Thence he proceeded to the University; his career there was a most brilliant one, and he soon gained a reputation as an elegant classical scholar. After some adaptations and occasional verse, he made his name in 1769 by the translation of the *Georgics*, Voltaire was delighted with it, and christened the author " Virgilius Delille ". The translation, which polished out of Virgil all the bolder and more poetic features, and reduced him to a poet after the heart of the eighteenth century, exactly met the taste of the time, and had a wonderful reception. A certain theoretical love of the country and of nature, as seen from the windows of a boudoir, was the fashionable craze of the time. This success settled Delille's poetic career, and he devoted the rest of his life to didactic and descriptive poetry, holding from the death of Voltaire in 1778 to the end of his life the undisputed position of the " prince of poets " of his time. Delille's best-known work is *Les Jardins* (1782), while others which had considerable vogue, in addition to the translation of the *Georgics*, were his *Énéide* and

Paradis Perdu. All these show the characteristics seen in the *Georgics*. He is entirely lacking in the imagination which sees nature at first hand, and he knows it only through the medium of literary commonplaces. Instead of the thing itself, he gives us an abstract idea; instead of a real description, an elegant combination of conventional expressions usually applied to the object. Hence his characteristic feature is artificiality, his characteristic method paraphrase. Two of his best-known " definitions " are perhaps those of glass, which becomes under his system, " *le sable, dissous par des feux dévorants (qui) pour les palais des rois brille en murs transparents* ", and sugar, " *le miel américain, que du suc des roseaux exprime l'Africain* ". Instead of a real and vivid picture, he gives a dull didactic recipe for the manufacture of the article in question. And this dealer in the commonplaces of literature, this compiler of verse compendiums, was for more than a quarter of a century regarded as a genius, and the unchallenged laureate of France!

A poet who gave great promise, but whose career was cut short at the early age of twenty-nine, was **Nicolas Gilbert** (1751–1780). The struggles and hardships with which his life was embittered find an echo in his poems, which have everywhere a strong undertone of melancholy. Of the little that he left the best is contained in the *Ode imitée de Plusieurs Psaumes*, which, however, was not, as is often stated, written on his death-bed. He has been to many, and especially to the Romanticists, a sympathetic figure, typifying, like the English Chatterton, youthful genius early succumbing in the pitiless struggle with fate.

Évariste de Parny (1753–1814) was a poet of the same school as Delille, and could boast of the friendship of the aged Voltaire. He was, like his master, deficient in pure imagination, and suffered like him from the artificial poetic taste of his day. Yet some of his early works have a severe and simple grace, and are of very considerable merit. At his best he is distinctly superior to Delille at his best. In his later years he wrote long didactic Voltairian poems, airing his philosophical and political views—dull and of no poetic value.

The only truly great poet of the period, **André Marie de Chénier,** does not appear till its very close.

Chénier was born in the year 1762 at Constantinople, where his father was French consul and commercial envoy. His mother was a Greek. In 1765, when André was two and a half years old, his father left Constantinople, and returned to France, taking with him the boy, who was never to see again the country of his birth. The mere place of his birth cannot then be reckoned among the influences which produced his so-called Hellenism, except in so far as it gave him his mother, and, through her, Hellenic blood and tastes. She was a learned and cultured woman, of a romantic disposition, and was doubtless of great importance in André's early training and development. On their return the Chénier family settled in Paris, and there, with the exception of a short absence, André spent the years of his boyhood. In 1773 he was sent by his father to the *Collège de Navarre*, where he made many friendships, of which several lasted throughout the remainder of his short life, while more than one of these school friends afterwards made some reputation as poets. It was while at school that he made his first essay in verse, with imitations of Homer and Virgil. After leaving school he served for six months in the army at Strasbourg, but the life was very distasteful to him, and he soon left the service.

In 1787 he went to London, where he was attached to the French embassy. He spent four years in England, and during that time studied carefully the great English poets, especially Milton, of whom he speaks with the greatest admiration. With his return in 1790 began his political career; he threw himself, like all his family, with ardour into the Revolutionary movement, but the excesses committed by the extremists terrified him, and he quickly identified himself with the moderate party, in the chief organ of which, the *Journal de Paris*, most of Chénier's political writings appeared. Of these the most important was the article of the 26th of February, 1792, entitled *De la cause des désordres qui troublent la France, et arrêtent l'établissement de la liberté*. This was practically a manifesto of the moderate Royalists, and attacked the Jacobins unmercifully. From this time Chénier was completely committed to his party, and when that party was defeated, and the King, Louis XVI, executed, his fate at the hands of the Jacobins was merely a matter of time.

On the 7th of March, 1794, he was suddenly arrested and imprisoned in St. Lazare, and four months later fell beneath the guillotine, two days only before the death of Robespierre, which would have saved him.

Chénier is incontestably the greatest French poet of the

eighteenth century, and its only poet of real worth. During his lifetime the only poems of his which appeared were his political ones, and it was not till 1819, long after his death, that anything like a representative edition was issued. Though coming at the very end of the century, he was more closely allied in spirit with the previous age than with the one about to dawn. He was a classicist, and differed only from the great Classicists whose line he ended in being more of an Hellene than they—a feature which he owed to his mother's nationality and influence. Yet at the same time it must not be supposed that he stood entirely apart from his own century and its materialistic and didactic tendencies. On the contrary, the only long works he planned were fully in the spirit of the eighteenth century and of the Encyclopedic movement.

His poetic work falls naturally into three divisions:

The short poems of classical form, style, and subject, which constitute the great bulk of his work;

The longer poems, planned and partly written, but all unfinished, conceived in the manner and spirit of the Encyclopedists;

The poems on political subjects, which occupied the last four years of his life.

It is the first of these divisions which contains Chénier's characteristic work. These short poems all bear classical names—Eclogues, Bucolics, Idylls, Elegies and Epistles, and are classical in spirit, conception, and expression. The language is throughout graceful and elegant, and often rises to great beauty, recalling the harmony and simplicity of Greek art.

Among the best known of these classical pieces are *La Jeune Tarentine*; *L'Aveugle*, the legend of Homer wandering, blind and a beggar, from land to land; and *Le Jeune Malade*.

The second division comprises works in the spirit of Voltaire and the Encyclopedists, in which we see Chénier treating the great scientific questions and problems of the day as they appealed to his imagination. The principal of these are *L'Amérique*, which was to be a poetic geography of the whole known world; *L'Hermès*, a universal philosophy in verse; *L'Astronomie*, and *La Superstition*. In all this part of his work he was not far superior to the many didactic poets of his age.

Lastly, we have to speak of his poems of the third period—those of his political career, when his attention was directed solely to the present. These are the *Odes* and *Iambes*, in which he expressed in nervous and often glowing language his earnest warnings to his countrymen, or passionate indignation at the excesses that were being committed in the name of liberty.

Of the Odes the best known are the Pindaric *Jeu de Paume*, and the eloquent one addressed to Charlotte Corday, under whose dagger Marat had fallen, expressing bitter indignation at her death.

The *Iambes*,[1] which contain some of his best verse, were all written during the four months of his imprisonment at St. Lazare, and reveal the bitter disappointment, the horror, revolt, and proud defiance which filled his heart during this last sad period of his life.

From the point of view of style, Chénier's importance lies in his frequent and bold use of *enjambement*, which, though not unknown before, was used by him much more frequently and in a more pronounced manner. He was the first since the *Pléiade*, with which he has many points in common, who in this way systematically broke the somewhat monotonous uniformity of the Alexandrine, and gave it greater flexibility and movement.

---

[1] *Iambes* are poems of indeterminate length, with verses of alternately eight and twelve syllables, and with irregular rhymes.

CHAPTER II

DRAMA

Earliest of the dramatists of any consequence in the century is **Prosper Jolyot de Crébillon** (Crébillon Père), born at Dijon in 1674. He began life as a lawyer's clerk, and his want of sound education and culture is traceable all through his work. Throughout the first half of the century he produced plays, and in his old age was set up as a rival to Voltaire, to the great annoyance of the latter. He died in 1762.

His best-known pieces are: *Atrée* (1707), *Électre* (1708), and *Rhadamiste et Zénobie* (1711), the most famous and most characteristic of all.

Crébillon's work is rather melodrama than genuine tragedy, and is founded in very great part on the usual melodramatic devices of incognitos, misunderstandings, mistakes, and recognitions. His guiding principle was to take some horrible and even atrocious subject, and by skilful manipulation of these devices to place it in a setting such as would satisfy the proprieties. Thus in presenting to us in *Oreste* a matricide, by making the son ignorant of the fact that it is his mother he is killing, he robs the act of its extraordinary atrociousness, while leaving the audience conscious of the double nature of the crime. On such complications Crébillion builds up most of his plays, and manages to extract from the scheme numberless telling effects and situations. Yet he is always artificial and conventional, never going direct to nature itself, and so never attains to real dramatic truth. His style is affected, bombastic, and pretentious.

> A writer who is of considerable importance for the history of the theatre in the eighteenth century, on account of the part he played in the revived dispute of the " Ancients and Moderns ", is **Houdar de La Motte,** previously mentioned. Taking his stand boldly on the side of the latter, he refused to admit the so generally assumed superiority of the ancients, and called in question the

accepted theories of the three Unities of time, place, and action, and the necessity of verse in tragedy. He wrote himself one tragedy, *Inès de Castro* (1723), which had a very considerable success, though that success is no argument in favour of his views, as he was inconsistent enough not to follow them in his own work. He was the great light of the *salon* [1] of the Marquise de Lambert, the successor of the *Hôtel de Rambouillet*, which supported him in his championship of the moderns against the ancients.

Voltaire, who comes next, was the only writer of tragedy of real merit the century produced. He wrote altogether more than twenty tragedies, many of which were acted with great success, and not in France alone, and of which the best can still be read and seen with pleasure. Although he is not entirely free from the conventionality and the melodramatic devices that we noticed in Crébillon, he is far more original, and made some innovations which were entirely for good. During his three years' stay in England, he learnt to know Shakespeare, and was much influenced by him, and it is to this influence that we owe the chief improvements which he attempted in French tragedy. The principal of these were increased psychological observation, greater life and action, and greater diversity in technique and local colour. Thus the scene is not confined to Greece and Rome, but we are transported to America (in *Alzire*), to Palestine (in *Zaïre*), to China (in *L'Orphelin de la Chine*). Yet Voltaire, in spite of his passion for the theatre and the excellence of his theory in many respects, had unfortunately very little real dramatic genius. His knowledge of the human heart was slight and superficial, and—a greater fault still in a dramatist—he was almost entirely incapable of objective treatment, that is to say, of laying aside his own personality and entering into the life and feelings of the characters he portrays. We are rarely allowed to forget that it is Voltaire who speaks; often indeed his plays are but instruments for the propagation of his rationalistic philosophy and ideas, and the characters the mouth-

---

[1] Fontenelle and La Motte reigned in this *salon*, while it was there that Marivaux made his *début*.

pieces that voice his words. As these theories and ideas were at that day matters of burning interest to all, they gave living significance to his plays, but now only serve to make them appear flat and lifeless. What gives his plays their undoubted value is the excellence of the workmanship, and the wonderful cleverness with which Voltaire, as an experienced playwright, was able to adapt them to the requirements of the stage. Consequently they give a much better impression when seen than when read.

The two plays which are universally admitted to be his best are *Zaïre* (1732) and *Mérope* (1743). *Zaïre* is noteworthy as being obviously inspired by the *Othello* of Shakespeare, with the rugged and terrible force of the English play toned down by artifices and devices worthy of Crébillon himself: *Mérope* as a play in which the love interest is excluded.

Among the other best-known plays of Voltaire are *Œdipe* (1719), his first, an imitation of Sophocles; *La Mort de César* (1732), another Shakespearean adaptation, and remarkable as being entirely without female characters; *Mahomet ou le Fanatisme* (1742), of which the secondary title sufficiently indicates the general trend.

With comedy we come to much more attractive and original work, not least so being that of **Pierre Chamblain de Marivaux,** born at Paris in 1688. He received a very moderate education, and early began to write, but his first attempt, a tragedy, was a complete failure. Admitted into the *salons* of the day, notably that of Madame de Lambert, he quickly found his true bent in comedies reflecting the tone of this side of Parisian life, most of which were produced at the *Comédie Italienne*. He was in somewhat straitened circumstances all his life, and lived principally by prose contributions to different papers or by ephemeral journals of his own. He died in 1763.

His best-known plays are: *La Surprise de l'Amour* (1722), his first great success; *Le Jeu de l'Amour et du Hasard* (1730), *Le Legs* (1736), *Les Fausses Confidences* (1737), *l'Épreuve* (1740), most of which were written and produced by the *Comédie Italienne*.[1]

Marivaux's avowed intention from the first was to belong to no school and to imitate nobody, and this originality he succeeded in achieving. His method consisted in taking love as the staple interest, as Racine had done before him in the seventeenth century, and in building up his plays around it. But as it was not tragedy at which he aimed, this love could not be the absolute and unconditional surrender which must inevitably lead to tragic issues, but the light and playful barter which was more suited to comedy. It is in this barter, in the first beginnings of the passion, in the reserve and caution, the gradual advances and prudent withdrawals, that his chief motives are found. Hence the action is almost exclusively interior. He represents the youth, beauty, and freshness of life, the young ideal, and in the presentation of this phase of existence Marivaux is a true poet. To the graceful, elegant, refined, and somewhat affected prose style in which these delicate plays were written was given the name of "*marivaudage*". That the invention of this term was justified by his creation of an individual style there is no doubt.

The name of **Alain René Le Sage** is one of very great importance in another connection, but by no means inconsiderable here. He was born in Brittany in 1668, went to Paris to study law, and became an advocate there. He gained his living by writing for the *Théâtre de la Foire* and the *Comédie Italienne*, and by composing novels, &c., being the first really great writer to depend on his pen for a regular livelihood. He spent the last years of his life in retirement at Boulogne-sur-Mer, and died in 1747.

His reputation as a writer of comedy depends upon two pieces, *Crispin Rival de son Maître* (1707), a farcical and extravagant but lively and most uncommonly witty play; and *Turcaret* (1709), his masterpiece, which is of much more solid

---

[1] *La Comédie Italienne*, an Italian company which appeared in France during the second quarter of the century.

and serious merit. It appeared in the middle of the war of the Spanish Succession, and gives a pitiless and scathing picture of the terrible corruption which prevailed in the world of finance at the time. Turcaret is a *traitant* and financier who is preying upon society, while he in turn is preyed upon by others, till we have a perfect cycle of plunder and peculation. *Turcaret* is historical, in that it represents in this way a condition rather than individual characters. In keenness of observation and realism of presentation it is a dramatic masterpiece.

Philippe Destouches (1680-1754) aimed at producing plays which should be serious and edifying, and only succeeded in being dull. His best are *Le Glorieux* (1732) and *Le Philosophe marié* (1727). His importance lies in the fact that in substituting the sentimental for the humorous interest in comedy he was the immediate precursor of La Chaussée and the *comédie larmoyante*.

More celebrated for his wit than for his dramatic production is **Alexis Piron** (1689-1773), whose *Métromanie* (1738), aimed at poetasters, is an excellent example of satiric comedy, full of spirit and wit, and containing many lines that have passed into proverbs.

Another writer who has earned a reputation as the author of one good play is **Jean Gresset** (1709-1777), to whom is due *Le Méchant*, which possesses much the same qualities as Piron's satire against poetasters. His best-known work, however, is the humorous burlesque *Vert-Vert* (1734), on a parrot's life.

Pierre Claude Nivelle de la Chaussée (1692-1754) went further than Destouches, and wrote plays in which the interest was exclusively pathetic and tragic. In his earliest comedies there was a certain mixture of the comic and pathetic, as in *Le Préjugé à la Mode* (1735), but this comic element gradually disappeared, and in 1741 he produced in *Mélanide* a play in which the pathetic reigned alone, and the *comédie larmoyante* was fully established. La Chaussée's comedy takes its subjects from ordinary domestic life, with its little tragedies and trials, and is really nearer to tragedy than comedy—a tragedy on a lower plane, a *tragédie bourgeoise*. Other plays of his are: *La Fausse Antipathie* (1733), *Paméla* (1743), *La Gouvernante* (1747), and *Le Retour Imprévu* (1756).

Diderot, of whom we shall have to speak at far greater length elsewhere, partly carrying on the work of La Chaussée, expounded the theory of the *drame* as a *genre* of dramatic writing intermediary between tragedy and comedy. He appealed for a closer following of the conditions of actual life, and greater realism in the externals of theatrical representation. Unfortunately, his theory was better than his practice, and his two dramas, *Le Fils Naturel* (1757) and *Le Père de Famille* (1758), are dull and declamatory, and without dramatic force.

Most famous among the writers of comedy of the century is **Beaumarchais,** a man whose importance in his own day was by no means solely literary.

> Pierre Augustin Caron was born at Paris in 1732, the son of a watchmaker, and he at first followed his father's trade. Soon, however, he transferred his energies to a larger sphere, managed to gain a footing in the world of finance, married a wife of noble family, became ennobled himself, and took the name of **Beaumarchais.** Into the many vicissitudes of his amazing life—more wonderful than any of his own plays—it is impossible to enter. It is sufficient to mention the sensational lawsuits which indirectly led him to fame through the four *Mémoires*, written in 1774–1775, in which he ridiculed his judges in such persistent and witty satire as to raise himself at once to the pinnacle of literary celebrity. To the end of his life he continued his madcap existence, now up, now down, now making fortunes, and now losing them—a striking instance of a man who preserved up to old age the buoyancy of spirits and recklessness of youth. He died in 1799.

Beaumarchais' dramatic work is of a piece with his life, and his great creation, the character of Figaro, we might almost call a dramatization of himself. The valet, capable, scheming, restlessly active, feeling his own ability and embittered by the want of recognition which he receives at the hands of society, is Beaumarchais himself, the man of humble birth whose life was a struggle to place himself on a level with men who, he felt, were not his equals, and even then with but half success. In the *Barbier de Séville* (1775) we have Beaumarchais' bold satire on politics and society in its earlier stage, already keen and biting, but not yet so relentless as it later becomes. The subject is old as Molière himself, and may be said to be the stock cast of the *Comédie Italienne*—the guardian, the ward, the lover, and the valet. All the characters are of the Molière school of comedy, and have nothing very original, if we except that of *Figaro*.

The *Mariage de Figaro* is the *Barbier de Séville* carried to a higher plane. What in the earlier play was scattered satire on social evils is here obvious and open derision of the whole state of society. The leading character, Figaro, has grown, is bolder, more determined, and also more acid. In the former, Figaro was not dangerous, so long as he could live and laugh at the expense of society, now he is a malcontent embittered against the society which has not recognized his merits at their true worth. It is often merely the voice of Beaumarchais himself that we hear, as in the most significant passage of all: "*Parce que vous êtes un grand seigneur, vous vous croyez un grand génie—vous vous êtes seulement donné la peine de naître—tandis que moi, parbleu!*"

The *Mariage de Figaro* was finished and ready for the stage in 1781, but permission for it to be acted was refused again and again; it was only in 1784 that Beaumarchais secured the license by irrepressible pertinacity and impudence. These three years of delay and intrigue had raised public curiosity to fever heat, and the play had unparalleled success, running to the then extraordinary length of a hundred representations. Its wonderful cleverness and brilliant wit were only in very small part responsible for this phenomenal reception, the real cause lying in the fact that it voiced the burning questions of the day, and expressed for many their own thoughts in vivid and telling form. It is this aspect of the Figaro plays which makes them not merely dramatic successes, but epoch-making works in the literature and history of France.

Many of the men who greeted with frantic applause Figaro's tirades against privilege and the privileged, his contrast of the solid virtues of the bourgeois and the arrogant assumption and selfish vices of the *grands seigneurs*, were to take part before many years were over in that terrible upheaval which was the necessary and inevitable result of the bitter ferment of hate and anger which underlay the fair exterior of society.

CHAPTER III

PROSE

First in order of the novelists of the eighteenth century, and on the whole first in importance, is **Le Sage**, of whose comedies we have already spoken. While most of his contemporaries turned towards England, he turned to Spain, and it is to the picaresque romance of Spain, a kind of belated romance of chivalry, that the inspiration of his two most famous works, *Le Diable Boiteux* and *Gil Blas*, is to be traced. But while the setting and many of the incidents are borrowed in this way, it is the originality of his novels which constitutes their importance, and it is as initiator of the *roman de mœurs* that he ranks as the leading novelist of his century.

Le Diable Boiteux (1707), of which both title and framework were suggested by the Spanish romancer Guevara, is a long string of adventures, in which a number of characters are brought before us in romantic and often whimsical, but always realistic fashion. This realism in the painting of the conditions of life is the original and characteristic feature of Le Sage's novels, and in his next and greatest work, *Gil Blas*, is much more strongly marked. Here *Gil Blas* in his many qualities and positions serves to portray so many conditions of human life. This attempt to represent universal humanity in the one novel is the cause of its greatest fault—diffuseness and want of plan and uniformity. Gil Blas himself really stands for a number of different persons, which have little in common but their name, while many of the minor characters have nothing whatever to do with the action; they are merely dragged in in order to contribute by the story of their own experiences another phase of the great comedy of life.

The first instalment of *Gil Blas* appeared in 1715, the last in 1735, so that it contains indirectly the reflections of the author during twenty years of his life. It is the story of how the hero Gil Blas left home a self-satisfied simpleton, with great ideas of what he was to accomplish, and a remarkably optimistic idea of life in general, and gradually came, through many ups and downs of fortune and the buffetings of fate, to realize his own insignificance, and to change his early optimism for the discretion and *savoir faire* of a man of the world. The great merits of Le Sage's novels, apart from their realism, the result of his wonderful observation of life and society, are their universality, their presentation of human nature in general rather than of the men of any particular time and country, and the simple and easy style in which they are written.

Marivaux, whose comedies have also been discussed in the preceding chapter, wrote novels which exhibit the same general characteristics as his plays, a light and subtle analysis of love and that combination of matter and manner to which the name of *marivaudage* was given. His two most important novels are *Marianne* (1731-1741), and the *Paysan Parvenu* (1735-1736). *Marianne* holds a high rank in the history of French fiction as being the first novel in which psychological analysis, the painting of the emotions and workings of the mind, really form the main interest. It is remarkable also for the exact and realistic portrayal of actual life, and that mostly of the life of the *bourgeois* class, or even the class below it.

A writer whose lasting fame depends almost entirely on a single book is the **Abbé Prévost,** the author of *Manon Lescaut*. Antoine François Prévost d'Exiles, born in Picardy in 1697, and usually known as the Abbé Prévost, was brought up by the Jesuits. He afterwards became a soldier, then a

Benedictine, left that order irregularly, and having in consequence to quit the country, spent several unsettled and adventurous years abroad. He was for many years a laborious writer, producing numerous novels, besides doing much translation, especially from English, and much mere hack work. He died in 1763.

Prévost's novels show signs of his unsettled and adventurous life, and also of the haste in which they were written. They are for the most part long and diffuse stories of adventure, in which love constitutes the main interest. This love, however, is not the light and playful philandering of Marivaux, but a serious and sometimes sombre passion, which is often meant to draw our tears, and occasionally is worthy of doing so. His masterpiece, and the only one of his many stories which is still read, is *Manon Lescaut*, which appeared in 1731 as the seventh part of the *Mémoires d'un Homme de Qualité*, of which the first part was issued in 1728. It is the story of a young girl, Manon Lescaut, and the chevalier Des Grieux, who love one another with an intensity which overcomes all obstacles, and outlives all the miseries into which it leads them. In this one story Prévost has laid aside all his usual diffuseness and sentimentality, and with absolute simplicity and unpretentious fidelity to nature carries on the touching and pathetic story to its sombre and tragic close.

His only other novels we need mention are *Cleveland* (1731–1738) and *Le Doyen de Killérine* (1735–1740).

As a mediator between English and French literature, and especially as the translator of Richardson's *Pamela* and *Clarissa Harlowe*, Prévost exercised a great influence on the literature of his day.

Voltaire tried his hand at novel writing as at all other branches of literary composition, and with great success, some of his short *contes* being, regarded purely as literature, among his very best work.

Like the other great leaders of the philosophic movement he made use of fiction as a vehicle for the propagation of his philosophic tenets, and found the form admirably adapted to carry the persiflage, innuendo and insinuation of satire which constitute his critical method.

Most famous of all his short stories is *Candide* (1759), suggested by the terrible earthquake which destroyed Lisbon in 1755. Candide, who has always been told by his preceptor that everything is for the best in this best of all possible worlds, is disillusioned by the misfortunes of his life, and the story develops into a comprehensive mockery of all existing institutions of society, and all the weaknesses and failings of mankind—a regular manifesto of pessimism.

Other well-known short *contes* of Voltaire are *Micromégas*, a satire on scientists, *Zadig*, and *L'Homme aux Quarante Écus*.

Diderot, of Encyclopedic fame, also attempted prose fiction, like all the leading men of letters of the time, and like theirs his novels all had a purpose. Three are deserving of mention—*La Religieuse*, an attack on the convents; *Jacques le Fataliste*, inspired by Sterne: the adventures of the valet Jacques and his master, with a running fire of stories told by Jacques, his master, and others; and last of all, and most significant, *Le Neveu de Rameau*, the most consistent and even of all his works. It takes the form of a dialogue between himself and the Bohemian who gives the piece its title, in which human nature is dissected and laid bare with a cynical frankness and total lack of ordinary conventional morality.

The writings of **Jean-Jacques Rousseau** are dominated throughout by so complete a unity of purpose, and his novels are so entirely concerned with the expression of his views and aspirations, that they will be more fitly treated in connection with his philosophic work, of which they form an integral part.

His most important disciple, however, **Jacques Henri Bernardin de St. Pierre**, naturally falls in this chapter.

Bernardin de St. Pierre was born at Le Havre in 1737. He early showed a passionate love of nature and animals; a famous story of his childhood illustrates aptly the turn of mind which afterwards declared itself in his work. His father had taken him to Rouen, and was pointing out the towers of the cathedral. All the boy saw, however, was the swallows flying round the lofty spires, and he broke silence with the exclamation, " *Mon Dieu! comme elles volent haut!*" After studying at the *École des Ponts et Chaussées*, he travelled as a kind of irregular engineer in many countries, visiting Germany, Holland, Poland, and Russia. In 1768 he was sent as *ingénieur des colonies* to l'Ile de France (Mauritius), but returned to France in 1771, where he made the acquaintance of Rousseau—the most important event of his life. His literary works brought him fame, wealth, and favour, and under Louis XVI, the Republic, and the Empire in turn, he held different posts and enjoyed great consideration. He died in 1814.

The importance of Bernardin de St. Pierre in literature is due above all to his pictures of scenery, in which, though inspired by Rousseau, he is nevertheless original. He depicts the Tropics as Rousseau the countryside, but his nature-painting is warmer, more sensuous, more passionate. His other literary characteristics, in which he is more or less still under the influence of Rousseau, are his revival of sentiment and emotion in opposition to the rationalism of the philosophic school; his picturesque, highly-coloured, and passionate style; his love of nature, and decrying of society and civilization, in which he almost outdid Jean-Jacques himself.

His vocabulary has always great local colour, due to the large number of words he borrowed from the arts and sciences, navigation, botany, and, in short, the technical expressions belonging to all the different subjects he was treating. Yet for all that his style is easy, clear, and harmonious.

His chief works are the *Voyage à l'Ile de France* (1773) and the *Études de la Nature* (1784), at the end of which appeared an extra volume, *Paul et Virginie* (1787), while *La Chaumière Indienne* was likewise introduced, in 1790.

By far the most famous is *Paul et Virginie*. It is the story, told in a direct and simple narrative, in clear and harmonious style, yet with all the warmth and colour of the tropical land in which it is placed, of the growth of love between a boy and girl, its simple course, and tragic end through the drowning of Virginie by shipwreck under the very eyes of Paul. Into this touching story is woven a picturesque description of the tropical scenery and nature of the Ile Bourbon, with its exotic wealth and warmth, forming altogether a setting which accounted largely for its wonderful success and popularity.

Such then was Bernardin de St. Pierre, a disciple of Rousseau in the painting of nature, an innovator himself in introducing to his countrymen pictures of landscapes in distant and unknown lands, and lastly the man who handed on the tradition from Rousseau his master to his disciple Chateaubriand.

The prose writing, other than fiction, of the period is so uniform in spirit that any sub-divisions would tend rather to confusion than to simplicity. The same scientific and enquiring spirit, which was so pronounced in the *philosophes* proper and Encyclopedists of the latter half of the century, animated the earlier writers of the period.

Bernard le Bovier de Fontenelle, half of whose life falls in the preceding age, and whose early work is in the manner of the seventeenth century, with the *Entretien sur la Pluralité des Mondes* (1686) entered upon the speculative and scientific period of his literary career, and gave the first indications of the spirit which was to dominate the whole of the eighteenth century.

> **Fontenelle** was born at Rouen in 1657. He was a nephew of Corneille, his mother being Corneille's sister. Educated by the Jesuits, he became a lawyer, but gave up his profession, and went to Paris with a tragedy which turned out a complete failure. However, he soon achieved literary success, and with the *Entretien sur la Pluralité des Mondes* firmly established his reputation and position. He entered the Academy in 1691, and in 1699 was made life secretary of the Academy of Sciences. He was a frequenter of all the most famous *salons*, and among the most brilliant and distinguished members of the intellectual society of the capital. He was a polished man of the world, a brilliant conversationalist, and, as a drawing-room philosopher and scientist, had great influence on his age in popularizing branches of learning which had not

before penetrated to the *salons* of the fashionable world. He lived to be nearly a hundred, universally esteemed, and recognized as a great man and leader of science and letters. He died in 1757.

Fontenelle began his literary work by writing plays, poetry, pastorals, and other compositions in the style of a seventeenth-century *précieux*. All this work was of little value, and he was severely handled, and with good reason, by the satirists of the time. J. B. Rousseau directed against him some of his most pointed epigrams, and he figures in one of La Bruyère's best-known *Caractères* as Cydias, the personification of the *bel esprit* and *précieux*.

However, with his *Entretien sur la Pluralité des Mondes* (1686) he found his true field, and entered upon the successful and useful part of his career. This work, in the form of conversations with a lady of quality, innocent hitherto of all scientific knowledge—" *une femme que l'on instruit, et qui n'a jamais ouï parler de ces choses-là* "—presents in easy form the entire system of the universe as understood in his day. It had the effect of spreading enormously interest in scientific matters, and is epoch-making as the first great work of popular science. His other notable works are the *Histoire des Oracles* (1687), which shows by examples taken from the ancient oracles the easy credulousness of mankind and the necessity for closer investigation before belief; the *Histoire de l'Académie* and the *Éloges des Académiciens*, the latter his most important and solid production. Taking advantage of the eulogies pronounced over the members of the Academy of Science at their death, he explained in clear and lucid language the scientific discoveries due to them, and utilized them as a medium for explaining and discussing the scientific theories and knowledge of his day.

Fontenelle's influence was very great on his contemporaries, partly owing to the length of his literary life, which left him at the beginning of the eighteenth century and till the rise of Voltaire's star, the unrivalled sovereign of letters.

In spite of his universality, and the elegance and clearness of his style, he was a man without true passion either for art or science; by his want of warmth he furthered the tendency towards artificiality from which the language and literature already suffered. His true significance is as a precursor of the scientific and philosophic spirit of the eighteenth century, not only as a popularizer of science, but also as the initiator of scientific doubt and destructive criticism. In his cold, dispassionate style and dread of over-credulousness we see the first signs of the spirit which animated Voltaire and the Encyclopedists.

Next in point of time of the great prose writers of the century is **Charles de Secondat de Montesquieu,** the founder of the philosophy of history and the father of modern scientific history. In his searching investigation and universal questioning of all phenomena and institutions we can see the workings of the whole *philosophe* movement in its early stages.

> **Montesquieu** was born at the Château de la Brède, near Bordeaux, in 1689. His family was of the *noblesse de robe*, with a descent traceable for two and a half centuries, and he was from the first destined for the profession of the law. In 1714 he became a councillor of the parliament of Bordeaux, and in 1716 president. In 1722, the year after the appearance of his *Lettres Persanes*, he came to Paris. In 1727 he was elected to the Academy. He had already given up the presidency of the Bordeaux parliament, and soon after set out on a series of travels, in order to gain the knowledge of the constitutions and conditions of the principal civilized countries which would be necessary for the great work on jurisprudence which he already contemplated. He visited in this way Germany, Austria, Italy, Switzerland, Holland, and last of all England, where he spent the years 1729–1731. The English constitution and English liberty made a profound impression upon him, and had very considerable influence on his writings. After his return to France he lived principally at La Brède, engaged in the composition of those books which formed the serious work of his life. He died at Paris in 1755.

Montesquieu's life has been happily compared with that of Montaigne, and a comparison of the two will afford an interesting parallel in many respects.

His early studies were directed to natural science, and in 1721 he published a *Discours sur les Causes de la Transparence des Corps*, and also *Observations sur l'Histoire Naturelle*. There was nothing remarkable in this aspect of his work, but in the same year (1721) appeared a book by him called *Lettres Persanes*, which achieved an immediate and very great success, and decided definitely his literary career.

The framework of the story is by no means original. A Persian, living in Paris from 1713 to 1720, writes letters to his friends describing French society in all its aspects, while his friends keep him posted in the news of his own household and seraglio. Thus there are two distinct parts—the letters of the Persian, of which the interest consists in the picture of the social life of France at the period; and the letters of his friends, through which runs the thread of an intrigue of gallantry, to which was due in a considerable measure the success of the book with the idle crowd. The essential part, however, is his criticism of French institutions, which, in the person of the Persian, he is able to make with great freedom, and from an independent and original point of view. Montesquieu always expressed the whole of his thought in all his books, and in the wide social and political satire and reflections on government and jurisprudence we already see the germs of *L'Esprit des Lois*. The description of Parisian society, though bright and clever, is more superficial.

Lastly, the style—brilliant, witty, and in brisk, short sentences—marks the transition from the long rhetorical period of the seventeenth century to the short, chopped phrase of the eighteenth, of which we have already noticed the beginnings in La Bruyère. Both from the point of view of style and also as the introduction to the famous *Esprit des Lois*, the light, witty, jesting *Lettres Persanes*, half-novel and half-treatise, mark a date to be remembered.

From 1728 Montesquieu turned to wholly serious work, and he may be said to have passed the next twenty years in the preparation and writing of his life's task, *L'Esprit des Lois*

(1748)—the *Considérations sur la Grandeur et Décadence des Romains*, which appeared in 1734, being only a preparation for the larger work—a part which absorbed all his interest and attention for a time, and developed to too great a length to be included in the general frame. In this work we get the wide and philosophic view of history, the drawing of broad generalizations, which forms the great importance and originality of his method. His endeavour was to explain everything, not merely to state, and even where he went wrong he showed marvellous ingenuity in inventing theories with which the facts could be made more or less convincingly to harmonize. He does not believe in blind chance. To quote his own words: " *Ce n'est pas la fortune qui domine le monde. Il y a des causes générales.*" And to give a typical case: " *Si le hasard d'une bataille, c'est-à-dire, une cause particulière a ruiné un état, il y avait une cause générale qui faisait que cet État devait périr par une seule bataille.*"

Montesquieu owed much to Bossuet's *Discours sur l'Histoire Universelle*, especially in the important sixth chapter, enumerating the causes of Roman greatness. These characteristics are: love of liberty and fatherland, constancy in difficulties, the feeling of honour, loyalty to leaders and to the State. The causes of the decadence: the cumbrous overgrowth of the Empire, distant wars, and the luxury which led to the general corruption of manners.

In style there is a great change from the lively maliciousness of the *Lettres Persanes*—here all is grave and dignified simplicity, relieved occasionally by a striking image or an unexpected turn.

Fourteen years later, in 1748, appeared *L'Esprit des Lois*, one of the most considerable books of the whole century. It is his life's work, the sum total of his observations and reflections, with the deductions he had drawn from the different facts and phenomena, historic, political, economic, and social, noted during a long life.

We shall easily understand the want of uniformity of the

whole when we remember that it shows the work of a long life, and reflects the many phases through which his character and opinions passed. But it is necessary first of all to have a clear idea of the exact meaning of the title, and the sense in which the author here uses the word *loi*, and with this object we cannot do better than to quote his own definition: "*Les lois dans la signification la plus étendue sont les rapports nécessaires qui dérivent de la nature des choses*": the necessary relations existing between different things resulting from the nature of the things themselves. Taking the word *loi*, then, in this sense, the title is broad enough to cover even the book for which it serves, and which in general terms we can best describe as a consideration of the different social and political conditions under which men have ever lived, and the effect on them of all the influences, moral or physical, which are capable of affecting them in any way.

> The work consists of thirty-one books. It begins with the formal division of governments into the three types—republic, monarchy, despotism—to each of which he attributes a typical principle—virtue, honour, and fear respectively. It then goes on to consider liberty in relation to government, and the way it is assured by the proper balance and adjustment of the legislative and executive power. In this connection he speaks in **Book XI** of the English constitution and English liberty, which he greatly admired.
>
> **Book XII** treats of the influence of external conditions, such as climate and the nature of the soil, on the constitution and forms of society, this being one of the best and most original parts of the whole; after which he discusses in turn the questions of commerce, finance, population, and religion.
>
> The last, **Books XXVI–XXXI,** are purely legal history, dealing with the Roman laws of succession, French law, and the feudal system.

Thus it will be seen that the work is no less stupendous in range than wanting in uniformity of plan. The fact is, that Montesquieu had no definite design for the whole, but put into it, as into an encyclopedia, all the thoughts, reflections, and deductions of the greater part of his life, without troubling about systematic arrangement and logical sequence. That he had himself but a vague general idea of the lesson he wished to convey is seen by the indefinite title he gave to the heterogeneous mass. It was this very discursiveness, together with the inventiveness and stimulating originality, the happy and piquant if often misguided generalizations, the mixture of philosophy and wit, which gave the book its enormous popularity in the eighteenth century. As Fontenelle had brought science, so Montesquieu brought history, and philosophic history to boot, into the life of ladies and men of fashion. Madame du Deffand hit off the popular appreciation when she called *L'Esprit des Lois* " *de l'esprit sur les lois* ".

Still, the book was an epoch-making one, desultory though it was, for it established the theory of the " continuity of history ", and founded the philosophy of history. It deserved its credit in its day; its subsequent loss of repute is easily to be understood, and is due not so much to any defect of its own, as to the advance of the science which it founded, which has made of one half of its theories and generalizations mere platitudes, while the other half it has discovered to be false.

Taken all in all, then, we must look upon Montesquieu as one of the weightiest and most significant French authors, not only of his own but of any century.

More important still is **Voltaire**, the most typical of the writers of the century, and the most versatile. Though Fontenelle and Montesquieu were the precursors of the *philosophe* movement, and show its earliest workings, it was Voltaire who brought it to maturity, and with whose name it is mainly identified. We will speak here of all his prose writings; this can the more readily be done owing to the uniformity of spirit which pervades them.

In the first rank among his serious prose must be placed his historical works. The first to appear was the *Histoire de Charles XII* (1731), a lively and brilliant narration, of which the interest consists not in any philosophic or political teaching or views, but in the stir of adventures and battles, and the romantic events amid which the life of the Swedish king was passed. It is the first instance of a historical work which is not merely history but literature. It is as interesting as a novel. Yet Voltaire did not knowingly sacrifice historical truth to narrative interest, but carefully examined all the documents and manuscripts within reach which bore on the subject.

This effort to obtain historical accuracy by going at first hand to the sources of information we see carried still further in his next work, *Le Siècle de Louis XIV* (1751), his historical masterpiece. His admiration for the monarch and his reign, the memory of its literary glories and the favour then shown to men of letters, made it for him a work of love. Looking upon the period with such sympathy as the climax of French glory, and as a golden age of ideal splendour and prosperity, he wished to give a full account of this society and civilization in all its many sides. He says in the introduction: " *Ce n'est pas seulement la vie de Louis XIV qu'on prétend écrire; on se propose un plus grand objet. On veut essayer de peindre à la postérité, non les actions d'un seul homme, mais l'esprit des hommes dans le siècle le plus éclairé qui fût jamais.*" And again: " *On ne s'attachera, dans cette histoire, qu'à ce qui mérite l'attention de tous les temps . . . à ce qui peut servir d'instruction, et conseiller l'amour de la vertu, des arts et de la patrie.*"

This being his ambition he spared no pains in acquiring the necessary knowledge of the period. In his youth he had met men who could give him first-hand information on the subject and this he supplemented by all the *mémoires* and manuscripts available, as well as the state archives to which as Historiographer Royal he had full access.

So we find a wonderful mass of information carefully sifted and arranged with great clearness and insight, an admirable adjustment of light and shade, and a careful distinction between the essential and unessential.

As a clear exposition of details and particulars the work could not be surpassed. But—and this qualification is an important one—it is almost entirely lacking in a conception of the unity of history, and the connection and relation of all the different forms of human activity; Voltaire follows the false and unnatural plan of isolating the different parts of what should be a complete and complex picture, as he announces himself in the introduction: "*Le gouvernement intérieur sera traité à part. La vie privée de Louis XIV . . . tiendra une grande place. D'autres articles . . . seront pour les arts, pour les sciences, pour les progrès de l'esprit humain dans ce siècle. Enfin on parlera de l'Église.*"

As might be expected from this artificial separation of things which show no such division in nature, the whole work is formal and dry; admirably clear, concise, and definite in particulars, but wanting in life and reality. One of its most important features is that it set the example of treating the arts, sciences, and letters as a corporate part of the history of a period.

The third notable historical work of Voltaire is the *Essai sur les Mœurs* (1756), a universal history of Europe from Charlemagne to Louis XIV. It takes up the subject where Bossuet leaves it in his *Discours sur l'Histoire Universelle jusqu'à l'Empire de Charlemagne*, but the spirit is entirely different. For Bossuet all things in the final issue were ordained by the hand of Providence; Voltaire eliminates the direct intervention of Providence as a factor in history, and sets himself the much harder task of finding the causes of events in the natural course of progress. So while Bossuet wrote theological, Voltaire wrote philosophic history.

Voltaire's main object in this work is to show the progress of reason and the advance of civilization, while representing Christianity rather as the obstacle in their way. It is this one-sidedness and prejudice which forms the weakness of the book, since it was impossible for anyone starting as the enemy of Christianity to write a just and sympathetic history of a period in which that religion formed the chief motive power.

It is this want of sympathy, this inability to place himself at the point of view of the times he deals with, which makes

Voltaire fall short of being a great historian. The same consideration accounts for the fact that *Le Siècle de Louis XIV*, which is nearer in point of time, and had his full interest, is his best historical work.

All Voltaire's prose works were written with a didactic purpose, and many with this object avowed and with eloquent titles. None of these were, however, of very great weight, and it is rather in his countless pamphlets and fugitive literature, in which he is, as it were, the journalist of the *philosophe* movement, that his importance as a reformer lies. In Switzerland, during the latter years of his life, he devoted himself principally to philosophy, and as leader of the Encyclopedic movement, which he joined, and of which he became virtual chief, exercised enormous influence.

It is impossible to enumerate the countless works of this kind which he produced during the last twenty years of his life—the list would be too long, and they are of too little consequence individually. We can only name the most significant. Immediately after his return from England appeared the *Lettres Philosophiques* (1734), containing his reflections on English institutions and his eulogies of English liberty. The *Dictionnaire Philosophique ou la Raison par Alphabet* (1764) explains itself and its purpose clearly enough; while his *Questions sur l'Encyclopédie* (1770-1772) comprises much of his best and most characteristic philosophic writing. Lastly, we may mention, as typical of his antichristian propaganda, such works as *Dieu et les Hommes* (1769), *La Bible enfin expliquée* (1776), *Traité sur la Tolérance* (1763).

The central point of Voltaire's philosophy is always the fight against intolerance—*l'Infâme*, the infamous thing. He does not deny the existence of a God or decry religion, but he repudiates all revealed religion. Christianity he treats without respect, submitting all things to the test of reason, and it is with this hard and unyielding criticism of religious matters that the name of Voltaire has come to be before all, and not without reason, identified. Yet it must always be remembered that Voltaire was not an atheist, and in this differed from many of the Encyclopedists. What he claimed was the right to examine all things independently of tradition and authority; to submit all things to the test of pure reason, and reject everything which did not satisfy its demands.

It is in this constitutional hatred of all merely traditional or hereditary authority, whether of Church or State, and in this demand for the right of free and universal inquiry and examination, that he is typical of the whole age.

Lastly, and not least important, we have to treat of Voltaire's enormous correspondence. We have no less than 12,000 letters of his, while others are still gradually coming to light, and many have been irretrievably lost.

As a great man of letters for half a century, and sovereign of European literature for half that time, as the correspondent of reigning monarchs, princes, and the most famous writers and intellectual leaders of every country in Europe, he built up in his letters an enormous compendium of the ideas of his day—a picture of the life and thought of the age drawn directly and at first hand by one in whose capacious mind every current of the time was reflected. In every conceivable style, addressed to people of almost every conceivable type, dealing with almost every kind of human condition, they show as nothing else could his ever-ready wit, his inexhaustible fertility of ideas, his wonderful adaptability and unparalleled many-sidedness.

So we take leave at length of Voltaire, after meeting him in every division of the literature of the century. Poetry, drama, fiction, history, philosophy, at all he tried his hand, his insatiable ambition making him aspire to rule in every domain. In all he produced work that was much above the average, and in none did he produce anything of outstanding merit. If he deserves a name among the first of French writers, it is not on account of any great original contribution to literature, but on account of his supreme genius as a popularizer of the results and thoughts of others. In this he has never been surpassed, and this it is which makes his name the most widely known in connection with the literature of his century. Though not a creator, he had a wonderful gift of assimilating the ideas of others and making them his own, and this astonishing facility being associated with an equal clearness of style, made him the universal spirit of his age.

In him the transition of style from seventeenth to eighteenth century is completed, and we have at its best the short, clear, lucid phrase; while in two respects, elegant simplicity and naturalness, he has probably never been equalled, even in that land where the writing of prose is a cult with every man of education.

One more name must be mentioned before we come to the Encyclopedic movement proper—that of **Luc de Clapiers de Vauvenargues** (1715–1747), of a poor but noble family of Provence. He entered the army, served in Italy and Germany, and in Bohemia, where his health was so far ruined as to necessitate his leaving the Service in 1743. Debarred by ill health from an active career, he turned his energies to literature, spending his last years in Paris, where he died at the early age of thirty-two.

His works are the *Introduction à la Connaissance de l'Esprit Humain* (1746), *Réflexions sur Divers Sujets, Conseils à un Jeune Homme*; and *Discours et Caractères*, in the manner of La Bruyère. Of these the only one finished was the *Introduction*.

All Vauvenargues' work breathes the longing for action, which he had been prevented from satisfying in the ordinary way, and to which he strove to give vent in his literary activity. His interest lies in the social institutions of man, and the play and development of human forces. He places sentiment and passion, as active forces, above reason, and in this is nearer akin to J.-J. Rousseau than to the speculative *philosophes*. In spite of his own unhappy fate, he was an optimist and fired by enthusiasm for humanity—a cheerful, honest, upright character, with something of the simplicity of all men of action, and a wholesomeness of view that might have exercised the best of influences on his century had he lived long enough to establish his literary position. As it was, he was almost unknown, and it was not till half a century later that he was fully appreciated. From his central doctrine, to which he loses no opportunity of giving prominence, the superiority of the passions to reason, he may be regarded, in a sense, as the Rousseau of the first half of the century.

The Encyclopedia.—The work in which all the philosophic tendencies of the century culminate is the *Encyclopédie*, the great literary monument of the second half of the century.

In 1740 a French bookseller, Le Breton, was offered a translation of the *English Cyclopedia* of Ephraim Chambers, which had appeared in 1728. However, he conceived the idea of making of it something more than a mere translation, and eventually induced Diderot and D'Alembert to undertake, as joint editors, the production of an encyclopedia which, while on the lines of the English one, should be an original and independent compendium of the letters, arts, and sciences of the day. The editors, and more especially Diderot, set to work to get together a set of contributors truly representative, and succeeded eventually in enrolling most of the famous names in all the different branches of letters. Among the regular collaborators were Condillac, Helvétius, D'Holbach, Grimm, Turgot, and Condorcet; and articles were received from Voltaire, Buffon, and Montesquieu; even Rousseau, though standing aloof on the whole, was represented in a certain degree.

A prospectus was drawn up by Diderot explaining the scheme and pointing out its twofold object, namely, as an Encyclopedia, giving an ordered and systematized account of all human learning; secondly, as a *Dictionnaire raisonné des Arts, des Sciences, et des Métiers*, recording the principles and essentials of all arts and sciences. This was repeated in the *Discours préliminaire* of D'Alembert, an introduction to the whole, and an excellent *résumé* of the state of the arts, science, and philosophy of the day.

The first two volumes appeared in 1751, but though at last under way the difficulties encountered were by no means over. Into the intrigues which led to its frequent suppression, and the opposition it met from many quarters, it is impossible to enter. D'Alembert lost heart or patience, and in 1759 resigned his post as joint editor, but Diderot toiled manfully on, and carried the work to completion.

The last and twenty-eighth volume appeared in 1772.

In spite of the many hands which took part in its composition, the *Encyclopédie* has a certain unity of spirit, due partly to the similarity of the philosophic creed of its contributors, and partly to the vigilant supervision and direction exercised by Diderot as editor. It was to be, to quote the words of Diderot's prospectus, a " *Tableau général des Efforts de l'Esprit Humain dans tous les Genres et dans tous les Siècles* ", and it was to show the progress of reason, the advance of civilization, and the growth of material prosperity and its advantages.

Rationalism, then, was its watchword, and the authorities were not far wrong, from their point of view, in their repeated attempts to suppress it, for its essential principle was destructive criticism of all established authority and traditional institutions. In religion its trend was still more revolutionary, as, even where frank atheism was not avowed, Christianity and revealed religion were ruthlessly set aside.

Its great importance lies in the fact that, taken as a whole, it shows the tendency of the period, forming a kind of manifesto or rather code of philosophism; in form, matter, and manner it is exactly typical of the age in which it was produced.

First and foremost among the *Encyclopédistes* comes **Denis Diderot.**

Diderot was born at Langres in Champagne in 1713, the son of a cutler. He was at first educated by the Jesuits of his native town, but finished his studies in Paris at the *Collège d'Harcourt*. Destined originally for the Church, and afterwards for medicine and the law, his love of letters made the adoption of any profession distasteful to him, and he finally settled down to support himself by literature, supplementing the scanty income this afforded by giving lessons and doing hack work of every description. In 1745 he was charged with the editing of the *Encyclopédie*, and this, in spite of the miserable pay, preserved him from actual want. Still, he was always in needy circumstances, and towards the end of his life was reduced to the necessity of selling even his library. From this calamity he was, however, preserved in an unexpected and pleasant way, for Catherine II, Empress of Russia, bought it, left him full and free enjoyment of it, and in addition gave him a salary as librarian. He died at Paris in 1784.

Diderot's works consist, in addition to the already-mentioned novels—*La Religieuse, Jacques le Fataliste, Le Neveu de Rameau*—of the *Essai sur le Mérite et la Vertu* (1745), *Pensées Philosophiques* (1746), *Lettre sur les Aveugles à l'Usage de ceux qui voient* (1749), and the *Salons* (posthumous); a large and varied *Correspondance*; a thousand and one fugitive and often unfinished writings; and last, and most important of all, his share in the *Encyclopédie*.

The *Essai sur le Mérite et la Vertu* still professes a kind of theism, but by the time the *Lettres sur les Aveugles* appeared in 1749, Diderot had become openly and avowedly an atheist. In this part of his work he is, in spite of some originality of ideas, a man of his age, expressing, though with greater insight than most, the thoughts with which the atmosphere of his day was charged.

The *Salons*, descriptions of the exhibitions of the years 1764-1767, forms some of his best work, and gave considerable impulse to art criticism in general, by establishing relations between art and literature, which had hitherto been almost entirely dissociated. Their chief defect is that they are too literary, laying undue stress on the subject, the story and idea of the picture, and taking too little account of the pictorial art itself. Yet his great gift of feeling and sympathy enabled Diderot, in spite of his lack of technical knowledge, to appreciate the spirit of the art with which he was dealing.

The key-note of all his artistic creed was strict truth to nature.

His *Corrrespondance*, and especially that with Mlle de Voland, in which he speaks without reserve of the society of the time, the doings and circumstances of his own personal friends, shows us the real Diderot, and enables us to learn and understand perfectly his true character.

But it is in the countless short fugitive pieces, which appeared in the *Encyclopédie* or otherwise, as pamphlets, dialogues, or in any other form which the thought might assume in his plastic imagination under the impulse of the moment, that we see the literary proclivities and typical work of Diderot. In them we find the universal sympathy and interest, and the rarely equalled versatility both of conception and style, which made him the great journalist and worthy editor of that great eighteenth-century storehouse, the *Encyclopédie*.

Of these shorter writings, many of which remained unfinished, while still more never received really literary shape and scarcely any literary finish, it is impossible to give a list. The two best-known, however, are probably the *Entretien d'un Philosophe avec la Maréchale de* ***, and *Le Rêve de D'Alembert*.

Of his importance as first joint and later sole editor of the *Encyclopédie* an account has already been given in connection with the Encyclopedia itself, with which he was indissolubly bound up, and which was to a great extent identified with his name.

Diderot's literary significance does not then depend on any great work or works, but upon his versatility and universality as a writer. Above all, as editor of the *Encyclopédie* for many years—as the man who carried on the arduous task in spite of all difficulties and even when forsaken by his discouraged partner, and as the man who gave to that epoch-making production such unity as it possessed, Diderot is of supreme importance for the history of eighteenth-century literature. On account of the unfinished and somewhat formless nature of much he wrote, it is not easy to understand the character of his literary genius. The main features of that genius were—firstly, a fiery and enthusiastic imagination, which impelled him to espouse all causes and interest himself in all matters that fell under his notice; and secondly, a peculiar literary impatience which made him indifferent to the form in which he clothed the thoughts and ideas of which he felt at the time such an irresistible necessity to disburden himself.

Such is Diderot in all his work—a brilliant extemporizer, a journalist of genius, but rarely an artist.

Next to Diderot the most important representative of the philosophic movement is **Jean le Rond d'Alembert.**

> D'Alembert, born in 1717, was a foundling exposed by his parents on the steps of the church of *St. Jean le Rond* in Paris. He was brought up by the wife of a poor glazier, and this foster-mother he honoured and respected as a real mother till her death. He was sent to the *Collège Mazarin*, and soon gave evidence of his great mathematical ability. At the age of twenty-four he was already a member of the Academy of Sciences. He was at first joint editor with Diderot of the *Encyclopédie*, but resigned official connection with the work in discouragement at the troubles and annoyances to which they were subjected. An invitation of Frederic II in 1752 to go to Berlin as president of the Berlin Academy, and that of Catherine II to go to Russia as tutor of her son, he refused. However, he accepted a pension from Frederic. In 1772 he became secretary of the Academy. He died in 1783.

A considerable part of his work consists of his contributions to the *Encyclopédie*. He wrote the famous *Discours Préliminaire*, which is, both as literature and philosophy, a work of very high merit. Besides editing the mathematical part and contributing mathematical articles, he furnished articles on general subjects, one, the article on Geneva, which elicited a reply from Rousseau—the *Lettre à M. D'Alembert sur les Spectacles*.

Apart from his many purely scientific and mathematical works, we owe to D'Alembert the *Éléments de Philosophie* and the *Éloges des Membres de l'Académie Française*, lives of all the members who had died since the beginning of the century, written in his capacity of secretary, the best-known and most readable of his writings. As literature, however, all he produced is open to the charge of dryness. It is too intellectual and formal. Indisputably great as a man of science and as a thinker, D'Alembert has few of the qualities that go to make literary greatness, and his position in the literature of his century is due rather to a conjunction of unusual circumstances, and to the esteem in which the sciences were held by the men of letters of his day, than to any purely literary merits of his own.

Among the remaining more important Encyclopedists, the most noticeable are Condillac, Helvétius, D'Holbach, and Grimm.

Étienne Bonnot de Mably de Condillac (1715–1780) was born of a noble family at Grenoble, was an Abbé, and lived for the most part quietly on his benefice, taking little part in the life of the great world of his day. His principal works are *Essai sur l'Origine des Connaissances Humaines* (1746), and *Traité des Sensations* (1754).

He was the greatest metaphysician of the century, the greatest philosopher among the *philosophes*. He took up the system of Locke, and carried it boldly to its logical extreme, deriving all ideas from the sensations directly. He was a man of strong, clear intellect, a great logician, the possessor of a lucid polished style, and in every way fitted to be, as he was, the representative in France of this " philosophy of the senses ".

This philosophy, which eliminates concrete facts, and deals only with sensations and ideas, was indeed the very philosophy of the eighteenth century.

Claude Adrien Helvétius (1715–1771) was born at Paris, became in 1738 farmer-general, and later chamberlain of the Queen's household. He was very rich, and also very liberal, and kept open house for the *philosophes*. His reputation depends on his two books: *De l'Esprit* (1758), and *De l'Homme* (1772). The former caused a great scandal, owing to the uncompromising frankness with which it professed materialism, proclaiming all thoughts and ideas to be due to different sensations, and so making all progress, civilization, and spiritual life merely the outcome of our physical conformation. It was condemned as immoral, and ordered to be publicly burnt by the common hangman. His second book, *De l'Homme*, was much inferior in power and merit, though it was no less fiercely assailed on its appearance.

The **Baron d'Holbach** (1723-1789) was born in the Palatinate. Coming to Paris, he became the intimate friend not only of the Encyclopedists, but also of Rousseau and Buffon, and the other intellectual leaders of the day. He was very hospitable and generous, ever ready to welcome the Encyclopedists, and was otherwise very beneficent.

His one work is the *Système de la Nature* (1770), an exposition of the egoistic philosophy, which establishes self-interest as the motive power of all actions, and does not admit the existence of a divine being.

As a bold proclamation of pure atheism and materialism it was of considerable account, and not only attracted much attention, but was the object of very bitter attacks.

Frédéric Melchior Grimm (1723-1807) was a German, educated at Leipzig, who came to Paris, made there the acquaintance of Rousseau in 1749, and later of most of the Encyclopedists. This wide circle of literary acquaintances, coupled with his own great talents, gave its value to his extensive *Correspondance*, which for a third of a century spread over a great part of Europe information and enlightened criticism on the state of contemporary French literature. The letters, which appeared once a fortnight, and were distributed to the different subscribers, among whom were Frederic the Great, Catherine II, the King of Poland, and other princes, were in reality more like the literary periodicals of to-day than letters, the only considerable difference being that these remarkable productions were not printed, but appeared in manuscript.

Other less considerable members of the same group are:

Anne Robert Jacques Turgot (1727-1781), appointed by Louis XVI comptroller-general of finance, much more famous as the man who attempted financial reforms which, if carried out, might have prevented the great Revolution, than as a man of letters. After the end of his political career Turgot devoted himself to literature and science.

His best-known contribution is the *Réflexions sur la Formation et la Distribution des Richesses* (1766). His work shows no great literary qualities, and it is more as a thinker and *philosophe* than a *littérateur* proper that his name deserves mention here.

Jean Nicolas Caritat, Marquis de Condorcet (1743-1794), a distinguished mathematician, a great leader of the Revolution in its early stages, and president of the Legislative Assembly, but afterwards, as a moderate, pursued, imprisoned, and probably done to death, wrote during his flight and concealment his *Esquisse des Progrès de l'Esprit Humain* (1794). This notable work, which is a summary and *résumé* of the philosophic ideas of the age, claims universal equality of privilege and rights, and with an optimism remarkable in a man in his time, traces the progress of humanity in face of tyranny and superstition, and argues the ultimate perfectibility of the human species.

Although **Jean-Jacques Rousseau** had frequent relations with the Encyclopedists, both hostile and friendly, he cannot be classed as an Encyclopedist, but, on the contrary, stands alone and independent—an original, and in many ways the most striking, figure of the century.

Rousseau (1712-1778) was born at Geneva of a French Protestant family. His mother died while he was still an infant, and he was left to the care of his father, a watchmaker, and the intermittent attentions of two aunts. His father was an idle, wayward character, whose one passion in life was reading, and that principally fiction and romance, a taste with which he early imbued his son.

In 1722 the father was compelled to move from Geneva, leaving his son behind in the care of an uncle. Thus began for Jean-Jacques the restless and ever-changing life which continued for the rest of his days. His uncle first placed him with a notary, but he was found utterly unfitted for his work; then he was apprenticed to an engraver, who ill-treated him, and Jean-Jacques, being very unhappy, in 1728 ran away, the manner of his flight being truly characterisic. He had rambled all day among the beauties of nature, which he already loved passionately, and on returning to the city in the evening found the gates shut. This he accepted as an omen, and resolved to return no more to the engraver and his uncle. After some wanderings, he attracted the interest of a Savoy priest, who sent him to Annecy to Madame de Warens, a Catholic convert who had in turn become a passionate proselytizer for her new-found religion. This was the beginning of a patronage which lasted for thirteen years, during which time Rousseau received oft-repeated assistance and kindness from his benefactress. By her he was first placed in the Romanist hospice at Turin, but his hopes of advancement from this quarter were vain, for he was baptized, and almost immediately afterwards discharged. He then for three years led a wandering and almost vagabond existence, gaining his livelihood in the most varied capacities—as footman, secretary, lackey, or by any other employment that came to hand. In 1731 he returned to Madame de Warens. The next ten years (1731–1741) were spent principally with his patroness, for whom he performed sundry services, becoming eventually a kind of factotum. At the same time he had various other employments, among them being the teaching of music. More important still, he continued his communion with nature and her beauties, and on this account this period of his life was of the greatest consequence to his further development.

In 1741 he went to Paris, taking with him a comedy, *Narcisse*, and also a new system of musical notation, neither of which, however, brought him either fame or profit. Still, he made the acquaintance of several people of mark, and managed to keep himself above actual want, principally by the copying of music; though it was not till 1750 that he became known with his *Discours sur les Sciences et les Arts*, which won the prize of the Dijon Academy, while in 1754 another essay for the prize of the same academy, the *Discours sur l'Inégalité*, finally established his independent position in literature.

The years 1756–1762 he passed at Montmorency in houses lent him by Madame d'Épinay and the Duc de Montmorency successively, and in spite of the annoyances which he created for himself wherever he went, these were among the happiest and most productive years of his life. In 1762, owing to the storm raised by the publication of the *Contrat Social*, he fled to Neuchâtel, but was driven from there by the peasants, and took refuge on the little Ile de St. Pierre in the Lac de Bienne. When the government of Berne made that asylum, too, impossible for him, he accepted, in 1766, the invitation of David Hume, with whom he stayed for eighteen months, at the end of which the inevitable quarrels reached a climax, and he left England and returned to France. In 1770 he was once more in Paris, keeping himself by copying music, all through his life his only stable means of subsistence. The gloominess which had been growing for many years was now becoming a veritable mania, and he looked upon himself as the victim of a universal plot to decry and dishonour him. Restless, suspicious, melancholy, and more than half mad, he led during the last years of his life a wretched existence. In 1778 he retired to a cottage in the park of Ermonville, lent him by the Marquis de Girardin, and there he died in July of that year, with a suddenness and under such suspicious circumstances as to lend probability to the belief that he took his own life.

Rousseau's principal works are:—*Discours sur les Sciences et les Arts* (1750), *Discours sur l'Origine et les Fondements de l'Inégalité parmi les Hommes* (1754), *Lettre à M. D'Alembert sur les Spectacles* (1758), *Julie ou la Nouvelle Héloïse* (1761), *Émile ou l'Éducation* (1762), *Le Contrat Social* (1762), and the *Confessions* (written between 1765–1770).

It was not till he was thirty-eight years of age that Rousseau's important literary work began with the *Discours sur les Arts et les Sciences* (1750), a prose essay crowned by the Dijon Academy as the best work presented on the theme proposed:—" *Si l'établissement des sciences et des arts a contribué à épurer les mœurs* ". In it the trend of Rousseau's thought is already plainly seen, and though Diderot asserts that he suggested to Rousseau a negative answer, it appears as if the mind of Rousseau would require no impulse to make it decide upon that line of argument. He contends that civilization is an evil because it leads man away from Nature, and that all the so-called progress of the human mind, its arts, sciences, and philosophy, have been in reality harmful, as sapping the original and primitive virtue of man.

In 1754 he carried on and still further developed the same theme in his *Discours sur l'Origine et les Fondements de l'Inégalité parmi les Hommes*, which finally established his position as a writer. In it he attributes to the institution of property all the ills which he argues to be the result of civilization. He says: " *Le premier qui, ayant enclos un terrain, s'avisa de dire: Ceci est à moi . . . fut le vrai fondateur de la société civile."* From the resulting inequality came tyranny and slavery, vice and unhappiness. And as the natural sequence of all this he goes on to assert his favourite doctrine of the perfection of the savage state, and the evils of civilization as leading man away from the condition of primitive simplicity.

In *Émile ou l'Éducation* (1762) we have this same teaching still further developed and elaborated, with an imaginary pupil Émile as the text of the lesson. The whole is divided into five Books, the contents of which are briefly given below.

> Émile is a rich orphan whose education Rousseau undertakes, devoting himself exclusively to the training of his body and mind. The fundamental idea of the book is that man is naturally good when leaving the hands of his Maker, and only becomes corrupted through the evil influences of civilization and society. Accordingly, all that has to be done is to let Nature work its own salvation in freedom, while warding off the evils of an artificial society. Hence he establishes the principle of a negative education as " *la meilleure ou plutôt la seule bonne* " not as teaching virtue, but as warding off error.
>
> **Book I** speaks of the plan of education proposed, the early life of the child chosen for the experiment, attacks many traditional practices, such as the use of swaddling-clothes, the putting out of children to nurse, &c.
>
> With **Book II** the child can already talk and his education is beginning. This, however, will not consist in the furnishing of any positive information, but in the preserving from error and from the danger of evil examples and counsels, the corruption of towns, and the harmful intercourse with unreliable servants. Émile is brought up in the country.
>
> **Book III** finds Émile at the age of twelve, but as yet unable to read books, which " *n'apprennent qu'à parler de ce qu'on ne sait pas* ". He does not learn by heart, he draws from Nature, and all he acquires is at first-hand. Also, though rich, he learns a trade—that of a carpenter—and we get the very significant words, " *nous approchons de l'état de crise et du siècle des révolutions* ". Thus up to the present all his lessons have been drawn from experience and from the necessary relations of things, not from ideas. He does not know the meaning of such abstract things as History and Metaphysics.
>
> **Book IV** shows Émile in his fifteenth year. Up to the present he has heard nothing of God, but here Rousseau places the famous

Profession de Foi du Vicaire Savoyard. One summer morning the *vicaire* leads the boy to the top of a hill overlooking the valley of the Po, and there, before the magnificent scene, reveals to him the all-powerful Will which created and governs the world he sees and knows. Yet no word is said of revelation—the religion is only natural, not revealed. As Émile approaches manhood his guardian at length leads him into the world and finds for him a wife. Only after Émile's marriage does the guardian relax his paternal cares.

Book V is devoted to the education of women.

Such was the book which had an enormous practical influence on its day and age, and an influence which on the whole was one for good. It performed a needful function in interesting men in the education of the young; it made it once more the fashion for mothers to rear and nurse their children. It is in fact marvellous how very much that is good and sensible the book contains, when we remember that the whole system on which it is built—the assumption of a human nature which is naturally perfect—is entirely false and unwarranted.

We have followed without interruption Rousseau's exposition of his theories on man and society—their development and education. Before *Émile*, however, had appeared two works of great import, *Julie* and the *Contrat Social*.

Julie ou la Nouvelle Héloïse (1761) is a novel in the form of letters, telling of the love of Julie and Saint-Preux. The whole, form and plot, shows clearly the influence of Richardson. Compelled by her father to renounce her lover, Julie marries a man whom she esteems though she does not love him. The novel had far-reaching effects, as the first example of Rousseau's peculiar sentimentality and descriptive powers. The word-painting has a wonderful charm, and warmth, vigour, and colour, much of it being inspired by the scenery of the Lake of Geneva and its neighbourhood.

Most important of all Rousseau's works in its after-effects however, was, the *Contrat Social*, which appeared in 1762, a few months before *Émile*, and was published in Amsterdam to avoid the censorship of the French press. Here again the fundamental idea is that of the original natural liberty of man, in contrast to the fetters with which society has bound him: "*L'homme est né libre et partout il est dans les fers.*" Rousseau proceeds from the premise that in forming the first political society each surrendered his own individual will for the sake of mutual protection, and that consequently man did not yield up his primitive liberty, and now remains as free as before. Thus sovereignty rests with the people, who have never renounced it. Obviously this theory demands a Republic with universal franchise, and it was his theory of such a " social contract ", and his assertion of the sovereignty of the People, which worked on men's minds and bore practical results in the Revolution, with its watchword of Liberty, Equality, and Fraternity.

Yet his assumption of this contract in which the primitive state originated is pure hypothesis, and many of his arguments, brilliant and specious as they are, are untenable.

Last of all Rousseau's notable works we must mention the *Confessions*, in which he claims to have portrayed himself without reserve, and which certainly speak with brutal frankness of very much that was low and shameful in his life.

He seems to glory in the tale of his meanness, and in the recording of things which most men would have preferred as far as possible to forget, rather than to rake them up from the ashes of the past and expose them to the public gaze. But Rousseau boasts that he is doing what was never done before, showing his very inmost life naked and entire to his fellow-men, and claims insolently that, bad as the story is, he would yet dare to appear before his Maker, and challenge any of his fellows to unfold a better tale. We can only in charity hope that his love of pose has betrayed him into attributing to himself vices for which he was not actually responsible.

Among his less weighty writings are sundry articles for the *Encyclopédie*; an opera, the *Devin du Village*, containing some airs, such as " Rousseau's Dream ", still popular to-day;

and lastly, one which is worthy of separate mention—the *Lettre à M. D'Alembert sur les Spectacles* (1758), a reply to a paper of D'Alembert in the *Encyclopédie* advocating the establishment of a theatre at Geneva, in which Jean-Jacques raises a vigorous protest against the introduction into the quiet town of Geneva of any such corrupting product of civilization.

Taken altogether, the influence of Rousseau on literature in general was the greatest of the century. His solemn note, almost that of the preacher, was at the opposite pole from the flippant cynicism of many of the Encyclopedists, and his own passionate conviction could not fail to touch the hearts of his readers. He had something of the wide declamatory eloquence of the seventeenth century, which we see also in the vehement oratory of Danton and other Revolutionists. His influence on his own time, and indeed not his own time alone, was twofold—it exerted itself forcibly on literature, and, in a practical way, on life and manners. In literature he virtually introduced two new features—the painting of nature and sentimentalism. Love of nature was throughout his life his one great passion, and lay at the root of all his characteristic views and philosophy.

In his peculiar kind of sentimentality, again, Rousseau was an innovator. Psychological analysis had already long ago invaded literature, it is true, but Rousseau's peculiar introspection, his brooding romanticism, his lyricism and subjectivity, were innovations. It was the first appearance in literature of that subtle evil known as " *le mal du siècle* ", which ran through all European literature, and gave birth in turn to Wertherism in Germany and to Byronism in England.

Among the practical results of Rousseau's work must be reckoned the revival of family feeling in France, of religious feeling, as well as an increased taste for simplicity of life and country pleasures. And lastly, in the great Revolution is seen the immediate and tangible outcome of ideas which largely owed their origin to his teaching, conveyed more or less indirectly in all his work, and directly in the *Contrat Social*.

Such was Rousseau, a writer who not only set on foot a literary movement which deeply influenced in turn the literature of the chief cultured peoples of Europe, but also by his eloquent teaching was the immediate forerunner of the greatest political and national upheaval the world has ever seen.

We now come, with **George Louis Leclerc, Comte de Buffon**, to a writer of a different type, one who was before all a scientist.

> **Buffon** (1707–1788) was born in Burgundy, son of a councillor of the Parliament of Bordeaux; studied at the Jesuit College of Dijon, travelled afterwards with a young Englishman, Lord Kingston, in Italy, Switzerland, and England, and subsequently settled in Paris in order to continue his mathematical and scientific studies. He became a member of the Academy of Sciences in 1733, and in 1739 was made *Intendant* of the *Jardin des Plantes*. Then it was that he conceived the plan of his great work, at which he laboured steadily for nearly half a century, making it, although he went into the world and was by no means a hermit, his one absorbing interest in life. He received many distinctions and honours, and was made Comte de Buffon by Louis XV, while his fame spread over the whole civilized world.

Buffon's life-work was his *Histoire Naturelle*, in 15 volumes, of which the first three appeared in 1749. The object which he proposed to himself was stupendous, for the work was to be an encyclopedia of all existing scientific knowledge concerning the earth and its vegetable and animal life. The whole of this colossal undertaking Buffon himself superintended, although he had collaborators who did much of the hack work, while he himself wrote the more striking and rhetorical parts.

By placing man at the centre of creation, and judging everything from his point of view and the way it affected him, Buffon gives his work an unsound and unscientific basis, yet by the very breadth of his scheme he widened the scientific horizon, and led the way to larger and more comprehensive views. At present, however, we are not so much concerned with Buffon's scientific as with his literary significance. This consists in his having won a new field for literature. He attached the utmost importance to style, as is expressed in his so well known, but often misquoted saying: "*Le style est l'homme même*." He wished to equal the dignity of his subject by the grandeur of his style, and even if this style is often inflated and bombastic, it has great merits, and showed for the first time the possibility of treating scientific subjects in clear and even eloquent language.

Before taking leave of the eighteenth century we must say a few words of the various women who played no unworthy part in their day.

In an age when the human interest was predominant, and the greatest weight was attached to matters of form and taste, it was only natural that ladies of refinement and culture should play a leading part in the intellectual life of the time. Such was the case; and we find many women, not so much because of their own writings as by the stimulating society which identified itself with their *salons*, who cannot be left out of account.

Madame du Deffand (1697–1780) may be taken first as being the most typical, not only on account of the famous men she gathered in her *salon*, but also because of the correspondence she maintained with some of the greatest, such as Voltaire, Montesquieu, D'Alembert, and the Englishman Horace Walpole. By her wonderful wit, shrewd and acute if narrow criticism of life and art, she won and maintained a position among thinkers and writers, for whom she furnished during many years, in her famous mansion of the Rue Saint-Dominique, a common meeting-ground.

The *salon* of **Madame Geoffrin** (1699–1777) formed a centre for the *philosophes* and Encyclopedists, among its frequenters being Diderot, D'Alembert, and D'Holbach. She was very rich, and not only entertained her *protégés*, but provided many of them with the very means of subsistence. While Madame du Deffand was a *grande dame*, Madame Geoffrin belonged to the *bourgeoisie*, and a somewhat analogous difference is to be traced in the characters of their *entourage*, the literary and æsthetic tone of the former being in marked contrast to the serious and business-like spirit by which the latter was on the whole animated.

Mademoiselle de Lespinasse (1732–1776), last but not least famous of those we have singled out for special remark, began as the friend and adviser of Madame du Deffand, and ended as her rival, taking away with her, after their quarrel in 1764, D'Alembert and not a few of the Encyclopedists. In addition to the importance of her *salon*, her name is remembered for the collection of love letters addressed to the Comte de Guibert, which form one of the rare expressions of genuine passion of the time, and in their warmth and fervour of feeling and glowing passionate language are not unworthy of being compared with the work of Rousseau himself.

Last of all may be mentioned the birth of a new *genre*, which was the direct outcome of political events—Political Eloquence.

Up till now the pulpit had been the only rostrum from which a direct appeal could be made, and it had produced very considerable oratorical eloquence, notably in the seventeenth century, with its long list of famous preachers. Now, however, a direct appeal had to be made to the people on other grounds, and the political tribune provoked a remarkable outburst of oratorical talent.

The list of famous speakers produced by the great national drama, and the stirring events to which it gave birth, is a long one, and we can speak only of the most conspicuous.

Gabriel Honoré De Riquetti, Comte de Mirabeau (1749–1791), is a personality so well known for other than literary reasons that it would be superfluous to give details of his life. Suffice it to say, that during the vicissitudes of a stormy career he had learnt much not only from men but also from books, especially during the periods of intermittent imprisonment for which he had to thank his various irregularities of conduct. His reading and experience served to develop his natural gift of eloquence. In the numerous speeches which he delivered before the *Assemblée Constituante* he displayed a wonderful power of improvisation, a fire and impetuosity of word and imagery exactly suited to carry away the audience to which they were addressed. He has been accused of over-emphasis, of bombast even, of want of polish in style, and of theatrical and commonplace metaphors and imagery, and from such faults he certainly was not free. Yet at the same time it must be remembered that such things were in the taste of the day, and that in oratory at any rate, where the object is to create a direct and immediate impression, the means must be at all costs adapted to the ends. Correctness of form and literary polish would have been poor substitutes for that powerful rush and impetus which carried the listeners away, and of which even to-day we can feel the power.

Besides his speeches we possess many letters, among them the *Lettres Originales écrites du Donjon de Vincennes*, and the *Lettre de Mirabeau à un de ses Amis en Allemagne*.

A collection of his *Œuvres Oratoires* was published in 1819.

Another striking orator of the Revolutionary epoch was **Robespierre** (1759-1794), who, in marked contrast to Mirabeau, delivered his most violent tirades in a phlegmatic and pedantic style that had more of the sermon than the popular oration—a style in which the ever-present striving after edification contrasts terribly with the undercurrent of relentless hatred of all those who in any way opposed him.

Lesser lights in the same field are **Danton, Saint-Just,** and **Hébert,** while a dozen more could be named, each of whom would stand out conspicuous at any other time, and who collectively illustrate the wonderful ferment produced in men's minds by the terrible events of the days in which they lived.

BOOK V
THE TRANSITION (1789–1820)

GENERAL VIEW

The period of the Revolution and the Empire was a time of transition between the eighteenth and nineteenth centuries belonging entirely to neither, but on the whole more akin in spirit to the latter than to the former. It marks the great change which came over literature from the time when the *Encyclopédie* still voiced the prevailing modes of thought and intellectual ideals, to the full outburst of the new art in the Romantic movement.

The distance traversed in this short time was great, and such rapid ripening and development of the germs of change would only have been possible in a time when the foundations of all institutions, and of society itself, were shaken, and men's minds correspondingly loosened from the bonds of old tradition and prejudice, and opened for the reception of new ideas.

We have seen that the *philosophes* and Encyclopedists of the eighteenth century, while questioning all merely traditional authority in religion and politics, remained on the whole fairly conventional in matters of literature. It was the task of the writers of the transition period of which we now speak to point out new ideals more in keeping with the times, and to pave the way for the great literary revolution which was to follow, while going a considerable part of the way themselves.

The two great names are those of **Madame de Staël** and **Chateaubriand,** who, though working along different lines, had very much in common, and in their different ways furthered the same tendency.

Madame de Staël, by directing the attention of her countrymen to the literatures of other lands, and above all to that of Germany, suggested a wider outlook, and struck the first note of that cosmopolitanism which was one of the proudest boasts of the Romantic school. She first drew attention to the Northern literatures as being especially worthy of consideration, and pointed out the romanticism which is their essential characteristic. It is, moreover, noteworthy that she was the first to use the word Romantic in its literary sense, as the opposite of Classic. Romanticism she declared to be the natural and only really living spirit of the time, Classicism having no longer anything but a borrowed and unnatural existence. In her the revolt from eighteenth-century Classicism and the advent of the new movement are very clearly and directly expressed.

Chateaubriand's share in the common task was the necessary complement of that of Madame de Staël; as she defined the characteristics of the change and established its theory, so he furnished it with ideals, and gave inspiration to the youthful reformers who were to carry the movement to its final realization. Like her he attached the greatest importance to the literature of other countries, and his own writings range over the widest variety of subjects and scenes. He has been called the Father of Romanticism, and the title is applicable both in the general and in the particular, for he both promoted by his general influence the tendency of the rising literature, and furnished the source of the many different currents which flowed from that tendency.

CHAPTER I

POETRY

Whatever may be the intrinsic merits of **Jean Pierre de Béranger** as a poet, he deserves special notice as the champion of the popular and middle-class sentiment of his day. He was born at Paris in 1780. Despite the noble particle, he belonged to the lower middle class, a fact which he never attempted to conceal. After various experiences he occupied, during the years 1807–1821, the unpretentious office of *commis expéditionnaire* at the University, and his daily bread being now assured, he devoted himself whole-heartedly to the writing of his famous songs. The first collection was published in 1815. The second volume, which appeared in 1821, contained political allusions for which he was punished by the loss of his post, a fine, and three months' imprisonment; while the fourth volume, in 1828, was taken still more seriously by the authorities. These persecutions naturally only increased his credit with the people, and his popularity became truly immense; but though he received repeated offers of advancement during the rest of his life, he chose to remain a private citizen. His last years were spent in retirement, and he died at Paris in 1857.

With the exception of *Ma Biographie*, published posthumously, Béranger's work consists exclusively of *chansons* (1815–1833). Among the best known are *Le Roi d'Yvetot, Roger Bontemps, Ma Vocation, Mon Habit, Le Dieu des Bonnes Gens, Waterloo, Le Vieux Drapeau, Les Deux Grenadiers*.

These songs range over a wide variety of subjects and tones, from the merely gay and jovial, through the amatory and convivial to the *chanson* of political satire, and even to a kind of half-philosophical ballad.

In all, the ideas, and philosophy, if such it can be called, are of the cheapest and most clap-trap order—the outlook of the popular orator or the tap-room politician. Even such as they are, his ideas have no stability or consistence, his politics being an incongruous mixture of imperialism and republicanism, his religious belief (if the expression may be pardoned) for the most part a curious mixture of paganism and Christianity.

Yet though not an ideal teacher, Béranger had all the qualities that go to make a popular poet—a ready wit, a lively fancy, force and directness of expression, and a happy knack of verse and rhyme which, though in fact the result of very great art and no little labour, has an air of perfect naturalness and spontaneity. Moreover, he expressed directly the views, if not of the people itself, of the great bourgeois majority of France, with its love for the *petite pointe* even at the expense of the idea, its essentially commonplace thought, its malicious fun, and lack of all real reverence—all traits of the *esprit gaulois*.

In a way he deserved his popularity, and in his day he was more popular even than the great leader of the Romantic school himself, for he was an artist in his kind. No one has ever understood better than he how to get the full value out of the refrain, no one better the secret of giving to each stanza its own individuality, no one better how to write the *chanson* of dramatic action.

CHAPTER II

DRAMA

The only dramatist of any consequence in this period is Casimir Delavigne (1793-1843), who enjoyed considerable reputation in his day, but who has not been kindly treated by time, his work appearing to us to-day unnatural and of little merit. As a poet he made himself famous with his *Messéniennes*, published in 1818, verse satires upon the Restoration, in which he celebrates liberty, and bewails the degradation and misfortunes of France. The best of his many plays are the *Vêpres Siciliennes* (1819), *Marino Faliero* (1829), *Louis XI*, produced in 1832, and *Les Enfants d'Édouard* (1833).

Delavigne was a writer of little originality, albeit of considerable technical skill, who wavered between Classicism and Romanticism, and possessed none of the best qualities of either. He was incapable of appreciating the sobriety and simplicity of the older art, and for the warmth and colour of the newer art he substituted commonplace rhetorical devices and exaggerated declamation.

CHAPTER III

PROSE

First in the list of great names of the period stands that of a famous woman-writer, **Madame de Staël**.

Anne Louise Germaine Necker (**Madame de Staël**) was born at Paris in 1766, the only child of a rich banker. She early gave proof of wonderful gifts, and at the age of eleven made the acquaintance in her mother's *salon* of some of the most distinguished men of the day. She showed marvellous precociousness; while still a mere child she read many English and French works, but devoted herself above all to Rousseau, with a critical essay upon whom she made her literary *début*.

At the age of twenty she married the Baron de Staël Holstein, the Swedish ambassador at Versailles, but the marriage, which lasted sixteen years, was not a happy one. She sympathized with the Revolution in its beginnings, but after the massacres of 1792, fled to her father's castle at Coppet, on the banks of the Lake of Geneva. Under the Directory she returned, but became suspect, and in 1803 received the order to leave Paris. She set off for Germany, and arrived at Weimar, where she charmed and was charmed by the brilliant literary society there, only leaving Weimar for Coppet to attend the deathbed of her father. In 1807 she paid a second visit to Germany, and it was after this that she wrote the greatest of her books, *De l'Allemagne*, published in 1813 by John Murray in England, where she was temporarily seeking a refuge. After the fall of Napoleon in 1814 she returned to Paris, and received a hearty welcome. The return of Napoleon again drove her from Paris, but she once more returned and died there, in 1817.

Her principal works are: *De la Littérature considérée dans ses Rapports avec les Institutions Sociales* (1800), *Delphine* (1802), *Corinne* (1807), *De l'Allemagne* (1810); and the unfinished *Considérations sur la Révolution Française*, published posthumously in 1818.

In *De la Littérature* she lays down principles of literary criticism in its relation to the laws and institutions of society. Literature, being intimately bound up with society, must change with it, and hence the great masterpieces of the past, however much we may admire them—and she expresses the warmest admiration for Racine and Corneille—are no longer suitable or possible models for the writers of to-day. Among the first, too, she points to the Northern and Germanic peoples as a source of inspiration for her generation—a message taken up and developed later in her greater work, *De l'Allemagne*.

Her two novels, *Delphine* (1802) and *Corinne* (1807), both present the author herself in different guises and situations, and both show the liberty of the individual in conflict with the fetters and restraints of society.

Delphine loves Léonce, who, though he returns her love, yet, under the pressure of convention and the persuasion of his family, marries Mathilde, to whom he is betrothed, but for whom he has no love. The novel develops the various miseries which are the consequences of this loveless marriage and of a true and genuine passion thwarted by the conventionalities of civilization.

The subject of *Corinne* is very much of the same nature, and treats of the barrier raised by false convention between the gifted and great-souled Corinne and the young Scottish noble, Lord Nelvil, whom she loves and who loves her in return, but who from selfish and worldly motives contracts a marriage of convenience with another woman. Fame is powerless to console the brilliant Corinne for her loss, and she dies of a broken heart.

The great and lasting work, however, on which her reputation depends is *De l'Allemagne* (1810). It consists of four parts, namely:—*De l'Allemagne et des mœurs des Allemands, De la littérature et des arts, La philosophie et la morale, La religion et l'enthousiasme.*

The first part bears in a more direct and concrete way on the nature of the country and the manners and habits of its people, showing the relation between the national character and literature, while in the second this direct consideration of the literature is carried still further. The third and fourth books treat of more abstract matters, pointing out the general principles and the great currents of German literature and thought, and establishing the essential characteristics of the Romanticism which it represents. Here, for the first time, the word Romantic was employed in a literary sense in opposition to Classic, and in the famous passage in which she expresses this we see formulated for the first time also the ideas which were eventually to result in the great Romantic movement in France. She says: "*La littérature romantique est la seule qui puisse croître et se vivifier de nouveau: elle exprime notre religion, elle rappelle notre histoire: son origine est ancienne mais non antique. Les poésies d'après l'antique sont rarement populaires, parcequ'elles ne tiennent dans le temps actuel à rien de national* ... *La littérature des anciens chez les modernes est une littérature transplantée, la littérature romantique ou chevaleresque est chez nous indigène, et c'est notre religion et nos institutions qui l'ont fait éclore.*"

In thus substituting a new ideal for the old classical one Madame de Staël breaks away completely from the eighteenth century, and prepares the way for that wider cosmopolitan conception of literature which was the ideal of the Romantic school, and in the birth and first beginnings of which lies the importance of the writers of the transition period. By thus widening the literary horizon, and creating the feeling of a larger intellectual fellowship, Madame de Staël rendered incalculable service.

The *Considérations sur la Révolution*, which was left unfinished at her death, is more directly concerned with the political than with the literary side of her activity. Though with the best and most humane of intentions, Madame de Staël is so hampered by class prejudice, and a kind of legislative liberalism, which sees in the application of a suitable constitution the only remedy for the curing of all social ills, that she fails to appreciate duly the Revolution with its deep underlying currents and workings. Yet the book is not without merit, and is still to-day of value for students of that eventful period.

It may safely be said that Madame de Staël is one of the most important women-writers the world has ever seen. Gifted as she was with an unbounded and many-sided enthusiasm, it was her mission to convince others of the things which she herself apprehended with such clearness and so much foresight. Endowed with a wonderful personality and great conversational powers, she exercised no less influence through the many men of distinction with whom she came in personal contact than by her writings. In opening up the wonderful treasure of German literature and thought, she conferred a great and lasting benefit on her country.

The new ideas and the theory of art defined by Mme de Staël were realized by **François René de Chateaubriand.**

Chateaubriand was born in 1768 at St. Malo in Brittany, as the tenth child of one of the most ancient families of the country. He was allowed to grow up, without much supervision or education, among the rude fisher-folk of his native place, and this free natural life had not a little to do with the character of his future work. For a short time he served as an ensign; in 1791 he went to America, but returned to France on hearing of the flight of Louis XVI, and joined the *émigrés*.

After being wounded at the siege of Thionville, he passed over to England, where in 1797 he published his *Essai sur les Révolutions*. He returned to France in 1800, and in 1801 published

Atala, which established once for all his literary position. In 1806 and 1807 he travelled in Greece, Palestine, and Egypt.

For a time he had been an admirer of Napoleon, and Napoleon would have been only too glad of his help in his endeavours to reinstate Christianity, but Chateaubriand definitively left him after the judicial murder of the Duc d'Enghien. With the Restoration, he became a warm supporter of the monarchy, and was raised to high honours. Into the many vicissitudes of his later political career it is impossible to enter. That his rapid and rather puzzling changes were due to change of conviction rather than to mere time-serving is, however, probable. He said of himself that he was "*Bourbonien par honneur, royaliste par raison et par conviction, républicain par goût et par caractère*". He died in 1848, and was buried at his birthplace.

His principal works are the *Essai sur les Révolutions* (1797), *Atala* (1801), *Le Génie du Christianisme* (1802), *René* (1805), *Les Martyrs* (1809), *Itinéraire de Paris à Jérusalem* (1811), *Les Natchez* (1826); and the *Mémoires d'Outre-Tombe*, which appeared partly before and partly after his death.

Chateaubriand's first literary venture, the *Essai sur les Révolutions*, published in England in 1797, is remarkable in that the ideas it expresses are the exact opposite of his later creed. The work is impregnated with pessimism and scepticism—a fact which is not so much to be wondered at when one reflects that the book was written when the author was a fugitive in London, poor, ill, disappointed, and wellnigh desperate. However, hardly was the work published when he turned round, influenced by the letters of a dead mother and sister: "*Les deux voix sorties du tombeau m'ont frappé: je suis devenu chrétien, j'ai pleuré et j'ai cru.*" This sentiment of religion, rather a sweet dream than a belief founded upon or requiring proofs, was for the rest of his life, with the royalism with which it was so closely connected, his faith and profession.

Moreover, hardly had he published his *Essai* than he set about its refutation in the *Génie du Christianisme*. From this he detached and published in 1801 *Atala*, a kind of prose poem, an episode from the mass of his American impressions and reminiscences, which had a great and immediate success, and established his literary reputation. He himself describes it as " *une sorte de poème moitié descriptif, moitié dramatique. J'ai essayé de donner à cet ouvrage les formes les plus antiques.*" The story tells how a young Indian, Chactas, who had fallen into the hands of a hostile tribe, is saved by an Indian girl, Atala. Each conceives for the other a passionate love, and Atala, feeling herself incapable of accomplishing the vow she made to her dying mother to devote herself to the service of the Virgin, poisons herself. The scenes which describe the wanderings of the lovers through the forests, and the adventures and dangers they encounter, show very great narrative skill and descriptive beauty.

The *Génie du Christianisme ou Beautés de la Religion Chrétienne* (1802) was intended before all to prove—to quote once more the author's own words—that " *de toutes les religions qui ont jamais existé, la religion chrétienne est la plus poétique, la plus humaine, la plus favorable à la liberté, aux arts et aux lettres; que le monde moderne lui doit tout, depuis l'agriculture jusqu'aux sciences abstraites, depuis les hospices pour les malheureux jusqu'aux temples bâtis par Michel-Ange et décorés par Raphaël . . . qu'elle favorise le génie, offre des formes nobles à l'écrivain, et des moules parfaits à l'artiste . . .*". Such is the vast design which the author proposes to himself, and we shall see how he carries it out. The work is divided into four parts: *Des Dogmes et de la Doctrine, Poétique du Christianisme, Beaux Arts et Littérature, Culte*.

The first part reviews the dogmas of a number of religions. In the second and third parts he compares Christianity with other religions from the artistic and poetic point of view, showing how sentiments and emotions have been raised by it to a higher plane; poetry, science, and art ennobled—how superior the Bible is to Homer, the characters of the Biblical patriarchs to those of the pagan heroes.

In the last part, *Culte*, he points out the beautiful and poetic character of the ceremonies of the Christian religion—its prayers, masses, processions, and the beauty of many of the buildings, churches and tombs, which are directly due to its influence.

What then was the value of this Christianity of Chateaubriand? Plainly he puts his main defence on no very high religious grounds, laying, as he does, more stress on its value as a poetic instrument than as a religion in the true sense. Sentiment plays too great, and reasoned argument too small a part. A contemporary well describes it in the words: " Le Génie du Christianisme *est un maître livre, mais par le sentiment qui y est fort, non par les raisons qui y sont faibles.*" The defence is, that an apology so conceived, though too sentimental and too little reasoned for our critical days, was the best and only suitable form under the circumstances in which it was written.

But whatever its value in other respects may be, the *Génie du Christianisme* will always mark an important date in the history of letters.

René was first published with the *Génie du Christianisme* in 1802, but afterwards appeared separately in 1805. It is the portrait not of a character but of a temperament, of the vague melancholy known as " *le mal du siècle* ", which had been already portrayed by Goethe in *Werther*, by Byron, and by Rousseau. As well as being a manifestation of a mode of thought of the period, *René* is a history of Chateaubriand's own inner life, of the indefinite fears and aspirations, and unmotived melancholy of the man who said that he had " *bâillé sa vie* ".

The story of René and his sister Amélie is in the essential the story of Chateaubriand's own youth, when he roamed the forests of his native country with his sister Lucile. René never knew his mother, and early loses his father. The only human being with whom he is happy is his sister. She saves him from many dangers, and even from suicide; but when she at length retires into a convent he seeks to forget his grief in the forests of the New World, where he joins a tribe of Indians, the Natchez. An old man, Chactas, becomes a father and confessor to him, and relates the story of his life, including the part already told in *Atala*.

In *Les Natchez* Chateaubriand later recounts the death of René.

Les Natchez, which did not appear till 1826, but of which we will speak in this connection, is divided into two parts, of which the first is a prose epic in twelve cantos, the second a prose novel.

The historical background is the destruction of a French colony in Louisiana by Indians in 1727, and the punishment of the Indians by the French. In the first part he introduces all kinds of personages of heaven and hell, the guardian angel of America, Satan, and even allegorical figures, Renown, &c. The work is full of weird and grotesque traits and unnatural imagery, and on the whole is somewhat of a failure, being only redeemed by an air of savage beauty and simplicity, and by the wonderful truth and picturesqueness of many of its descriptive passages.

Les Martyrs (1809) is important as being an attempt on the author's part to carry into execution the literary principles which he had laid down in the *Génie*. *Les Martyrs ou Triomphe de la Religion Chrétienne* is a large prose epic in twenty-four cantos.

The subject is the persecution of the Christians in the time of Diocletian, in the beginning of the fourth century A.D. Eudore, a noble Greek, loves Cymodocée, the daughter of a priest of Homer, and she is converted in order to marry him. Eudore, who after his return to Rome has made himself conspicuous by his Christian zeal, is condemned to die in the arena, where at the last moment Cymodocée joins him, and they die together. A cross of light and thunder announce that the persecutions are at an end.

The work, which was written with the purpose of demonstrating a theory—a fact which we are in no danger of forgetting—contains, along with the beauties of style and of natural description which are always to be associated with the author's name, much that is merely formal and insipid, much that is exaggerated and unreal. The influence of Milton is strongly marked—we are given views of heaven and hell, of God and Satan, angels and demons. As an epic it has many shortcomings; there is too much that is merely conventional, and more that is not true to the epic spirit, faults which cannot be fully compensated by the beauties of description and the excellence of certain episodes.

L'Itinéraire de Paris à Jérusalem (1811) gives the story of Chateaubriand's journey to the Holy Land by way of Greece, and the return through Egypt, Barbary, and Spain, undertaken after he had broken with Napoleon in disgust at the murder of the Duc d'Enghien. Here we see the author at his best; the varied and interesting countries which he visited, the old-world customs of the peoples, the legends and historical associations of the different places seen, called forth as no other scenes could have done his remarkable powers as a master of eloquent and picturesque prose.

Lastly, we must mention the *Mémoires d'Outre-Tombe*, which was not to appear till after his death, but of which he was compelled by pecuniary difficulties to sell the rights during his lifetime, or, as he put it, to " *hypothéquer sa tombe* ", in consequence of which a part actually appeared before his death. Written in the last period of his life, during which he remained aloof from politics and loyal to the legitimate monarchy, these memoirs abound in eloquent and touching passages, but are dominated and marred by his excessive self-appreciation and sensitive, almost morbid, pride.

Chateaubriand exercised on the literature of the beginning of the nineteenth century an ascendancy only paralleled by that of Madame de Staël. He has been justly called " the last of the Classicists and the first of the Romanticists ". Like Madame de Staël he drew the attention of his fellow-countrymen to foreign literatures, and so anticipated what was, if not the practice, at any rate the profession of the Romantic school. By the importance which he attached to the *ego*, by his sentimentalism and self-questioning, he showed the path which modern lyricism was to pursue.

He wrote three works, each of which formed a school—a thing which could be said of few writers, and which of itself shows the wide range of his influence, apart from the question of the value of these works. To quote the words of Théophile Gautier: " *Dans le* Génie du Christianisme, *il restaura la cathédrale gothique*; *dans* Les Natchez, *il rouvrit la grande nature fermée; dans* René, *il inventa la mélancolie et la passion moderne.*"

It is not as a thinker that he is pre-eminent in the annals of French literature; he deals too much in sentiment, and not infrequently false sentiment, and lapses occasionally into exaggerations prompted by his fervid imagination. Where his genius is best displayed is in the glowing diction of his descriptive writings, in which he surpasses even his masters, Rousseau and Bernardin de St. Pierre; in the majestic language in which he speaks of some of the great and noble enthusiasms of life, and which acted like a trumpet call and an inspiration to the young and impressionable leaders of the Romantic school. On them Chateaubriand's ascendancy can be traced, not in one style or in one direction alone, but in the most comprehensive fashion.

> The influence of Rousseau and of Chateaubriand combined in the writings of **Étienne de Sénancour** (1770–1846), whose fame rests securely on *Obermann* (1804), a romance in epistolary form, in which the hero expresses so effectively the desolating *maladie du siècle*, that disgust of life before having lived, of which Rousseau may be called the creator.

A writer who made up in quality for lack of quantity is **Joseph Joubert** (1754–1824). He had a most peculiar literary career, if the term may be used of one whose literary labours were not known till after his death. He was born in Perigord, but at the age of twenty-two came to Paris, and went through all the terrors of the Revolution. At Paris he spent most of the remainder of his life, in correspondence and personal intercourse with many men of letters, and was well known for his criticisms of the writings of others, though he put forward nothing of his own.

It was not till 1838, fourteen years after his death, that his friend Chateaubriand issued a volume of *Pensées*, collected from the papers he had left behind, which at once established his reputation as one of the greatest writers of *pensées* of the world, worthy to rank beside even Pascal and La Rochefoucauld. They are remarkable for their wide range, embracing theology, politics, social questions, and ethics, as well as literature; and still more for their wonderful condensation of thought, which is attained without obscurity or any sacrifice of style. His *Pensées* are the product of a cultured mind which was happily capable of matching refinement and delicacy of thought with equal refinement and delicacy of expression.

A hatred of all new ideas, and of the institutions called forth by the Revolution, is the key-note of the work of **Joseph de Maistre** (1753–1821), born at Chambéry, a son of the President of the Senate of Savoy. When Savoy became French in 1792 he withdrew to Lausanne, and there wrote his first treatise of importance, the *Considérations sur la France*. From 1802 to 1817 he lived at St. Petersburg as minister of the King of Sardinia. In 1817 he returned to Turin, and died there in 1821.

His chief works are *Considérations sur la France* (1796), *Du Pape* (1819), *De l'Église Gallicane* (1820), and the uncompleted *Soirées de St. Pétersbourg*, in the same year. All his writings are dominated by one guiding idea—the most absolute ultramontanism, that is to say, the theory which sees in the Pope the only final and supreme source of all earthly power, while temporal princes only hold a certain degree of authority as his deputies. In this logical uniformity he sought the remedy for all the strife and complexities of civilized life, and for what the idea was worth he supported it with exceptional argumentative force. Paradoxical he was in a great degree, and few will agree with his fundamental principle, but none can deny his very remarkable powers of close and consistent reasoning, which remind one of the best traditions of the eighteenth century in this its finest quality.

The same doctrines, though in a different way, were set forth by the **Vicomte de Bonald** (1754–1840), to whom Joseph de Maistre could write: " *Je n'ai rien pensé que vous ne l'ayez écrit; je n'ai rien écrit que vous ne l'ayez pensé.*"

His principal writings, composed in a firm and vigorous style, are *La Théorie du Pouvoir Civil et Religieux* (1796), and *La Législation Primitive* (1802), in which his views are summed up.

Another polemical writer of note is **Benjamin Constant** (1767–1830), who led the liberals in politics and religion. His ideal was a government strong enough to protect the individual, yet sufficiently limited not to be able to oppress him. But his fame, in literature at all events, rests on *Adolphe* (1816), the only great psychological novel of the century before Stendhal, in which the hero is none other than Constant himself, and the heroine, Ellénore, is perhaps Madame de Charrière, of Neuchâtel.

Joseph's brother, **Xavier de Maistre** (1763–1852), a soldier who served in his youth in the Piedmontese, and later in the Russian army, wrote simple tales and sketches which attained, and still hold, a certain reputation. The *Voyage autour de ma Chambre* (1794), most charming of all, written when the author, then a young officer, was confined to his room during six weeks for some trifling offence, tells how he whiled away the monotony by making the tour of his room, looking at every object with new eyes, and making the commonplace and familiar things around him serve as the theme for remarks and reflections of the most delicate and charming fancy. His other best-known tales are *La Jeune Sibérienne* and *Le Lépreux de la Cité d'Aoste*, in both of which a simple and touching story is told in a delightfully naïve way.

For brilliancy and scathing irony the first place among French pamphleteers is occupied by **Paul Louis Courier** (1772–1825), born in Paris, the son of a wealthy bourgeois, and educated at the *Collège de France* and a military academy. He was a passionate student of Greek literature, to which he devoted himself both at school and at the academy to which he afterwards passed. He had a great distaste for business, and as his father would not hear of letters as a profession, he entered the army in 1793, and served on and off for seventeen years. After the battle of Wagram, in which he was severely wounded, he finally abandoned the Service, and devoted himself entirely to literature, which had been all through his life his only real interest. For a time he lived in Florence, where the accidental blotting of a page in a manuscript of Longus led to the *Lettre à M. Renouard* (1810), which first revealed his literary powers. In 1814 he settled on his small estate in Touraine, occupying himself with its management and with vine culture, and lived there, with frequent visits to Paris, for the remainder of his life. In 1825 he was shot a few yards from his house by a farm hand whom he had dismissed from his service.

Courier's best-known writings are the *Lettre à M. Renouard*, already mentioned; *Pétition aux deux Chambres* (1816), in which he describes the wrongs and grievances of the peasants; *Lettre à Messieurs de l'Académie des Inscriptions et Belles Lettres* (1819), the wittiest and most brilliant of all his productions, in which he castigates that learned body for having preferred to him in their last election a man whose only merit was noble birth; a series of *Pamphlets* addressed to his fellow villagers, and signed " Paul Louis Vigneron ", among which the most famous is his *Simple Discours*, published in 1821, protesting against the subscription raised to present the castle of Chambord to the Duc de Bordeaux, and which brought him a couple of months' imprisonment. His private letters are delightful.

All his typical writings were in short pamphlet form. He neither wrote nor attempted a greater work in any of the more serious forms of literary composition. The man who started life as a pure *bellelettrist*, as a passionate lover of Greek literature, was turned by force of circumstances and by the chicanery of politics into a journalist, and the most considerable of his time. Beginning with a strong fund of Voltairianism, as a liberal *bourgeois* of the old school, he became after the Restoration what we might call a professional oppositionist.

Brought up on the beauty and simplicity of his beloved Greek, and steeped in the great writings of the classical literature of his own land, this pamphleteer was, however, something more. His thought is narrow, his ideas are one-sided and never far-reaching, but in finish of expression and incisive argument he has rarely been surpassed. He excels in staging his effects; he understands perfectly how to put each thought in its most telling form. Add to this, that in irony he has had few superiors and not many equals, that he is a master of the sly comic spirit which delights in sudden and unexpected sallies, and that over all is shed a certain subtle suggestion of archaism which is not without its charm, and we shall understand the delight with which he was read by his contemporaries and is still read to-day.

One of the most original writers of the day was **Félicité de Lamennais,** a poet in prose, and the earliest preacher of what has since been called " Christian socialism ". Born at St. Malo in 1782, after an irregular education he became first of all a schoolmaster, and later a priest. From 1817 to 1823 appeared his *Essai sur l'Indifférence*, which at once made him a marked man. In 1830 he started a paper, *L'Avenir*, with the motto " *Dieu et Liberté* " which sums up his ideas, but it was censured by Gregory XVI, and suspended in the following year. Starting as an Ultramontane, he gradually drifted farther and farther away, disgusted to find material interests preponderating even in Rome itself, and eventually rejected orthodoxy completely. He died, without being reconciled to the Church, in 1854.

Lamennais is even more important for the history of religious thought than for the history of literature, but at the same time his two most significant works, the *Essai sur l'Indifférence en Matière de Religion* (1817-1823) and the *Paroles d'un Croyant* (1834), are of great literary merit.

He began his career very much as Joseph De Maistre had done, but with the difference that while De Maistre lays greater stress on the temporal power of the Papacy and based social and political uniformity on complete submission to its authority, Lamennais seeks from the same unquestioned supremacy religious uniformity and peace. This is the subject of the *Essai*, in which he argues the necessity, for the sake of unity, of renouncing private opinion and judgment, and regarding the one will as infallible.

Profoundly disappointed in his high conception of papal aims and methods, he denied all spiritual authority in his embitterment, and in the *Paroles d'un Croyant* proclaimed in impassioned and eloquent words, and in a wonderful rhythmical diction, nearer akin to poetry than prose, a kind of natural religion outside all formulas and creeds.

Lamennais was an enthusiast, and for that very reason apt to rush to extremes. He demanded perfection from those who were for the time being the object of his passionate devotion, and when the inevitable disappointment followed, was equally impassioned in his disgust and condemnation. He made the mistake of judging causes by their representatives, of confounding persons and ideas. Yet most of his faults were founded on true nobility of purpose, and there is much that is great in this dreamer of dreams.

BOOK VI
NINETEENTH CENTURY

GENERAL VIEW

The nineteenth century is the time of a great revival in French literature, known as the **Romantic Movement,** a kind of second Renaissance, in which, after a period of preparation, there appeared a number of men of great and varied genius, whose united labours resulted in the production of a body of literature remarkable alike in quality, quantity, and range. After Romanticism had held undisputed sway during the first part of the century, there arose in the latter half a second movement, known as **Realism,** which in its later and exaggerated phase was styled **Naturalism.** Lastly, during the last two decades of the century, a third movement developed known as **Symbolism,** a reaction against Naturalism, felt chiefly in poetry, and which by the end of the century had ceased to be an active force.

First Period (1820 c.–1850 c.). — **Romanticism,** of which the first germs are to be traced back to the eighteenth century, and which during the period of transition had been slowly gaining ground, declared itself in the third decade of the nineteenth century, and by 1830 was firmly established.

We must examine what was the nature of this revolution and what is understood by the term Romantic literature. To give a short comprehensive definition is impossible, for it possesses many more negative than positive features, and was by no means understood by all its adherents in one clearly defined and indisputable sense. We shall then have to speak of its general traits and also of its negations, rather than to lay down a hard and logical definition.

Romanticism was, as has been already said, largely negative, consisting in the rejection of the classical creed and a breaking up of the bonds under which classical literature laboured. It demanded greater freedom in all branches, a greater recognition of the personal element, more play for the individual imagination, a more lyrical spirit in general. Its reforms bore on all branches of the literary art—subject, language, and form.

In subject it demanded the right to represent not only the beautiful, which was solely admissible under the strictly classical canon, but also the ugly and even the repulsive, claiming by the contrast, by this duality in art, to obtain a closer presentation of the many-sidedness of actual life.

Thus, in the preface to *Cromwell*, the great manifesto of the Romanticists, which appeared in 1827, **Victor Hugo** says: "*Tout dans la création n'est pas humainement beau, le laid y existe à côté du beau, le difforme près du gracieux, le grotesque au revers du sublime, le mal avec le bien, l'ombre avec la lumière*"; and he goes on to say that romantic poetry "*se mettra à faire comme la nature, à mêler dans ses créations . . . l'ombre à la lumière, le grotesque au sublime*".

Not only did they vindicate the right of taking up any subjects, but they also chose their subjects from the most varied sources and regarded the whole universe as their legitimate field. They chose by preference unfamiliar places and people for their themes, and endeavoured at the same time to render faithfully the local colour of such places and peoples. On this they laid the greatest stress: "*On commence à comprendre de nous jours que la localité exacte est un des premiers éléments de la réalité. . . . Le lieu où telle catastrophe s'est pàssée en devient un témoin terrible et inséparable . . . .*"[1]

[1] Victor Hugo, Preface to *Cromwell*.

To the importance of foreign literatures attention had already been called by the two great authors of the Transition, Madame de Staël and Chateaubriand. The lesson they had taught was taken to heart by the Romanticists, who prided themselves on their acquaintance not only with the great names of the great literatures, not only with Shakespeare, Goethe, Schiller, and Byron, but also with less famous names and with the literatures of more obscure nations. In keeping with the great importance attached to modern foreign literatures at the expense of the classics was the substitution of medieval and Christian art for pagan mythology. This tendency had received a great impulse from the numerous translations of foreign works, and from the collections of popular songs and studies on medieval literature and manners, published during the first thirty years of the century.[1]

In language the reform aimed at was also considerable; in place of the classical formality and simplicity they sought to obtain the highest possible degree of colour and brilliancy, using every freedom in treatment, daring contrast and antithesis, and startling turns of expression. Not least revolutionary was their vocabulary itself; the classical exclusiveness and selectness disappeared, and words of every sort and description were employed with the most supreme and joyous exuberance. Of this side of the reform Victor Hugo speaks in the *Réponse à un Acte d'Accusation*:[2]

> *Les mots, bien ou mal nés, vivaient parqués en castes;*
> *Les uns, nobles, hantant les Phèdres, les Jocastes,*
> *Les Méropes, ayant le décorum pour loi,*
> *Et montant à Versailles aux carrosses du roi;*
> *Les autres, tas de gueux, drôles patibulaires,*
> *Habitant les patois; quelques-uns aux galères,*

---

[1] The following is a list in chronological order of the most important of these works: (1809) Schiller's *Wallenstein*, translated by B. Constant; (1816–1821) Raynouard, *Choix de Poésies Originales des Troubadours*; (1821) translation of Shakespeare by Guizot; (1822–1825) translation of Byron by Pichot; (1823) translation of Manzoni's tragedies by Fauriel; (1825) Lœve-Veimars, *Ballades, Légendes et Chants Populaires de l'Angleterre et de l'Écosse*; (1828) translations of *Faust* by Nodier and Gérard de Nerval; (1829) of *La Divine Comédie de Dante* by A. Deschamps.

[2] *Contemplations*, vol. i, 7.

> *Dans l'argot; dévoués à tous les genres bas;*
> *Déchirés en haillons, dans les halles; sans bas,*
> *Sans perruque; créés pour la prose ou la farce;*
> *Populace du style, au fond de l'ombre éparse;*
> *Vilains, rustres, croquants, que Vaugelas leur chef*
> *Dans le bagne Lexique avait marqués d'une F;*
> . . . .
> *Alors, brigand, je vins; je m'écriai: " Pourquoi*
> *Ceux-ci toujours devant, ceux-là toujours derrière?"*
> *Et sur l'académie aïeule et douairière,*
> *Cachant sous ses jupons les tropes effarés*
> *Et sur les bataillons d'alexandrins carrés,*
> *Je fis souffler un vent révolutionnaire,*
> *Je mis un bonnet rouge au vieux dictionnaire.*

Though the change in this respect was not wholly beneficial, and the new-found liberty was rather apt to be carried to excess and to lead to a motley confusion in vocabulary, yet in so far as it drove out conventionality and meaningless paraphrase by the use of the *mot propre* it conferred a priceless boon on the language.

This use of the *mot propre*[1] was one of the things on which the Romanticists prided themselves, and V. Hugo boasts of it in the already-mentioned poem:

> . . . . *Le mot propre ce rustre*
> *N'était que caporal, je l'ai fait colonel.*
> . . . .
> *Je nommai le cochon par son nom; pourquoi pas?*
> . . . .
> *On entendit un roi dire: Quelle heure est-il?*

To form they devoted no less attention. In drama the Unities were severely examined, those of Time and Place being rejected emphatically: " *Croiser l'unité de temps à l'unité*

---

[1] In order to avoid the hated *mot propre* writers, and more especially the pseudo-classicists of the eighteenth century, had resorted to the most absurd circumlocutions; Belloy in the tragedy *Le Siège de Calais* (1765), wishing to inform the audience that the besieged had been reduced to eating rats and dogs, expresses himself as follows:

> *Le plus vil aliment, rebut de la misère,*
> *Mais, aux derniers abois, ressource horrible et chère,*
> *De la fidélité respectable soutien,*
> *Manque à l'or prodigue du riche citoyen.*

de lieu comme les barreaux d'une cage, et y faire pédantesquement entrer, de par Aristote, tous ces faits, tous ces peuples, toutes ces figures que la providence déroule à si grandes masses dans la réalité! c'est mutiler hommes et choses, c'est faire grimacer l'histoire!" [1] The third, the unity of Action, is as important as the others are harmful: " *Celle-là est aussi nécessaire que les deux autres sont inutiles. C'est elle qui marque le point de vue du drame.*" [1]

In the structure of the verse the tendency is all towards freer and more supple rhythmical combinations, a more daring use of *enjambement*, not only between line and line, but also between one stanza and the next, and a less rigid application of the cæsura, which, instead of being placed uniformly in the middle of the Alexandrine, was variously shifted in such a way as to break the monotonous pendulum-like action of the classical standard verse, one pronounced type being the employment of the double cæsura in such a way as to secure the frankly ternary line. As Victor Hugo says:[2]

Nous faisons basculer la balance hémistiche.
. . . . . . Le vers, qui sur son front
Jadis portait toujours douze plumes en rond,
Et sans cesse sautait sur sa double raquette,
Qu'on nomme prosodie et qu'on nomme étiquette,
Rompt désormais la règle et trompe le ciseau,
Et s'échappe, volant qui se change en oiseau,
De la cage césure . . .

Rhyme, " *cette esclave-reine, cette suprême grâce de notre poésie, ce générateur de notre mètre* ",[3] they endeavoured to render full and rich by identifying it with a really significant word in the verse.

The opening in earnest of the Romantic campaign dates from 1820, in which year appeared the *Méditations* of **Lamartine,** followed in 1822 by the *Odes* of Victor Hugo. About the time of the appearance of the *Odes* was formed the society of young authors known as the **Cénacle,** the members of which

[1] V. Hugo, Preface to *Cromwell*.   [2] *Réponse à un Acte d'Accusation*.
[3] Preface to *Cromwell*.

had, however, as yet no definitely polemical purpose. At length in 1827 Victor Hugo, in the resounding Preface to *Cromwell*, flung down the Romantic challenge, and established himself as the natural leader of the movement. The *Orientales* (1829) furnished a brilliant justification of the theories of the *Préface*, and with the representation of *Hernani* on the stage of the *Théâtre Français* in 1830 the important vantage-ground of the theatre was won and the reform accomplished.

Beginning with the *belles lettres*, Romanticism was extended first of all to the drama, and from that to the other literary forms. Still its strongest point was the lyric, while the predominant characteristic of the whole movement was throughout lyrical.

The poetry of the Romantic period shows a wonderful wealth, an unrivalled lyrical outburst of song. One man, **Théophile Gautier,** with his motto of " art for art " and excessive attention to form, gives the earliest indication of the chief poetic school of the next period. The Drama is on the whole the weakest part of its work. The Novel develops extraordinary fertility and originality, while in three writers, and particularly in **Balzac,** we find the forerunners of that literary bent which has dominated the greater part of the latter half of the century. In history a striking revival takes place, which in quantity, quality, and solid worth so far surpasses all that had preceded, that French history may be practically dated from its achievements. Of Scientific Criticism the period furnishes the founder and greatest exponent in **Sainte-Beuve.**

Second Period (1850 c.–1885 c.).—Realism, Naturalism. The literature of the second half of the century shows a double reaction—that against Romanticism in the so-called Realism, followed in turn by a reaction against exaggerated Realism. The same trend appears towards the middle of the century in all parts of the literature in different forms, its general characteristics being a change from lyricism to positivism, from subjectivity to objectivity, from idealism to realism.

The personal note becomes less apparent, and in lieu of the romantic ideals truth and nature are removed to the centre of interest, and more importance is attached to facts. In short, the path followed is one that leads, on the whole, to a more prosaic conception of literature.

In poetry the reaction is represented by the group of poets known as the **Parnassiens,** after the collection of poems issued by them in 1866 under the title of *Parnasse Contemporain.* Inspired by Théophile Gautier, in whose poetry the transition from the personal to the impersonal is already observable, the *Parnassiens* took up the cry of " art for art "; they not only preserved the impersonal and realistic element, but strove for perfection of artistic form and greater precision in diction and rhyme. Almost from the beginning they branched off, however, in different directions; some, contrary to the tenets of the school, devoted themselves to the analysis of the emotions, while others sought inspiration in the life of the humbler classes.

In the Novel, the most important literary branch of the period, realism pursued the course already marked out in the previous period by Stendhal, Mérimée, and especially Balzac, its characteristics becoming more and more marked. The great novelist of this stage is **Flaubert.**

Towards 1870 another phase is entered upon with the so-called Naturalism, an exaggerated Realism, the main features of which are a linking of science and letters and the painstaking and professedly scientific analysis of repulsive and unwholesome subjects. The name with which this school is identified is that of **Zola.**

Third Period (beginning 1885 c.).—Finally, in the last years of the century a reaction set in against Naturalism itself. The positive aims of this movement are, however, not easy to determine.

In poetry, the new group is known as the **Décadents** or **Symbolistes,** and as far as their aims can be definitely stated at all, they are of a twofold nature, affecting both matter and form.

In matter they react against the unemotionalism, the *impassibilité* of the *Parnassiens*, and the scientific spirit of Naturalism, and endeavour to substitute for it vast but vague ideas on the emotions of the soul in contact with the unfathomable problems of life and being. The direction is, however, very undefined, and the prevailing tone is one of vagueness, obscurity, and occasionally eccentricity.

In form they protest against the plastic art of Gautier and the *Parnassiens*, with its preciseness of outline and sculptural hardness of form. They strive to bring poetry more into affinity with music [1] than painting, and so leave more room for the vague, the dreamy, and the mystical. The theme by them is often treated as a symbol, which may suggest some idea to the esoteric enthusiast, but gives little direct impression to the uninitiated. At the same time they continue the breaking up of the line which Victor Hugo had begun. In the Alexandrine the last traces of regularity in the use of the cæsura vanish; new combinations are attempted, sometimes what appears to be an arbitrary mixture of long and short measures, the so-called *vers libre*, or a sort of half-way form between poetry and prose.

Incomparably the greatest among them is **Verlaine**, a true poet in spite of himself, and who on the whole remained free from the extravagances of the school which claimed him as its chief.

In the Novel, Realism and Naturalism are both exhausted, and the only positive result that can be chronicled is the liberty in which each writer is left to pursue his own ideal in his own way. The only definite tendencies that can be observed are certain symptoms of neo-christianity and religious mysticism, and at the same time an interest in the supernatural and transcendental, the most important influence during the last two decades having been that received from foreign literatures, and above all from George Eliot, Tolstoi, and the Scandinavians Ibsen and Bjœrnson.

---

[1] Cp. Verlaine's *Art Poétique: De la musique avant toute chose.*

In the Theatre the day of Naturalism is no less over. The *Théâtre Libre*, founded to champion Naturalistic art, wearied the public with its dreary pessimism, and conscientious but monotonous exactitude of brutal detail; its only merit was that it set the fashion of truthfulness of representation and general *mise en scène*.

This third period may be said to end with the nineteenth century. Since then, until the present day, there has been no movement sufficiently strong to give the lead, or any genius great enough to gather around him what might be called a new school. In poetry diversity and independence reign supreme, in spite of certain small groups pursuing more or less identical aims. In the theatre, after the sensational success achieved by Rostand's romantic plays, Realism and Naturalism, albeit in a modified form, are again preponderant, while in fiction, which is extending its scope more and more, a still greater variety than in poetry, if that were possible, holds sway and riots. Thus, at the present day, though certain currents are discernible in the general dissolution, it is impossible to say whither they may lead ultimately.

FIRST PERIOD (1820–1850)

CHAPTER I

POETRY

The first decided note of the new movement was struck by **Alphonse de Lamartine**.

Lamartine was born at Mâcon, in Burgundy, in 1790, at the family home of Milly, whither his father, an officer and an ardent Royalist, had retired after the Terror, to which he nearly fell a victim. There, in a united domestic circle and in close touch with nature, he grew up amid influences which had much to do with forming his future poetical characteristics. He was first under the charge of a priest, and afterwards sent to different schools, none of them of the first quality, but left at fifteen, and for some years continued his own education both at home and on his travels in Italy and France, by a course of the most wide and varied reading. Like his father, an enthusiastic Royalist, he joined the Garde Royale on the fall of Napoleon, but soon left the Service. In 1820 he published the *Méditations*, which not only announced the new school, but won him very great fame and popularity. In 1821 he joined the diplomatic service, which took him in turn to Naples and Florence. In 1830 appeared his *Harmonies*, which led to his unanimous election to the Academy. Naturally Lamartine disapproved of the July Revolution,[1] and refusing to recognize the new order, set out on a tour to the East, visiting Greece, Syria, Palestine, and Arabia, the result being the production on his return of the *Voyage en Orient*. However, political life had irresistible attractions for him, and in 1833 he entered the Chamber. His *Histoire des Girondins* (1847) contributed greatly to the downfall of the July Monarchy, but after the outbreak of the revolution of 1848 he did much, as a member of the provisional government, to prevent excesses and preserve order. With the establishment of the Empire under Napoleon III, he retired from public life and devoted himself entirely to literary work. During the last part of his life he was greatly troubled by money difficulties, which compelled him to do much that was little better than literary hack work. Even thus, however, he could not meet his obligations, and had to be relieved by the charities of the nation and government. He died in 1869.

His principal works are: *Méditations Poétiques* (1820), *Nouvelles Méditations* (1823), *Harmonies Poétiques et Religieuses* (1830), *Voyage en Orient* (1835), *Jocelyn* (1836), *La Chute d'un Ange* (1838), *Recueillements Poétiques* (1839), *Histoire des Girondins* (1847), *Confidences* (1849), and *Nouvelles Confidences* (1851).

The first to appear of Lamartine's works, and the most important for the history of literature, was the *Méditations* in 1820, which alone would suffice to give him a leading position in the literature of the century These poems were the spontaneous expression of his most intimate thoughts and

---

[1] The Revolution by which, in 1830, the Bourbon dynasty was overthrown, Charles X forced to abdicate, and the Orleanist Louis Philippe, eldest son of the Duc d'Orlèans, known as Philippe Égalité, or the Citizen King, raised to the throne.

emotions, composed not with a view to literary effect, but under the necessity of giving shape and form to his own spiritual experiences, and it was this very spontaneity, this pure lyricism, which made them appeal so forcibly to their first readers. Their success and popularity were enormous; they came like a revelation to those who found here voiced what had so long been unconsciously present in their own hearts. It was the first step towards the literary revolution, and with it the lyrical character of Romanticism was once and for all established. But not only did the poet speak of the workings of his own soul, he touched also on nature, religion, and all the themes which are the natural domain of lyric art. Among the best known of these poems are *Le Lac*, *L'Automne*, *La Prière*, *Immortalité*. But true and admirable as is the inspiration of the *Méditations*, the language and form are by no means perfect. An amateur in poetry, as he called himself, Lamartine cared less for the manner than the matter of his lyrics, and the consequence is that we find many surface flaws—repetitions, technical faults and imperfections. And these failings unfortunately grow more pronounced in his later works. The *Nouvelles Méditations* (1823) and the *Harmonies* (1830) are a continuation of the same strain, only that, owing to the want of novelty as compared with the first outburst, the inferior spontaneity, and an increased faultiness of workmanship and manner, they produced, and still produce, a weaker and less favourable impression. Yet this modified praise must not be misunderstood, for they possess the great and original merits of the first *Méditations* if in a lesser degree, the *Harmonies* ranking after them as the author's second-best work. *Jocelyn* (1836), a kind of epic idyll written in Alexandrines, passes from the purely personal to the symbolic and human note. It is, like *La Chute d'un Ange* which followed it, a fragment, as it were, of a great epic on the spiritual destinies of mankind; but though the poet may have had vaguely the conception of such a work it was never carried into execution. *Jocelyn* is the story of a man who sacrifices his vocation, his ambitions, his heart's desires, whose whole life is a sacrifice, and who in this renunciation finds peace and rest. In *La Chute d'un Ange* (1838), renunciation is once more the theme. In *Jocelyn* we see the peasant's son who gives up his inheritance to provide his sister's dowry, and sacrifices his love to a sense of duty; while in the former poem the angel Cédar is represented as renouncing heaven itself, and consenting to live on earth for the love of Daïdha, a daughter of the giants. But the subject was not suited to Lamartine's genius, and the work, in spite of the beauty of certain passages, is on the whole a failure—often exaggerated and unreal and in great part tedious. With the *Recueillements* (1839) Lamartine returns to his earlier inspiration, but this collection has nothing of moment to add and can claim no striking merit.

As a prose writer Lamartine is of little significance comparatively, although a few words may be said of three of his various prose writings.

The *Voyage en Orient* (1835) shows the same character of improvisation that is apparent throughout his work, and along with many striking passages of description contains much that is trivial.

The *Histoire des Girondins* (1847), his most notable work in prose, which exercised great influence in its day, has little purely historical value, but is redeemed by some admirable examples of dramatic narrative, and is an eloquent expression of the democratic ideas of the time.

Lastly, the *Confidences* (1849-1851) necessarily contains very much that is interesting, but suffers from the fault of being too confidential, the trivial and the essential being confounded with a strange want of discrimination.

Lamartine is a striking instance of a man who with his first literary venture produced his best and most important work. In the spontaneity of these first lyrics, their simple communion with nature, the gentle, mildly-melancholy outpourings that come straight from the heart, in a word, in their personal note and their pure lyricism the true significance of Lamartine is to be found. God in nature and the whole of nature in man's soul—this is the theme which inspires him and which was to be an inspiration to others. " *Quelle qu'ait été,*" he says himself, " *quelle que puisse être encore la diversité de ces impressions jetées par la nature dans mon âme, et par mon âme dans mes vers, le fond en fut toujours un profond instinct de la Divinité dans toutes choses.*"

Such was the one true and original message he had to tell, which in its first telling was so admirable, but in the conscious and voluntary negligences that followed gained nothing and had much to lose. In spite of the reiteration that was the natural accompaniment of his improvised and unlaboured composition, his verse has a delicate harmonious beauty hitherto unknown in French poetry. Lamartine's place among the greatest lyric poets is secure.

In striking opposition to Lamartine stands another great Romantic poet, **Alfred de Vigny,** born at Loches in Touraine in 1797. In 1814 he became a sub-lieutenant in the Guards, and remained in the army for fourteen years, leaving it at the age of thirty-one in order to devote himself exclusively to literature. The latter part of his life he spent mostly in seclusion, his natural melancholy embittered by the want of recognition which he suffered at the hands of his contemporaries. He died in 1863.

The writings of De Vigny comprise his poetical works, which consist of the *Poèmes Antiques et Modernes* (1822–1826), and the collection known as *Destinées*, not published under this title till 1864; his prose works, consisting of plays, the best being *Chatterton* (1835), and novels—*Cinq-Mars* (1826), *Stello* (1832), *Servitude et Grandeur Militaires* (1835).

Among the *Poèmes Antiques et Modernes* (1822–1826) the finest are *Moïse*, which describes the last moments of the great lawgiver, weary of the isolation which has been the necessary condition of his greatness—the moral being that genius predestines to sorrow; *Éloa*, a mystic story of a sister of the angels, sprung from a tear of Christ, who is seized with pity and sympathy for the fallen archangel, and descends with him to his place of torture; and *Le Déluge*, which tells in beautiful and touching language how a shepherd and a maiden, after watching from the top of Mount Ararat the rising of the waters, are eventually swallowed up in them.

In this first volume the author's pessimistic outlook and melancholy are already strongly marked; and in each of the poems some one idea is taken and treated from the philosophic point of view.

Of similar nature is the collection entitled *Destinées*, his only other considerable poetic production. In this the note of despair and disenchantment, and the necessity for stoicism and resignation, are even more strongly emphasized.

The subject of the prose drama *Chatterton* (1835) is the sad life of the wonderful boy-poet. The miseries to which he was subjected by his sensitive pride, and the want of appreciation of the material world around him, are very sympathetically treated by one who had much in common with his hero.

Cinq-Mars (1826) is a historical novel, somewhat in the style of Scott. Cinq-Mars, a brilliant young nobleman, is brought to court by Richelieu, but leaves him for the King, and on the failure of a plot to overthrow the Cardinal, is executed. It is valuable as containing a lively and fairly reliable picture of the life of the period it treats.

Alfred De Vigny was before all a thinker; nearly every one of his works is guided by some clearly conceived idea, while the direction which his thought took was a very pronounced one. All life seemed to him to be an evil, all our noblest feelings and faculties only instruments of suffering. A reasoned pessimism was his doctrine, and his remedy for it, or rather the attitude he recommended towards it, haughty resignation.

The essence of his philosophy is eloquently summed up by himself in these four lines of *La Mort du Loup*, one of his finest shorter poems:

> *Gémir, pleurer, prier est également lâche.*
> *Fais énergiquement ta longue et lourde tâche*
> *Dans la voie où le sort a voulu t'appeler.*
> *Puis, après, comme moi, souffre et meurs sans parler.*

His style is sober and of severe simplicity, delicate and at the same time strong; yet though with him the thought is always uppermost, he laboured to give it an appropriate setting, and the artistic value of much of his work stands very high.

We now come to the leader, the embodiment of the Romantic school, **Victor Hugo**, the greatest of all French poets, and one of the greatest in the world's literature. For convenience sake we shall take the whole of his work together—poetry, drama, and fiction.

Marie Victor Hugo was born at Besançon in 1802, the son of a distinguished officer of the Empire, while his mother was a Vendean and of royalist sympathies. During his childhood he was taken with the rest of the family to Italy and Spain, seeing in this way Rome, Florence, Naples, and Madrid. However, he was educated principally at Paris, though the formal education he received was not very considerable. Already when very young he competed and won prizes in literary competitions, notably those of the Academy and the Jeux Floraux of Toulouse. In 1822 appeared his *Odes et Poésies Diverses*, when he was only twenty years of age, which at once made him famous and won for him the protection of Chateaubriand and the favour of Louis XVIII. Of the part this collection played in the rise of the Romantic party and how Hugo, though standing somewhat aloof from the earlier *Cénacle*, became by right of genius the avowed leader of the movement on the appearance of the *Odes et Ballades* (1826), *Cromwell* (1827), and, above all, the *Orientales* (1829) and *Hernani* (1830), we have already spoken elsewhere.

Meantime his political creed had been undergoing a transformation; from being an ardent Royalist he became an enthusiastic admirer of Napoleon. In 1845, under the July monarchy, he entered the Chamber as a Peer of France, and in 1849 was sent to the *Chambre Constituante* as a representative of the capital. There he sat till 1851, his sympathies more and more inclining to the extreme Republicans. Being included in the proscription which followed the *Coup d'État*, he fled to Brussels, and thence to

Jersey and afterwards to Guernsey, where he spent the next eighteen years. On the fall of the Empire he returned to Paris, from which time till his death he played a very considerable political part as member of the National Assembly and later as senator. He died on 22nd May, 1885, and was buried amid funeral ceremonies that were a veritable apotheosis.

The following is a classified list of the principal works of Victor Hugo:

Poetry:—*Odes et Ballades* (1826), *Les Orientales* (1829), *Les Feuilles d'automne* (1831), *Les Chants du Crépuscule* (1835), *Les Voix Intérieures* (1837), *Les Rayons et les Ombres* (1840), *Les Châtiments* (1853), *Les Contemplations* (1856), *La Légende des siècles* (in three parts: 1859-1883), *Les Chansons des Rues et des Bois* (1865), *L'Année terrible* (1872), *L'Art d'être grand-père* (1877), *Les Quatre Vents de l'Esprit* (1881), &c.

Drama:[1] — *Cromwell* (1827), *Hernani* (1829), *Marion Delorme* (1829), *Le Roi s'amuse* (1832), *Lucrèce Borgia* and *Marie Tudor* (1833), *Ruy Blas* (1838), *Les Burgraves* (1843), &c.

Prose Writings:—*Han d'Islande* (1823), *Bug-Jargal* (1819), *Notre-Dame de Paris* (1831), *Napoléon le Petit* (1852), *Les Misérables* (1862), *William Shakespeare* (1864), *Les Travailleurs de la Mer* (1866), *L'Homme qui rit* (1869), *Quatre-vingt-treize* (1873), *Histoire d'un crime* (1852-1877), &c.

It is as a poet that Victor Hugo is most important, and the quantity as well as quality of his poetic achievement is remarkable. Already at the age of twenty he produced, in the *Odes et Poésies Diverses*, a collection of verse which, if it did not show the power and originality of his later work, displayed a wonderful fertility of imagination, adaptability of form, and command of rhyme and rhythm. The *Odes et Ballades* in 1826 showed a marked advance in every aspect of the poetic art, and won the warmest praise from the already aged Chateaubriand, still the acknowledged sovereign of letters. With the *Orientales*, which followed three years later, Hugo stepped

---

[1] *Lucrèce Borgia, Marie Tudor,* are in prose.

right to the very forefront, and was hailed as the greatest poet of the day, while by their wealth of imagination, glow of colour, and brilliance of form these poems revealed clearly the true aspirations of the rising Romantic school.

The four following collections, which all appeared in the decade from 1830 to 1840, *Les Feuilles d'automne, Les Chants du Crépuscule, Les Voix Intérieures,* and *Les Rayons et les Ombres,* show the poet arriving at the full command of his powers, with both his characteristic virtues, and also his faults and mannerisms, growing more pronounced. They evince a closer sympathy with human joys and sufferings than had been revealed in the previous volumes, and strike on the whole a deeper and truer note.

Les Châtiments, which was issued from Guernsey in 1853, after Hugo's forced departure from Paris, was launched against Napoleon III, the cause of his exile. In spite of the exaggerated tone, and the somewhat unconvincing mass of unflattering epithets with which Hugo fairly overwhelms the unfortunate object of his attack, who becomes in his heated imagination a living example of every conceivable vice, they are in the main very brilliant satire, and attain at times true eloquence. Speaking of his resolution still to defy the tyrant, in spite of exile and persecution, and even though abandoned by his fellows, he makes a fine point in the lines:

> *Si l'on n'est plus que mille, eh bien! j'en suis. Si même*
> *Ils ne sont plus que cent, je brave encore Sylla;*
> *S'il en demeure dix, je serai le dixième;*
> *Et s'il n'en reste qu'un, je serai celui-là.*

Les Contemplations, of which both volumes appeared in 1856, contains poems of more or less personal character, dealing with the years from 1830 to 1856. Those of the first period, down to 1843, bear the title of *Autrefois*; those of the second, that of *Aujourd'hui*. The author himself calls them *Les Mémoires d'une Ame,* and tells us that " *une destinée est écrite là jour à jour* ". The year of division is the date of the drowning of his daughter Léopoldine, with her husband M. Vacquerie, during a pleasure trip on the Seine: "*La joie . . . s'effeuille page à page dans le tome premier qui est l'espérance, et disparaît dans le tome second, qui est le deuil. . . . Autrefois, Aujourd'hui. Un abîme les sépare, le tombeau.*" The first volume contains the famous *Réponse à un Acte d'Accusation*, and in both volumes are found pieces of remarkable beauty.

In 1859 appeared the first two volumes of *La Légende des siècles*, the third not till eighteen years later. In these memorable collections of poems Hugo brings before our eyes typical scenes from the history of the world down to the present time, his purpose being to set forth in striking and dramatic pictures scenes illustrative of the great epochs of human life on earth. They display fully his marvellous narrative power, and in their variety of music, range of theme, and alternate dignity and tenderness have seldom been rivalled. Among the most famous and the best is the one called *Ruth et Booz*, which gives contradiction to the often-repeated statement that Victor Hugo was incapable of simplicity. Exquisitely sober and delicate are the words in which we are told how Ruth, lying at the feet of Boaz,

> *se demandait,*
> *Immobile, ouvrant l'œil à moitié sous ses voiles,*
> *Quel dieu, quel moissonneur de l'éternel été*
> *Avait, en s'en allant, négligemment jeté*
> *Cette faucille d'or dans le champ des étoiles.*

None of the remaining verse reveals any strikingly original qualities or advance on his previous work.

L'Année terrible gives a series of stirring pictures of the war of 1870; *L'Art d'être grand-père* exhibits in a very human way the sympathetic interest he took in all the pursuits and in the society of his two little grandchildren; *Les Quatre Vents de l'Esprit*, representing Hugo's four main inspirations —the lyric, epic, satiric, and dramatic, written in 1881, when he was verging on his eightieth year, shows at times his wonderful powers still unimpaired.

We will next speak of the dramas, all the best of which were written in the fourth decade of the century, and which, even the most successful, are not to be compared in intrinsic worth with his poetic accomplishment. The most successful, the only real survivors—on the stage at any rate—and the best are *Hernani* (1829) and *Ruy Blas* (1838). The first of the series, *Cromwell* (1827), was less remarkable for the play itself than for the Preface, the importance of which in connection with the early Romantic movement has been already discussed. *Cromwell* was never acted, and it is almost incapable of production, being in fact less a play than a romance in dramatic form. Already in *Cromwell*, however, Hugo's great dramatic principle is apparent—the blending of two opposite elements for the attainment of what he considered a higher dramatic truth. Thus we have Cromwell the stern Puritan and strong leader of men, who is at the same time a buffoon in his moments of privacy; or, to quote the author's own words: " *C'est un être complexe . . . composé de tous les contraires . . . plein de génie et de petitesse . . . hypocrite et fanatique . . . grotesque et sublime.*" This dramatic conception is seen in all his later plays, and is the root-idea of all Hugo's dramatic creations: *Hernani* is both a bandit and a hero; *Ruy Blas*, a lackey, and a model of greatness and virtue—the highest moral worth in the lowest social station; *Marion Delorme*, the noble passion of love in the heart of a courtesan; *Le Roi s'amuse* presents in the court fool, Triboulet, the most degraded of human natures, redeemed by paternal love; *Lucrèce Borgia*, all the vices, and a great example of maternal devotion, or, in Victor Hugo's own words: " *La maternité purifiant la difformité morale* ". As already said, the two most famous and the best are *Hernani* and *Ruy Blas*.

Hernani, who is an outlaw and bandit, and at the same time a duke and grandee of Spain, is the successful rival of Ruy Gomez for the hand of his niece and ward, Doña Sol. Pressed by the officers of the King, Hernani is successfully concealed by Ruy

Gomez in his castle and saved. The latter, however, has discovered his love for his niece, and Hernani is only allowed to depart with his life on vowing by the head of his father to take the life so spared with his own hand whenever he shall hear the sound of the horn which he detaches from his waist and hands to Ruy Gomez. Hernani is restored to favour and regains his estates, and with his betrothal to Doña Sol the cup of his happiness seems to be full, when at the masquerade which follows their betrothal a sinister figure appears. Hernani hears the fatal Horn, and in the presence of Ruy Gomez both he and Doña Sol poison themselves.

Ruy Blas is a lackey who is introduced to court by a grandee, Don Salluste, in the name of his cousin, Don César, with the object of entangling and ruining the Queen. Ruy Blas, well educated and possessed of great talents, rapidly rises, and under his assumed name and quality becomes minister. He is madly in love with the Queen, and the falseness and hopelessness of his position, together with the pitiless humiliations to which Don Salluste subjects him, at last exhaust his endurance, and he first slays his persecutor and afterwards poisons himself.

Les Burgraves (1843), the last, was more extravagantly antithetical and full of surprises than all the others, and with its lavish use of the most ordinary stage tricks, meetings, recognitions and coincidences, is the purest melodrama as far as its merely dramatic side is concerned, though even the worst of Victor Hugo's plays abound in fine lyrical passages.

Of his prose writings by far the most impressive is the novel *Notre-Dame de Paris* (1831), a historical romance of Paris in the time of Louis XI, in which the ancient capital of the fifteenth century, with all the different classes of its inhabitants, nobility, clergy, citizens, and people, are brought in a very graphic way before our eyes. Naturally it is full of the characteristic antitheses and startling contrasts, with a grotesqueness which at times makes it more like a phantasmagoria than living reality. The personages themselves have little individuality. More real are the city itself and its teeming population; but the central figure of the whole is the sombre cathedral, which looms vast, mysterious, and incommen-

surable, like a personification of the Middle Ages themselves.
Already before *Notre-Dame* had appeared the two wildly romantic novels, *Han d'Islande* (1823) and *Bug-Jargal* (1819). *Napoléon le Petit* (1852) was the prose equivalent of the *Châtiments* in the castigation of his enemy. But after *Notre-Dame* the most important of Victor Hugo's romances is *Les Misérables*, of which the ten volumes appeared in 1862. It is a comprehensive picture of the life of the day, into which the author, no longer fettered by the limitations of the stage, poured the most varied elements, with little care to fit them suitably into the framework of the story, the result being a mass of digressions and irrelevancies which at times is almost chaotic.

The story woven through the whole is briefly as follows:

> Jean Valjean, a released convict, repents, and under the name of M. Madeleine becomes a rich and respectable member of society. To save another from suspicion he denounces himself, and is once more imprisoned, but escapes. He rescues and adopts a young girl, Cosette, whom he marries to Marius, confessing to the latter who he is, but not making any mention of his good deeds. Leaving the young couple he withdraws from the world, but before he dies learns that his nobility is recognized and appreciated by those he loves.

Along with inevitable improbabilities and exaggerations this enormous work has many purely admirable passages, the struggle in the soul of the hero as he is fighting his way back to virtue being told with a delicacy and psychological insight which the author has nowhere else attained.

Les Travailleurs de la Mer (1866) is an exquisite little idyll of passion and adventure; *L'Homme qui rit* (1869), an extravagant but powerful romance, which purports to be historical; *Quatre-vingt-treize* (1874), another historical romance; and the *Histoire d'un crime* (1877) has been described as the "apotheosis of the Special Correspondent".

Much as Victor Hugo liked to pose as the *penseur*, convinced as he undoubtedly was that therein lay his strength and his importance for the human race, there is nothing very remarkable in his thought or ideas. Though his constant endeavour is to teach and enlighten, his belief not that of "*l'art pour l'art*", but rather of "*l'art pour l'humanité*", he has nothing very new or original to tell, and what message he has to deliver is obscured and distorted from the teacher's point of view by his characteristic bias towards antithesis and exaggeration. His mind does not work by the logical processes of thought habitual to a philosopher, but by the intuitive methods of the poet—he thinks not in ideas but in images. With rare exceptions, he shows very little power of reading the innermost workings of the human heart—little psychological insight. Where his great and surpassing merit lies is in his command of form, and there he displays not merely skill but genius. He had one of the largest vocabularies that ever mortal employed, and his mastery of it is always supreme and unerring. For "the word" he had a special sense, feeling it as an entity with laws and properties of its own, possessing not only meaning and sound, but as it were colour and individuality. The gift of personifying imagination and imagery he possessed in the highest degree, being often indeed tempted by it to the excesses of exaggeration and meaningless antithesis. All contrasts and reliefs of light and shade appealed forcibly to his nature, and such, both in the literal and figurative, are everywhere found throughout his work.

He is a master of rhyme and rhythm, while of his innovations in versification mention has already been made elsewhere. He has an inexhaustible capacity of inventing new rhythms and strophic combinations, and his gift of adapting sound to sense, poetic form to subject, reveals the consummate artist.

His prose is on the whole far inferior to his verse, and naturally so, as some of his greatest qualities—those of the harmonist and technical artist—are not brought into play; his drama, apart from the beautiful lyrical passages with which it abounds, is of no exceptional merit, and is only too apt to be suggestive of melodrama. Where he is really great, probably greater than any other Frenchman, and certainly surpassed by none, is in lyric poetry; the range and variety of subjects, the music and grace of form and versification, the warmth and colour of style and the spontaneity of the emotions, constitute a combination of qualities that are only found in the supreme masters of the art.

In spite of his faults he has left a body of work wonderful in its quantity and in many of its qualities, in the universality of its interests, the variety of its music, and above all in its rare lyrical beauties. His is a figure which looms large not only in the literature of France but of the world.

Probably the greatest lyric poet of France, in the narrower sense, is **Alfred de Musset.**

> De Musset was born at Paris in 1810. In 1828 he was already at the age of eighteen introduced into the *Cénacle*, and in 1830, with the *Contes d'Espagne et d'Italie*, became famous, and one of the recognized Romantic leaders. However, his enthusiasm for the new creed did not last, and except at the outset of his career he was only a half-hearted Romanticist, avowing his admiration for their *bête-noire*—Racine, and mildly poking fun at some of their extravagances. In 1833 took place his meeting with George Sand, and during the years 1833 and 1834 they were together in Italy, but in the latter year De Musset left her and returned to Paris, and in the following year, 1835, the final rupture occurred. This episode left indelible traces on his life and writings. Most of his best work was done before the age of thirty, after which, with energies and strength exhausted by the irregularities of his life, he produced comparatively little. He died in Paris in 1857, at the early age of forty-six.

His principal works are *Contes d'Espagne et d'Italie* (1830), *Le Spectacle dans un Fauteuil* (1832), *Rolla* (1833), *Les Nuits* (1835–1837), *La Confession d'un Enfant du Siècle* (1836), in prose; and among his prose comedies, which he collected in 1856 under the comprehensive title of *Comédies et Proverbes*, *On ne badine pas avec l'amour*, and *Il ne faut jurer de rien*. He also wrote two prose dramas—*André del Sarto* (1833) and *Lorenzaccio* (1834).

The *Contes d'Espagne et d'Italie*, which were written in the ardour of his early romantic enthusiasm, are lyrics and verse tales glowing with all the warmth and colour of the South, in which, at the same time, licence and extravagance run riot.

The *Spectacle dans un Fauteuil* is remarkable for one of its two dramatic pieces, *La Coupe et les Lèvres*, a Faust-like theme, the execution of which is unfortunately far inferior to its conception.

The four *Nuits—De Mai et de Décembre* (1835), *d'Août* (1836), and *d'Octobre* (1837)—reflect the bitterness of soul and disillusionment which followed his rupture with George Sand, and the ending of those romantic dreams of ideal love which they had founded on that relationship. The personal allusions with which they abound make them often obscure, but there is no mistaking their delicate analysis and fine insight into the human heart. They contain much that is purely admirable as lyricism of the passion and sufferings of love.

In the *Confession d'un Enfant du Siècle*—the story of a young man who has exhausted before his prime all the pleasures the world has to offer and his own power of enjoyment, and, young in years, finds himself old at heart, without ambition, faith, or hope—we cannot but trace the picture of De Musset himself.

Of Musset's comedies some few are among his very best work. They have, on the whole, comparatively little action, their interest lying more in the delicate analysis of human feelings and emotions, while he often shows himself a master of dramatic dialogue, and his wit is lively and never-failing. Some of the pieces, remarkable for their intensity and graceful fantasy, as, for instance, *On ne badine pas avec l'amour* and *Il ne faut jurer de rien*, still maintain their hold on the stage.

Alfred de Musset was before all a great lyricist, whose source of inspiration was the human heart, and whose one absorbing theme was love in its varied manifestations. All his work is strongly subjective; nowhere do we long forget the personality of the author. Beginning life as an enthusiast, fired with ambition and hope, he early underwent a sad disillusionment, owing principally to his unhappy relations with

George Sand, and his later work is inspired by a melancholy which broods upon the darker problems of life, and ends by caressing a despair which sees in its very regrets and bitter-sweet memories the only thing worth having lived for.

His style is on the whole careless and wanting in artistic finish, showing imperfections and faults which he had not the patience or inclination to avoid, but attaining at times, when inspired by genuine passion, a simple directness and force which make it a perfect medium of expression.

A comparison with Byron is one which will naturally suggest itself to the student of comparative literature.

In contrast to De Musset, detachment from self is the keynote of the poetry of **Théophile Gautier** (1811–1872), who began by the study of art, to become later an artist in literature. He was the youngest of the Romanticists, and the most noisy in his enthusiasm, making himself conspicuous for his eccentricity in manner and dress, although it should not be overlooked that at bottom he was a conscientious and indefatigable worker.

Gautier's chief works comprise his poetry, published in 1845 under the title of *Poésies Complètes*, and which includes the *Poésies* (1830), *La Comédie de la Mort* (1838) and *España*; also the later collection *Émaux et Camées* (1852); his fiction, the most important being *Mademoiselle de Maupin* (1835), *Le Roman de la Momie* (1858), *Le Capitaine Fracasse* (1863), and a number of short stories second only to those of Mérimée; his account of his travels, the best of which are *Tra los Montes* (1843), his journey to Spain, and *Voyage en Russie* (1867); his critical works, including *Les Grotesques* (1853) and *Histoire du Romantisme* (1874).

Already, with his first poems in 1830, the cult of form and colour which he brought over from painting to the sister art was apparent,[1] and announced the great colourist and artist

---

[1] Cf. his own words:

Laisse-moi faire, ô grand vieillard,
Changeant mon luth pour ta palette,
Une transposition d'art.

in style of the Romantic school. In his most typical collection, which he published in 1852 under the characteristic title of *Émaux et Camées*, this feature is pronounced, and we find everything regarded from the point of view of the painter. The centre of interest is removed from the subjective sentimentality of the Romanticists to that of objective beauty, and in the field of ethics we have the corresponding change from the consciously moral or immoral, to the neither moral nor immoral, the neutral, with its cry of " art for art ". This theory and creed of the all-importance of form in art at the expense both of sentiment and ideas, was the side of Gautier's work which inspired those who were later known as the *Parnassiens*.

That this doctrine was essentially false, as confounding the relative spheres of two complementary but not interchangeable arts, is beyond dispute, and in this respect Gautier had a harmful influence in lending the weight of his example to an unsound tendency. At the same time he exerted a very wholesome influence on literature in liberating Romanticism from what was rapidly inclining to become an over-subtle and morbidly introspective sentimentalism. Of the *Émaux et Camées* he says himself: " *Ce titre exprime le dessein de traiter sous forme restreinte de petits sujets, tantôt sur plaque d'or ou de cuivre avec les vives couleurs de l'émail, tantôt avec la roue du graveur de pierres fines sur l'agate, la cornaline ou l'onyx.*"

The same peculiarities of style are seen in his prose writings, the same firmly chiselled reproduction of the objects which struck the painter's eye, everywhere the point of view of the man " *pour qui le monde extérieur existe* ", to quote his definition of himself. The best of them, apart from the travels, are *Mademoiselle de Maupin*, which, with its defiant polemical preface, marks the transition to Realism in fiction; *Le Capitaine Fracasse*, a kind of romantic adaptation of Scarron's *Roman Comique*; *Les Grotesques*, on the minor poets of the reign of Louis XIII, in whom, with surer instinct than Sainte-Beuve, he recognized the ancestors of Romanticism; and *Histoire du*

Romantisme, still indispensable for a detailed and anecdotic knowledge of that movement.

For good or for bad, Gautier has to be reckoned with as a very important factor in the literature of the middle decade of last century. With him ends the line of the great masters of the new poetic movement. Among the lesser lights may be noted:

> **Marceline Desbordes-Valmore** (1786–1859), one of the best of French women-poets, whose verse is remarkable for its sincerity and poignancy, if occasionally marred by vagueness and prolixity.
>
> **Auguste Brizeux** (1806–1858), a graceful idyllist who, in *Marie* (1831) and *Les Bretons* (1845), has sung the praises of Breton wilds and ways.
>
> **Auguste Barbier** (1805–1882), inspired by the July Revolution, wrote a series of nineteen satires, published under the title of *Iambes* (1831). They are somewhat violent in tone, but several and especially *La Curée*, are good examples of spirited satire.
>
> His other poems, *Il Pianto*, on the misfortunes of Italy, and *Lazare*, a picture of the misery among the working-classes in England, are far inferior to the *Iambes*.
>
> **Hégésippe Moreau** (1810–1838), whose sad death in a hospital at the early age of twenty-eight has lent additional interest to a collection of his poetry published after his death, under the title of *Le Myosotis*. Moreau's range is not wide, but his verse is always the result of a true passion felt. A few of his best pieces, like the charming elegy *La Voulzie*, have found a place in the standard anthologies.

CHAPTER II

DRAMA

The dramatic work of Victor Hugo having been already discussed, the name of **Alexandre Dumas père,** the second dramatist of eminence among the Romanticists, naturally opens this chapter.

Alexandre Dumas was born in 1803 at Villers-Cotterêts, a little Picardy town, and was the son of a general of the Revolution, and grandson of a creole. He received a very scanty and irregular education, and came to Paris at twenty to make his fortune. The future novelist began with verse, and then being seized with a passion for the theatre, entered upon his serious literary career with the writing of several dramas, with which he achieved considerable success, though nothing like the success he attained subsequently once he found in the novel his true sphere. *Henri III et sa Cour*, his first important play, was produced at the Théâtre Français shortly before *Hernani*. About 1840 Dumas went over to the novel, and partly alone and partly in collaboration with a number of others, who helped to make up the *Maison Dumas et Cie*, turned out an incredible number during the remaining thirty years of his life. Nor was his literary activity confined to novel-writing; he wrote memoirs, travels, and any other form of saleable composition, adapted his novels for the stage, lectured both in France and abroad, and in fact turned his facile pen to any labour which could raise the sums necessary to meet the expenses into which he was led by his reckless extravagance. In the midst of these untiring labours he died in Normandy in 1870.

His principal plays are *Henri III* (1829), *Antony* (1831), *La Tour de Nesle* (1832), *Mademoiselle de Belle-Isle* (1839).

Though not endowed with any great power of character-drawing and wanting in psychological insight, Dumas is remarkable as introducing on the stage the treatment of historical subjects, afterwards taken up with such avidity by other Romanticists. At the same time Dumas possesses in a high degree the dramatic instinct; all is action, and the characters fitly explain themselves by their deeds and not their words. He fully understood the requirements and conventions of the stage, and to his power of adapting himself to its conditions is to be ascribed the success of his plays, in spite of their lack of all the highest dramatic qualities.

Of his novels we shall speak in the next chapter.

The greatest name of the period in comedy is that of **Augustin Eugène Scribe** (1791–1861), an author whose productivity was phenomenal.

Beginning his work as a dramatist when hardly out of his

teens, he had at first little success, but gradually came to the front, and for some fifty years figured largely in the repertoire of several theatres, beginning with the *Gymnase* from its opening in 1820, and being admitted some seven or eight years later to the stage of the *Théâtre Français*.

Among his best-known pieces are *Le Mariage de Raison* (1826), one of the earlier pieces written for the Gymnase; *Bertrand et Raton* (1833), a story of revolutions and conspiracies; *La Camaraderie* (1837), a satire on the coteries of the *bourgeoisie*; and possibly best-known of all, *Le Verre d'Eau* (1840), the historical setting of which is the series of intrigues which led to the fall of the Duchess of Marlborough.

Scribe is a remarkable instance of a writer who was a playwright before everything. His comedies have no purely literary qualities, and their thought is insignificant. All the interest is centred in the intrigue; he takes any situations and any characters, and, setting them in motion with the greatest skill, manipulates them with unerring instinct for dramatic effect. Without genius or originality, he was possessed of great shrewdness, and exactly hit the tastes of the public for which he wrote—the great well-to-do middle class of Parisian society. Alone, or in collaboration, he wrote some hundreds of plays; and, unlike Dumas, with whom he may be compared in point of fertility and productiveness, not only made but kept a very considerable fortune.

> Among his many collaborators might be mentioned **Ernest Legouvé** (1807–1903), in conjunction with whom he wrote *Bataille de Dames*, one of the best, if not the best of all his comedies.

The only other dramatist of any importance in this first half of the century is **François Ponsard** (1814–1867), who, after the appearance of *Lucrèce* (1843), was hailed as the founder of the "*école du bon sens*", which, though showing traces of Romanticism in picturesqueness and colour, as also in versification, had much of the regularity of the old classical tragedy. However, he did not keep to this style, which he had himself originated, but in *Charlotte Corday* (1850) wrote what was to all intents a romantic play. In 1853 he passed over to social comedy with *L'Honneur et L'Argent*, but in his last piece, in 1866, *Le Lion Amoureux*, he reverted to more serious drama. In spite of the considerable reputation he enjoyed in his day, Ponsard has not left any great work in any one of his different pieces. His plays are written in verse, but contain no real poetry, and their psychological interest is very small.

His historical plays, of which the principal are *Charlotte Corday* and *Le Lion Amoureux*, have an air of actuality which is due to their coldness and want of imagination. His one merit is that he provided, by the solidity of his style and the regularity of his well-turned couplets, an influence which served, at least for a time, to check the extravangances of some of the Romanticists.

CHAPTER III

PROSE

After poetry, fiction is the most important branch of Romantic literature. Of the novels of **Victor Hugo** we have already spoken in conjunction with the rest of his work, but it may be again remarked in this connection how momentous they were in directing the Romanticists to this form, while the greatest of all, *Notre-Dame de Paris*, was the first notable example of the historical novel, which flourished in France during the early part of this period, owing in large measure to the fame which Sir Walter Scott had since 1814 achieved with his historical romances.

The most remarkable writer of novels of this kind was **Alexandre Dumas**, who turned from the theatre to fiction in 1844, and during the next decade composed his best stories. Among the enormous number which he wrote, either with or without the help of collaborators, the most famous perhaps are

Le Comte de Monte Cristo (1844–1845), *Les trois Mousquetaires* (1844), *Vingt Ans Après* (1845), *La Reine Margot* (1845).

Dumas' novels have no great literary qualities, and show little art in arrangement and development of plot; they all betray that want of finish which is only to be expected from the haste with which they were written, and the little labour that was bestowed upon them. Nevertheless they reveal a wonderful wealth of imagination, a never-failing faculty of invention, and their unrivalled narrative-power carries the reader irresistibly along through the endless series of stirring scenes and situations, which are rather strung together than subordinated to any ruling motive.

The main developments of the Romantic novel are often divided into two currents—Idealism and Realism, and although the distinction might be misleading if interpreted too literally, it contains a great deal of truth, and may be a helpful generalization if supplemented by a closer examination of the facts of the case.

With such qualifications we may describe **George Sand** as a representative of Idealism.

Lucile Aurore Dupin, Baronne Dudevant, was born at Nohant in the year 1804. Her father was a grandson of the Maréchal de Saxe, her mother a Parisian bourgeoise, and on her father's death she lived principally with her grandmother on her estate at Nohant in Berri. At eighteen she married M. Dudevant, and after living with him nine years she separated from him, abandoned her fortune, and went to Paris to make her living by literature. She began by collaborating with Jules Sandeau under the pseudonym of Jules Sand, from which, by the change of Jules to George, was derived her famous *nom de plume*. For some twenty years she lived in the Bohemian society of the capital, under the influence, during the first part of the time, of various distinguished artists and men of letters; notably Alfred de Musset and Chopin; during the later part, more especially of the philosophers, socialists, and politicians. In the years 1833 and 1834 she made, in the company of Alfred de Musset, the journey to Italy, which is reflected in the work of both, and left so deep a mark on his life.

In 1839 she withdrew from the life of the capital to her beloved Berri, where as châtelaine of Nohant she passed the rest of her days, engaged with but short intervals in steady and untiring literary toil. She died in 1876.

Her work may be divided into four periods, and the principal writings of each are respectively the following: *Indiana* (1831), *Valentine* (1832), *Lélia* (1833), *Jacques* (1834); *Spiridion* (1839), *Consuelo* (1842-1843), *La Comtesse de Rudolstadt* (1844), *Elle et Lui* (1859); *La Mare au Diable* (1846), *La Petite Fadette* (1849), *François le Champi* (1850); *Les Beaux Messieurs de Bois Doré* (1858), *Jean de la Roche* (1860), *Le Marquis de Villemer* (1860).

The novels of the first period reflect clearly the Romantic tendencies of the day, together with a very strong Rousseau influence, and gain their distinctive character from the prominence they give to the marriage question, the unsatisfied yearnings of the *femme incomprise*, and the sacredness of true love, which is superior to all obligations.

Elle et Lui (1859) deals with the Musset episode.

In the second period the influence of her philosophic friends, the most important of whom was Lamennais, is apparent, and she produced novels which were mainly rhapsodies on social questions, treating largely of the relations between the classes, and drawing wonderfully idealized pictures of fusion between the different ranks effected by the all-potent influence of love.

The best book of this period, and one of the best she wrote, is *Consuelo* (1842).

In the third period, inspired by her beloved Berri, she turns to scenes of rural simplicity and simple faith, and creates some idylls that are pure masterpieces, and in which, though both scenes and personages are largely idealized, yet the whole is inspired by the highest degree of poetic truth. Many regard the works of this period as her greatest, and we are inclined to agree with them.

Lastly, towards the close of her life she returns to storytelling pure and simple, and leaves Berri for other scenes, which she uses as the background for romantic tales told with the calm and smiling serenity of her own placid old age.

To the large number of George Sand's novels, several of which have been omitted, must be added a considerable quantity of dramatic work, in addition to a voluminous *Histoire de ma Vie, Lettres*, and much miscellaneous work.

George Sand is one of the most considerable of woman writers of any age and country. Gifted with a wonderfully ready and fertile imagination, and a no less marvellous facility of composition, she seemed to produce her works with little or no effort. Nor did the quality suffer as much as might have been expected from this free and unlaboured method, for what she gave to the world in this way as the spontaneous emanation of her genius has qualities both of matter and style. Though she no more makes an effort to excel in psychological analysis than in any other direction, her insight into human nature is not inconsiderable, and not to be concealed by the halo of idealism which she throws around her characters. Thus it would be wrong to call her an idealist if using the term implied the total exclusion of realism; the work of George Sand may best be described as a fusion of the two, her conception and mental vision being in the highest degree true to nature, while her optimistic woman's nature leads her to invest her characters with rather more of poetry and romance than is justified by the hard facts of actual life.

Among the Realists, three figures stand out conspicuously. We will speak first of **Stendhal** (1783-1842), the originator of the movement.

Marie Henri Beyle, who wrote under the name of Stendhal, was a person who saw much active life, trying his hand at more than one profession, and among other things taking part in the Russian campaign. He lived for several years in Italy, for which country he had a passionate preference.

His fame depends upon two novels: *Le Rouge et le Noir* (1831), and *La Chartreuse de Parme* (1839).

The former takes for its hero a man of unscrupulous ambition, Julien Sorel, who in the troublous times which followed the Revolution resolves by his own energy and ability to carve out for himself a position, but whose career of vice is cut short on the scaffold.

The latter is almost entirely occupied with the painting of Italian life, but is best known for the description of the field of Waterloo, given in realistic fashion from the point of view of a conscript who fought in the great battle. In its cold, unimpassioned detail it is a model of realism, no less by what it omits than by what it tells.

In both, Stendhal shows his two main characteristics, the love of action and energy, and the observation of the human heart, which makes him the first in point of time of the great modern psychological novelists. His influence was very considerable, especially on Balzac and Mérimée, his two immediate successors in the earlier part of the century.

Prosper Mérimée was born at Paris in 1803, and began by studying law. Abandoning this occupation, he held various government posts, and became finally Inspector of Historical Monuments. Under Napoleon III he was made a senator, and was a great favourite both of the Emperor and of the Empress Eugénie. He died in 1870.

His chief writings are *Théâtre de Clara Gazul* (1825), *La Chronique du Règne de Charles IX* (1829); and among his short stories, *La Vénus d'Ille* (1837), *Colomba* (1840), *Tamango, Carmen* (1845), *Matteo Falcone, L'Enlèvement de la Redoute*.

Beginning his literary career at twenty-two with some dramatic pieces professing to be from the Spanish of an imaginary Clara Gazul, he followed in 1830 with another mystification in the form of a collection of pretended Illyrian folk-songs, signed with an anagram of the previous name, La Guzla. Up to this time his work had borne a decided romantic imprint both in matter and form, but he then turned to the writing of those stories on which his lasting fame depends.

Though still in keeping with romantic traditions in their predilection for strange and less civilized countries, and the interest they display in foreign languages and literatures, they are in the best sense of the word realistic in their exact and picturesque portrayal of the local setting, and in the truth of their artistic, historical, and archæological descriptions.

Mérimée stands midway between Stendhal and Balzac in the history of the Realistic novel, having many points in common with both, though he is a greater artist than either. The influence of Stendhal he himself acknowledges: "*Les idées de Stendhal sur les hommes et sur les choses ont singulièrement déteint sur les miennes*", he says, and that influence is clearly to be seen in his preference for lands whose primitive force and energy have not been affected by the influences of civilization, while he resembles Balzac in the importance he attaches to the painting of externals, and the connection he establishes between the mind and its surroundings.

Most remarkable in his method is the striking objectivity of treatment; he seeks to efface himself, concealing his own personality behind his work, which is allowed to speak for itself. His style is clear and polished, and even when he is recounting the horrors and mysteries in which he takes delight, the tone never loses its elegance and urbanity. Mérimée is, in short, an artist, and one whose reputation will gain much more than it will lose with the progress of time.

Lastly, we must speak of the third of the group, **Honoré de Balzac,** the founder proper of the modern social Realistic novel, and one of the greatest names in French literature.

Balzac was born at Tours in 1799, studied law for three years at the Sorbonne, his father wishing him to become a notary. In 1819 he left his native town to try his fortune in Paris, where his life for the first ten years was a long struggle in which he contracted debts which hampered him for the rest of his life. He wrote during this period several novels of little worth, and it was not till the publication of *Les Chouans* (1829) that he met with any real success. Soon after appeared *La Peau de Chagrin*, the first of his great works, and his reputation was established. From that time on till his death he brought out a continuous stream of novels, working with phenomenal industry and endurance, his hours varying, according to his own account, from fifteen to eighteen a day, turning night into day, and often shutting himself up from the world for weeks at a time. This unnatural labour, to which he devoted himself partly under the pressure of a load of debts, and partly from the necessity which he felt of realizing his artistic conceptions, exhausted his strength, and he died in 1850 at the early age of fifty-one.

In 1841, when he had already written several of his best works, Balzac conceived the idea of a gigantic gallery of novels representing contemporary life, into the framework of which he fitted many of those he had already written, and which was to be completed by a great number of others of which some were actually written and some never went beyond their conception in the author's brain. To this unique work he gave the title of *La Comédie Humaine*, and divided it into six groups: *Scènes de la Vie Privée*, comprising among others *La Femme de Trente Ans* (1832), *Le Colonel Chabert*, *Le Père Goriot* (1835); *Scènes de la Vie de Province: Le Lys dans la Vallée* (1835), *Eugénie Grandet* (1833), *Le Curé de Tours*, *Illusions Perdues* (1837); *Scènes de la Vie Parisienne: César Birotteau* (1837), *La Cousine Bette* (1846); *Scènes de la Vie Politique: Une Ténébreuse Affaire* (1841); *Scènes de la Vie Militaire: Les Chouans* (1827-1829); *Scènes de la Vie de Campagne: Les Paysans* (1844), *Le Médecin de Campagne* (1833), *Le Curé de Village* (1839). He wrote also Philosophical studies: *La Recherche de l'Absolu* (1834); and Analytical studies.

This great creation in which society is approached from so many sides, from the point of view of so many ranks, professions, and situations, in which the characters are connected and their relations with one another and with the rest of their imaginary society fully and minutely portrayed, places Balzac by the side of the great creative geniuses, the Shakespeares and Molières, who have produced from their own consciousness a world as actual and living as the world in which we live.

The society that Balzac places before us is essentially that of the France of Louis Philippe, and more particularly the *bourgeoisie*, with its ignoble striving after wealth and position its intrigues and egoisms, its trivialities and low ideals. Doubtless that society was not one of the most encouraging to the student of sociology, yet we have every reason to believe that it was not as bad as Balzac paints it, for as he himself declared, he occupied himself by preference with the mean and sordid in human life and character. " *Les êtres vulgaires m'intéressent plus qu'ils ne vous intéressent,*" he said to George Sand. " *Je les grandis, je les idéalise, en sens inverse, dans leur laideur ou dans leur bêtise.*"

Accordingly he is best in his pictures of doubtful and more than doubtful characters. He cannot paint a gentleman, an honest man, or a virtuous woman, but he is excellent in his villains and victims of human folly and vice. His favourite method is to take one character who has become, through addiction to some besetting sin, a human monster, and trace in all its ramifications the ravages effected in him and in the society that is dependent upon him or exposed to his influence. His own peculiar types of character he draws with a marvellous realism, and with a command of detail which has never been equalled. Externals and material surroundings form an important part of his method, and are regarded as an index to character and an essential element in its formation. Yet he is no thinker—much less so than Victor Hugo—and not infrequently his minute descriptions, as well as his pseudo-philosophical dissertations, tend to make his novels wearisome. Although Balzac showed a marked preference for the baser side of nature, the fact must not be lost sight of that he is in part a Romanticist, a Realist haunted by phantasms of romance, as is well illustrated by such of his works as *Séraphita* and *Le Lys dans la Vallée*.

Both in its qualities and failings his influence is everywhere traceable in the fiction of the latter half of last century.

Among the numerous lesser novelists and writers of stories the most noticeable in this period are:

Charles Nodier (1783–1844), whose literary importance lies in the fact that he was the centre around which, in the library of the Arsenal, gathered the advanced guard of the young Romantic revolters—De Vigny, Sainte-Beuve, **Émile Deschamps** (1791–1871), who translated from Shakespeare, his brother **Antony Deschamps** (1800–1869), who turned part of Dante into French—in fact, all those who are known as the first *Cénacle*. Nodier's achievement is considerable, but the only portion of it likely to live are a few admirable short stories, such as *Trilby* (1822), and perhaps *Le Peintre de Salzbourg* (1803), in the German sentimental manner.

Eugène Sue (1804–1859), the author of a number of novels, most of which teem with absurdities and various objectionable qualities, but of which at any rate two, *Les Mystères de Paris* (1843) and *Le Juif Errant* (1845), achieved great success.

Émile Souvestre (1806–1854) to whom we owe some charming stories of Breton life, the best known being *Les Derniers Bretons*, *Les Derniers Paysans*, and *Foyer Breton*. Another book of his which has gained a certain reputation is *Le Philosophe sous les Toits*, the reflections of a young man on the every-day events of his life, mingled with some unobtrusive moralizing thereupon, the whole written in an easy and graceful style that makes it not without interest.

Alphonse Karr (1808–1899), who made his reputation with *Sous les Tilleuls* (1832), followed by a long series of novels, the best being *Geneviève* (1838), though none equalled either the merit or popularity of his first work. His characteristics are a strong feeling for the picturesque, blended with a wit and irony which possess a distinct attraction of their own.

Henri Murger (1822–1864), whose reputation rests on the *Scènes de la Vie de Bohème* (1851), humorous descriptions of the life of the needy student population of Parisian Bohemia, in which the fantastic and the real are delightfully blended. He wrote also many other novels dealing with the vagabond life of the *Quartier Latin*, the romance of which he did more than anyone else to create.

Not least important of the literary branches of the period is history, which can point to half a dozen famous names, and to a revolution in method which prepared the way for the historians of to-day.

The father of modern French history is **Augustin Thierry**, who, with the *Lettres sur l'Histoire de France* (1820), gave the first indication of the new trend.

Born at Blois in 1795, he became in 1815 the secretary of Saint-

Simon; but from 1817 turned to political writing. In 1820 he published in the *Courrier Français* the first ten *Lettres sur l'Histoire de France*, to which fifteen more were afterwards added. Although defective sight, aggravated by excessive application, ended in blindness, he continued his labours and researches with a fine courage and perseverance, till his death in 1856.

His works comprise, in addition to the already mentioned *Lettres*, the *Histoire de la Conquête de l'Angleterre par les Normands* (1825), *Dix Ans d'Études Historiques* (1834), and the *Récits des Temps Mérovingiens* (1840).

In all he wrote Thierry seeks by the aid of a vivid imagination to make history live again before our eyes in a series of pictures that shall be full of animation and colour, and yet possess the fidelity and truth which can only be founded on patient and careful investigation. His aims can best be given in his own words: " *J'avais l'ambition de faire de l'art en même temps que de la science, de faire du drame à l'aide de matériaux fournis par une érudition sincère et scrupuleuse.*"

The main influences by which he was inspired were the writings of Chateaubriand, whose *Martyrs* gave him the first impulse in the direction of his future career, and Walter Scott, for whom he entertained a no less ardent admiration.

His best works are the *Conquête de l'Angleterre* and the *Récits des Temps Mérovingiens*, in the latter of which especially he evokes, with striking force and picturesqueness, the sturdy semi-barbarous princes, warriors, and people of those turbulent times. It is the masterpiece of the new narrative school of history initiated by Thierry.

As Thierry was the leader of the Descriptive school, **François Guizot** is the undoubted chief of the Philosophic group of historians.

> **Guizot** was born in Nîmes, at 1787, of a Protestant family, and after being brought up at Geneva, came to Paris, studied law, and became a professor at the Sorbonne, forming in the last years of the Restoration, with Villemain and Cousin, a kind of intellectual triumvirate. His lectures, which were mainly on French institutions, were suspended in 1822, and were not resumed till 1828.

Under Louis Philippe he was twice Minister of Public Instruction; in 1840 he was sent as French Ambassador to London, but after the fall of Thiers, returned and became President of the Council and chief adviser of Louis. By his steady opposition to all reasonable reforms he was largely instrumental in bringing about the Revolution of 1848. After that event he was for a short time in exile in England, but returned to France, and from 1851 on devoted himself entirely to his literary labours. He died in 1874.

His four principal works are the *Histoire de la Révolution d'Angleterre* (1826–1856), *Histoire Générale de la Civilisation en Europe* (1828), *Histoire Générale de la Civilisation en France* (1829–1832), *Mémoires pour servir à l'Histoire de mon Temps* (1858–1868).

Guizot's leading ideas are the superiority of constitutional government to even a legitimate and enlightened monarchy, and the necessity of religious faith, not only from the moral, but also from the social point of view. His method sacrifices the narrative and picturesque interest to a cold unimaginative exposition of facts. His works are models of order, system, and clearness, but not great examples of literary composition and style, and interesting rather to the student of history than to the general reader. His merits are those of the thinker and logician; events and characters are of secondary importance; his main concern everywhere centres in the ideas of which outward events and circumstances are, as it were, the symbol and expression.

Realism in history is represented by **Louis Adolphe Thiers** (1797–1877), who began by the study of law, but afterwards came to Paris and busied himself with literature and journalism. In 1823 appeared the first two volumes of his *Histoire de la Révolution Française*. Both under Louis Philippe and Napoleon III he played an important political *rôle*, and from 1871 to 1873 he was President of the Republic.

He wrote two great historical works, the already mentioned *Histoire de la Révolution Française* (1823–1827), and the *Histoire du Consulat et de l'Empire* (1845–1855).

Thiers is neither a painter like Thierry nor a philosopher

like Guizot, but before all a patient and reliable dealer in facts. Of his own untiring investigation he speaks himself: "*Je n'ai aucun repos que je n'aie découvert la preuve du fait . . . et je ne m'arrête que lorsque je l'ai trouvée ou que j'ai acquis la certitude qu'elle n'existe pas.*"

He was gifted with an excellent fund of sense and a marvellous facility of comprehension, coupled with a rare faculty for expounding and elucidating. Even the most difficult subjects give the impression of simplicity and ease under his treatment. He has been accused of cynical indifference towards the merits or demerits of the actions he relates, but this is due rather to his desire to give a faithful reproduction of reality, without philosophic deductions or bias of any kind, than to any want of moral sympathy. Through the prominence he gave to his admiration for Napoleon, he was one of those who helped to build up the Napoleonic legend, and indirectly collaborated in bringing about the Second Empire.

A friend and intimate of Thiers was **François Auguste Mignet** (1796–1884), whose fame rests on the *Histoire de la Révolution Française*, which appeared in 1824. He represents the Revolution as the natural outgrowth of the different conditions of time, place, climate, and national temperament. This endeavour to explain all effects as the necessary and inevitable result of their respective causes has led to the charge of fatalism being laid against him—a charge which is partly justified, though he by no means fails to recognize the power of human will and energy to modify the course of events. At the same time, he ascribes to them a limited *rôle*, or, as he himself says: "*Ce sont moins les hommes qui ont mené les choses, que les choses qui ont mené les hommes.*"

His *French Revolution* is a concise but admirably clear account of the great events of which it treats, giving a vivid picture, and at the same time sober and philosophic deductions, the value of the whole being heightened by the excellence of the form. His style is a model of conciseness and concentration without obscurity.

The greatest of all French historians, and unrivalled as an evocator of the past, is **Jules Michelet.**

> Michelet (1798–1874) was born in Paris, the son of a printer, and was brought up amid scenes of poverty and privation. In 1833 he became assistant Professor of History under Guizot at the Sorbonne; in 1837 professor at the Collège de France. Refusing to swear allegiance to Napoleon, he was deprived of his chair in 1851, and henceforward devoted himself entirely to his literary labours. During the last twenty years of his life he did not confine himself to history, but wrote many works in which philosophy, the love of nature, and poetry are delightfully blended.

His principal historical writings are the great *Histoire de France*, begun in 1833, in ten years brought up to the Renaissance, and continued later, after the appearance of the *Histoire de la Révolution* (1847–1853), and the *Des Jésuites* (1843), written in collaboration with Quinet. Of his other works, among the best known are *Du Prêtre, de la Femme, de la Famille* (1845), *L'Oiseau* (1856), *L'Insecte* (1857), *La Bible de l'Humanité* (1864), *La Montagne* (1868).

Of his historical writings the best is the part of his *Histoire de France* which deals with the Middle Ages. Here his gift of imagination and picturesque and vivid description have full play, and he is not led astray by the party feelings and prejudices which make him so partial in his treatment of periods nearer to his own day.

The *Histoire de la Révolution*, in spite of its brilliant pictures and literary merits, has little value as history. The writer is too much influenced by his passionate democratic sympathies to give a cool and impartial account of the period with which he is concerned. *Des Jésuites* shows the same failing from the historical point of view; it is also written in a pronounced party spirit—that of hostility to the famous order.

Michelet's pre-eminence as a historian lies in his picturesque revival of the past, in which he resembles Augustin Thierry, but far surpasses him in imaginative power, brilliance, and colour. In his later work, when he turns from history to the innate lyricism and poetry which had always been his passion, his faults of partisanship disappear, and his gifts of imagination and style are fully revealed. For glow and colour of form he is second only to Victor Hugo in the century, and the best of his wonderful prose poetry has permanent qualities that will only gain in reputation when time has allowed them to be placed at the right perspective.

Of the disciples of Guizot in the historical field the most conspicuous is, without contention, **Alexis de Tocqueville** (1805–1859), the author of two historical works which achieved a merited reputation—*De la Démocratie en Amérique* (1835–1840) and *L'Ancien Régime et la Révolution* (1856).

Both are excellent as philosophic history, and show great impartiality and freedom from prejudice and prepossession. De Tocqueville is a deep, original, and logical thinker, and performed a real service by his cool and objective examination of democracy.

With the growth of the new spirit in literature went hand in hand, as the necessary counterpart, a new conception of criticism, which found complete expression in **Charles Augustin Sainte-Beuve** (1804–1869), the great literary critic of the Romantic school.

Born at Boulogne-sur-Mer, he began life by the study of medicine, but, abandoning that profession, made his literary appearance by articles in the *Globe* on Victor Hugo, and formally joined the Romanticists, becoming one of the inner *Cénacle*.

Sainte-Beuve's works comprise his poems, *Joseph Delorme* (1829), *Les Consolations* (1830), and *Les Pensées d'Août* (1837); one novel, *Volupté* (1834); his critical essays, of which the most important are the *Tableau de la Poésie Française au XVIe Siècle* (1828), the *Portraits Littéraires* (1844–1852), the *Causeries du Lundi*, begun in the *Constitutionnel* (1857), and continued as *Nouveaux Lundis* in the *Moniteur*, and his great work *L'Histoire de Port-Royal* (1840–1860).

Apart from the intrinsic merit of his verse, which is not

great, his real significance as a poet is to be sought in the fact that he was the first to teach the Romanticists the value and importance of form, and especially of rhyme, in French poetry:

> Rime, qui donnes leurs sons
> Aux chansons;
> Rime, l'unique harmonie
> Du vers, qui sans tes accents
> Frémissants,
> Serait muet au génie, &c.

It was Sainte-Beuve, too, in the *Pensées d'Août*, who first struck the popular note afterwards carried to greater perfection by Manuel and Coppée, as we shall see later.

Nevertheless his fame will always rest on his achievement as a critic, for here he was a reformer and an innovator, and opened up a new era in the science of criticism. Instead of estimating all literary productions according to certain preconceived standards, he showed that they should be judged on their own merits, and that those merits depend not on their resemblance to some famous previous exemplar of their own literary kind, but on the value of the ideas expressed, and the way in which form and expression are adapted to the rendering of those ideas. In order to fully appreciate the conception from which the work has arisen, he proceeds from the work to the man, tries to get an insight into his personality and the different influences to which he has been subjected, and thus as it were to trace back the work under consideration through every process of its genesis. The purely human plays a very great part in his method, and his delicate and subtle appreciation of character, and wide, almost universal, sympathies, give a breadth and stability to his generalizations which make them of the very highest worth.

The gap between the old school and Sainte-Beuve's method had been partly bridged by **Abel François Villemain** (1790–1870), professor of Rhetoric at the Sorbonne, afterwards Ministre de l'Instruction Publique under Louis Philippe. His best-known work is *Cours de Littérature Française* (1828–1830).

Basing his literary judgments on a knowledge both of ancient and modern languages and literatures, he wrote much comparative criticism that was both valuable and impressive. By identifying literature with history, he represents the first step from that criticism which judged merely from a comparison of previous recognized models to the more modern scientific school.

Edgar Quinet (1803-1875), Michelet's collaborator in his attack on the Jesuits, and like him violently anti-clerical though imbued with deep religious feeling, tried his hand at many subjects, but was a complete master of none. Of his early works the most remarkable is *Ahasuérus* (1833), a kind of wildly romantic imitation, in prose, of the ancient mysteries, in which the Creation, the birth of our Lord, the Day of Judgment, the Leviathan, the stars, sphinxes, &c., are represented in a strange medley. This was followed by *Prométhée*, in verse (1838), and subsequently by *Merlin l'Enchanteur* (1860), a vast prose allegory. His prose is far superior to his poetry; in fact his studies on German literature and philosophy, and on medieval French literature—*Idées sur la Philosophie de l'Histoire de Herder*, 1825; *Les Épopées Françaises*, 1831; *Allemagne et Italie*, 1839—can still be read with profit, as also his letters to Michelet, and indeed all his various volumes of correspondence.

From a literary point of view, undoubtedly the most considerable of philosophers must be accounted **Victor Cousin** (1792-1867), born at Paris, the son of a jeweller. Educated at the *École Normale*, he became a professor of Greek at the age of twenty, but early turned his attention to philosophy. He first studied the Scottish metaphysicians, and afterwards devoted himself to the great German philosophers—Kant, Fichte, Schelling, and Hegel, visiting Germany in 1817. His lectures at the *Sorbonne* were only rivalled in popularity by those of Guizot.

He was the founder of philosophical eclecticism, which binds itself unreservedly to the tenets of no particular school, but chooses the best from all, and compounds therefrom a system of its own.

His principal philosophical writings are: *Sur le Fondement des Idées Absolues, Cours d'Histoire de la Philosophie Moderne* (1827); *Du Vrai, du Beau, et du Bien* (1836), and *Histoire Générale de la Philosophie*. With the last work Cousin was the initiator of the history of philosophy. He also wrote literary studies and criticism, principally on the early part of the seventeenth century in France, the best known of these being the *Études sur Pascal* (1842–1844), and *La Société Française au XVIIᵉ Siècle d'après le Grand Cyrus* (1858).

By his brilliant lectures and wonderful personal ascendancy he did more than anyone to revive the study of his subject in France.

Lastly, pulpit oratory found a worthy representative in **L'Abbé Lacordaire** (1802–1861), who revived religious eloquence, and introduced Romanticism in the pulpit. He was a born orator, full of fire, and gifted with a poetic utterance that won and carried away his auditors. During the years 1835 and 1836, and again from 1843 to 1851, he delivered the series of sermons famous as the *Conférences de Notre-Dame*.

SECOND PERIOD (1850–1900)

CHAPTER I

POETRY

All the chief poets of the opening years of this period belong to the group known as the *Parnassiens*. Among them the first to come forward was **Théodore de Banville** (1823–1891), the most direct and obvious disciple of Théophile Gautier, the founder of the school.

Already before 1850 he had published two volumes of verse: *Les Cariatides* (1842) and *Les Stalactites* (1846); which were followed by *Odelettes* and *Odes Funambulesques* (both in 1857), *Les Exilés* (1874), and *Les Princesses* in the same year. He also composed numerous plays: *Gringoire* (1866), *Socrate et sa Femme* (1885), *Le Baiser* (1888)—all of no great merit.

The names that De Banville gives to the majority of his collections show plainly the characteristics of his verse. He carries still further the principles of Gautier, reducing the cult of art for art's sake to that of art for the sake of artificiality. With Gautier the idea had after all counted for something, but with De Banville all traces of it vanish before his excessive worship of poetic form, and more especially of rhyme,[1] on which, according to him, the value of verse solely depends. " *La rime* ", he informs us in his curious *Petit Traité de Poésie Française*, " *est l'unique harmonie du vers et elle est tout le vers. . . . Dans la poésie française, la rime est le moyen suprême d'expression et l'imagination de la rime est le maître-outil. . . . C'est une loi absolue, comme les lois physiques; tant que le poète exprime véritablement sa pensée, il rime bien; dès que sa pensée s'embarrasse, sa rime aussi s'embarrasse, devient faible, traînante et vulgaire.*" He is even prepared to uphold the use of the *cheville* or padding in the body of the line, although it should be stated that in nearly every case it is impossible to detect it in De Banville's verse, so great is his metrical skill.

Such a conception of verse explains his fondness for the most complicated old French poetic forms, such as the *rondeau*, the *ballade*, and the *triolet*, which afforded excellent opportunities for the special display of his virtuosity. From its very nature De Banville's poetry excites surprise rather than admiration, and he shows a true appreciation of his talent when he ingenuously confesses that his ambition was to ally the buffoon element to the lyric, by curious combinations of rhymes or peculiar effects of sounds. To sum up, we cannot do better than to quote Jules Lemaître's witty definition of Théodore de Banville: " *Un poète lyrique hypnotisé par la rime, le dernier venu, le plus amusé et dans ses bons jours le plus amusant des romantiques, un clown en poésie qui a eu dans sa vie plusieurs idées, dont la plus persistante a été de n'exprimer*

[1] Cp. Sainte-Beuve.

aucune idée dans ses vers." In spite of these reservations, some of his trifling *odelettes*, or mocking *vers de société*, where verbal and metrical skill are a help and not a hindrance, are unsurpassed in their kind. In the *Exilés* and *Princesses*, his later collections, De Banville showed that he was capable of writing stately descriptions in the manner of the later *Parnassiens* (cp. *Le Sanglier, Andromède, Némée*, &c.).

The morbid and decadent tendency found an early and intense expositor in Banville's unfortunate friend **Charles Baudelaire** (1821–1867), whose works, in addition to the translations from Edgar Poe and the prose *Paradis Artificiels*, consist of the poems published in 1857 under the title of *Fleurs du Mal*. In this collection he gives form to his paradoxical theory that everything in nature is evil, and all that is natural is hateful, although it should not be overlooked that much of his so-called *satanisme* is pure pose; in fact, Baudelaire himself warns us that " a little of the charlatan is always permissible to genius ". His principal idea is that of death, and death not as a symbolic conception, but in its sensations of decay and corruption. As an artist he is painstaking and powerful, and amid the fungous growths or noxious bacilli of his *Flowers of Evil*, can be found curiously idealistic or symbolical poems, such as *L'Idéal du Poète, Correspondances*, and *Harmonie du Soir*, remarkable for compactness and finish, as well as for the great influence they exercised on the succeeding generation.

The greatest poet of the second half of the nineteenth century is probably **Charles Marie Leconte de Lisle** (1818–1894), the acknowledged leader of the *Parnassiens*, the second clearly-defined poetic school of the century. He was born in the island colony of Réunion, and did not remove permanently to France till 1847. After his political hopes had been dashed by the *Coup d'État*, he settled down in Paris to a life of literary work. Apart from his translations from Homer, Hesiod, and Æschylus, Leconte de Lisle's poetry consists of *Poèmes Antiques* (1853), *Poèmes Barbares* (1862), and *Poèmes*

Tragiques (1884), besides a volume of posthumous verse, *Derniers Poèmes*, published in 1895.

Like all the school of which he was the undisputed chief, Leconte de Lisle attaches very great importance to the poetic art itself, and his form is wholly admirable in its flawless plasticity, while his language exhibits wonderful precision, enhanced by a never-failing instinct for the telling word, and enriched by fine, expressive imagery. His poetry is characterized by a well-marked and avowed disinclination to make a show of his personal feelings; he always protested against the professional use of tears, the cry of the heart, or other such like Romantic devices, which to him appeared a cheapening and corruption of art. In that respect the piece entitled *Les Montreurs* might serve as an epigraph to the whole of his poems:

> *Tel qu'un morne animal, meurtri, plein de poussière,*
> *La chaîne au cou, hurlant au chaud soleil d'été,*
> *Promène qui voudra son cœur ensanglanté*
> *Sur ton pavé cynique, ô plèbe carnassière!*
>
> . . . .
>
> *Je ne livrerai pas ma vie à tes huées,*
> *Je ne danserai pas sur ton tréteau banal,* &c.

Yet in spite of the lack of subjectivity in his work, he is by no means the " impassible " that is sometimes imagined. He felt only too deeply, but instead of indulging in the everlasting self-contemplation of a Lamartine or a Musset, he thought it was a nobler task for the poet to give expression to the more general and less ephemeral sufferings of humanity. Behind his apparent cold callousness the careful reader can divine the most hopeless despair, the most profound aspiration after the nihility of the Buddhistic *nirvâna*, that impassable barrier beyond which the mind of man can conceive nothing. Nothing exists, all is illusion and dream; such, in short, is the basis of Leconte de Lisle's philosophy, as reflected not only in the poems inspired by Hindoo subjects (*Vision de Brahma, Baghavat, Çunacepa*), but also in *La Ravine Saint-*

Gilles, *La Dernière Vision*, *Fiat Nox*, and more especially in the last twelve verses of the *Poèmes Tragiques*, where it is so eloquently summed up:

> *Maya! Maya! torrent des mobiles chimères,*
> *Tu fais jaillir du cœur de l'homme universel*
> *Les brèves voluptés et les haines amères,*
> *Le monde obscur des sens et la splendeur du ciel.*
> *Mais qu'est-ce que le cœur des hommes éphémères,*
> *O Maya! sinon toi, le mirage immortel?*
> *Les siècles écoulés, les minutes prochaines,*
> *S'abîment dans ton ombre en un même moment,*
> *Avec nos cris, nos pleurs et le sang de nos veines;*
> *Éclair, rêve sinistre. éternité qui ment,*
> *La Vie antique est faite inépuisablement*
> *Du tourbillon sans fin des apparences vaines.*

The philosopher of the *Parnassiens* is **René Sully-Prudhomme** (1839–1907), who, with his *Stances et Poèmes* (1865), won a warm eulogy from Sainte-Beuve. Other volumes which followed were entitled *Les Solitudes* (1869), *Les Vaines Tendresses* (1875), *La Justice* (1878), and *Le Bonheur* (1888).

He began with a fine and delicate analysis of the inner life, the prevailing tone of which is a deep-seated but serene melancholy. In *La Justice* and *Le Bonheur*, the two greatest French philosophic poems of this century, he attempted a larger manner. The former, which speaks of the search for justice, teaches that it is only to be attained in the human conscience; the latter, that happiness can only be reached through self-abnegation and love. Though he attaches more importance to the moral significance of his work than his fellow *Parnassiens*, like them he attains very great precision and finish of form.

Altogether his poetry, with its union of subtlety and exactness, delicate psychology and science, has very great originality and distinction.

Following in the footsteps of Sainte-Beuve, **Eugène Manuel** (1823–1901) has acquired a well-deserved reputation for some charming pictures of the everyday life of the lower classes in

Paris—*Pages Intimes* (1866), *Poèmes Populaires* (1871), *Pendant la Guerre* (1872), and *En Voyage* (1882).

The same conditions of life form the favourite theme of **François Coppée** (1842-1908), a very popular poet in his day. With *Le Reliquaire* (1866) and *Les Intimités* (1868) he won for himself a distinguished place among the *Parnassiens*. Other noteworthy collections of his are: *La Grève des Forgerons* (1869), *Les Humbles* (1872), *Promenades et Intérieurs* (1872), *Contes en Vers* (1881 and 1887).

Devoid of any great original power, Coppée nevertheless displays a delicate skill and a fund of graceful sentiment in the treatment of those subjects which he has made particularly his own. His style has an easy simplicity, due to his perfect mastery of all the artifices of rhyme and rhythm, although it cannot be said that he always succeeds in avoiding the prosaic and trivial in his treatment of popular themes.

Among the adherents of Leconte de Lisle none was a more faithful disciple than **José Maria de Heredia** (1842-1905), though he never shared his master's pessimistic outlook on life. Born at Santiago in Cuba of a French mother and claiming descent from the old *conquistadores*, he migrated to France at an early age and subsequently became a student at the École des Chartes, and there can be little doubt that his training and the scholarship of the famous school influenced his conception of the poetic art. His poems were not collected in book form until 1893, in a small volume of some two hundred pages, entitled *Les Trophées*, and consist almost entirely of sonnets, which form Heredia adopted deliberately as most worthy of the perfect artist he aimed to be. The sonnets were arranged by the author himself in separate sections, each section representing in a succession of pictures or portraits, typical phases of the history of civilization: Greece and Sicily; Rome and the Barbarians; the Middle Ages and the Renaissance; the East and the Tropics; with a concluding section entitled Nature and Dreams. Heredia may be said to have realized the Parnassian ideal—perfect form and absolute objectivity. Though some may find the highly wrought medallions of the *Trophées* somewhat cold in their formal beauty, their craftsmanship is such as to entitle Heredia to be ranked among the greatest sonnet writers, not only of France, but of the world. He is original too in having enlarged the horizon of the idea in the concluding lines of the sonnet, instead of compressing it. Take, for instance, the last lines of *Antoine et Cléopâtre*, where the Roman imperator, bending over the Egyptian Queen,

> *Vit dans ses larges yeux étoilés de points d'or*
> *Toute une mer immense où fuyaient des galères.*

Or again, the wide vistas opened up in the last tercet of *Les Conquérants*:

> *Chaque soir, espérant des lendemains épiques,*
> *L'azur phosphorescent de la mer des Tropiques*
> *Enchantait leur sommeil d'un mirage doré;*
>
> *Ou, penchés à l'avant des blanches caravelles,*
> *Ils regardaient monter dans un ciel ignoré*
> *Du fond de l'Océan des étoiles nouvelles.*

Of the school known as *Symbolistes* or *Décadents* the greatest by far is **Paul Verlaine**, that second Villon, born in 1844, who, after a vagabond life spent between workhouses, cafés, and hospitals, died in January, 1896. He made his literary début in 1866 with a volume entitled *Poèmes Saturniens*, followed by *Fêtes Galantes* (1869), and *La Bonne Chanson* (1870), all of which show in various ways the influence of Banville, Baudelaire, and Leconte de Lisle. He first struck a distinctively personal note in *Romances sans Paroles* (1874). Then, after a long period of silence, during which he had suffered a term of imprisonment and been converted to the Catholic faith, appeared *Sagesse* (1881), verses of humble and sincere penitence, unsurpassed in the French language, and which have been called by a great contemporary critic " the first in French poetry that express truly the love of God ".

Other collections were *Jadis et Naguère* (1885), *Bonheur* (1889), *Parallèlement* (1890), the latter a strange conception, in which the theme is alternately sin and repentance.

Verlaine's position and the character of his poetry have been frequently misunderstood, even by those who called themselves his disciples. As a matter of fact, he was a considerable innovator. At bottom Verlaine's idea, stripped of its antic garb, was to replace the rhetoric and rigorously disciplined rhythm of French poetry, which the Romantic school, in spite of its innovations, had left almost unimpaired, by the dreamy suggestiveness which English or German poetry so admirably conveys. Although the inherent limpidity of the French language that makes of it an incomparable vehicle for prose or certain kinds of poetry renders rivalry with the Germanic languages almost impossible in this respect, yet Verlaine showed that partial success was possible, and thus rendered a great service to French lyric poetry. This will be readily realized by a comparison of the following little gem with Victor Hugo's characteristic verse, or still better with that of Leconte de Lisle:

> *Il pleure dans mon cœur*
> *Comme il pleut sur la ville,*
> *Quelle est cette langueur*
> *Qui pénètre mon cœur?*

> *O bruit doux de la pluie*
> *Par terre et sur les toits!*
> *Pour un cœur qui s'ennuie*
> *O le chant de la pluie!*

> *Il pleure sans raison*
> *Dans ce cœur qui s'écœure.*
> *Quoi! nulle trahison?*
> *Ce deuil est sans raison.*

> *C'est bien la pire peine*
> *De ne savoir pourquoi,*
> *Sans amour et sans haine*
> *Mon cœur a tant de peine.*

In this connection Verlaine's *Art Poétique*, a short poem of thirty-six lines, should be carefully read. We quote the two stanzas which best illustrate our meaning:

> *Il faut que tu n'ailles point*
> *Choisir tes mots sans quelque méprise;*
> *Rien de plus cher que la chanson grise*
> *Où l'Indécis au Précis se joint...*
>
> *De la musique encore et toujours!*
> *Que ton vers soit la chose envolée*
> *Qu'on sent qui fuit d'une âme en allée*
> *Vers d'autres cieux, à d'autres amours.*

In versification his reforms were likewise aimed at the directness and excessive cult of rhyme of his predecessors. Hence his fondness for uneven measures, such as lines of nine, eleven, or thirteen syllables.

> *De la musique avant toute chose,*
> *Et pour cela préfère l'Impair*
> *Plus vague et plus soluble dans l'air,*
> *Sans rien qui pèse ou qui pose.*
> —*Art Poétique.*

He also used the cæsura with great freedom, and restored the hiatus of old French poetry.

In spite of the unevenness of his work, Verlaine is in reality a great poet, in turn simple and complex, strong and yet capable of unexpected depths of tenderness. He has left some poems which are masterpieces of mystic fervour and deep human sympathy. He is a decadent in the super-sensitiveness and morbid sentimentality of a portion of his verse, but it is erroneous to imagine that his work consists mainly of symbolical oddities. That he did write a few such poems, thus giving the Symbolist school the opportunity of claiming him as their leader, is undeniable, but he wrote his best poetry when recreant to the theories of the Symbolists, whose endeavour it was, while accepting Verlaine's teaching, to manifest physically by means of symbols what is spiritually accessible only to the few.

The theorist of the true Symbolists, who may be called their leader with much more right than Verlaine, was **Stéphane Mallarmé** (1842-1898). He produced very little himself (some hundred poems in all, a single volume of prose, a few pamphlets, and a prose translation of the poems of Poe); but by his lofty conception of the poetic art and his wonderful personal ascendancy he exercised a powerful influence on the young poets of his time who used to foregather Tuesday by Tuesday to listen to the Master in his rooms in the Rue de Rome, where he lived a quiet and studious life on his modest stipend as Professor of English in one of the Paris *lycées*. In spite of his habitual obscurity it is to Mallarmé, strange to say, that we owe the most lucid definition of Symbolism. It runs as follows: " *La contemplation des objets, l'image s'envolant de rêveries suscitées par eux, sont le chant: les Parnassiens, eux, prennent la chose entièrement et la montrent; par là, ils manquent de mystère; ils retirent aux esprits cette joie délicieuse de croire qu'ils créent. Nommer un objet, c'est supprimer les trois-quarts de la jouissance du poème qui est faite du bonheur de deviner peu à peu; le suggérer, voilà le rêve. C'est le parfait usage de ce mystère qui constitue le symbole; évoquer petit à petit un objet pour montrer un état d'âme, ou, inversement, choisir un objet et en dégager un état d'âme par une série de déchiffrements.*" The symbol disengages from the mystic signs of nature a hidden soul, or rather *états d'âme*, to use Amiel's expression, which are very similar to ours, and which at least belong to the same category of sensibilities. Baudelaire had already been struck by these " *correspondances* ":

> *La Nature est un temple où de vivants piliers*
> *Laissent parfois sortir de confuses paroles;*
> *L'homme y passe à travers des forêts de symboles*
> *Qui l'observent avec des regards familiers.*

Nature must yield her secrets, and the universal life blend with the life of him who questions her. It matters little whether the emotions of the reader differ in detail from those of the poet provided they flow from the same state of sensibility. Not only does the reader "think" that he is creating life, as Mallarmé puts it, but he does so in reality from the moment the symbol suggests and evokes emotion. It is this endless, inexhaustible, creative power that distinguishes Symbolism from allegory. Such then is the theory in outline. With Mallarmé the symbol or *motif* is clear enough as a rule, but the emotions called forth in his mind by the symbol, especially in some of his later sonnets, are often so subtle and complex that they find no echo in the mind of the ordinary mortal. In this he was perfectly consistent, for he addressed himself to the select few only and exclusively; "without a musical education", he said once, "you would not pretend to understand a Beethoven symphony or a Mozart sonata. Why, then, without any education in the art of poetry should one pretend to understand poetry." Another cause of his obscurity, which this remark explains, is that in his attempt to rival music he choses his words and phrases for their musical and evocative value alone, and here again his verbal sonorities, in keeping with the emotions they suggest to him, make no appeal save to the initiated. The result is that the bulk of his verse will always be a closed book to most of us, though he did write, before he had fallen a victim to the fatal enchantments of a theory, a few poems which are assured of literary longevity.

The most versatile of the group is without doubt **Henri de Régnier** (born 1864). His earlier collections of verse are written almost exclusively in the so-called *vers libres*, in the handling of which none of the Symbolists have equalled him, unless it be Verhaeren. This kind of verse, which unlike Symbolism itself has still adherents among present-day poets, was probably suggested by the example of Walt Whitman, and was first erected into a prosodic system by **Gustave Kahn** (born 1859), one of the most extravagant of the then young reformers. The lines of *vers libres* may vary from one to fourteen or more syllables, mixed in any order, according, so runs the theory, to the promptings of poetic inspiration or the changing aspect of the subject in hand. No heed is paid to syllabism or number, one of the fundamental principles of regular French prosody, so that the *vers libre* as practised by the Symbolists differs profoundly from the *vers libre* of La Fontaine's *Fables* for example, in which the different measures are never blended in such a way as to obliterate number. The *vers libristes*, as they styled themselves, make as free with rhyme, which with them is frequently replaced by mere assonance or mixed in any order, as they do with syllabism. According to them the initial impulse determines the rhythm of the strophe. Rhythm is the one important factor; nothing else matters.

De Régnier's best work in *vers libres* will be found in *Sites* (1887), *Poèmes Anciens et Romanesques* (1890), *Tel qu'en Songe* (1892), and in *Les Jeux Rustiques et Divins* (1897). In his subsequent work de Régnier, under the influence of Heredia, whose daughter he married in 1896, has discarded that form of prosody and turned to a technique more or less borrowed from the *Parnassiens* and to a classical conception of poetry, as a result of which he can no longer be accounted a Symbolist in that part of his work. The change is evident already in *Les Médailles d'Argile* (1900), and becomes more pronounced in the volumes which have appeared since (*La Sandale Ailée*, *La Cité des Eaux*, &c.).

Henri de Régnier has shown his versatility in prose as well as in verse by writing a large number of short stories and novels in a style free from any Symbolist peculiarities.

With more of genius in him though less productive was **Jean Moréas** (1856–1910), born at Athens, and whose real name is Jean Papadiamantopoulos. He also gradually drifted from Symbolism, and by a curious evolution, due no doubt in part at least to his Hellenic origin, became the founder and leader of the *École Romane*, whose ambition it was to rival the sixteenth-century *Pléiade*, and by so doing to revert to the Romance tradition, the only true guide. Conscious after a time of the futility of writing what were in fact nothing but pastiches of Ronsard and his followers, he showed himself a remarkable poet in his wholly admirable *Stances* (1899–1901), classic both in form and inspiration and one of the supreme achievements of modern French lyricism, as also in the tragedy *Iphigénie* (1903).

Here too a place should be found for **Émile Verhaeren** (1855–1916), the greatest of the Belgian poets who have written in French, and generally recognized as one of the outstanding poets of modern Europe. Beginning as a Realist, he was attracted for a time by Symbolism, which he soon renounced, however, in favour of a larger and more lofty conception of the poet's mission. His first noteworthy collection of verse was *Les Flamandes* (1883), realistic sketches of the life and people of his native Flanders in the manner of Teniers. This was followed year after year by a constant stream of other remarkable poems till the year of his death, amounting in all to some score of substantial volumes, showing that Verhaeren was not one of those who toyed with his art, like so many of the Symbolists. Of these by far the most important are the two great trilogies. The first consists of the three volumes: *Les Soirs* (1887), *Les Débâcles* (1888), and *Les Flambeaux Noirs* (1890), in which the poet, lately recovered from a long and painful illness, is seen struggling out of gloom and darkness to renewed hope and faith. Verhaeren's masterpiece is his second trilogy, comprising *Les Campagnes Hallucinées* (1893), *Les Villages Illusoires* (1895), and *Les Villes Tentaculaires* (1895), a picture of the countryside swallowed up by the tide, rising relentlessly, of the great manufacturing towns. Here we have not only great poetry, but poetry that is truly modern, such as Walt Whitman might have penned, reflecting one of the most striking phenomena of a modern civilization with all it implies—the naked, abandoned fields; the deserted homes; the huge and grim cities of refuge, with smoke and carbon flames shooting out, where life riots and swelters. The style too matches the matter—vigorous and direct, brutal at times, teeming with popular metaphors. Among the later works should be mentioned *La Multiple Splendeur* (1906), dealing with the problems of modern industrialism in the spirit of the convinced Socialist Verhaeren had become, and *Les Ailes Rouges de la Guerre* (1916), a scathing indictment of German atrocities as well as a tragic presentation of the horrors of war, which has been compared not inaptly to Victor Hugo's *Châtiments*. Verhaeren also wrote a few plays (*Philippe II, Le Cloître, Hélène de Sparte*), more remarkable for their lyric than for their dramatic qualities.

Verhaeren is essentially a Northern genius; he has not the French refinement and sense of proportion, but on the other hand he stands head and shoulders above any of the French Symbolists by the massive splendour of his work.

Among the lesser lights of Symbolism may be mentioned: **Francis Vielé-Griffin** (born 1864), a Gallicized native of the United States, who sings exclusively in *vers libres*. His cheery optimism contrasts pleasantly with the hopelessness of many of his fellows. **Albert Samain** (1858–1900), a delicate though somewhat langorous elegiac, too obviously inspired by Baudelaire and Verlaine, whose successive *recueils* (*Au Jardin de l'Infante*, 1893; *Aux Flancs du Vase*, 1898; *Le Chariot d'Or*, 1901) encourage the belief that he might have developed greater originality had he not died so young.

Finally, a few poets who do not belong to any particular school deserve passing recognition: **Jean Lahor** (1840–1909), whose real name is Cazalis, continues the philosophy of Leconte de Lisle in his Buddhistic poetry (*L'Illusion*, 1888, and enlarged 1893), but differs from him in that his verse is more truly lyrical. **Maurice Rollinat** (1846–1903) commenced by composing poems under the influence of George Sand's rustic novels (*Dans les Brandes*, 1877), but afterwards fell under the spell of the morbid Baudelaire (*Les Névroses*, 1883), though his last collection, *La Nature* (1892), testifies to a serener frame of mind. **Jean Richepin**, born in 1849 in Algeria, had experiences during his youth of the realities of life as a *franc-tireur* and as a sailor, which are reflected in his early poems. He began by an attempt to introduce the baser side of Naturalism into poetry, in *La Chanson des Gueux* (1876), and in *Les Blasphèmes* (1884). Abandoning this, he wrote descriptions of sailor life and remarkable seascapes in *La Mer* (1886), which display to the full his wonderful verbal invention and metrical agility, though not always free from eccentricities. His later poems, *Mes Paradis* (1894), share the clearly-marked tendency of recent literature towards an idealistic reaction.

Before the beginning of the present century Symbolism, which it must be remembered never had any real hold on the drama and still less on prose writings, is a spent force. Although certain general tendencies and more or less definable groups emerge in the general disintegration none of these can be said at the present day to have won in the domain of poetry anything like general acceptance. Nevertheless the cult of poetry has continued to flourish, and the first two decades of the present century have brought to light a considerable number of poets of undoubted talent, of which those only can be mentioned who appear to be the most significant: **Paul Valéry** (born 1871) continues the tradition of Mallarmé in his noble and dignified *Odes* (1920), and in *Charmes ou Poèmes* (1922). Had he published more he would perhaps be ranked as the greatest of contemporary French poets. **Francis Jammes** (born 1868), on the contrary, is very prolific and has exercised very great influence. He is the chief representative of the Catholic revival and of the return to Nature. He sings with somewhat affected simplicity, and not without a touch of irony, the praises of the rustic folk and countryside of his beloved Orthez in *De l'Angélus de l'Aube à l'Angélus du Soir* (1898), and in *Les Géorgiques Chrétiennes* (1913). He excels chiefly as an elegiac (*Le Deuil des Primevères*, 1902). Another Catholic and rural poet is **Louis Mercier** (born 1870), but being of peasant stock and a peasant himself, the notes of his rustic reed have a truer ring than those of Jammes. Starting as a too obvious imitator of Baudelaire and the *Parnassiens* in *L'Enchantée* (1897), he found the true path in his admirable *Les Voix de la Terre et du Temps* (1903). The Catholic revival is also apparent, in a very different aspect however, in the verse of **Paul Claudel** (born 1868), a synthetic and obscure writer, who has adopted a form of verse recalling that of the Psalms and sometimes that of Walt Whitman. An important part in the religious renascence was also played by **Charles Péguy** (born 1873), who fell at Plessy-l'Évêque in September, 1914. His best poetry centres round the national legends of Jeanne d'Arc and Sainte-Geneviève, though he is best known for a lofty patriotic poem. The group of the self-styled *Humanistes* is headed by **Fernand Gregh** (born 1873), originally a follower of Verlaine, and includes Abel Bonnard, the novelist Henri Barbusse, and Léo Larguier. Weary of the aloofness of the *Parnassiens* and of Symbolist obscurity, they dreamed of an art which should be " more enthusiastic and more tender at the same time, more active and less narrow, direct, living, an art in a word which should sum up everything—a *human* art ". The ideal of another group, the Neo-Classicists, whose guides are Moréas and Maurras and of whom we have already spoken, is best represented in this period by the work of **Jean Marc Bernard** (born 1881), a poet of the greatest promise, who fell in action on the Somme, in July, 1915. His *Sub Tegmine Fagi* (1913) recalls Horace, and in its descriptions of country, Virgil. Here also must be classed the later work, notably *L'Homme Intérieur* (1905), inspired by Chénier, of **Charles Guérin** (1873–1907), who had begun as a disciple of the Symbolists. The society of the *Unanimistes*, grouped round **Jules Romains** (born 1885) and **Charles Vildrac** (born 1883), influenced by the example of Verhaeren and Walt Whitman, seeks poetic truth in the glorification of groups and collective masses in which individuality must be merged and absorbed. Despite his theories Jules Romains is no mean exponent of his art as his various collections show, of which the most characteristic are *La Vie Unanime* (1908), *Odes et*

Prières (1913), and *Europe* (1919). Vildrac, who upholds the use of *vers libres*, is of less moment, except perhaps in his *Chants du Désespéré* (1920). Of the self-styled *Fantaisistes*, who often hide their disillusionment under the cloak of irony or sarcasm, the widest appeal is made by **Tristan Derème** (born 1889), in *La Verdure Dorée* (1922). Among the independents who have refused to identify themselves either with the modernists or the traditionalists **Paul Fort** (born 1872), the author of *Les Ballades Françaises*, of which some twenty-nine volumes have appeared up to date, stands out. Fort expresses himself in a kind of rhythmic prose—" *un style pouvant passer au gré de l'émotion de la prose au vers et du vers à la prose* ". His compositions, ranging over a wide and varied field, are reminiscent of folk-songs and at another time of the minor poets of the seventeenth century.

Lastly a few lines should be reserved for the poetesses of the present day, who, both in number and excellence, have never been equalled at any other period in the annals of French literature. Among them the outstanding figure is undoubtedly **La Comtesse Mathieu de Noailles** (born 1876), of Greek and Roumanian ancestry, who has written the most beautiful feminine poems of the century. She is essentially lyric, ultra-emotional perhaps, pursuing love and all that life and nature have to give with a sort of frenzy, but haunted by the idea of death. This antinomy between the joy of life and the fear of death, and her love of nature, are her chief characteristics. She proceeds directly from the great Romanticists of 1830, particularly Musset, while her supersensitiveness she inherited from Baudelaire. Her most representative verse is contained in *L'Ombre des Jours* (1902), *Les Éblouissements* (1907), and *Les Forces Éternelles* (1920). Romantic also, but more in the vein of de Vigny, is the poetry of **Madame Henri de Régnier** (born 1875), wife of the poet and second daughter of de Heredia, who writes under the pen-name of Gérard d'Houville. In sharp contrast to that of the Comtesse de Noailles, her verse breathes a spirit of virile and noble stoicism not untempered by a touch of discreet emotion. **Madame Lucie Delarue-Mardrus** (born 1880) has sung the flowers, the sea, and the landscapes of her native Normandy (*Horizons*, 1905; *Par Vents et Marées*, 1911; *Souffles de Tempête*, 1918) with an intoxication purely physical.

Though the poetry of these three (they can be taken as representative) differs widely, they have this in common, that they each continue some aspect of Romanticism and by so doing react against Symbolist idealism.

CHAPTER II

DRAMA

The second half of the nineteenth century is one of the most brilliant periods of the French theatre, the prevailing dramatic type being the realistic *comédie de mœurs*, in sharp contrast to Scribe's shallow comedy of imbroglio. The principal representative of the new type is **Alexandre Dumas fils**, son of the novelist, who was born in Paris in 1824, and after a good education, early turned to literature, publishing in 1848 his novel *La Dame aux Camélias*, which he dramatized in the following year. In addition to novels, with which he began his literary career, and dramas, which form the bulk of his work, he wrote a large number of essays, letters, prefaces, and pamphlets. He died in 1895. Of his seventeen plays, among the best-known are *La Dame aux Camélias* (1852), *Le Demi-Monde* (1855), *La Question d'Argent* (1857), *Le Fils Naturel* (1858), *Un Père Prodigue* (1859), *Les Idées de Madame Aubray* (1867), *Une Visite de Noces* (1871), *Denise* (1885).

In the first of his plays, *La Dame aux Camélias*, Dumas both displayed the moralizing tendency which inspired all his dramatic work, and gave the first intimation of the kind of moral problems with which he was to occupy himself. The subject is the same as that of Victor Hugo's *Marion Delorme*

—the rehabilitation of a fallen woman through pure love. In the *Demi-Monde* he likewise treats the social question arising through the existence in society of this class, and handles the subject with the greatest realism and outspokenness, though it is doubtful if his crusade had much practical effect. The same note of warning to the youth of France is the burden in *L'Ami des Femmes*, *Une Visite de Noces*, *La Princesse Georges*, and *L'Étrangère*, while other reforms in the social or legal fabric are also advocated in *Le Fils Naturel*, *Les Idées de Mme Aubray*, and *M. Alphonse*.

Everywhere, in fact, Dumas insists on the moral significance of the stage, maintaining that it is the duty of the dramatist to expose the burning social evils of his day, using his position for the improvement and edification, and not merely for the amusement, of society. Yet commendable as is this theory, it has its dangers, from which, moreover, Dumas does not escape, and the *pièce à thèse*, the problem play, is only too apt to acquire an air of premeditation, and lose in life and movement what it gains in moral worth. Nevertheless, although the didactic purpose is sometimes too prominent, his plays are, without exception, worthy of being ranked as literature, and they reveal everywhere a perfect understanding of the requirements of the stage. Dumas is a born dramatist, and knows how to give the action the highest degree of movement and life, and to keep the interest of the public rooted to the dramatic business in hand. His style is vigorous and often brilliant, while in the art of sustained dramatic dialogue he is, thanks to his inexhaustible wit and verve, successful in a rare degree. In short, his work has many qualities of real greatness, and was not unworthy of its success, and of the influence it exercised. The only pity is that in the inculcation of the particular moral lessons to which he devoted his gifts and energies he should not have chosen a less paradoxical method, and one less apt to defeat the very ends he was seeking to attain.

The second in importance of the dramatists of the period

is **Emile Augier** (1820-1889), who, after producing some pleasant and not unsuccessful comedies and verse pieces, was directed by the appearance of the *Dame aux Camélias* to his true field, the representation of contemporary manners—the *comédie de mœurs*. In 1854 appeared *Le Gendre de M. Poirier*, written in collaboration with Sandeau, one of the classics of the modern French stage. It treats the familiar theme of the evils resulting from unions between needy aristocrat and wealthy *bourgeois*. His other representative pieces are *Ceinture Dorée* (1855), *Le Mariage d'Olympe* (1855), a sort of counterpart of *La Dame aux Camélias*, showing the disasters which result from the attempted rehabilitation of Olympe; *Les Lionnes Pauvres* (1858), *Maître Guérin* (1864), *Le Fils de Giboyer* (1863), and his last piece, certainly one of his best, *Les Fourchambault* (1878), a powerful picture of the miseries which arise from marriages of money or convenience.

It was Augier's boast that his life had been one free from events, and his type of mind is just what would be expected from a regular, successful life—solid healthy good sense and mental balance. It is from an eminently sensible and practical point of view that he regards that society of his own day which forms the subject-matter of his drama, and though he too, like Dumas, has a moral lesson to convey, it is no revolutionary or paradoxical one. He is before all the painter of the *bourgeoisie*, not only of Paris but of the provinces, and both in that respect, and also on account of many similarities in subject and treatment, has been compared with Balzac. He treats nearly all the questions which were agitating the particular society of his choice, and without display of didactic purpose, honestly strives by the ridicule of its weaknesses and vices to bring about its moral improvement.

Eugène Labiche (1815-1888) produced between 1848 and 1876 a number of vaudevilles, the best known being *Le Chapeau de Paille d'Italie* (1851) and *Le Voyage de M. Perrichon* (1860), in which a wonderful gift of invention and the most fertile fancy and wit were combined with a certain reasonableness even in the wildest farce. His best comedies contain shrewd observation, and even behind his caricatures is to be discerned great delicacy of tone and accuracy of expression.

The tradition of Scribe was continued by **Victorien Sardou** (1831–1908), who, after some preliminary failures, won immense success in his day in all branches of dramatic art— vaudevilles (*Divorçons*, 1880); comedies of manners (*Nos Intimes*, 1861; *La Famille Benoîton*, 1865); comedies of intrigue (*Les Pattes de Mouche*, 1861); political comedies (*Rabagas*, 1872); historical dramas (*Patrie*, 1869; *La Haine*, 1874; *Fédora*, 1884; *Thermidor*, 1891; *Madame Sans-Gêne*, 1893). Sardou is above all a past-master in stagecraft, and outdoes even Scribe in the truly amazing skill with which he weaves and unravels the most complicated intrigues and plots. On the other hand his characters, more particularly in the comedies, are shallow and unconvincing, in spite of the smart dialogue and undeniable wit. Nevertheless a few of his dramas, remarkable for their unity of action, have something of universal truth, and did not owe their success alone to Sarah Bernhardt's acting in the title *rôle*. Sardou then does not deserve all the unkind things certain critics have written about him, which is not to say, of course, that he can be called a dramatist of the first rank.

Far less copious, but possessing literary gifts of a much higher order, **Édouard Pailleron** (1834–1899) will always be remembered for his satirical comedy *Le Monde où l'on s'ennuie* (1881), which has been not inaptly compared with *Les Femmes Savantes*, with the necessary differences of time and circumstance. His other pieces, of which the most noteworthy are *L'Étincelle* (1879) and *Cabotins* (1894), do not reach the same high level.

Jules Lemaître (1853–1914), better known as a literary critic, has written some dozen plays which, though they did not obtain great popularity, have given him a high rank among modern dramatists. They all reveal an exceptionally keen sense of psychology and unusual skill in portraying simply and unostentatiously the more delicate emotions of the human heart. The best are *Le Député Leveau* (1890), *Mariage Blanc* (1891), *Le Pardon* (1895), *La Princesse de Clèves* (1908).

The problem play continues to flourish, albeit in a modified form, in the work of **François de Curel** (born 1854), who, taking up large social and philosophic questions (*L'Envers d'une Sainte*, *L'Amour brode*, *Les Fossiles*, &c.), will always remain too difficult and abstract ever to win popular approval; and more especially in that of the more accessible **Eugène Brieux** (born 1858), the author of some two dozen plays dealing with the ordinary problems of society, particularly the lower and middle classes, and characterized by sound common sense and a high ideal of the playwright's *rôle* as a social reformer. His best is seen in *La Robe Rouge* (1900), one of the most powerful modern plays. He is less happy when his good intentions become too obvious, and occasionally his insistent preaching is apt to pall, as in *Les Remplaçantes* (1901), which teaches the humble lesson that it is better for a mother to suckle her own baby than to hand it over to a wet nurse, or in *La Française* (1907), depicting, for the benefit of foreigners, the typical French wife of the *bourgeoisie*, not as she appears in so many novels and plays, but as she exists in real life. As a thinker Brieux, the son of working-class parents, is never profound, but he is sane and shrewd.

Despite Brieux's somewhat shallow psychology and laboured style, it is a relief to turn to his plays after reading those of the more gifted **Henry Becque** (1837-1899), the leader of the new tendency in the theatre towards Naturalism. In his cruel pessimism and uncommented observation of the sordid and ugly aspects of life Becque typifies the reaction against the optimistic morality of the school of Scribe and Sardou, and for their technically correct plays he substituted what he called " slices of life ", presented in all their incoherence with just enough intrigue to connect the successive scenes. Unlike Brieux, Becque is not prolific; he wrote some half-dozen plays only, of which *Michel Pauper* (1870), *Les Corbeaux* (1882), and *La Parisienne* (1885), best illustrate his outlook on life and his dramatic technique.

To the category of the problem play belong also the dramas of **Paul Hervieu** (1857–1915), the novelist, dealing with the injustice of the laws that govern society or with the cruel workings of Nature's laws. *La Course du Flambeau* (1901), of which the motto could be "*quasi cursores vitai lampada tradunt*", shows each generation of humanity sacrificed to the selfish one that follows. Earlier plays are *Les Tenailles* (1895), the " pincers " being the marriage bond holding as in a vice the unhappy couple, and *La Loi de l'Homme* (1897), in which the injustice of the marriage laws is the theme. *Le Dédale* (1903) and *Le Réveil* (1905) are more melodramatic; and in *Connais-toi* (1909) a return is made to a more human kind of play. Hervieu's pieces grip the audience and have undoubted power, but, like those of De Curel, they are gloomy and depressing. His chief failing is that he creates types rather than individuals.

Becque's most objectionable features were encouraged and developed still further by an enterprising actor André Antoine, who in 1887 founded at Montmartre the **Théâtre Libre,** so called because it was a semi-private venture, dependent on subscribers and thus not subject to censorship, and because it welcomed those playwrights whose ideas were too advanced for the general public. Through lack of support the *Théâtre Libre* was forced to close its doors after a run of no more than ten years, but in the meantime it had exercised a considerable, and on the whole pernicious, influence on the French theatre, plainly perceptible in the work of such prominent present-day playwrights as **Henry Bataille** (1872–1922) and **Henry Bernstein** (born 1876), to name two only, who have too often devoted their talent to the portrayal of unhealthy emotions and vicious instincts. On the other hand it rendered appreciable service by liberating the stage from the routine of Conservatoire tradition, and also by introducing

DRAMA

to the French public the chief representatives of the new drama abroad, such as Tolstoi, Ibsen, and Hauptmann.

The romantic drama in verse, as opposed to the *drame naturaliste* in the manner of Becque and his adherents, burst into renewed life in the plays of **Edmond Rostand** (1868–1918), known the world over as the author of *Cyrano de Bergerac* (1897). He began his dramatic career with a pretty comedy, *Les Romanesques* (1894), recalling Musset in its graceful fantasy, followed by *La Princesse Lointaine* (1895), a dramatization of the story of the troubadour Jaufre Rudel, and by *La Samaritaine* (1897), a religious play of no great merit. Then came *Cyrano*, a "*comédie héroïque*", the most brilliant theatrical success of modern times and acclaimed at once as a masterpiece by critics of authority. The view, often expressed, that in *Cyrano* Rostand inaugurated a new epoch in the history of French dramatic art is untenable; it represents Romanticism renewed in its more flamboyant aspect, allied to Banvillesque metrical virtuosity in the grand manner, with a good deal of Gautier's *Capitaine Fracasse* in the hero's magnificent swagger. But the truly amazing fireworks of wit with which the whole play is sprinkled is all Rostand's own. *L'Aiglon* (1900), his next play, in which the hero is the son of Napoleon I, has no real life in it and only kept the stage for a while, thanks to the wonderful acting of Sarah Bernhardt and Coquelin. *Chantecler* (1910), with its characters disguised as birds and beasts and its lagging plot, showed that Rostand had reached his highest level in *Cyrano*.

The romantic drama in verse, which started with Victor Hugo's *Cromwell*, found other exponents, beside Rostand, in **Henri de Bornier** (1825–1901), whose *La Fille de Roland* (1875) still keeps the stage; **François Coppée** (he also wrote some delightful lyrical dramas, such as *Le Passant*), the author of *Les Jacobites* (1880), *Severo Torelli* (1883), and *Pour la Couronne* (1895), his masterpiece in this *genre*; in the equally versatile **Jean Richepin**, already noticed, to whom we owe *Nana Sahib* (1883), *Par le Glaive* (1892), and in the lighter vein of comedy *Le Chemineau* (1897), a very dashing and spirited performance.

Despite the brilliant success achieved not so long ago by Rostand, the romantic play in verse has again fallen into disfavour and there is no demand at the present day for dramatic work on those lines.

We have seen that Symbolism was primarily a poetic movement; it produced very little drama of note, except the earlier plays of **Maurice Maeterlinck** (born at Ghent in 1862)—*La Princesse Maleine* (1889), *L'Intruse* (1890), *Les Aveugles* (1890)—which owe their fame to the extravagant praise bestowed upon them at the time rather than to their intrinsic merit, which is very slight. In them he attempted to put into practice his theory of the " static drama ", relieved of what he called the disturbing element of action. The plots unroll in an atmosphere of mysteriousness and vague symbolism, the object of which is, in true Symbolist fashion, to evoke certain moods in the spectator rather than to say anything direct. His next plays show him less faithful to his earlier ideal, while in *Monna Vanna* (1902), returning to the dramatic traditions he had disowned, he wrote a frankly romantic drama inspired in part by Browning's *Luria*. *L'Oiseau Bleu* (1908), suggested perhaps by Barrie's *Peter Pan*, revealed another side of Maeterlinck's talent; it is a charming fairy play, free from all Symbolist intention—simple allegory such as children, for whom it was intended, can readily follow.

Maeterlinck is also the author of numerous essays, of which *Le Trésor des Humbles* (1896), *La Sagesse et la Destinée* (1898), and *La Vie des Abeilles* (1901), semi-philosophical disquisitions, alone possess general interest. His later treatises, from *Le Temple Enseveli* (1902) to *Le Grand Secret* (1921), reveal other moods and points of view more difficult to follow.

More pleasing aspects of the dramatic art of to-day than those typified by Bataille and Bernstein and their followers are represented in the work of such writers as the following, to mention the most important only, though even in their hands the treatment of certain questions and problems is apt to be somewhat too free: **Maurice Donnay** (born 1860), a master of brilliantly witty dialogue, has displayed his many-sided talent in pure comedy (*La Douloureuse*, 1897; *L'Affranchie*, 1898); social satire (*La Clairière*, 1900; *Oiseaux de Passage*, 1904); high comedy (*L'Autre Danger*, 1902; *Paraître*, 1906); verse comedy (*Le Ménage de Molière*, 1912), besides many lighter pieces merely intended to amuse. **Henri Lavedan** (born 1859), noted especially for amusing but cynical pictures of the smart and fast set of Parisian life, such as *Le Nouveau Jeu* (1906), *Viveurs* (1904), *Le Marquis de Priola* (1902), the latter depicting a kind of modern Don Juan, and one of his best in that kind, though his masterpiece is the more serious *Le Duel* (1905), the struggle between religious faith and free thought in the heart of a woman. **Octave Mirbeau** (1848–1911) has written one vigorous social play, one of the finest of the modern stage, *Les Affaires sont les Affaires* (1903), and before that (1897) *Les Mauvais Bergers*, depicting the struggle between capital and labour. **Émile Fabre** (born 1870) is also interested in social problems, and likewise takes the corrupting influence of money as his theme in *L'Argent* (1895), and in *Les Ventres Dorés* (1905); while in his other plays the political interest is uppermost—*La Vie Publique* (1902), *Les Vainqueurs* (1909), *Un Grand Bourgeois* (1914). **George de Porto-Riche** (born 1849) can be described as an elegiac analyser of sensual love and its sufferings in his *Théâtre d'Amour*, of which the best plays are *La Chance de Françoise* (1889), *Amoureuse* (1891), *Le Passé* (1897). **Alfred Capus** (1858–1922) is a prolific author of witty light comedies, an optimist without a spark of malice who just sought to amuse his audiences. His greatest successes were *La Veine* (1901), and *Notre Jeunesse* (1904). **Robert de Flers** (born 1872) and **Armand de Caillavet** (1869–1915) have collaborated in a series of cleverly constructed and side-splitting comedies of a lighter kind—*L'Ane de Buridan* (1909), *Le Roi* (1908), *Le Bois Sacré* (1910), *Papa* (1912). **Pierre Wolf** (born

1865) and **Romain Coolus** (born 1868), the best perhaps of the former being *Le Secret de Polichinelle* (1903), and of the latter, *Petite Peste* (1905). **Georges Courteline** (born 1861) among the writers of pure farces, a genre which rarely attains the standard of literature, must be mentioned for his remarkable gifts of penetrating observation—*Boubouroche* (1893), *Le Gendarme est sans Pitié* (1900), *L'Ami des Lois* (1905), *Messieurs les Ronds de Cuir* (1911).

CHAPTER III

PROSE

The novel is the most important and characteristic branch of literature in the Realistic period, both the quantity and quality of the writers being truly remarkable.

The greatest of these, and probably the greatest French novelist next to Balzac, is **Gustave Flaubert** (1821–1880), the initiator of Naturalism, which, as we have already noticed, is merely Realism exaggerated, and striving, or rather pretending, to adopt the methods of science.

His principal novels are *Madame Bovary* (1856), *Salammbô* (1862), *L'Éducation Sentimentale* (1870), and *La Tentation de Saint Antoine* (1874).

Madame Bovary is the story of an unhappily married wife, who is driven by the tedium of her existence and the reading of unhealthy sentimental novels into vice, followed by despair and suicide. It is a painful story, but the penetrating analysis of morbid mental conditions, and the vigour and at the same time reality of the descriptions, have strength and genius. The subject of *Salammbô* is the final struggle of Rome and Carthage, the scene being placed in Carthage, in which, with the help of a mass of historical and archæological detail, the life of far-off times and strange and savage peoples is painted with astonishing life and realism. Where his history and archæology fail, Flaubert draws on his artistic imagination, and whatever may be the judgment of men of learning on the scientific aspect of the work, there is no mistaking the extraordinary artistic sympathy which, hand in hand with a rare creative power, makes this rude and distant humanity live and move before our eyes. The *Tentation de St. Antoine* is an extraordinary combination of the realistic and fantastic, a masterpiece in its kind.

Flaubert combines the qualities of Romanticism and Realism, and in that consists his great individuality. He was a fervent admirer of the great Romantic leaders and an idolizer of Victor Hugo, and Romantic influences are strongly marked on all his work. But with the verve of sentiment and imagination of the Romanticists he combined the Realist's conception of art in the order and solidity of his work and great patience and faithfulness in the reproduction of nature. In glow and colour of style and in wealth of word and imagery he is purely Romantic, but he is before all things a Realist in his studied elimination of self, and purely objective impersonal presentation of life.

Flaubert is not copious, but he took the pains to give a lasting shape to his work, and he has left one or two masterpieces of fiction unsurpassed and probably unrivalled in the century.

The same tendencies, but with important modifications, are represented by the brothers **Edmond de Goncourt** (1822–1896) and **Jules de Goncourt** (1830–1870), one of the many examples in French literature of successful collaboration. They began by appreciative studies of the art and manners of the eighteenth century, but afterwards turned to fiction, writing together *Charles Demailly* (1860), *Sœur Philomène* (1861), *Renée Mauperin* (1864), *Germinie Lacerteux* (1865), *Manette Salomon* (1867), and *Mme Gervaisais* (1869). After Jules' death Edmond continued to write novels, of which the most noticeable are *Les Frères Zemganno* (1879) and *La Faustin* (1882), and also published the *Journal des Goncourt*

(1887–1894), invaluable for a study of the two brothers and their literary *entourage*.

The de Goncourts lay great stress on the minute and accurate description of the environment of their characters, seeking reality in the introduction of a weight of detail, in which they show a marked preference of the odd to the typical in life, which is equivalent to saying that they replaced real psychology by the methods of reporting. Secondly, they endeavoured, in *Germinie Lacerteux*, to set up the principle that the coarser the matter the more realistic the work, thus establishing a precedent which unfortunately was destined to find too many adherents even among the more gifted of their followers.

Their chief originality, however, lies in their "impressionist" style, which attempts by a capricious use of the word and a subtle, irregular, arbitrary language, to give rather the suggestion of the idea than its direct expression. Although frequently overwrought and finical, their style is always graceful, and admirably fitted for rendering certain very delicate shades.

The processes of Naturalism were erected into a system and carried to extremes by **Émile Zola** (1840–1902), the acknowledged leader of the Naturalistic school of fiction, born at Paris of an Italian family. After trying his hand without success at journalism and the drama, he turned to the writing of fiction. Of his earlier work the best is found in some of his short stories, and especially the charming *Contes à Ninon* (1864), which demonstrate that he could have excelled in this branch of literature if he had chosen to lay aside his theories and his rather ponderous style.[1] After 1870 he entered upon an enormous gallery of novels, conceived on the plan of Balzac's *Comédie Humaine*, entitled *Les Rougon-Macquart* (1871–1893), the chief being *La Curée* (1872), *La Faute de l'Abbé Mouret* (1875), *L'Assommoir* (1877), *Nana* (1880),

---

[1] Another proof is the delightful *Attaque du Moulin* in the *Soirées de Médan*, a collection by a group of Naturalists.

Germinal (1885), *La Terre* (1887), *La Bête Humaine* (1890), *La Débâcle* (1892). Between 1894 and 1898 Zola wrote his trilogy of the " Three Cities "—*Lourdes, Rome,* and *Paris*—three very long books, in which he appears as a moralist and preacher rather than as a writer of fiction. The same attitude is also apparent in his " Three Gospels "—*Fécondité, Travail, Vérité*—to which was to be added a fourth " gospel ", *Justice*, which never saw the light.

Les Rougon-Macquart, Histoire Naturelle et Sociale d'une Famille sous le Second Empire, to give it its full title, comprises in all a score of volumes, to which Zola pretends to give a sort of unity by means of the appearance and reappearance of members of the same family, but between which the connection is not very real or essential. They treat of life on all its sides and in all its phases, and show how thoroughly the author has carried out his own Naturalistic theory of the study of the " *document humain* ". For not only is Zola the principal exponent of the Naturalist school, but he is also its theorist and doctrinaire; the chief of the principles which he lays down for the writer of Naturalist fiction is the necessity of that preliminary study of life and humanity which consists in noting down at first hand characteristic and individual phases and details of existence, and building up from them a sort of notebook on life for future use. This and another feature, his pretensions to science, in which for Zola there is one question of supreme interest, that of heredity, are characteristic of the school, and are fully illustrated in its leader.

Zola's work shows great power and vigour of treatment applied to the most trivial or unworthy subjects. He has a rare gift of evoking the life of humanity in the mass, and a wealth of description which reminds one of the best days of Romanticism; but at the same time he presents the most brutal and sordid conception of man, with a fulness of ugly and revolting detail which, though it may have its counterpart in life, does not represent the experience of the normal being, but the results of a search undertaken with an express purpose. Intentionally or not, his work is of the most gloomy and dispiriting pessimism, and leaves behind upon the reader, if not a demoralizing, at any rate a most depressing impression.

Among the Realists must be counted **Alphonse Daudet** (1840–1897), although he offers many points of divergence. He was born at Nîmes, and at the age of seventeen set out for Paris, where he became a secretary of the Duc de Morny. His travels in Corsica and Algeria are worthy of mention on account of the influence they had on his literary work. His fiction falls naturally into three divisions: novels, dealing especially with Parisian life: *Fromont Jeune et Risler Aîné* (1874), *Jack* (1876), *Le Nabab* (1877), *Les Rois en Exil* (1879), *Numa Roumestan* (1881), *Sapho* (1884); short stories: *Lettres de mon Moulin* (1869), delightful sketches of the life of Provence, *Contes du Lundi* (1873), mostly reminiscences of the Franco-Prussian War; humorous stories, the Tartarin series: *Tartarin de Tarascon* (1872), *Tartarin sur les Alpes* (1886), and *Port Tarascon* (1890), the amusing story of the typical *méridional*, loquacious, good-humoured, and boastful, full of enthusiasms and illusions, who has only to recount some imaginary adventure of his own in order to believe it the next moment, and which for its quiet, half-satirical humour and caricatured reality, as it were, has been not without reason compared with the manner of Dickens.

Daudet reveals the influence of Realism in his preference for subjects taken from low life, and in his marked fondness for treating life's failures and bankrupts. Yet though debased and depraved characters are found in his works in plenty, they are placed at the right perspective, while by predilection and instinct he avoids all that is merely disgusting and repulsive. His main characteristics are to be found in a delicate, and on the whole optimistic outlook, which is mingled with a gentle irony, and expressed in a charmingly light, vivacious, and graceful style. His novels and short stories by the human and sympathetic note they strike, as well as by their personal touch, make a strong appeal to English readers; their admixture of humour and pathos, found to the same degree in no other French writer, recalls the English Realists.

Guy de Maupassant (1850–1893), a godson of Flaubert, fought in the Franco-Prussian War, and after writing verse, some of which possessed admirable lyrical qualities, turned to the writing of short stories and novels. The most famous of the *contes* are the collections, entitled in most cases after the opening story of each volume: *La Maison Tellier* (1881), *Mlle Fifi* (1882), *Toine* (1885), *Contes du Jour et de la Nuit* (1885), *La Petite Roque* (1886), *Le Horla* (1887), *L'Inutile Beauté* (1890); of the novels, six in all: *Une Vie* (1883), *Bel-Ami* (1885), *Pierre et Jean* (1888), *Notre Cœur* (1890). Maupassant has also left travel impressions, delightful in themselves, and important for the study of his stylistic workmanship: *Au Soleil* (1884), *Sur l'Eau* (1888), *La Vie Errante* (1890), and one comedy, *Musette* (1891), which shows that his bent was not that way.

The merit of Maupassant's novels is great, and some of them, especially *Une Vie*, are among the most powerful that French narrative art has produced, but it is as the greatest representative of the short story that he occupies a unique position in French literature. It is no exaggeration to assert that to his influence is due the great spread of this *genre* both in England and Germany. He has written in all over a hundred of these *contes*, dealing with the most varied themes, and covering a wide range of tone, but all showing the keen insight and analysis of a master. His command of language is no less remarkable, and his concise and yet vivid expression places him high among the great French stylists. Of his choice of subject a less favourable story is to be told, and he not infrequently represents Naturalism in its grossest form, while the springs of human action he generally finds in the requirements of the different physical appetites.

Joris Karl Huysmans (1848–1907), though born in Paris,

was, as his name suggests, of Flemish origin. He began as a direct imitator of Zola at his worst, in *Marthe* (1878), *Les Sœurs Vatard* (1879), and other filthy novels. Then he passed on to the abnormal in *A Rebours* (1884), the hero of which, Des Esseintes, experiments in every anti-natural sensation he can devise. The love of the abnormal and of pose, for part of the whole thing was pose, is further exemplified in *Là-bas* (1891), which dabbles in the morbid Satanism of Baudelaire and of Barbey d'Aurevilly. Finally, by way of æsthetic mysticism (*En Route*, 1895), Huysmans evolved to a kind of Catholic sacerdotalism, preaching his doctrine in a series of wearisome volumes which partake of the character of proselytizing treatises rather than of fiction in the proper sense—*La Cathédrale* (1898), *Sainte-Lydwine de Schiedam*, *L'Oblat*. As a stylist Huysmans is occasionally powerful, but more often heavy and truculent.

Auguste Villiers de l'Isle Adam (1840–1888) is another not insignificant figure in the later years of the nineteenth century, who, like Huysmans, had considerable influence in his day and on the next generation. He was a visionary who dwelt in a strange and fantastic world created by his imagination, despising the Philistines and weaving his dreams in obscurity and poverty. Some of his works, notably *Tribulat Bonhomet* (1887) and the posthumous *Axel*, though the style is often obscure and involved, verge on genius.

Outside the ranks of Naturalism fiction has found many notable representatives. The novel of Romantic idealism, inaugurated by George Sand, was continued by **Octave Feuillet** (1821–1890), who was born in Normandy, but early went to Paris, where, after beginning as one of Dumas' assistants, he started his independent literary career with comedies and other dramatic pieces, and later gained popularity with the idealistic novel *Le Roman d'un Jeune Homme Pauvre* (1858), followed by *M. de Camors* (1867), *Julia de Trécœur* (1872), *La Morte* (1886), *Honneur d'Artiste* (1890), and others.

In his later novels Feuillet shows traces of the prevailing

spirit of Realism, and paints often enough with a very vigorous and daring touch, though what he gains in force he loses in that elegance which is one of his best qualities. He is distinguished above all for his delicate charm of sentiment, the placid optimism of his conception of human nature, and especially his portrayal of the manners of aristocratic society, in which at the same time he is doubtless guilty of a certain degree of idealization, and not innocent of insipidity.

Edmond About (1828–1885), born in Lorraine, followed up a brilliant career at the Lycée Charlemagne and the *École Normale* by studying archæology in Athens, and on his return to Paris made his name by the publication of the study *La Grèce Contemporaine* (1855). Of his works of fiction the best are *Tolla* (1855), *Les Mariages de Paris* (1856), *Le Roi des Montagnes* (1856), *Trente et Quarante* (1865), *Le Roman d'un Brave Homme* (1874).

Without any particular depth, the novels of About show abundant wit and an amount of light and genial satire which, combined with a talent for lively description, gave them a considerable and not unmerited vogue.

Victor Cherbuliez (1829–1899) was born at Geneva, educated at Paris and in Germany, and in 1864 was called to Paris to join the staff of the *Revue des Deux Mondes*. Among his many novels might be mentioned *Le Comte Kostia* (1863), *Le Roman d'une Honnête Femme* (1867), *L'Aventure de Ladislas Bolski* (1870), *Méta Holdénis* (1873), *L'Idée de Jean Têterol* (1878).

His novels are clever, and show great taste and wide and varied knowledge. By their mixture of narrative and philosophic reflection, and their amusing if somewhat eccentric originality, they have appealed to a large class of readers, though they are not calculated to attain universal popularity. To them is due the introduction of a certain type of fantastic novel into French literature.

Émile Erckmann (1822–1899) and **Alexandre Chatrian** (1826–1890), two natives of Lorraine, entered in 1847 upon a collaboration which met with no considerable success till the publication of *L'Illustre Docteur Mathéus* (1859). Among their many stories the best are *Histoire d'un Conscrit de 1813* (1864), *Waterloo* (1865), *Le Blocus* (1867), *Histoire d'un Paysan* (1868), *Les deux Frères* (1873), *Le Banni* (1882). Their reputation is due mainly to the simple and truthful presentation of the homely conditions of life in Lorraine, in which they are unique in French literature.

A foremost position in French fiction is occupied by **Pierre Loti** (1850–1923), who in real life was Julien Viaud and a naval officer, born at Rochefort. His first novel of mark, *Le Mariage de Loti* (1880), from which his pseudonym is taken, was followed by a number of others, of which the best are the earliest: *Le Roman d'un Spahi* (1881), *Mon Frère Yves* (1883), *Pêcheur d'Islande* (1886), *Madame Chrysanthème* (1888), *Ramuntcho* (1896). During the Balkan War his sympathy with the Turks called forth *La Turquie Agonisante* (1913), and at the time of the Great War he flayed the aggressor with his usual lyric powers, kindled by righteous indignation, in *La Hyène Enragée* (1916), *L'Outrage des Barbares* (1917), and *L'Horreur Allemande* (1918).

Loti's distinctive place in contemporary literature is due to his brilliant and original pictures of natural scenery, in which he is the successor of Bernardin de St. Pierre and Chateaubriand. He manages to convey a wonderful impression of sensuous and emotional sympathy with nature in all the forms in which he had learnt to know her in his long years of travel on many seas and in many lands. There is something elemental in the way in which he interprets, for example, the significance of the misty rainy coast of Brittany in its melancholy and grey monotony, or the dead expanse of a wide unbounded plain of waters.

Loti by his gift of imagination, his power of poetic suggestion, and his haunting style, is one of the greatest word-painters in the whole of French literature.

The outstanding figure in French literature in recent years

has undoubtedly been **Anatole France** (1844–1924), whose real name is Anatole Thibault, the author of numerous novels which are better described as conversations or disquisitions on a variety of topics than pure fiction, with no regular plot to speak of, and which he used as a convenient vehicle to express his thoughts and feelings, either directly or by the mouth of the characters he created. A profound scholar and great browser in the byways of literature and forgotten lore, his penetrating mind ranges over a vast field of inquiry, including Christian antiquity, the Italy of the Middle Ages, the French eighteenth century, and, in later years, the history of contemporary France. From this extensive inquiry he draws the conclusion that man is incapable of apprehending truth and reality—that all is vanity. But it must not be thought for all that that he is a pessimist; rather is he a dilettante and a sceptic, recalling Montaigne and Renan with whom he has much in common, who delights in noting the contradictory aspects of human nature and in demolishing ideas and principles commonly accepted as true—a subtle and ironical intellectual nihilist, whose love of beauty and sympathy with man's helplessness saved from arid pessimism. His first noteworthy success came with *Le Crime de Sylvestre Bonnard* (1881), which remains, at least outside France, his most popular work, the story of a simple old recluse and bookworm (the hero is none other than Anatole France himself) and a young orphan, granddaughter of his former sweetheart. This was succeeded by the semi-autobiographical *Le Livre de mon Ami* (1885), one of his most delightful books. *Thaïs* (1890), which followed next, is a psychological analysis of asceticism, on which is grafted a kind of historical novel, offering the author ample scope for the display of erudition. In *La Rôtisserie de la Reine Pédauque* and in its sequel *Les Opinions de M. Jérôme Coignard* (both issued in 1893), Anatole France's anti-Christian attitude finds a sympathetic spokesman in the reprobate eighteenth-century monk and his faithful pupil Jacques Tournebroche. *Le Lys Rouge* (1894), the scene of which is set in modern Florence, is less characteristic, though better constructed; it may be described as a psychological novel of the world of fashion, not unlike those of Bourget, with the usual excursions on various extraneous matters and contemporary personages, such as the amusing portrait of the poet Choulette, in whom we readily recognize some of the vagaries of Verlaine. The year 1897 which saw the appearance of the first volume of *Histoire Contemporaine* (1897–1901), consisting of *L'Orme du Mail*, *Le Mannequin d'Osier*, *L'Anneau d'Améthyste*, and *M. Bergeret à Paris*, marks a new phase in Anatole France's outlook on life, provoked, though always latent, by the bitter controversies of the Dreyfus affair. He is no longer the detached sceptic of his earlier work; his irony, now harsher and more acid, becomes the weapon of a believer in reason and justice. *L'Histoire Comique* (1903), dealing with the life of actors, displays the same bitterness, as does also *L'Ile des Pingouins* (1909), a satire of French history in the tone of Voltaire. The year before he had published his *Histoire de la Vie de Jeanne d'Arc*, which had occupied him for many years and aroused a violent controversy on account of the author's rationalistic explanation of the spiritual elements in the Maid's character. In the closing years of his life Anatole France turned more and more towards Socialism and international pacificism, a tendency already apparent in some of his earlier political writings.

As a stylist Anatole France stands very high in a literature which counts so many great literary artists; the classical purity of his style, its perfect simplicity, the ease and grace with which he expresses the subtlest conceptions, have not been equalled in modern times. He is sure of a place among the great prose writers of France.

With a fame in his own country scarcely inferior to that of Anatole France, but far less considerable in other countries on account of the peculiarly French characteristics of his genius, another dominant personality in the history of contemporary French literature and French thought is **Maurice Barrès**, born in 1862 at Charmes-sur-Moselle, in Lorraine. After studying law for some time at Nancy, where he had received his early education, he came to Paris in 1883 on the advice of Anatole France and Leconte de Lisle who had seen some of the young man's manuscripts, determined to devote himself to literature. His first success came with *Sous l'Œil des Barbares*, which appeared late in 1888. With *Un Homme Libre* (1889) and *Le Jardin de Bérénice* (1891) it forms a trilogy entitled *Le Culte du Moi*—the cult of self or the cult of the *ego*—the first stage in his mental development. In these three " metaphysical novels ", or rather metaphysical essays—for like most of his other works they hardly belong to the domain of pure fiction—Barrès interprets in the person of the twenty-year-old boy Philip the state of mind of the young generation of Frenchmen which came to its majority in the early and middle eighties of last century, at a time when the morale of his young countrymen stood at a very low ebb. Religion, ethics, the sentiment of nationality, having been destroyed, Barrès seeks salvation in self-knowledge and self-culture, in the full development of the individual regardless of the interests of his fellows. The same outlook is seen in his next work, *L'Ennemi des Lois* (1892), in which the object is to demonstrate how society may be organized in such a way as not to sacrifice individuality to the benefit of the community. But in Barrès there is a man of action as well as a metaphysician, and by a strange though not unintelligible process he came to see that the *ego* could not be paramount in life, and turned to the glorification of local and national patriotism in a second trilogy—*Le Roman de l'Énergie Nationale*, consisting of *Les Déracinés* (1897), *L'Appel au Soldat* (1900), and *Leurs Figures* (1903). In the first of these, *Les Déracinés*, he relates, recalling the memories of his early days in Paris, the story of seven young Lorrainers of different temperament and station in life though brought up under the same influences, uprooted from their native soil and cast into the maelstrom of the metropolis—how some perish tragically and miserably, and how those who do finally reach the shore do so only at the expense of their hopes and illusions. The moral lesson is that man should remain faithful to his native soil. The other two volumes bring vividly before our eyes the various political dramas which agitated France between 1880 and 1895, such as the Boulanger affair and the Panama scandal. Then by a further and final development Barrès reached the conviction that if a race wishes to survive it can only do so by considering itself as the heir of the dead buried in its soil, and by never departing from the customs and traditions accumulated through the centuries of the past. This doctrine of the subjection of the individual to " *la terre et les morts* " he expounded in a third trilogy—*Les Bastions de l'Est*, which includes *Les Amitiés Françaises* (1903), *Au Service de l'Allemagne* (1905), and *Colette Baudoche* (1909). The second describes the sufferings of the young men of Alsace-Lorraine, compelled to serve in the German army. *Colette Baudoche*, his greatest achievement, slight though the plot is, shows, under the guise of a novel with a love plot, the superiority, as opposed to German Kultur, of French culture, stoutly maintained against the Teutonic oppressor. Barrès is the author of numerous other works in which he continues in different ways to preach the principle and cult of Nationalism, of which from now on he became one of the resolute advocates outside and above all political parties. His remarkable descriptive powers, for he is more than a polemist, are best illustrated by the *Le Voyage de Sparte* (1905), and by *Greco ou Le Secret de Tolède* (1912), written in a style of classical chasteness contrasting with the somewhat mannered expression of the earlier period. The character and trend of his many militant writings during the war, by which he did so much to maintain the morale of the people in the rear, is sufficiently indicated by their collective title—*L'Ame Française et La Guerre*.

By the mass and excellence of his literary work, as well as by the influence he exercised on the younger generation, Maurice Barrès remains one of the most representative figures of contemporary France, and one whose work no foreigner can afford to neglect. His writings showed the young men of France the right road at a time when they were distracted and dispirited, and played no small part in the moral resurrection of which the Great War gave to the world so splendid a manifestation.

Another author who stands out among present-day writers of fiction is **Paul Bourget** (born 1852), the recognized head of the so-called Psychological school, and the greatest master of the novel of mental and moral analysis since Stendhal. His principal works are *Cruelle Énigme* (1885), *Un Crime d'Amour* (1886), *Mensonges* (1887), *Le Disciple* (1889), *Cosmopolis* (1893), *Une Idylle Tragique* (1896). Of those written in the present century the most typical perhaps are: *L'Étape* (1902), *L'Émigré* (1907), *Le Sens de la Mort* (1915), and *L'Écuyère* (1921). He has also published numerous collections of short stories, from *Pastels* (1889) to *Anomalies* (1920), and also accounts of travels abroad—*Sensations d'Oxford* (1888), *Outre-Mer* (1895), &c., apart from significant and highly suggestive volumes of literary criticism, noticed subsequently.

Instead of limiting his observations to the externals of life, like Zola and his followers, he applies the methods of Naturalism to purely psychological subjects, and laboriously and carefully, with a mass of detail, builds up the history of human souls. Although his minute dissection of character is apt at times to become tedious, he has rendered no small service in dragging the novel from the bog of animalism.

Bourget's work deals almost exclusively with Parisian high life, and the cosmopolitan types studied during his travels.

To the category of the psychological novel belongs also *Dominique* (1863) by **Eugène Fromentin** (1820–1876), the painter and art critic, based on personal experience, and which, by its penetrating analysis of delicate feeling and the charm of its style, allied to beautiful descriptions of nature in perfect harmony with the melancholy tone of the narrative, attains the first rank.

The enormous output in the field of contemporary French

fiction has been increased by a number of less considerable though not unimportant writers: **Ferdinand Fabre** (1830–1898) deserves a greater reputation among modern French novelists for his profound studies of clerical life and his delicate delineations of peasant character. His best-known novels are *Les Courbezon* (1862), *Le Chevrier* (1868), *L'Abbé Tigrane* (1873), *Barnabé* (1875), *Mon Oncle Célestin* (1881), *Lucifer* (1884), and *Xavière* (1890). Fabre is one of the earliest representatives of " Regionalism ", which sprang from the feeling that the life of the metropolis is not the only one worthy of attention, and a desire to depict provincial life and local scenes and ways. This tendency has developed considerably in recent years, and is seen at its best in some of the novels of René Bazin and of Henry Bordeaux notably, to be mentioned subsequently. **André Theuriet** (1833–1907) first made his mark by various collections of verse, revealing a real and genuine love of the country and its glades and woods. He is best known, however, as a graceful painter of the intimacies of provincial life in the small towns of Eastern France, particularly the Ardennes, which he depicts with contagious sympathy and with a realism free from any objectionable features—as in *Raymonde* (1877), *Le Fils Maugars* (1879), *La Maison des deux Barbeaux* (1879), *Sauvageonne* (1880), *Bigarreau* (1885). **Émile Pouvillon** (1840–1906) has chosen as his particular domain the rustic scenes and manners of Rouerge and Quercy. *Césette* (1881) is an exquisite idyll, and in *Les Antibel* (1892), his best novel, simplicity and pathos are allied in a way rare in modern fiction. **Léon Cladel** (1834–1892), who also wrote stories located in Southern France, on the other hand, displays all the brutality of the Naturalists in truly terrifying novels, written in a style which has undeniable vigour, but is too often marred by puerile mannerisms. His merits as well as his demerits are best illustrated by *Le Bouscassié* (1869), his first, and *Celui de la Croix-aux-Bœufs* (1885). **Édouard Rod** (1857–1910), a Swiss like Cherbuliez, was at first a Naturalist, but soon overcame the tendency. He is a psychologist, heavy, albeit very earnest, fond of analysing the struggle between duty and the passions. His best novels are those in which he depicts life not in its violent crises, but in its more homely and intimate aspects. Representative are *La Course à la Mort* (1885), *Le Sens de la Vie* (1889), *La Vie Privée de Michel Tessier* (1893), *Le Ménage du Pasteur Naudié* (1898), *L'Incendie* (1906), *Les Unis* (1909). **Margueritte, Paul** (1860–1918) and **Victor** (born 1866), sons of the heroic General Margueritte of Reichhoffen fame, offer another example of literary collaboration in a quartet of novels on the war of 1870— *Le Désastre* (1898), which may profitably be contrasted with Zola's *La Débâcle*, *Les Tronçons du Glaive* (1901), *Les Braves Gens* (1901), and *La Commune* (1904), all containing many vigorous passages, but in which the narrative is not infrequently impeded by a tiresome multiplicity of unnecessary detail. The elder brother had previously written independently other contributions to fiction, such as *Jours d'Épreuve* (1889), in which realism is attenuated by heart-felt sympathy, *La Force des Choses* (1891), poignant in its simple pathos, *Ma Grande* (1893), a combination of the idyllic and dramatic, and *La Tourmente* (1894), a psychological study, keen yet delicate. **Paul Hervieu** (1857–1915), who abandoned the novel at the moment when he was about to take a high place in contemporary fiction, is the author of powerful indictments of society in *Peints par eux-mêmes* (1893), portraying the moral decadence of the aristocracy, and in *L'Armature* (1895), in which the theme is the all-pervading influence of money as the "framework" of the life of to-day. **Marcel Prévost** (born 1862) has made a speciality of the analysis of feminine sentiments, and in that sense he is what the French call a "moralist". Of his score of novels his best by far is *Les Vierges Fortes* (1900), championing women's rights and the feminist movement generally. **Édouard Estaunié** (born 1862) has produced little. All his novels, however, merit attention, and some, such as *L'Empreinte* (1896), *Le Ferment* (1899), *L'Épave* (1902), have high social and moral import. **Maurice Maindron**

(1857–1911) has revived successfully the historical novel proper in *Le Tournoi de Vauplassans* (1895), *Saint-Cendre* (1902), *Blancador l'Avantageux* (1900), and *Monsieur de Clérambon* (1904), which are not only minute reconstitutions but vigorous evocations of the past, especially the French sixteenth century. Here too should be mentioned *La Force* (1899) of **Paul Adam** (1862–1920), dealing with the period of the Revolution and the First Empire, and far superior to his other novels.

Fiction within the last twenty-five years continues to bulk so largely that it is impossible in a manual of this scope to notice any but the essential names—those novelists whose work is not unlikely to survive either for intrinsic merit or as indicating a new departure.

The " *roman à thèse* ", or problem novel, is continued by **Henri Bazin** (born 1853), the novelist particularly of provincial and rustic life, which he describes realistically, but without overstepping the bounds of decency (*Ma Tante Giron*, *Les Noellet*, *La Sarcelle Bleue*, *Madame Corentine*, &c.). He takes up a higher theme in *La Terre qui Meurt* (1899), one of the finest works of contemporary fiction, the subject being the migration from the land to the cities. In *Les Oberlé* (1901) and *Les Nouveaux Oberlé* (1919) we see the consequences to the Alsatians of the Franco-Prussian War and of the Great War respectively. Other notable novels of his are *Donatienne* (1903) and *Stéphanette* (1920). **Henry Bordeaux** (born 1878) writes problem novels, with considerable power and increasing sympathy, upholding the rights of the family, as in *La Maison* (1912) and *Les Roquevillard* (1906), and in the more recent series entitled *La Vie Recommencée* (1920–1922). **Claude Farrère** (born 1876), a naval officer like Loti, has written like him, but in a more violent style, brilliant descriptions of the Near and Far East: *L'Homme qui assassina* (1907) and *Les Civilisés* (1905). In *La Bataille* (1911) he shows, under the veneer of Western culture which the Japanese affect, the persistence of their old traditions. **André Gide** (born 1869) is a penetrating psychologist, a master of the novel of observation. His characteristics appear most clearly in *La Porte Étroite* (1909) and in *Les Caves du Vatican* (1914), which place him among the foremost of present-day novelists. **Charles-Louis Philippe** (1874-1909), an important author, though his reputation has been chiefly posthumous, not only on account of the intrinsic merit of his work but also of the influence he has had on many of the younger writers. His social studies of the miseries and hardships of the poor among whom he was born and reared, told in a style of remarkable sobriety (*La Mère et L'Enfant*, 1900; *Bubu de Montparnasse*, 1901; *Croquignole*, 1906; &c.), are sure to live. **Marcel Proust** (1873-1922), whom his admirers place in eminence next to Anatole France, though he differs profoundly from him, is a psychologist, or rather a pathologist, who dissects souls and delights in following in minute detail the reaction on himself. His long series *A la Recherche du Temps perdu*, of which some twenty volumes have so far appeared, has been not inaptly described as " *mémoires d'un esprit* ", and has had an influence greater than its intrinsic merits justify. His style, never easy to follow, is often discursive and digressive. **Romain Rolland** (born 1866), started as a writer on music, and sprang into prominence as the author of *Jean-Christophe* (1904-1912), a voluminous biographical romance, in ten books, describing the youth and adolescence of a musical genius, and showing how, in the end, the hero, purified by suffering of his passions, reaches a loftiness of soul that recognizes no national distinctions. Here we already see appearing the internationalist and pacifist proclivities which have made the name of Rolland notorious, and which he preached openly in his two later novels, *Clérambault* and *Pierre et Luce* (both in 1920). **J.-H. Rosny** is the collective pseudonym of Justin (born 1859) and Joseph-Henry (born 1856) Boëx, powerful and forceful, though very uneven, writers, whose subjects range from the Salvation Army (*Nell Horn*, 1886) to prehistoric times (*Les Xipchuz*, 1887; *Vamireh*, 1892). The elder brother is also the author of *Marthe Barraquin*

(1909), on the life of the *apache* class, interesting to the student of a special brand of *argot*.

Of the novels called forth by the war two stand out as real works of art—*La Vie des Martyrs* of the poet **Georges Duhamel** (born 1884), and *Les Croix de Bois* by **Roland Dorgelès** (born 1886), noble and touching in its classical simplicity, far superior to the Zolaesque and depressing *Le Feu* of **Henri Barbusse** (born 1874), which had such a phenomenal sale.

Among the foremost women novelists of the day may be reckoned: **Marguerite Audoux**, whose *Marie-Claire* (1910) is already a classic; **Colette** (Madame Henri de Jouvenel); the poetess, **Comtesse Mathieu de Noailles**; **Rachilde** (Madame Alfred Vallette); **Marcelle Tinayre**, the leading woman writer of to-day; **Colette Yver**.

A rigid application of the modern scientific spirit to the history of religion is the keynote of the most remarkable among the works of **Ernest Renan**, born at Tréguier in Brittany, in 1823, and at the time of his death in 1892 universally regarded as the first man of letters in France, and as one of her greatest prose writers. He was intended for the Church, and educated accordingly, first in his native town, and later at the seminary of Saint-Sulpice. Gradually, however, his naturally critical spirit, strengthened by the study of ancient and modern philosophy, undermined his religious beliefs, and he renounced the idea of the priesthood. Continuing, meanwhile, his critical study of Christianity, and aided in his methods by a mission to the East in 1860, during which he visited Syria and the Holy Land, he began the publication of his works, the first of his important books being the *Vie de Jésus* in 1863. His principal work is contained in the *Origines du Christianisme*, which comprises the *Vie de Jésus* (1863), *Les Apôtres* (1866), *Saint Paul* (1869), *L'Antéchrist* (1873), *Les Évangiles* (1877), *L'Église Chrétienne* (1879), and *Marc Aurèle* (1881). This had been preceded by the *Histoire Générale des Langues Sémitiques* (1857), *Études d'Histoire*

Religieuse (1857), and was followed by the important *Histoire du Peuple d'Israël* (1887–1892).

Renan's importance does not lie in any great originality either in the results of his research or in his religious doubt, but in the way in which he established the relativity of religion, and in the fact that he may be almost said to have created the history of religion. He has once for all settled the question of revelation, giving to all the choice between an acceptation of revealed religion as a pure act of voluntarily unreasoning faith, and its rejection on philosophic and scientific grounds. Religion which is permanent and eternal in humanity, although its symbols are ever changing, is for him the imperishable ideal, the highest beauty in the moral world. Renan has made of this science of the history of religion a true literary branch. He is capable both of eloquent passages of appeal and of picturesque description. His style has the indescribable quality of charm, and in its discreet irony and easy pliability it is perfectly adapted to his subtle treatment of a difficult subject.

Sainte-Beuve's method of criticism was reduced to mathematical precision by **Hippolyte Taine** (1828–1893), born at Vouziers, in the Ardennes, and educated at the *École Normale*. In 1853 he entered upon his important literary career with a brilliant thesis, *La Fontaine et ses Fables*. Apart from his two great works, the *Histoire de la Littérature Anglaise* (1863–1864), and the *Origines de la France Contemporaine*—comprising *L'Ancien Régime* (1876), *La Révolution* (1878–1885), and *Le Régime Moderne* (1890–1894)—his remaining works include the *Voyage aux Pyrénées* (1855), *Les Philosophes Français du XIXe Siècle* (1856), *Essais de Critique et d'Histoire* (1858), *Nouveaux Essais* (1865), *Voyage en Italie* (1866).

Although he has won a high place both as a historian and a philosopher, Taine is more notable as a literary critic. The originality of his critical theories, as first expounded in his preface to the *Histoire de la Littérature Anglaise* in 1863, consists in the application of the scientific and Naturalistic method to literature, following which he regards all literary works as the necessary products of certain general causes capable of being traced by proper method and investigation. These are: nationality; conditions in general, such as climate, political, social, and historical circumstances; the psychological moment. These principles he applies notably to English literature, and in such a way as to betray the element of weakness in the theory, which consists in the want of allowance made for the individual and the deviation from the type, and its tendency to regard literary genius too much as the mechanical resultant of certain known and clearly-defined productive forces. He undoubtedly gave considerable impetus to the Naturalistic movement, but it is entirely unfair to make him responsible for its exaggerations and excesses.

Taine applies the same methods of deduction and systematization to history, and falls, as in literature, into the faults of mechanical symmetry and artificial unity, which are inevitable consequences of the system.

He possesses a vigorous and pregnant style, which, though capable of great concentration of thought, is saved from dryness by his imaginative faculty. In some of his descriptive passages, and especially in the *Voyage aux Pyrénées* (1855), he shows the power of writing with admirable colour and relief.

Among the number of noteworthy names by which literary criticism since Taine has been represented the most famous is that of **Ferdinand Brunetière** (1849–1906), whose importance for French literature is twofold. Firstly, as the champion of the classical tradition he attacked Naturalism, especially in *Le Roman Naturaliste* (1883), and was largely instrumental in hastening its end. Secondly, pursuing but at the same time modifying the system of Taine, he applied the theory of evolution to literary criticism, showing how, as in living organisms, the different types in turn spring from one another, develop, compete, and die. Where he improves on Taine is in making more allowance for the personal element, the phenomenon of individual genius. Beside the already-mentioned *Roman Natu-*

raliste, his principal works are *Histoire et Littérature* (1884–1886), *Études Critiques sur la Littérature Française* (1880–1899), *L'Évolution des Genres dans l'Histoire de la Littérature Française* (1890), *Les Époques du Théâtre Français* (1892), *L'Évolution de la Poésie Lyrique* (1894), *Discours de Combat* (1900).

Diametrically opposed to Brunetière is **Jules Lemaître,** already mentioned in another connection, who thinks more of enjoying, and helping others to enjoy, than of classifying, weighing, and comparing, to paraphrase some words of his own. He has no system or theory to expound, but treats literature purely from the subjective standpoint. He describes criticism as a representation of the world, like other branches of literature, and hence by its nature as relative, as vain, and therefore as interesting as they. Consequently, instead of deducing literary productions, he contents himself with defining them and giving the impressions they produce upon himself. He is attracted especially by modern authors, on whom he has written a series of remarkable essays, *Les Contemporains* (1885–1899), in a terse, subtle, and wittily ironical style which frequently recalls Renan. His *Impressions de Théâtre* appeared from 1888 to 1898, while of his dramatic work mention has already been made. Literary criticism is also avowedly treated as a record of personal taste, as we might expect, in *La Vie Littéraire* (1887–1893) of **Anatole France.**

To **Paul Bourget,** on the other hand, the task of the critic —here again as we might expect—is that of an experimental psychologist; in his *Essais* and *Nouveaux Essais de Psychologie Contemporaine* (1883–1885) he endeavours to bring out the characteristic tendencies of the second half of the nineteenth century—the period selected by him—such as pessimism, dilettantism and cosmopolitanism, by means of a minute and systematic examination of the mental and moral qualities of certain typical authors.

The method of **Émile Faguet** (1847–1922), one of the most copious and suggestive writers on French literature, is interpretation. He is best known for his attractive though quite substantial series of *Études Littéraires* on the great writers of the last four centuries and for his study of *Les Politiques et Moralistes du XIXe Siècle*, as well as for monographs on individual authors and a concise *History of French Literature*. Though rarely constructive, he is a critic who makes one think.

The most authoritative of present-day critics in academic circles is **Gustave Lanson** (born 1857), Professor of French Literature at the Sorbonne, and, since the death of Brunetière, the chief influence in guiding students of French literature. His method is now essentially one of historical and biographical research; in his hands literary criticism has become literary history, which in less skilled hands than his ceases to be literature and leads to the worship of the card catalogue and the *fiche*. His compendious *Histoire de la Littérature Française* is unequalled by any other work of similar compass. In addition he has written important studies of Nivelle de la Chaussée, Boileau, Bossuet, and Corneille, not to mention his numerous contributions to periodical literature.

Another critic, but not an academic one, who should not be left out of account, is **Charles Maurras** (born 1868), a friend of Moréas on whom he has written some illuminating pages, one of the leaders of the neo-classical movement in literature and of aggressive Nationalism in life and politics. Most of his critical essays have not yet been collected in book form, while many others have appeared in volumes whose titles are not sufficiently indicative of their contents. This is to be regretted, not only because Maurras is acknowledged by friend and foe to be one of the greatest prose writers of to-day, but because some of his studies, such as that on various writers of the nineteenth century from Chateaubriand to Madame la Comtesse de Noailles, are indispensable. His method is one of selection; by sifting the chaff from the grain he attempts to reduce the variety of literary production to a few stable and guiding principles.

Amid the poverty of historical production which followed

the remarkable outburst of the earlier part of last century, **Fustel de Coulanges** (1830–1889) has with good cause been hailed as a great historian and a great writer. He has left two works of great importance: *La Cité Antique* (1864), an attempt at a full and profound investigation of ancient states of society, and the *Histoire des Institutions Politiques de l'Ancienne France* (1875–1889), his masterpiece, which was unfortunately left unfinished at his death.

The characteristics of his method are to be found in the honesty with which he examines all documents and texts that bear on the epochs with which he is concerned, and in the resolve to lay aside all preconceptions and modern prejudices before approaching them. For him history is one of the exact sciences, and the historian's task consists " *à constater des faits, à les analyser, à les rapprocher, à en marquer le lien. Il se peut, sans doute, qu'une certaine philosophie se dégage de cette histoire scientifique; mais il faut qu'elle s'en dégage naturellement, d'elle-même, presque en dehors de la volonté de l'histoire.*" His main interest lies in the growth and development of states of society, and his two great works treat of the great changes which prepared the way for the rise of the society of to-day, namely, the transformation of ancient forms of belief and the growth of feudalism.

His style is severe and concise; unembarrassed by any meretricious ornament it attains great effects by simple means.

Fustel de Coulanges is the protagonist of the modern scientific school of historians, in whose hands history has ceased to be an art, although the chief representative of that school in France to-day, **Ernest Lavisse** (born 1842), has shown, like Fustel de Coulanges, that it is possible, while not departing from the strictest scientific methods, to write history that may still be called literature.

INDEX

NOTE.—The article and its compounds are treated as integral parts of names, but not the preposition "de".

About, Edmond, 323.
Academy, The French, 98, 126.
Adam, Jeu d', 23.
Adam, Paul, 332.
Adam de la Halle, 21, 26.
Aimeri de Narbonne, 12.
Albéric de Briançon, 14.
Alembert (D'), 208, 212.
Alexandre de Bernai, 14.
Aliscans, 12.
Amis et Amiles, 12.
Amyot, 46, 78.
Ancients and Moderns, Quarrel of the, 163.
André de Coutances, 32.
Arnauld, Antoine, 130, 131, 132.
Aubanel, 4.
Aubigné (D'), 70.
Aucassin et Nicolette, 38.
Audoux, Marguerite, 334.
Augier, Émile, 309.

Baïf, Antoine de, 62, 68.
Balzac, Guez de, 98, 127.
Balzac, Honoré de, 98, 250, 279.
Banville, Théodore de, 290.
Barbier, Auguste, 271.
Barbusse, Henri, 334.
Barrès, Maurice, 326.
Basoche (La), 27.
Bataille, Henry, 312.
Baudelaire, Charles, 292.
Bayle, 100, 162.
Bazin, Henri, 332.
Beaubreuil, Jean de, 115.
Beaumarchais, 173, 189.
Becque, Henry, 311.
Belleau, Remi, 62, 69.

Benoît de Sainte-More, 14, 35.
Béranger, 228.
Bernard, Jean Marc, 305.
Bernardin de Saint-Pierre, 174, 194.
Bernier, 31.
Bernstein, Henry, 312.
Béroul, 16.
Bertaut, 72.
Berte au Grand Pié, 12.
Berzé, Hugues de, 32.
Beyle. See *Stendhal*.
Bèze (De), 74.
Bodel, Jean, 21, 23, 31.
Bodin, Jean, 82.
Boileau, 133, 164, 165.
Boisrobert (De), 143.
Bonald (De), 241.
Bordeaux, Henry, 332.
Bornier, Henri de, 313.
Boron, Robert de, 18.
Bossuet, 96, 155.
Bourdaloue, 159.
Bourget, Paul, 329, 337.
Brantôme, 81.
Brieux, Eugène, 311.
Brizeux, 271.
Brunetière, 336.
Brunetto Latini, 38.
Buffon, 171, 222.

Caillavet, Armand de, 315.
Calvin, Jean, 45, 59.
Capus, Alfred, 315.
Cénacle (Le), 249, 281.
Chantelouve, 74.
Chapelain, 109, 115.
Charles d'Orléans, 39.
Charroi de Nîmes, 12.

341

Charron, Pierre, 94.
Charte aux Anglais, 32.
Chartier, Alain, 22.
Chateaubriand, 227, 233.
Châtelain de Coucy. See *Gui de Coucy*.
Chatrian, 323.
Chénier, André, 180.
Cherbuliez, Victor, 323.
Chesnaye, Nicole de la, 53.
Chrétien, Florent, 85.
Chrétien de Troie, 17.
Christine de Pisan, 22.
Chronique de Du Guesclin, 11.
Cladel, Léon, 330.
Claudel, Paul, 305.
Colette (Mme Henri de Jouvenel), 334.
Combat des Trente, 11.
Commines, 6, 37, 44.
Condillac, 213.
Condorcet, 215.
Confrérie de la Passion, 26, 73.
Conon de Béthune, 20.
Conrart, Valentin, 126.
Constant, Benjamin, 241.
Coolus, Romain, 316.
Coppée, François, 295, 313.
Corneille, Pierre, 96, 115.
Corneille, Thomas, 152.
Courier, Paul Louis, 241.
Courtebarbe, 31.
Courteline, Georges, 316.
Cousin, Victor, 289.
Covenant Vivien, 12.
Crébillon père, 184.
Crétin, 42.
Curel (De), 311.

Dacier (Mme), 165.
Daigaliers, Pierre de Laudun, 115.
Dancourt, 161.
Danton, 225.
Daudet, Alphonse, 320.
Daurat (or Dorat), 62.
Décadents (Les), 251, 296.
Delarue-Mardrus (Mme), 307.
Delavigne, Casimir, 229.
Delille, 172, 179.
Derème, Tristan, 306.
Desbordes-Valmore (Mme), 271.
Descartes, 96, 128.
Deschamps, Antony, 282.
Deschamps, Émile, 282.
Deschamps, Eustache, 22, 27.
Desmarets de Saint-Sorlin, 109, 163.
Desmasures, Louis, 75.
Des Periers, Bonaventure, 58.

Desportes, 72.
Destouches, 188.
Diderot, 174, 189, 194, 208, 209.
Dit de la Rébellion d'Angleterre, 32.
Donnay, Maurice, 315.
Doon de Mayence, 11.
Dorgelès, Roland, 334.
Du Bartas, 69.
Du Bellay, Joachim, 62, 63, 67, 73.
Du Deffand (Mme), 223.
Duhamel, Georges, 334.
Dumas fils, Alexandre, 307.
Dumas père, Alexandre, 271, 274.
Durant, Gilles, 85.
Du Vair, 94.

Encyclopédie (L'), 174, 208.
Enfances, Ogier (Les), 12.
Erckmann, 323.
Estaunié, Édouard, 331.
Étienne, Henri, 46, 86.
Évangile des Femmes, 32.

Fabre, Émile, 315.
Fabre, Ferdinand, 330.
Fabri, 114.
Faguet, Émile, 337.
Farrère, Claude, 332.
Fastoul, Baude, 21.
Fauchet, 87.
Fénelon, 165.
Feuillet, Octave, 322.
Flaubert, Gustave, 251, 316.
Fléchier, 160.
Flers, Robert de, 315.
Fontenelle, 100, 164, 174, 196.
Fort, Paul, 306.
Fougères, Étienne de, 32.
Fournival, Richard de, 33.
Franc Archer de Bagnolet (Le), 27.
France, Anatole, 325, 337.
Froissart, 7, 21, 36.
Fromentin, Eugène, 329.
Furetière, 155.
Fustel de Coulanges, 339.

Gace Brulé, 20.
Garin de Monglane, 10.
Garin le Loherain, 12.
Garnier, Robert, 76.
Garnier de Pont Sainte-Maxence, 35.
Gautier, Théophile, 250, 269.
Gautier le Long, 31.
Geoffrei Gaimar, 35.
Geoffrey of Monmouth, 15.
Geoffrin (Mme), 223.

INDEX

Gerson, 38.
Gide, André, 332.
Gilbert, 180.
Gomberville, 125.
Goncourt, Edmond de, 317.
Goncourt, Jules de, 317.
Greban, Arnoul, 24.
Greban, Simon, 25.
Gregh, Fernand, 305.
Gresset, 188.
Grévin, 76, 77, 114.
Grimm, Melchior, 214.
Gringoire, 28.
Griselidis, Histoire de, 24.
Guérin, Charles, 305.
Gui de Coucy, 20.
Guillaume le Maréchal, 21.
Guiot de Provins, 32.
Guizot, 283.

Hardy, 110.
Hébert, 225.
Helvétius, 213.
Herberay des Essarts, 61.
Heredia (De), 295.
Heroët, 51.
Hervieu, Paul, 312, 331.
Holbach (D'), 214.
Hotman, 83.
Houville, Gérard d' (Mme Henri de Régnier), 306.
Hugo, Victor, 246, 259, 274.
Huon de Bordeaux, 12.
Huon le Roi, 31.
Huysmans, 321.

Jacot de Forest, 15.
Jacquemart, Gelée, 29.
Jammes, Francis, 304.
Jansenist Movement (*The*), 130.
Jasmin, 4.
Jean de Froissart, 21.
Jean de Tuin, 15.
Jodelle, 62, 73, 74, 75, 76.
Joinville, 36.
Joubert, 239.

Kahn, Gustave, 300.
Karr, 282.

Labé, Louise, 52.
Labiche, 309.
La Boétie, 82.
La Bruyère, 161, 165.
La Calprenède, 125.
La Chaussée, 173, 188.

Lacordaire, 290.
La Fayette, Comtesse de, 155.
La Fontaine, 96, 136, 138, 165.
La Fosse, Antoine de, 161.
Lahor, Jean, 303.
Lamartine, 249, 253.
Lambert le Tort, 14.
Lamennais, 243.
La Motte, Houdar de, 165, 178, 184.
Lancelot, 130.
La Noue, 81.
Lanson, Gustave, 338.
Larivey, 78, 143.
La Rochefoucauld, 153.
La Salle, Antoine de la, 38.
La Taille, Jean de, 76, 78, 115.
Lavedan, Henri, 315.
Lavisse, Ernest, 339.
Lebrun, 172, 179.
Leconte de Lisle, 292.
Legouvé, 273.
Le Maire de Belges, Jean, 47.
Lemaître, Jules, 310, 337.
Le Maistre, 130.
Leroy, Jean, 84.
Le Sage, 173, 187, 191.
Lespinasse (Mlle de), 223.
L'Hôpital, Michel de, 83.
Lorris, Guillaume de, 33.
Loti, Pierre, 324.
Louis, Le Roi, 9.

Machaut, 21.
Maeterlinck, 314.
Maillart, 38.
Maindron, Maurice, 331.
Mairet, 112, 115.
Maistre, Joseph de, 240.
Maistre, Xavier de, 241.
Malherbe, 97, 101.
Mallarmé, 299.
Manuel, Eugène, 294.
Margaret of Navarre, 50, 58.
Margueritte, Paul, 331.
Margueritte, Victor, 331.
Marie de France, 16, 29.
Marivaux, 173, 186, 192.
Marot, Clément, 44, 48.
Massillon, 168.
Maupassant, Guy de, 321.
Maurras, Charles, 338.
Meigret, 85.
Ménippée, La Satire, 83.
Menot, 38.
Mercier, Louis, 304.
Mérimée, 278.

INDEX

Meschinot, 42.
Meung, Jean de, 6, 33.
Michelet, 286.
Mignet, 285.
Mirabeau, 224.
Mirbeau, Octave, 315.
Mistral, 4.
Molière, 96, 139.
Molinet, 42.
Monluc, Blaise de, 80.
Montaigne, 46, 88.
Montchrétien, 77.
Montesquieu, 171, 198.
Moréas, 301.
Moreau, Hégésippe, 271.
Murger, 282.
Musset, Alfred de, 267.

Nicole, 130.
Noailles (La Comtesse Mathieu, de). 306, 334.
Nodier, Charles, 281.

Ogier, François, 111, 115.
Orléans, Siège d', 25.

Pailleron, 310.
Paix aux Anglais (La), 32.
Parnassiens (Les), 251, 290.
Parny, 180.
Pascal, Blaise, 98, 130, 131.
Pasquier, Étienne, 87.
Passerat, 72, 85.
Patelin, 27.
Péguy, Charles, 305.
Pèlerinage de Charlemagne, 9.
Perrault, Charles, 100, 164.
Philippe, Charles-Louis, 333.
Philippe de Thaon, 33.
Piron, 176, 188.
Pithou, 85.
Pléiade (La), 45, 62, 68, 114.
Ponsard, 273.
Pontus de Thyard, 62.
Porto-Riche, George de, 315.
Port-Royal, 130.
Pourtalis, Jean de, 53.
Pouvillon, Émile, 330.
Pradon, 149.
Précieuses (Les), 97, 105.
Prévost d'Exiles, 173, 192.
Prévost, Marcel, 331.
Proust, Marcel, 333.

Quête du Saint-Graal (La), 18.
Quietists (The), 166.

Quinault, 139.
Quinet, Edgar, 289.

Rabelais, 44, 53.
Racan, 112.
Rachilde (Mme Alfred Vallette), 334
Racine, Jean, 96, 99, 145.
Rambouillet, Hôtel de, 105.
Ramus (or Ramée), 85.
Raoul de Cambrai, 11.
Rapin, Nicolas, 85.
Regnard, 161.
Régnier, Henri de, 300.
Régnier, Mathurin, 97, 103.
Régnier, Mme Henri de. See *Houville, G. de.*
Renan, 334.
Renard, Roman de, 29.
Retz, Cardinal de, 153.
Richelieu, 115, 126
Richepin, 303, 313.
Robespierre, 225.
Rod, 330.
Roland, Chanson de, 12.
Rolland, Romain, 333.
Rollinat, 303.
Romanticism, 245, 249.
Romains, Jules, 305.
Ronsard, 45, 62, 65, 69, 115.
Rosny, J.-H., 333.
Rostand, Edmond, 313.
Rotrou, 122.
Roumanille, 4.
Round Table (The), 16.
Rousseau, Jean Baptiste, 175.
Rousseau, Jean-Jacques, 171, 194, 215.
Rutebeuf, 24, 31.

Sablé (Mlle de), 108.
Saint-Cloud, Pierre de, 14.
Saint-Cyran, 131.
Saint-Evremond, 122.
Saint-Gelais, Melin de, 51.
Saint-Just, 225.
Saint-Pierre. See *Bernardin.*
Saint-Simon, Duc de, 169.
Saint-Sorlin. See *Desmarets.*
Sainte-Beuve, 250, 287.
Sales, Saint François de, 123.
Samain, Albert, 303.
Sand, George, 275.
Sardou, Victorien, 310.
Saurin, 160.
Scaliger, 114.
Scarron, 109, 126.
Scève, Maurice, 51.

INDEX

Schélandre, 111.
Scribe, 272.
Scudéry, Georges de, 109.
Scudéry, Madeleine de, 125.
Sénancour, 239.
Sévigné (Mme de), 154.
Sibilet, 114.
Simon, Richard, 156.
Sorel, 126.
Souvestre, 282.
Sponsus, 23.
Staël (Mme de), 227, 230.
Stendhal, 277.
Sue, Eugène, 282.
Sully, Maurice de, 38.
Sully-Prudhomme, 294.
Symbolistes (Les), 251, 298, 299.

Taine, 335.
Théâtre Libre (Le), 312.
Theuriet, 330.
Thibaut de Champagne, 20.
Thierry, Augustin, 282.
Thiers, 284.
Thomas, 17.
Thou (De), 82.
Tinayre, Marcelle, 334.
Tocqueville (De), 287.
Troie, Destruction de, 25.
Turgot, 214.

Turnèbe, Odet de, 78.

Unities, Rules of the Three. 113.
Urfé (D'), 124.

Vair, Guillaume Du, 94.
Valéry, Paul, 304.
Vaugelas, 98, 127.
Vauquelin de la Fresnaye, 72.
Vauvenargues, 207.
Verhaeren, 302.
Verlaine, 252, 296.
Viau, Théophile de, 97, 105, 112.
Viélé-Griffin 303.
Vigny, Alfred de, 257.
Vildrac, Charles, 305.
Villehardouin, 36.
Villemain, 288.
Villiers de l'Isle Adam, Auguste, 322.
Villon, 40, 44.
Vivonne, Catherine de, 106.
Voiture, 107.
Voltaire, 171, 172, 176, 185, 193, 202.

Wace, Robert, 35.
Wolf, Pierre, 315.

Yver, Colette, 334.

Zola, 251, 318.